# 2016

# TEXAS
## *Courthouse Guide*

**TEXAS LAWYER**
An **ALM** Publication

# 2016

# TEXAS

## *Courthouse Guide*

## TABLE OF CONTENTS

## Courts & Agencies

TEXAS LAWYER

978-1-62881-109-4 (print) | 978-1-62881-110-0 (eBook)
Printed in the United States of America

Note: This volume was published in April 2016 with information gathered beginning in December 2015. Because the courts are constantly in flux, ALM Media and its employees do not warrant, either expressly or implied, that the information in this volume has not been subject to change, amendment, or revision.

Texas Lawyer Staff
Projects Manager: Anna Liza Burciaga
Marketing Assistant: Dalila Macias
Data Collection and Customer Care: Steven House

For additional information on any of the Texas Lawyer books contact:
ALM Media, LLC
c/o Texas Lawyer
1999 Bryan St., Suite 825, Dallas, Texas 75201
(214) 744-9300 • (800) 456-5484
www.texaslawyerbooks.com

Other Titles From Texas Lawyer Books:
*Directory of Corporate Counsel*
*Harris County Bench Book*
*How to Recover Attorneys' Fees in Texas*
*Lanier's Texas Personal Injury Forms*
*Library of Texas Employment Law Forms*
*Legal Writing for the Rewired Brain*
*Maslanka's Field Guide to the Fair Labor Standards Act*
*Maslanka's Field Guide to the Family & Medical Leave Act*
*Maslanka's Guide to Employment Law*
*North Texas Bench Book*
*Pronske's Texas Bankruptcy — Annotated*
*Texas Business Litigation*
*Texas Criminal Codes and Rules — Annotated*
*Texas Insurance Coverage Litigation*
*Texas Legal Malpractice and Lawyer Discipline*
*Texas Litigator's Guide to Departing Employee Cases*
*Texas Personal Automobile Insurance Policy —Annotated*
*Texas Practitioner's Guide to Civil Appeals*
*What Judges Want: A Former Judge's Guide to Success in Court*

*For Returns: In Care of: ALM Media*
*545 Wescott Road, Eagan, MN 55123*

*For QUESTIONS please contact Customer Service at 1-877-256-2472*

*Subscriptions to books are auto-renewed to avoid disruptions in service.*
*Print editions must be returned within 30 days in resalable condition for refund.*
*For downloadable eBook or online products, a refund will be granted*
*if the eBook or online product has not been downloaded.*

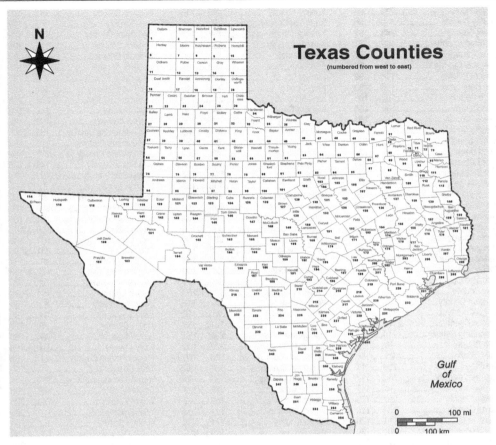

## Texas Counties
(numbered from west to east)

Gulf of Mexico

N

0    100 mi
0    100 km

| County | | |
|---|---|---|
| Dimmit County | 233 | 96 |
| Donley County | 19 | 96 |
| Duval County | 243 | 97 |
| Eastland County | 101 | 97 |
| Ector County | 120 | 97 |
| Edwards County | 186 | 98 |
| El Paso County | 114 | 99 |
| Ellis County | 106 | 103 |
| Erath County | 102 | 103 |
| Falls County | 152 | 104 |
| Fannin County | 50 | 104 |
| Fayette County | 199 | 105 |
| Fisher County | 78 | 105 |
| Floyd County | 30 | 106 |
| Foard County | 33 | 106 |
| Fort Bend County | 220 | 106 |
| Franklin County | 70 | 108 |
| Freestone County | 136 | 108 |
| Frio County | 224 | 109 |
| Gaines County | 74 | 109 |
| Galveston County | 221 | 110 |
| Garza County | 57 | 111 |
| Gillespie County | 190 | 111 |
| Glasscock County | 122 | 112 |
| Goliad County | 227 | 112 |
| Gonzales County | 216 | 112 |
| Gray County | 14 | 113 |
| Grayson County | 49 | 113 |
| Gregg County | 110 | 114 |
| Grimes County | 175 | 115 |
| Guadalupe County | 214 | 115 |
| Hale County | 29 | 116 |
| Hall County | 25 | 116 |
| Hamilton County | 130 | 117 |
| Hansford County | 3 | 117 |
| Hardeman County | 34 | 117 |
| Hardin County | 207 | 118 |
| Harris County | 204 | 118 |
| Harrison County | 111 | 130 |
| Hartley County | 6 | 130 |
| Haskell County | 60 | 130 |
| Hays County | 194 | 131 |
| Hemphill County | 10 | 132 |
| Henderson County | 108 | 132 |
| Hidalgo County | 252 | 133 |
| Hill County | 133 | 135 |
| Hockley County | 38 | 135 |
| Hood County | 103 | 136 |
| Hopkins County | 69 | 136 |
| Houston County | 155 | 137 |
| Howard County | 96 | 138 |
| Hudspeth County | 115 | 138 |
| Hunt County | 67 | 139 |
| Hutchinson County | 8 | 139 |
| Irion County | 145 | 140 |
| Jack County | 63 | 140 |
| Jackson County | 229 | 140 |
| Jasper County | 180 | 141 |
| Jeff Davis County | 160 | 141 |
| Jefferson County | 208 | 142 |
| Jim Hogg County | 248 | 143 |
| Jim Wells County | 244 | 144 |
| Johnson County | 105 | 144 |
| Jones County | 79 | 145 |
| Karnes County | 226 | 146 |
| Kaufman County | 87 | 146 |
| Kendall County | 191 | 147 |
| Kenedy County | 250 | 147 |
| Kent County | 58 | 148 |
| Kerr County | 188 | 148 |
| Kimble County | 166 | 149 |
| King County | 42 | 149 |
| Kinney County | 210 | 149 |
| Kleberg County | 246 | 149 |
| Knox County | 43 | 150 |
| La Salle County | 234 | 150 |
| Lamar County | 51 | 151 |
| Lamb County | 28 | 151 |
| Lampasas County | 150 | 152 |
| Lavaca County | 208 | 152 |
| Lee County | 198 | 152 |
| Leon County | 154 | 153 |
| Liberty County | 205 | 153 |
| Limestone County | 135 | 154 |
| Lipscomb County | 5 | 154 |
| Live Oak County | 236 | 155 |
| Llano County | 168 | 155 |
| Loving County | 118 | 156 |
| Lubbock County | 39 | 156 |
| Lynn County | 56 | 157 |
| Madison County | 174 | 157 |
| Marion County | 93 | 158 |
| Martin County | 95 | 158 |
| Mason County | 167 | 158 |
| Matagorda County | 231 | 159 |
| Maverick County | 222 | 159 |
| McCulloch County | 148 | 160 |
| McLennan County | 134 | 160 |
| McMullen County | 235 | 161 |
| Medina County | 212 | 161 |
| Menard County | 165 | 162 |
| Midland County | 121 | 162 |
| Milam County | 171 | 163 |
| Mills County | 129 | 163 |
| Mitchell County | 97 | 164 |
| Montague County | 47 | 164 |
| Montgomery County | 203 | 165 |
| Moore County | 7 | 166 |
| Morris County | 72 | 167 |
| Motley County | 31 | 167 |
| Nacogdoches County | 139 | 168 |
| Navarro County | 107 | 168 |
| Newton County | 181 | 169 |
| Nolan County | 98 | 169 |
| Nueces County | 245 | 170 |
| Ochiltree County | 4 | 171 |
| Oldham County | 11 | 172 |
| Orange County | 209 | 172 |
| Palo Pinto County | 82 | 173 |
| Panola County | 113 | 173 |
| Parker County | 83 | 174 |
| Parmer County | 21 | 175 |
| Pecos County | 161 | 175 |
| Polk County | 178 | 176 |
| Potter County | 12 | 176 |
| Presidio County | 182 | 177 |
| Rains County | 88 | 178 |
| Randall County | 17 | 178 |
| Reagan County | 144 | 179 |
| Real County | 187 | 179 |
| Red River County | 52 | 179 |
| Reeves County | 117 | 180 |
| Refugio County | 239 | 180 |
| Roberts County | 9 | 180 |
| Robertson County | 153 | 181 |
| Rockwall County | 86 | 181 |
| Runnels County | 125 | 182 |
| Rusk County | 112 | 182 |
| Sabine County | 159 | 182 |
| San Augustine County | 158 | 183 |
| San Jacinto County | 177 | 183 |
| San Patricio County | 238 | 184 |
| San Saba County | 149 | 184 |
| Schleicher County | 163 | 185 |
| Scurry County | 77 | 185 |
| Shackelford County | 80 | 185 |
| Shelby County | 140 | 186 |
| Sherman County | 2 | 186 |
| Smith County | 109 | 187 |
| Somervell County | 104 | 188 |
| Starr County | 251 | 188 |
| Stephens County | 81 | 189 |
| Sterling County | 123 | 189 |
| Stonewall County | 59 | 189 |
| Sutton County | 164 | 190 |
| Swisher County | 23 | 190 |
| Tarrant County | 84 | 190 |
| Taylor County | 99 | 197 |
| Terrell County | 184 | 198 |
| Terry County | 55 | 198 |
| Throckmorton County | 61 | 198 |
| Titus County | 71 | 199 |
| Tom Green County | 146 | 199 |
| Travis County | 195 | 200 |
| Trinity County | 156 | 205 |
| Tyler County | 179 | 205 |
| Upshur County | 92 | 206 |
| Upton County | 143 | 206 |
| Uvalde County | 211 | 206 |
| Val Verde County | 185 | 207 |
| Van Zandt County | 89 | 208 |
| Victoria County | 228 | 208 |
| Walker County | 171 | 209 |
| Waller County | 202 | 210 |
| Ward County | 141 | 210 |
| Washington County | 200 | 210 |
| Webb County | 242 | 211 |
| Wharton County | 230 | 212 |
| Wheeler County | 15 | 213 |
| Wichita County | 36 | 213 |
| Wilbarger County | 35 | 214 |
| Willacy County | 253 | 214 |
| Williamson County | 170 | 215 |
| Wilson County | 215 | 216 |
| Winkler County | 119 | 216 |
| Wise County | 64 | 217 |
| Wood County | 90 | 217 |
| Yoakum County | 54 | 218 |
| Young County | 62 | 218 |
| Zapata County | 247 | 220 |
| Zavala County | 223 | 220 |

## FEDERAL COURTS AND AGENCIES

## STATE ADMINISTRATIVE REGIONS

## STATE APPELLATE COURTS

## STATE AND FEDERAL COURTS AND AGENCIES

# FEDERAL COURTS AND AGENCIES

## U.S. SUPREME COURT

1 First St. NE
Washington, DC 20543
www.supremecourt.gov

**Clerk: Scott Harris**
Phone: 202-479-3011

**Chief Justice: John G. Roberts, Jr.**
Counselor to the Chief Justice:
Jeffrey P. Minear

**Associate Justices:**
Anthony M. Kennedy
Clarence Thomas
Ruth Bader Ginsburg
Stephen G. Breyer
Samuel A. Alito, Jr.
Sonia Sotomayor
Elena Kagan

# 5TH U.S. CIRCUIT COURT OF APPEALS

600 S. Maestri Place
New Orleans, LA 70130
www.ca5.uscourts.gov

**Clerk: Lyle W. Cayce**
Phone: 504-310-7700
ca05ac_clerksoffice@ca5.uscourts.gov

**Chief Deputy Clerk: Thomas Plunkett**
Phone: 504-310-7700

**Case Administration Manager: Peggy Keller**
Phone: 504-310-7708

**Case Managers**
Southern and Eastern Districts: Amanda Sutton-Foy

Phone: 504-310-7670
**Northern and Western Districts: Peter Conners**
Phone: 504-310-7685

**Louisiana/Mississippi Agency Matters: Connie Brown**
Phone: 504-310-7671

**Senior Staff Attorney: Michael Schneider**

**Circuit Librarian: Sue Creech**
Law Library, Room 106
Phone: 504-310-7797
Fax: 504-310-7578

## CIRCUIT JUDGES
IN ORDER OF SENIORITY

**Chief Judge Carl E. Stewart**
300 Fannin St., Suite 5226
Shreveport, LA 71101-3074
Phone: 318-676-3765

**Circuit Judge E. Grady Jolly**
501 E. Court St., Suite 3.850
Jackson, MS 39201
Phone: 601-608-4745

**Circuit Judge W. Eugene Davis**
800 Lafayette St., Suite 5100
Lafayette, LA 70501
Phone: 337-593-5280

**Circuit Judge Edith H. Jones**
515 Rusk Ave., Room 12505
Houston, TX 77002-2655
Phone: 713-250-5484

**Circuit Judge Jerry E. Smith**
515 Rusk Ave., Room 12621
Houston, TX 77002
Phone: 713-250-5101

**Circuit Judge James L. Dennis**
600 Camp St., Room 219
New Orleans, LA 70130
Phone: 504-310-8000

**Circuit Judge Edith Brown Clement**
600 Camp St., Room 200
New Orleans, LA 70130
Phone: 504-310-8068

**Circuit Judge Edward C. Prado**
755 E. Mulberry Ave., Suite 350
San Antonio, TX 78212
Phone: 210-472-4060

**Circuit Judge Priscilla R. Owen**
903 San Jacinto Blvd., Room 434
Austin, TX 78701-2450
Phone: 512-916-5167

**Circuit Judge Jennifer Walker Elrod**
515 Rusk Ave., Room 12014
Houston, TX 77002
Phone: 713-250-7590

**Circuit Judge Leslie H. Southwick**
501 E. Court St., Suite 3.750
Jackson, MS 39201
Phone: 601-608-4760

**Circuit Judge Catharina Haynes**
1100 Commerce St., Room 1264
Dallas, TX 75242
Phone: 214-753-2750

**Circuit Judge James E. Graves, Jr.**
501 E. Court St., Suite 3.550
Jackson, MS 39201
Phone: 601-608-4775

**Circuit Judge Stephen A. Higginson**
600 Camp St., Room 300
New Orleans, LA 70130-3425
Phone: 504-310-8228

**Circuit Judge Gregg J. Costa**
515 Rusk St., Room 4627
Houston, TX 77002
Phone: 713-250-5030

**SENIOR JUDGES:**
**Circuit Judge Rhesa H. Barksdale**
501 E. Court St., Suite 3.800
Jackson, MS 39201
Phone: 601-608-4730

**Circuit Judge Fortunato P. Benavides**
903 San Jacinto Blvd., Room 450
Austin, TX 78701
Phone: 512-916-5796

**Circuit Judge (Vacant)**
515 Rusk Ave., Room 12015
Houston, TX 77002
Phone: 713-250-5462

**Circuit Judge Patrick E. Higginbotham**
903 San Jacinto Blvd., Room 400

Austin, TX 78701
Phone: 512-916-5723

**Circuit Judge Carolyn Dineen King**
515 Rusk Ave., Room 11020
Houston, TX 77002
Phone: 713-250-5750

**Circuit Judge Thomas M. Reavley**
515 Rusk Ave., Room 11009
Houston, TX 77002
Phone: 713-250-5185

**Circuit Judge Jacques L. Wiener, Jr.**
600 Camp St., Room 244
New Orleans, LA 70130
Phone: 504-310-8098

# U.S. COURT OF APPEALS FOR THE FEDERAL CIRCUIT

717 Madison Place NW
Washington, DC 20439
www.cafc.uscourts.gov

**Circuit Executive and Clerk of Court: Daniel E. O'Toole**
Room 401
Phone: 202-275-8000
Fax: 202-275-9678

**Chief Judge: Sharon Prost**

**JUDGES:**
William C. Bryson
Raymond T. Chen
Timothy B. Dyk
Todd M. Hughes
Richard Linn
Alan D. Lourie
Kimberly A. Moore
Pauline Newman
Kathleen M. O'Malley
Jimmie V. Reyna
Kara F. Stoll
Richard G. Taranto
Evan J. Wallach

**SENIOR JUDGES:**
Raymond C. Clevenger, III
Haldane Robert Mayer
S. Jay Plager
Alvin A. Schall

# U.S. COURT OF INTERNATIONAL TRADE

One Federal Plaza
New York, NY 10278-0001
Phone: 212-264-2800
Fax: 212-264-4138
www.cit.uscourts.gov

**Clerk: Tina Potuto Kimble**
Phone: 212-264-2908
clerk@cit.uscourts.gov or
tina_kimble@cit.uscourts.gov

**Chief Deputy Clerk: Mario Toscano**
Phone: 212-264-2826
chief_deputy_clerk@cit.uscourts.gov or
mario_toscano@cit.uscourts.gov

**Administrative Manager: Brian Young**
Phone: 212-264-2831
Fax: 212-264-2803
brian_young@cit.uscourts.gov

**Operations Manager: Scott Warner**
Phone: 212-264-2031
Fax: 212-264-1085
scott_warner@cit.uscourts.gov

**Systems Manager: Bienvenido Burgos**
Phone: 212-264-1868
bienvenido_burgos@cit.uscourts.gov

**Director, Library and Attorney Services:
Daniel R. Campbell**
Phone: 212-264-2804
daniel_campbell@cit.uscourts.gov

**Chief Judge: Timothy C. Stanceu**
Case Manager: Cynthia Love
Phone: 212-264-2923

**JUDGES:**
**Delissa A. Ridgway**
Case Manager: Casey Cheevers
Phone: 212-264-1615
**Leo M. Gordon**
Case Manager: Steve Taronji
Phone: 212-264-1611
**Mark A. Barnett**
Case Manager: Rebecca Demb
Phone: 212-264-1628
**Claire R. Kelly**
Case Manager: Steve Taronji
Phone: 212-264-1611

**SENIOR JUDGES:**
**Jane A. Restani**
Case Manager: Rebecca Demb
Phone: 212-264-1628
**Thomas J. Aquilino, Jr.**
Case Manager: Steve Taronji
Phone: 212-264-1611
**Nicholas Tsoucalas**
Case Manager: Cynthia Love
Phone: 212-264-2923
**R. Kenton Musgrave**
Case Manager: Geoffrey Goell
Phone: 212-264-2973
**Richard W. Goldberg**
Case Manager: Casey Cheevers
Phone: 212-264-1615
**Donald C. Pogue**
Case Manager: Geoffrey Goell
Phone: 212-264-2973
**Richard K. Eaton**
Case Manager: Casey Cheevers
Phone: 212-264-1615

**Inactive Senior Judges**
**Gregory W. Carman**
Case Manager: Cynthia Love
Phone: 212-264-2923
**Judith M. Barzilay**
Case Manager: Steve Taronji
Phone: 212-264-1611

# U.S. TAX COURT

400 Second St. NW
Washington, DC 20217
Phone: 202-521-0700
www.ustaxcourt.gov

**Clerk: Stephanie A Servoss**
**Chief Judge: Michael B. Thornton**

**JUDGES:**
Tamara Ashford
Ronald L. Buch
John O. Colvin
Maurice B. Foley
Joseph H. Gale
Joseph Robert Goeke
David Gustafson
James S. Halpern
Mark V. Holmes
Kathleen Kerrigan
Albert G. Lauber
Richard T. Morrison
Joseph W. Nega

Elizabeth Crewson Paris
Cary Douglas Pugh
Juan F. Vasquez

**SENIOR JUDGES:**
Herbert L. Chabot
Carolyn P. Chiechi
Mary Ann Cohen
Howard A. Dawson, Jr.
Joel Gerber
Harry A. Haines
Julian I. Jacobs
David Laro
Robert P. Ruwe
Thomas B. Wells
Laurence J. Whalen

**SPECIAL TRIAL JUDGES:**
Peter J. Panuthos, Chief Special Trial Judge
Robert N. Armen
Lewis R. Carluzzo
Daniel A. Guy, Jr.

# U.S. COURT OF FEDERAL CLAIMS

717 Madison Place NW
Washington, DC 20439
Phone: 202-357-6400
Fax: 202-357-6401
www.uscfc.uscourts.gov

Clerk: Hazel C. Keahey

Chief Judge: Patricia E. Campbell-Smith

**JUDGES:**
Susan G. Braden
Lydia Kay Griggsby
Marian Blank Horn
Elaine D. Kaplan
Charles F. Lettow
Margaret M. Sweeney
Thomas C. Wheeler
Mary Ellen Coster Williams
Victor J. Wolski

**SENIOR JUDGES:**
Eric G. Bruggink
Lynn J. Bush
Edward J. Damich
Nancy B. Firestone
James F. Merow
John Paul Wiese

# U.S. DISTRICT COURT

## EASTERN DISTRICT

Headquarters for the Eastern District
211 W. Ferguson St., Room 106
Tyler, TX 75702
903-590-1000
www.txed.uscourts.gov

Chief Judge: Ron Clark
300 Willow Street, Suite 221
Beaumont, TX 77701
Phone: 409-654-2800

## Beaumont Division

300 Willow St., Suite 104
Beaumont, TX 77701
www.txed.uscourts.gov

Counties Served: Hardin, Jasper, Jefferson,
Liberty, Newton and Orange.

Deputy-in-Charge: Kyla Dean
Phone: 409-654-7000
Fax: 409-654-7080

Chief Judge Ron Clark
Suite 221
Phone: 409-654-2800
Fax: 409-654-6280
Court Administrator: Brandy O'Quinn
Court Reporter: Chris Bickham
chris_bickham@txed.uscourts.gov
Phone: 409-654-2891
Law Clerks: Brian Cannon and Valerie Lewis
Deputy: Faith Ann Laurents
Phone: 409-654-7030

Judge Thad Heartfield
Suite 212
Phone: 409-654-2860
Fax: 409-654-2874
Secretary/Case Manager: Kristi Wernig
Law Clerk: Mary Margaret Groves
Deputy: Jill Veazey

Judge Marcia A. Crone
Suite 239
Phone: 409-654-2880
Fax: 409-654-2888
Court Administrator: Patricia Leger

Law Clerks: Marianne Laine, Tanner Franklin and Julie Goodrich
Court Reporter: Tonya Jackson
tonya_jackson@txed.uscourts.gov

*Note: Any inquiries made should be directed to the court administrator.*

**Magistrate Judge Zack Hawthorn**
Suite 234
Phone: 409-654-2815
Fax: 409-654-6274
Court Administrator/Law Clerk: Jennifer Fisher
Law Clerks: Molly Moore and Phil Morgan
Deputy: Tonya Piper

**Magistrate Judge Keith Giblin**
Suite 118
Phone: 409-654-2845
Fax: 409-654-6271
Judicial Assistant: Sherre White
Law Clerk: Alexandra McNicholas
Deputy: Kyla Dean

## Lufkin Division

104 N. Third St.
Lufkin, TX 75901
www.txed.uscourts.gov

Counties Served: Angelina, Houston, Nacogdoches, Polk, Sabine, San Augustine, Shelby, Trinity and Tyler.

**Deputy-in-Charge: Kyla Dean**
Phone: 936-632-2739
Fax: 936-632-1210

**Judge Michael Schneider**
**Magistrate Judge Keith Giblin** *sits as scheduled.*
**Magistrate Judge Zack Hawthorn** *sits as scheduled.*

## Marshall Division

100 E. Houston St., Room 125
Marshall, TX 75670
www.txed.uscourts.gov

Counties Served: Camp, Cass, Harrison, Marion, Morris and Upshur.

**Deputy-in-Charge: Mel Martin**
Phone: 903-935-2912
Fax: 903-938-2651

**Judge Rodney Gilstrap**
Phone: 903-935-3868
Fax: 903-935-2295
Judicial Assistant: Sandre Goldsby
Law Clerk: Rudy Fink
Term Law Clerk: Michael Dean
Court Reporter: Shelly Holmes
Deputy: Jan Lockhart

**Magistrate Judge Roy Payne**
Phone: 903-935-2498
Fax: 903-938-7819
Law Clerks: Christopher First and Craig Walker
Deputy: Becky Andrews

**Judge Caroline Craven** *sits as scheduled.*

## Sherman Division

101 E. Pecan St., Room 216
Sherman, TX 75090

The Sherman Divisional Annex
7940 Preston Rd.
Plano, TX 75024
Phone: 214-872-4800
www.txed.uscourts.gov

Counties Served: Collin, Cooke, Delta, Denton, Fannin, Grayson, Hopkins and Lamar.

**Deputy-in-Charge: Patricia Manning**
Phone: 903-892-2921
Fax: 903-892-6801

**Judge Richard A. Schell**
7940 Preston Rd., Suite 111
Plano, TX 75024
Phone: 214-872-4820
Fax: 214-872-4828
Secretary: Lori Bates
Law Clerks: Aileen Durrett and Amber Reece
Courtroom Reporter: (Vacant)
Deputy: Bonnie Sanford

**Magistrate Judge Don D. Bush**
7940 Preston Rd., Suite 110
Plano, TX 75024
Phone: 214-872-4840
Fax: 214-872-4846
Judicial Assistant: Lori Muñoz
Law Clerk: Kirstine Rogers
Deputy: Toya McEwen

**Magistrate Judge: (Vacant)**
200 N. Travis St.
Sherman, TX 75090
Phone: 903-893-7008
Fax: 903-893-9067
Judicial Assistant: Terri Scott
Law Clerk: Emileigh Hubbard
Deputy: Debra McCord

**Chief Judge Ron Clark** sits as scheduled.

**Judge Marcia A. Crone** sits as scheduled.

## Texarkana Division

500 N. State Line Ave.
Texarkana, TX 75501
www.txed.uscourts.gov

Counties Served: Bowie, Franklin, Titus and
Red River.

**Magistrate Judge Caroline Craven**
Room 401
Phone: 903-792-6424
Fax: 903-792-0367
Secretary: Nicole Peavy
Law Clerk: Jennifer Orgeron
Deputy: Lynn Siebel

**Honorable Robert W. Schroeder, III**
Judicial Assistant: Shedera Combs
Courtroom Deputy: Betty Schroeder
Court Reporter: Brenda Smith
Law Clerks: Boone Baxter, Elizabeth Chiaviello
and Jenna Rea

## Tyler Division

211 W. Ferguson St.
Tyler, TX 75702
www.txed.uscourts.gov

Counties Served: Anderson, Cherokee,
Gregg, Henderson, Panola, Rains, Rusk,
Smith, Van Zandt and Wood.

**Clerk: David A. O'Toole**
Phone: 903-590-1000
Fax: 903-590-1015
Chief Deputy: Maria Dozauer

**Judge Michael H. Schneider**
Room 100
Phone: 903-590-1091
Fax: 903-590-1095
Law Clerk: Ray Warner
Phone: 903-590-1097
Law Clerk: Melissa Butler
Phone: 903-590-1088
Law Clerk: John Pace
Phone: 903-590-1093
Court Reporter: Shea Sloan
Phone: 903-590-1096
Court Administrator: Rosa Ferguson
Phone: 903-590-1094

**Magistrate Judge John D. Love**
Room 210
Phone: 903-590-1164
Fax: 903-590-1168
Judicial Assistant: Sharon Guthrie
Law Clerks: Jenna Gillingham and Samantha
Pace
Deputy: Mechele Morris

**Magistrate Judge K. Nicole Mitchell**
Room 300
Phone: 903-590-1077
Fax: 903-590-1081
Law Clerk: Terri Good
Deputy: Lisa Hardwick

## Northern District

Headquarters for the Northern District
1100 Commerce St.
Dallas, TX 75242-1003
www.txnd.uscourts.gov

**Clerk: Karen Mitchell**
Room 1452
Phone: 214-753-2200
Fax: 214-753-2155

**Chief Deputy: Jim Barton**
Phone: 214-753-2200

**Chief Judge Jorge A. Solis**
Room 1654
Phone: 214-753-2342
Fax: 214-753-2352
Case Letter Designation: P
Court Reporter: Shawn McRoberts
Phone: 214-753-2349
Deputy: Kevin Frye
Phone: 214-753-2346

STATE AND FEDERAL COURTS AND AGENCIES

## Abilene Division

341 Pine St.
Abilene, TX 79601
www.txnd.uscourts.gov

Counties Served: Callahan, Eastland, Fisher, Haskell, Howard, Jones, Mitchell, Nolan, Shackelford, Stephens, Stonewall, Taylor and Throckmorton.

**Deputy-in-Charge: Marsha Elliott**
Phone: 325-677-6311

**Chief Judge Jorge Solis**

**Magistrate Judge E. Scott Frost**
Room 2313
Phone: 325-676-4582
Fax: 325-672-6895
Case Letter Designation: BL
Deputy: Dianna Davis
Phone: 325-690-3972

## Amarillo Division

205 SE 5th Ave., Room 133
Amarillo, TX 79101-1559
CM/ECF Help: 800-596-9414
www.txnd.uscourts.gov

Counties Served: Armstrong, Briscoe, Carson, Castro, Childress, Collingsworth, Dallam, Deaf Smith, Donley, Gray, Hall, Hansford, Hartley, Hemphill, Hutchinson, Lispcomb, Moore, Ochiltree, Oldham, Parmer, Potter, Randall, Roberts, Sherman, Swisher and Wheeler.

**Deputy-in-Charge: Daniel Aguilera**
Phone: 806-468-3800

**Judge Mary Lou Robinson**
Room 226
Phone: 806-468-3822
Case Letter Designation: J
Judicial Paralegal: Melba Fenwick
Court Reporter: Stacy Morrison
Phone: 806-672-6219
Deputy: Delynda Smith
Phone: 806-468-3831

**Magistrate Judge Clinton E. Averitte**
Room 123
Phone: 806-468-3832
Case Letter Designation: BB
Deputy: Elodia Breto
Phone: 806-468-3811

## Dallas Division

1100 Commerce St.
Dallas, TX 75242-1003
www.txnd.uscourts.gov

Counties Served: Dallas, Ellis, Hunt, Johnson, Kaufman, Navarro and Rockwall.

**Clerk: Karen Mitchell**

**Chief Deputy: Jim Barton**

**Chief Judge: Jorge A. Solis**

**Judge Jane Boyle**
Room 1376
Phone: 214-753-2740
Fax: 214-753-2744
boyle_clerk@txnd.uscourts.gov
Case Letter Designation: B
Court Reporter: Shawnie Archuleta
Phone: 214-753-2747
Deputy: Jenelle Wilson

**Judge Sidney A. Fitzwater**
Room 1528
Phone: 214-753-2333
Case Letter Designation: D
Judicial Secretary: Debra Eubank
Court Reporter: Pamela Wilson
Phone: 214-622-1557
Deputy: Pat Esquivel
Phone: 214-753-2336

**Judge David C. Godbey**
Room 1505
Phone: 214-753-2700
Case Letter Designation: N
Judicial Assistant: Donna Hocker Beyer
Court Reporter: Linda Robbins Langford
Phone: 214-748-8068
Deputy: Carla Moore
Phone: 214-753-2706

**Judge Ed Kinkeade**
Room 1627
Phone: 214-753-2720
Case Letter Designation: K
Judicial Assistant: Cheri Leatherwood
Court Reporter: Todd Anderson
Phone: 214-766-2170
Deputy: Ronnie Jacobson
Phone: 214-753-2166

**Judge Sam A. Lindsay**
Room 1546
Phone: 214-753-2365
Fax: 214-753-2372
Case Letter Designation: L
Judicial Assistant: Michelle Marshall-Goode
Court Reporter: Charyse Crawford
Phone: 214-753-2373
Deputy: Tannica Stewart
Phone: 214-753-2368

**Judge Barbara M.G. Lynn**
Room 1572
Phone: 214-753-2420
Case Letter Designation: M
Judicial Assistant: Judy Flowers
Court Reporter: Keith Johnson
Phone: 214-753-2325
Deputy: Lori Ann Greco
Phone: 214-753-2421

**Senior Judge A. Joe Fish**
Room 1404
Phone: 214-753-2310
Case Letter Designation: G
Judicial Assistant: Eleanore Piwoni
Phone: 214-354-3139

**Senior Judge Robert B. Maloney**
Room 1452
Chambers Phone: 214-753-2201
Case Letter Designation: T

**Magistrate Judge David L. Horan**
Room 1549
Phone: 214-753-2400
Fax: 214-753-2407
Case Letter Designation: BN
Deputy: Vila Fisher
Phone: 214-753-2165

**Magistrate Judge Irma C. Ramirez**
Room 1567
Phone: 214-753-2393
Case Letter Designation: BH
Deputy: Marie Castaneda
Phone: 214-753-2167

**Magistrate Judge Renee H. Toliver**
Room 1407
Phone: 214-753-2385
Fax: 214-753-2390
Case Letter Designation: BK
Deputy: Jane Amerson
Phone: 214-753-2169

**Magistrate Judge Paul D. Stickney**
Room 1611
Phone: 214-753-2410
Case Letter Designation: BF
Deputy: Lavenia Price
Phone: 214-753-2168

# Fort Worth Division

501 W. 10th St.
Fort Worth, TX 76102-3673
Phone: 817-850-6600
CM/ECF Help: 800-240-7240
or 817-850-6733
www.txnd.uscourts.gov

Counties Served: Commanche, Erath, Hood,
Jack, Palo Pinto, Parker, Tarrant and Wise.

**Divisional Manager: Edmond Dieth**
Room 310
Phone: 817-850-6600

**Judge John H. McBryde**
Room 401
Phone: 817-850-6650
Fax: 817-850-6660
Case Letter Designation: A
Judicial Assistant: Diane Terry
Court Reporter: Debbie Saenz
Phone: 817-850-6661
Deputy: Fleather Arnold
Phone: 817-850-6659

**Senior Judge Terry R. Means**
Room 201
Phone: 817-850-6670
Case Letter Designation: Y
Judicial Assistant: Brenda Bishop (Civil Docket)
Court Reporter: Ana Warren
Phone: 817-850-6681
Deputy: Carmen Bush (Criminal Docket)
Phone: 817-850-6673

**Magistrate Judge Jeffrey L. Cureton**
Room 520
Phone: 817-850-6690
Case Letter Designation: BJ
Judicial Assistant: Margarita Koye
Deputy: Julie Harwell
Phone: 817-850-6697

**Judge Reed O'Connor**
Room 310
Phone: 817-850-6788
Fax: 817-850-6787

Case Letter Designation: O
Deputy: Tyler Crowley
Phone: 817-850-6781
Courtroom Reporter: Denver Roden
Phone: 214-753-2298

## Lubbock Division

1205 Texas Ave.
Lubbock, TX 79401
806-472-1900
CM/ECF Help: 806-472-1905
www.txnd.uscourts.gov

Counties Served: Bailey, Borden, Cochran, Crosby, Dawson, Dickens, Floyd, Gaines, Garza, Hale, Hockley, Kent, Lamb, Lubbock, Lynn, Motley, Scurry, Terry and Yoakum.

**Deputy Clerk-in-Charge: Erik Paltrow**
Room 209

**Senior Judge Sam R. Cummings**
Room C-210
Phone: 806-472-1922
Case Letter Designation: C
Judicial Assistant: Delva Hernandez
Court Reporter: Mechelle Daniel
Phone: 806-744-7667
Deputy: Criss Flock
Phone: 806-472-1925

**Magistrate Judge Nancy M. Koenig**
Room 211
Phone: 806-472-1933
Case Letter Designation: BG
Deputy: Lana Waits
Phone: 806-472-1914

## San Angelo Division

33 E. Twohig Ave., Room 202
San Angelo, TX 76903-6451
www.txnd.uscourts.gov
325-655-4506
Fax: 325-658-6826

Counties Served: Brown, Coke, Coleman, Concho, Crockett, Glasscock, Irion, Menard, Mills, Reagan, Runnels, Schleicher, Sterling, Sutton and Tom Green.

**Deputy Clerk-in-Charge: Erik Paltrow**
Room 202

**Senior Judge Sam R. Cummings**

**Magistrate Judge E. Scott Frost**

## Wichita Falls Division

1000 Lamar St.
Wichita Falls, TX 76301
www.txnd.uscourts.gov

Counties Served: Archer, Baylor, Clay, Cottle, Foard, Hardeman, King, Knox, Montague, Wichita, Wilbarger and Young.

**Deputy Clerk-in-Charge: Teena Timmons**
Room 203
Phone: 940-767-1902
Fax: 940-767-2526

**Judge Reed O'Connor** *sits as scheduled.*

**Part-Time Magistrate Judge Robert K. Roach**
P.O. Box 8445
Wichita Falls, TX 76307
Phone: 940-767-1902
Fax: 940-767-2526
Case Letter Designation: KA
Courtroom Deputy: Paige Lessor

## Southern District

Headquarters for the Southern District
515 Rusk Ave.
Houston, TX 77002
www.txs.uscourts.gov

**Clerk: David J. Bradley**
Room 5300
Phone: 713-250-5500

**Chief District Judge Ricardo H. Hinojosa**

## Brownsville Division

600 E. Harrison St.
Brownsville, TX 78520
www.txs.uscourts.gov

Counties Served: Cameron and Willacy.

**Deputy-in-Charge: Rosy D'Venturi**
Room 101
Phone: 956-548-2500

**Judge Hilda G. Tagle**
Room 306
Phone: 956-548-2510
Case Manager: Stella Cavazos
Phone: 956-548-2628

**Judge Andrew S. Hanen**
Room 301
Phone: 956-548-2591
Case Manager: Cristina Sustaeta
Phone: 956-548-2629
Court Reporter: (Vacant)
Phone: 956-548-2629, ext. 9668

**Judge Rolando Olvera**
Phone: 456-548-2545
Case Manager: Sandra Spinoza
Phone: 956-982-9685

**Magistrate Judge Ronald G. Morgan**
Room 204
Phone: 956-548-2570
Case Manager: Bertha Vasquez
Phone: 956-982-9657

**Magistrate Judge Ignacio Torteya, III**
Phone: 956-548-2564
Case Manager: Sally Garcia
Phone: 956-982-9659

## Corpus Christi Division

1133 N. Shoreline Blvd.
Corpus Christi, TX 78401
www.txs.uscourts.gov

Counties Served: Aransas, Bee, Brooks,
Duval, Jim Wells, Kenedy, Kleberg, Live Oak,
Nueces and San Patricio.

**Deputy-in-Charge: Marianne Serpa**
Phone: 361-888-3142

**Senior Judge Hayden Head**
Phone: 361-888-3148
Case Manager: Arlene Rodriquez
Phone: 361-888-3369

**Senior Judge Janis Graham Jack**
Phone: 361-888-3525
Case Manager: Linda R. Smith

**Judge Nelva Gonzales Ramos**
Phone: 361-693-6455
Case Manager: Brandy Cortez
Phone: 361-693-6457

**Magistrate Judge B. Janice Ellington**
Phone: 361-888-3291
Case Manager: Leticia Garza
Phone: 361-888-3432

**Magistrate Judge Jason B. Libby**
Phone: 361-888-3550
Case Manager: Kendra Bledsoe
Phone: 361-888-3445

## Galveston Division

601 Rosenburg St.
Galveston, TX 77550
www.txs.uscourts.gov

Counties Served: Brazoria, Chambers,
Galveston and Matagorda.

**Deputy-in-Charge: Lucia Smith**
Room 411
Phone: 409-766-3547

**Judge George C. Hanks, Jr.**
Phone: 409-766-3737
Case Manager: Dana Perez
Phone: 409-766-3547

**Magistrate Judge John R. Froeschner**
Phone: 409-766-3729
Case Manager: Sheila Anderson
Phone: 409-766-3533

## Houston Division

515 Rusk Ave.
Houston, TX 77002
www.txs.uscourts.gov

Counties Served: Austin, Brazos, Colorado,
Fayette, Fort Bend, Grimes, Harris, Madison,
Montgomery, San Jacinto, Walker, Waller and
Wharton.

**Clerk: David J. Bradley**

**Deputy-in-Charge: Darlene Hansen**
Phone: 713-250-5500

**Judge Nancy F. Atlas**
Phone: 713-250-5300
Case Manager: Shelia Ashabranner
Phone: 713-250-5407

**Judge Keith P. Ellison**
Phone: 713-250-5181
Case Manager: Stephanie Vaught

**Judge Vanessa Gilmore**
Phone: 713-250-5512
Case Manager: Byron Thomas

**Judge Melinda Harmon**
Phone: 713-250-5518
Case Manager: Rhonda Hawkins

**Judge David Hittner**
Phone: 713-250-5511
Case Manager: Ellen Alexander

**Judge Kenneth M. Hoyt**
Phone: 713-250-5884
Case Manager: Cynthia Horace

**Judge Lynn N. Hughes**
Phone: 713-250-5516
Case Manager: Glenda Hassan

**Judge Sim Lake**
Phone: 713-250-5514
Case Manager: Andrew Boyd

**Judge Gray Miller**
Phone: 713-250-5129
Case Manager: Rhonda Moore-Konieczny

**Judge Lee Rosenthal**
Phone: 713-250-5517
Case Manager: Lisa Eddins

**Judge Ewing Werlein, Jr.**
Phone: 713-250-5533
Case Manager: Marilyn Flores

**Magistrate Judge Nancy K. Johnson**
Room 7019
Phone: 713-250-5703
Case Manager: Shannon Jones

**Magistrate Judge Mary Milloy**
Room 7007
Phone: 713-250-5158
Case Manager: Cynthia Jantowski

**Magistrate Judge Stephen Wm. Smith**
Room 7720
Phone: 713-250-5148
Case Manager: Jason Marchand

**Magistrate Judge Francis H. Stacy**
Room 7525

Phone: 713-250-5565
Case Manager: Beverly White

## Laredo Division

1300 Victoria St.
Laredo, TX 78040
www.txs.uscourts.gov

Counties Served: Jim Hogg, La Salle,
McMullen, Webb and Zapata.

**Deputy-in-Charge: Rosie Rodriguez**
Room 1131
Phone: 956-723-3542
Fax: 956-726-2289

**Judge Marina Garcia Marmolejo**
Phone: 956-726-2209
Case Manager: Angie Trevino
Phone: 956-790-1364

**Judge Diana Saldana**
Phone: 956-790-1381
Case Manager: Sara Medellin
Phone: 956-790-1377

**Senior Judge George P. Kazen**
Phone: 956-726-2237
Case Manager: Veronica Caballero
Phone: 956-790-1351

**Magistrate Judge Guillermo R. Garcia**
Phone: 956-790-1757
Case Manager: Aimee Veliz
Phone: 954-726-5229

**Magistrate Judge Diana Song Quiroga**
Phone: 956-726-2242
Case Manager: Cindy Dominguez-Deleon
Phone: 956-790-1372

**Magistrate Judge J. Scott Hacker**
Phone: 956-790-1750
Case Manager: Debbie Flores
Phone: 956-790-1363

## McAllen Division

1701 W. Highway 83
McAllen, TX 78501
www.txs.uscourts.gov

Counties Served: Hildalgo and Starr.

**Deputy-in-Charge (Acting): Sally Henry**
Suite 1011
Phone: 956-618-8065

**Chief Judge Ricardo H. Hinojosa**
Phone: 956-618-8100
Case Manager: Alex De La Garza
Phone: 956-618-8474

**Judge Randy Crane**
Phone: 956-618-8083
Case Manager: Ludi Cervantes
Phone: 956-618-8473

**Judge Micaela Alvarez**
Phone: 956-618-8220
Case Manager: Iris Belmares
Phone: 956-618-8470

**Magistrate Judge Peter E. Ormsby**
Phone: 956-618-8080
Case Manager: Carmel Ramirez
Phone: 956-618-8431

**Magistrate Judge Dorina Ramos**
Phone: 956-618-8060
Case Manager: Lupita Corbett
Phone: 956-618-8428

## Victoria Division

312 S. Main St.
Victoria, TX 77902
www.txs.uscourts.gov

Counties Served: Calhoun, DeWitt, Goliad, Jackson, Lavaca, Refugio and Victoria.

**Deputy-in-Charge: Lana Tesch**
Room 406
Phone: 361-788-5000

**Judge John D. Rainey**
Phone: 361-788-5030
Case Manager: Stacie Marthiljohni

**Judge Gregg Costa** sits as scheduled.

**Magistrate Judge Nancy K. Johnson** sits as scheduled.

## WESTERN DISTRICT

Headquarters for the Western District
655 E. Cesar E. Chavez Blvd., Room G65

San Antonio, TX 78206
www.txwd.uscourts.gov

**Clerk: Jeannette J. Clack**
Room A-500
Phone: 210-472-4955, ext. 2811
Chief Deputy: Philip Devlin
Phone: 210-472-4955, ext. 2812

**Chief Judge Fred Biery**
Phone: 210-472-6505
Judicial Assistant: Gilbert Rodriguez
Court Reporter: Chris Poage
Phone: 210-244-5036
Deputy: Gloria Vela
Phone: 210-472-6550, ext. 5022
gloria_vela@txwd.uscourts.gov

## Austin Division

501 W. 5th St.
Austin, TX 78701
www.txwd.uscourts.gov

Counties Served: Bastrop, Blanco, Burleson, Burnet, Caldwell, Gillespie, Hays, Kimble, Lampasas, Lee, Llano, Mason, McCulloch, San Saba, Travis, Washington and Williamson.

**Divisional Office Manager: Annette French**
Suite 1100
Phone: 512-916-5896

**Judge Robert Pitman**
Suite 5310
Deputy: Julie Golden
julie_golden@txwd.uscourts.gov

**Judge Sam Sparks**
Phone: 512-916-5230
Judicial Assistant: Linda Mizell
Court Reporter: Lily Reznik
Phone: 512-391-8792
Deputy: Alexis Montgomery
alexis_montgomery@txwd.uscourts.gov

**Judge Lee Yeakel**
Phone: 512-916-5756
Court Reporter: Arlinda Rodriguez
Phone: 512-391-8791
Deputy: Janie Jones
janie_jones@txwd.uscourts.gov

**Senior Judge James R. Nowlin**
Suite 6400

Phone: 512-916-5675
Fax: 512-916-5680

**Magistrate Judge Andrew W. Austin**
Phone: 512-916-5744
Fax: 512-916-5750
Deputy: Zing Cheng
Phone: 512-916-5896, ext. 8713

**Magistrate Judge Mark Lane**
Phone: 512-916-5679
Fax: 512-916-5668
Deputy: Jennifer Williams
jennifer_williams@txwd.uscourts.gov
Phone: 512-916-5896, ext. 8719

## Del Rio Division

111 E. Broadway St., Room L100
Del Rio, TX 78840
www.txwd.uscourts.gov

Counties Served: Edwards, Kinney, Maverick,
Terrell, Uvalde, Val Verde and Zavala.

**Divisional Office Manager: Rebecca Moore**
Room L100
Phone: 830-703-2054
Fax: 830-703-2071

**Judge Alia Moses**
Phone: 830-703-2038
Fax: 830-703-2159
Court Reporter: Vicki Lee Garza
Phone: 830-703-2054
Deputy: Debbie Green
Phone: 830-703-3754
debbie_green@txwd.uscourts.gov

**Magistrate Judge Victor Roberto Garcia**
Phone: 830-703-2170
Deputy: Carmen Levrie
Phone: 830-703-2111
carmen_levrie@txwd.uscourts.gov

**Magistrate Judge Collis White**
Phone: 830-703-2050
Deputy: Veronica Sobrevilla
Phone: 830-703-3753
veronica_sobrevilla@txwd.uscourts.gov

## El Paso Division

525 Magoffin Ave.
El Paso, TX 79901
www.txwd.uscourts.gov

Counties Served: El Paso and Hudspeth.

**Divisional Office Manager: Laura Gonzales**
Suite 105
Phone: 915-534-6725
Fax: 915-534-6722

**Judge Kathleen Cardone**
Phone: 915-534-6740
Deputy: Javier Martinez
Phone: 915-534-6725, ext. 1517
javier_martinez@txwd.uscourts.gov

**Judge David C. Guaderrama**
Phone: 915-534-6005
Fax: 915-534-6724
Deputy: Greg Duenas
Phone: 915-534-6725, ext. 1509
greg_duenas@txwd.uscourts.gov

**Judge Philip R. Martinez**
Phone: 915-534-6736
Court Reporter: Laura Stewart
Phone: 915-534-6725, ext. 1553
Deputy: Roberto Velez
Phone: 915-534-6725, ext. 1538
roberto_velez@txwd.uscourts.gov

**Judge Frank Montalvo**
Phone: 915-534-6600
Courtroom Reporter: Nalene Benavides
Phone: 915-534-6725, ext. 1563
Deputy: Adriana Quezada
Phone: 915-534-6725, ext. 1532
adriana_quezada@txwd.uscourts.gov

**Senior Judge David Briones**
Phone: 915-534-6744
Court Reporter: Maria del Socorro Briggs
Phone: 915-534-6725, ext. 1568
Deputy: Ruben Cabrera
Phone: 915-534-6725, ext. 1506
ruben_cabrera@txwd.uscourts.gov

**Magistrate Judge Anne T. Berton**
Phone: 915-834-0579
Fax: 915-834-0665
Deputy: Cecilia Rodriguez
Phone: 915-534-6725, ext. 1534
cecilia_rodriguez@txwd.uscourts.gov

**Magistrate Judge Robert F. Castaneda**
Phone: 915-534-6028
Deputy: Veronica Montoya
Phone: 915-534-6725, ext. 1520
veronica_montoya@txwd.uscourts.gov

**Magistrate Judge Leon Schydlower**
Phone: 915-534-6980
Deputy: Aida Radke
Phone: 915-534-6725, ext. 1533
aida_radler@txwd.uscourts.gov

**Magistrate Judge Miguel A. Torres**
Phone: 915-534-6732
Deputy: Rita Velez
Phone: 915-534-6725, ext. 1519

## Midland-Odessa Division

200 E. Wall St.
Midland, TX 79701
www.txwd.uscourts.gov

Counties Served: Andrews, Crane, Ector,
Martin, Midland and Upton.

**Divisional Office Manager: Jaye Kissler**
Room: 222
Phone: 432-686-4001

**Judge Robert A. Junell**
Phone: 432-686-4020
Court Reporter: Ann Record
Phone: 432-686-0605
Deputy: Monica Ramirez
Phone: 432-686-4004
monica_ramirez@txwd.uscourts.gov

**Magistrate Judge David Counts**
Phone: 432-570-4439
Deputy: Cristina Lerma
Phone: 432-686-4001
cristina_lerma@txwd.uscourts.gov

## Pecos Division

410 South Cedar St.
Pecos, TX 79772
www.txwd.uscourts.gov

Counties Served: Brewster, Culberson, Jeff
Davis, Hudspeth, Loving, Pecos, Presidio,
Reeves, Ward and Winkler.

**Office Manager: Michael Benavides**
Phone: 432-445-4228
michael_benavides@txwd.uscourts.gov

**Magistrate Judge David Fannin**
Suite 222

Phone: 432-837-9740
Fax: 432-837-9780
Judicial Assistant: Susan Williams
Deputy: Aida Bueza

## San Antonio Division

655 E. Cesar E. Chavez Blvd.
San Antonio, TX 78206
www.txwd.uscourts.gov

Counties Served: Atascosa, Bandera, Bexar,
Comal, Dimmit, Frio, Gonzales, Guadalupe,
Karnes, Kendall, Kerr, Medina, Real and
Wilson.

**Divisional Manager: Michael F. Oakes**
Room G65
Phone: 210-472-6550
Fax: 210-472-6513

**Judge Fred Biery**
Phone: 210-472-6505
Court Reporter Chris Poare
Phone: 210-244-5036
Deputy: Sylvia Ann Fernandez

**Chief Judge Orlando L. Garcia**
Phone: 210-472-6565
Court Reporter: Leticia Rangel
Phone: 210-244-5039
Deputy: Jessica Urrutia
Phone: 210-472-6550, ext. 5020
jessica_urrutia@txwd.uscourts.gov

**Judge Xavier Rodriguez**
Phone: 210-472-6575
Court Reporter: Karl Myers
Phone: 210-244-5037
Deputy: Becky Greenup
Phone: 210-472-6550, ext. 5011
becky_greenup@txwd.uscourts.gov

**Senior Judge David A. Ezra**
Phone: 212-472-5870
Deputy: Tiffany Ramaekers
Phone: 210-472-6550, ext. 5016
tiffany_ramaekers@txwd.uscourts.gov

**Magistrate Judge Pamela A. Mathy**
Phone: 210-472-6350
Deputy: Kathy Hicks
Phone: 210-472-6550, ext. 5005
kathy_hicks@txwd.uscourts.gov

**STATE AND FEDERAL COURTS AND AGENCIES**

**Magistrate Judge Henry J. Bemporad**
Phone: 210-472-6363
Deputy: Kriston Hunt
Phone: 210-472-6550, ext. 5013
kriston_hunt@txwd.uscourts.gov

**Magistrate Judge John W. Primomo**
Phone: 210-472-6357
Deputy: Magda Muzza
Phone: 210-472-6550, ext. 5012
magda_muzza@txwd.uscourts.gov

## Waco Division

800 Franklin Ave.
Waco, TX 76701
www.txwd.uscourts.gov

Counties Served: Bell, Bosque, Coryell, Falls, Freestone, Hamilton, Hill, Leon, Limestone, McLennan, Milam, Robertson and Somervell.

**Office Manager: Mark G. Borchardt**
Room 380
Phone: 254-750-1501

**Judge Walter S. Smith**
Phone: 254-750-1501
Court Reporter: Kristie M. Davis
Phone: 254-754-7444
Deputy: Debbie Galler
debbie_galler@txwd.uscourts.gov

**Magistrate Judge Jeffrey C. Manske**
Phone: 254-750-1501
Deputy: Lisa Trotter
Phone: 254-750-1511
lisa_trotter@txwd.uscourts.gov

# U.S. BANKRUPTCY COURTS

## EASTERN DISTRICT
www.txeb.uscourts.gov

## TYLER OFFICE
Serving Marshall and Tyler Divisions

Headquarters for the Eastern
Bankruptcy District
110 N. College Ave. 9th Floor
Tyler, TX 75702

**Judge Bill Parker**
Phone: 903-590-3200
Judicial Assistant: Sandy Johnson
Phone: 903-590-3240
Law Clerk: Jane Gerber
Phone: 903-590-3242

## Marshall Division
Counties Served: Camp, Cass, Harrison, Marion, Morris, Upshur.

## Tyler Division
Counties Served: Anderson, Cherokee, Gregg, Henderson, Panola, Rains, Rusk, Smith, Van Zandt, Wood.

**Clerk of Court: Jason K. McDonald**
Phone: 972-509-1240
Fax: 972-509-1253
jason_mcdonald@txeb.uscourts.gov
Deputy in Charge: Mark Taylor
mark_taylor@txeb.uscourts.gov
Courtroom Deputy: Chasha Traylor
chasha_traylor@txeb.uscourts.gov

**Case Administrator: Brandon Davis**
Phone: 903-590-3213 (Digits 50 – 99)
brandon_davis@txeb.uscourts.gov

**Case Administrator: Debbie Duke**
Phone: 903-590-3232
debbie_duke@txeb.uscourts.gov

**Case Administrator: Vicki Hand**
Phone: 903-590-3231 (Digits 00 – 49)
vicki_hand@txeb.uscourts.gov

Voice Case Information: 1-866-222-8029
PACER: 800-676-6856

## BEAUMONT OFFICE
Serving Beaumont and Lufkin Divisions

300 Willow St., Suite 100
Beaumont, TX 77701

## Beaumont Division
Counties Served: Hardin, Jasper, Jefferson, Liberty, Newton, and Orange.

## Lufkin Division
Counties Served: Angelina, Houston, Nacogdoches, Polk, Sabine, San Augustine, Shelby, Trinity and Tyler.

**Deputy-in-Charge: Mona Doyle**
Phone: 409-654-7064
mona_doyle@txeb.uscourts.gov

**Case Admin/Intake/ECRO: Shannon Britten**
Phone: 409-654-7070 (Digits 00-49)
shannon_britten@txeb.uscourts.gov

**Case Admin/Intake/ECRO: JoAnne Judice**
Phone: 409-654-7065 (Digits 50-99)
joanne_judice@txeb.uscourts.gov

## PLANO OFFICE
Serving Sherman and Texarkana Divisions

660 N. Central Expy., Suite 300B
Plano, TX 75074

**Chief Judge Brenda Rhoades**
Judicial Assistant: Marianne Denning
Phone: 972-509-1250
Law Clerk: Leslie Masterson
Phone: 972-509-1252

## Sherman Division
Counties Served: Collin, Cooke, Delta, Denton, Fannin, Grayson, Hopkins and Lamar.

## Texarkana Division
Counties Served: Bowie, Franklin, Red River and Titus.

**Deputy-in-Charge: Sheryl Denham**
Phone: 972-633-4757
Courtroom Deputy (Ch. 12 and 13):
Sheryl Denham
Phone: 972-633-4751
sheryl_denham@txeb.uscourts.gov
Courtroom Deputy (Ch. 7, 11, and Adversary Proceedings): Shirley Rasco
Phone: 972-509-1246
shirley_rasco@txeb.uscourts.gov

**Intake Clerk: Maria Sheppard**
Phone: 972-633-4730
maria_sheppard@txeb.uscourts.gov

**Case Administration Leader: Lori Carter**
Phone: 974-633-4724 (Digits 00-09)
lori_carter@txeb.uscourts.gov
**Case Administrator: Jennifer Childs**
Phone: 972-633-4727 (Digits 10-39)
**Case Administrator: Sandie Tyrone**

Phone: 972-633-4725 (Digits 40-69)
sandie_tyrone@txeb.uscourts.gov
**Case Administrator: Betty Lee**
Phone: 972-633-4742 (Digits 70-99)
betty_lee@txeb.uscourts.gov

## U.S. Trustee's Office
## Tyler Field Office

110 N. College Ave., Room 300
Tyler, TX 75702
www.justice.gov/ust

*See Northern District for Regional Office (Dallas) of Region 6 U.S. Trustee Program.*

**Assistant U.S Trustee: Timothy W. O'Neal**
Room 300
Phone: 903-590-1450
Fax: 903-590-1461

**Trial Attorney: Marc F. Salitore**
Phone: 903-590-1450, ext. 216
marc.f.salitore@usdoj.gov

**Trial Attorney: John M Vardeman**
Phone: 903-590-1450, ext. 218
john.m.varderman@usdoj.gov

**Bankruptcy Analyst: Samuel M. Baker**
Phone: 903-590-1450, ext. 213
samuel.m.baker@usdoj.gov

## NORTHERN DISTRICT

Headquarters for the Northern
Bankruptcy District
1100 Commerce St., Room 1254
Dallas, TX 75242
Phone: 214-753-2000
Voice Case Information System (VCIS):
Phone: 866-222-8029
www.txnb.uscourts.gov

**Bankruptcy Clerk of Court: Jed G. Weintraub**
Phone: 214-753-2012
Fax: 214-753-2038
Chief Deputy: Rob Colwell
Phone: 214-753-2017
Deputy-in-Charge: Lisa Holmes
Phone: 817-333-6017

**Chief Judge Barbara J. Houser**
Room 1421
Phone: 214-753-2055/2056

Case Identifier: BJH
Law Clerk: Michaela Crocker
Deputy: Dawn Harden
bjh_settings@txnb.uscourts.gov
Phone: 214-753-2059
Transcripts/ECRO: Nicole Whittington
Phone: 214-753-2064

## Amarillo Division
205 South East 5th, Room 133
Amarillo, TX 79101-2389

Counties Served: Armstrong, Briscoe, Carson, Castro, Childress, Collingsworth, Dallam, Deaf Smith, Donley, Gray, Hall, Hansford, Hartley, Hemphill, Hutchinson, Lipscomb, Moore, Ochiltree, Oldham, Parmer, Potter, Randall, Roberts, Sherman, Swisher and Wheeler.

Clerk's Office
Phone: 806-324-2302
Fax: 806-468-3862

**ECF Help Desk: 800-442-6850**
ecfhelp@txnb.uscourts.gov

**Judge Robert L. Jones** *sits as scheduled.*

## Dallas Division
Counties Served: Dallas, Ellis, Hunt, Johnson, Kaufman, Navarro and Rockwall.

Wichita Falls Jurisdiction Counties also filing in Dallas: Archer, Baylor, Clay, Cottle, Foard, Hardeman, King, Knox, Montague, Wichita, Wilbarger and Young.

**ECF Help Desk: 800-442-6850**
ecfhelp@txnb.uscourts.gov

**Chief Judge Barbara J. Houser**

**Judge Harlin D. Hale**
Case Identifier: HDH
Phone: 214-753-2015
Law Clerk: Stephan Manz
Phone: 214-753-2015
Deputy: Jenni Bergreen
Phone: 214-753-2060
hdh_settings@txnb.uscourts.gov
Judicial Support Specialist:
Erica Adams- Williams
Phone: 214-753-2088

**Judge Stacey G.C. Jernigan**
Case Identifier: SGJ
Phone: 214-753-2040
Judicial Assistant: Anna Saucier
Law Clerk: Laura Smith
Deputy: Traci Davis
sgj_settings@txnb.uscourts.gov
Transcripts: 214-753-2065

## Fort Worth Division
501 W. 10th St.
Fort Worth, TX 76102-3643

Counties Served: Comanche, Erath, Hood, Jack, Palo Pinto, Parker, Tarrant and Wise.

**Divisional Manager: Lisa J. Holmes**
Phone: 817-333-6000
Fax: 817-333-6001

**ECF Help Desk: 800-442-6850**
ecfhelp@txnb.uscourts.gov

**Judge Mark X. Mullin**
Case Identifier: MXM
Phone: 817-333-6020
Law Clerk: Paul Lopez
Deputy: Jennifer Calfee
Phone: 817-333-6016
dml_settings@txnb.uscourts.gov
Transcripts/ECRO: Sandy Maben
Phone: 817-333-6015

**Judge Russell F. Nelms**
Case Identifier: RFN
Phone: 817-333-6025
Law Clerk: Laurie Babich
Deputy: Jana McCrory
rfn_settings@txnb.uscourts.gov
Judicial Assistant: Barbara Groves
Transcripts: Amanda Shelby
Phone: 817-333-6014

## Lubbock Division
1205 Texas Ave., Room 306
Lubbock, TX 79401-4002

Counties Served: Bailey, Borden, Cochran, Crosby, Dawson, Dickens, Floyd, Gaines, Garza, Hale, Hockley, Kent, Lamb, Lubbock, Lynn, Motley, Scurry, Terry and Yoakum.

San Angelo Jurisdiction Counties also filing in Lubbock: Brown, Coke, Coleman, Concho, Crockett, Glasscock, Irion, Menard, Mills,

Reagan, Runnels, Schleicher, Sterling, Sutton and Tom Green.

Abilene Jurisdiction Counties also filing in Lubbock: Callahan, Eastland, Fisher, Haskell, Howard, Jones, Mitchell, Nolan, Shackelford, Stephens, Stonewall, Taylor, and Throckmorton.

**Divisional Manager: Tina Stevens**
Phone: 806-472-5000
Fax: 806-472-5004
Case Information System: 866-222-8029

**ECF Help Desk: 800-442-6850**
ecfhelp@txnb.uscourts.gov

**Judge Robert L. Jones**
Case Identifier: RLJ
Phone: 806-472-5020
Judicial Assistant: Shelby Wimberley
Law Clerk: John Eisler
Deputy: Christi Graham
Phone: 806-472-5006
rlj_settings@txnb.uscourts.gov

## U.S. Trustee's Office
## Dallas Field Office

1100 Commerce St., Room 976
Dallas, TX 75242
Phone: 214-767-8967
Fax: 214-767-8971
www.usdoj.gov/ust

**U.S. Trustee (Region 6): William T. Neary**
Phone: 214-767-8967

**Assistant U.S. Trustee: Lisa L. Lambert**
Phone: 214-767-1080

**Bankruptcy Analyst: Bradley D. Perdue**
Phone 214-767-1087

**Bankruptcy Analyst: Kendra M. Rust**
Phone: 214-767-1240

**Bankruptcy Analyst: Cheryl H. Wilcoxson**
Phone: 214-767-1243

**Bankruptcy Analyst: Susan G. Young**
Phone: 214-767-1246

**Trial Attorney: Mary Frances Durham**
Phone: 214-767-1241
maryfrances.durham@usdoj.gov

**Trial Attorney: Meredyth Kippes**
Phone: 214-767-1079

**Trial Attorney: Nancy S. Resnick**
Phone: 214-767-1088

**Trial Attorney: Erin Schmidt**
Phone: 214-767-1075

**Trial Attorney: Elizabeth Ziegler**
Phone: 214-767-1247

# SOUTHERN DISTRICT

Headquarters for the Southern Bankruptcy District
515 Rusk Ave.
Houston, TX 77002-2604
www.txs.uscourts.gov/bankruptcy

**Clerk: David J. Bradley**
P.O. Box 61010
Houston, TX 77208
Phone: 713-250-5500

**Judge Marvin Isgur**
Phone: 713-250-5421
Case Manager: Anita Dolezel
cmA671@txsb.uscourts.gov

## Brownsville Division
600 E. Harrison St., Room 101
Brownsville, TX 78520
www.txs.uscourts.gov/bankruptcy

Counties Served: Cameron and Willacy.

**Deputy-in-Charge: Rosy D'Venturi**
Phone: 956-548-2500

**Judge Marvin Isgur** *sits as scheduled.*

**Judge Eduardo V. Rodriguez** *sits as scheduled.*

## Corpus Christi Division
1133 N. Shoreline Blvd., Room 208
Corpus Christi, TX 78401
www.txs.uscourts.gov/bankruptcy

Counties Served: Aransas, Bee, Brooks, Duval, Jim Wells, Kenedy, Kleburg, Live Oak, Nueces and San Patricio.

**Deputy-in-Charge: Marianne Serpa**
Phone: 361-888-3142

STATE AND FEDERAL COURTS AND AGENCIES

**Assistant Deputy-in-Charge: Sondra Scotch**
Phone: 361-888-3142

# Galveston Division
601 Rosenburg St., Room 411
Galveston, TX 77550
www.txs.uscourts.gov/bankruptcy

Counties Served: Brazoria, Chambers, Galveston and Matagorda.

**Deputy-in-Charge: Cathy Carnew**
Phone: 409-766-3547

**Judge Letitia Z. Paul** *sits as scheduled.*
Phone: 713-250-5410
Case Manager: Maria Rodriguez
Deputy: Tracey Conard
Phone: 713-250-5772

# Houston Division
515 Rusk Ave.
Houston, TX 77002
www.txs.uscourts.gov/bankruptcy

Counties Served: Austin, Brazos, Colorado, Fayette, Fort Bend, Grimes, Harris, Madison, Montgomery, San Jacinto, Walker, Waller and Wharton.

**Deputy-in-Charge: Darlene Hansen**
Phone: 713-250-5500

**Chief Judge Jeff Bohm**
Phone: 713-250-5470
Case Manager: Vangie Attaway
cmA679@txs.uscourts.gov
Deputy: Kimberly Picota
Phone: 713-250-5405

**Judge Karen K. Brown**
Phone: 713-250-5250
Secretary: Maureen Bryan
Case Manager: Ruben Castro
Phone: 713-250-5449
cmA487@txs.uscourts.gov
Deputy: Annarose Harding

**Judge Marvin Isgur**
*See Southern District Headquarters.*

**Judge David Jones**
Phone: 713-250-5713

Case Manager: Albert Alonzo
albert_alonzo@txs.uscourts.gov
Phone: 713-250-5417
Deputy: Diyana Staples
Phone: 713-250-5779
diyana_staples@txs.uscourts.gov

**Judge Letitia Z. Paul**
*See Galveston Division.*

# Laredo Division
1300 Victoria St., Suite 1131
Laredo, TX 78040
www.txs.uscourts.gov/bankruptcy

Counties Served: Jim Hogg, La Salle, McMullen, Webb and Zapata.

**Deputy-in-Charge: Rosie Rodriguez**
Phone: 956-723-3542

**Judge David Jones** *sits as scheduled.*

**Judge Marvin Isgur** *sits as scheduled.*

# McAllen Division
1701 W. Business Highway 83, Suite 1011
McAllen, TX 78501
www.txs.uscourts.gov/bankruptcy

Counties Served: Hidalgo and Starr.

**Deputy-in-Charge: Velma Varnera**
Phone: 956-618-8065

**Judge Marvin Isgur** *sits as scheduled.*

**Judge Eduardo V. Rodriguez** *sits as scheduled.*

# Victoria Division
312 S. Main, Room 406
Victoria, TX 77901
www.txs.uscourts.gov/bankruptcy

Counties Served: Calhoun, De Witt, Goliad, Jackson, Lavaca, Refugio and Victoria.

**Deputy-in-Charge: Lana Tesch**
Phone: 361-788-5009
Fax: 361-788-5045

**Judge David Jones** *sits as scheduled.*

## U.S. Trustee's Office
## Houston Regional Office

515 Rusk St., Suite 3516
Houston, TX 77002-2604
Phone: 713-718-4650
Fax: 713-718-4670
www.usdoj.gov/ust

The Houston office of the U.S. Trustee serves Houston, Galveston, Laredo, Victoria and Corpus Christi Divisions of the Southern District of Texas.

**U.S. Trustee (Region 7): Judy A. Robbins**
Phone: 713-718-4650
judy.robbins@usdoj.gov

**Assistant U. S. Trustee: Diane Livingstone**
diane.g.livingstone@usdoj.gov

**Assistant U. S. Trustee: Nancy Ratchford**
Phone: 210-472-4640

**Bankruptcy Analyst: Barbara L. Griffin**
Phone: 713-718-4650, ext. 225
barbara.l.griffin@usdoj.gov

**Bankruptcy Analyst: Glenn D. Otto**
Phone: 713-718-4650, ext. 226
glen.d.otto@usdoj.gov

**Bankruptcy Analyst: Clarissa Waxton**
Phone: 713-718-4650, ext. 231
clarissa.waxton@usdoj.gov

**Trial Attorney: Hector Duran, Jr.**
Phone: 713-718-4650, ext. 241
hector.duran.jr@usdoj.gov

**Trial Attorney: Ellen Hickman**
Phone: 713-718-4650, ext. 250
ellen.hickman@usdoj.gov

**Trial Attorney: Nancy L. Holley**
Phone: 713-718-4650, ext. 232
nancy.holley@usdoj.gov

**Trial Attorney: Christine A. March**
Phone: 713-718-4650, ext. 239
christine.a.march@usdoj.gov

**Trial Attorney: Stephen Statham**
Phone: 713-718-4650

## U.S. Trustee's Office
## Corpus Christi Field Office

606 N. Carancahua Street, Suite 1107
Corpus Christi, TX 78401
Phone: 361-888-3261
Fax: 361-888-3263
www.usdoj.gov/ust

The Corpus Christi office of the U.S. Trustee serves Corpus Christi, Brownsville, McAllen, Laredo and Victoria Divisions of the Southern District of Texas.

**Assistant U.S. Trustee: Diane Livingstone**
Paralegal Specialist: Adrian Duran
Regional Auditor: Valerie Goodwin
Legal Assistant (Bankruptcy/OA):
Genny Henicke
Trial Attorney: Stephen Statham

## Western District

Headquarters for the Western Bankruptcy District
615 E. Houston St., Room 597
San Antonio, TX 78205
www.txwb.uscourts.gov

**Clerk: Yvette M. Taylor**
Phone: 210-472-6720

**Chief Judge Ronald B. King**
Phone: 210-472-6609
Judicial Secretary: Tricia K. Haass
Law Clerk: Jason Enright
Deputy: Jana Brisiel
Phone: 210-472-6720, ext. 5735

## Austin Division

903 San Jacinto Blvd., Suite 322
Austin, TX 78701
www.txwb.uscourts.gov

Counties Served: Bastrop, Blanco, Burleson, Burnet, Caldwell, Gillespie, Hays, Kimble, Lampasas, Lee, Llano, Mason, McCulloch, San Saba, Travis, Washington and Williamson.

**Deputy-in-Charge: Theresa Mills**
Phone: 512-916-5237, ext. 2707

**Judge Tony M. Davis**
Suite 332
Phone: 512-916-5237
Law Clerks: Christopher Bradley, Sarah Wood and Robert Shannon
Phone: 512-916-5875
Deputy: Jennifer Lopez
Phone: 512-916-5237, ext. 2711

**Judge H. Christopher Mott**
Suite 326
Phone: 512-916-5237
Law Clerks: Jennifer Wuebker and Sarah McHaney
Phone: 512-916-5800
Deputy: Ronda Farrar
Phone: 512-916-5237, ext. 2712
ronda_farrar@txwb.uscourts.gov

## El Paso Division
511 E. San Antonio Ave., Room 444
El Paso, TX 79901
www.txwb.uscourts.gov

County served: El Paso.

**Deputy-in-Charge: Julie Herrera**
Phone: 915-779-7362, ext. 6575
**Case Managers:**
Rachel Cardenas, ext. 6571
Laura Resendez, ext. 6573
Bobby Yarbrough, ext. 6572

**Judge H. Christopher Mott** *sits as scheduled.*

## Midland-Odessa Division
100 E. Wall St., Room P-163
Midland, TX 79701
www.txwb.uscourts.gov

Counties served: Andrews, Brewster, Crane, Culberson, Ector, Hudspeth, Jeff Davis, Loving, Martin, Midland, Pecos, Presidio, Reeves, Upton, Ward and Winkler.

**Unstaffed Office** as of 5/25/15

**Chief Judge Ronald B. King** *sits as scheduled.*

## San Antonio Division
615 E. Houston St., Room 597
San Antonio, TX 78205
www.txwb.uscourts.gov

Counties Served: Atascosa, Bandera, Bexar,

Comal, Dimmit, Edwards, Frio, Gonzales, Guadalupe, Karnes, Kendall, Kerr, Kinney, Maverick, Medina, Real, Terrell, Uvalde, Val Verde, Wilson and Zavala.

**Deputy-in-Charge: Christy Carouth**
Phone: 210-472-6720, ext. 5747

**Judge Craig A. Gargotta**
Room 505
Phone: 210-472-6720
Law Clerks: Amelia Hurt and Megan Young
Deputy: Lisa Elizondo
Phone: 210-472-6720, ext. 5736

**Chief Judge Ronald B. King** *sits as scheduled.*

## Waco Division
800 Franklin Ave., Suite 140
Waco, TX 76701

Counties Served: Bell, Bosque, Coryell, Falls, Freestone, Hamilton, Hill, Leon, Limestone, McLennan, Milam, Robertson and Somervell.

**Office Manager: Mark G. Borchardt**
Room 380
Phone: 254-750-1501

**Judge Walter S. Smith**
Phone: 254-750-1501
Court Reporter: Kristie M. Davis
Phone: 254-754-7444
Deputy: Suzanne Miles
suzanne_miles@txwd.uscourts.gov

**Magistrate Judge Jeffery C. Manske**
Phone:254-750-1501
Deputy: Lisa Trotter
Phone: 254-750-1511
lisa_Trotter@txwd.uscourts.gov

## U.S. Trustee's Office
## Austin Field Office

903 San Jacinto Blvd., Suite 230
Austin, TX 78701-2450
Phone: 512-916-5328
Fax: 512-916-5331
www.usdoj.gov/ust

The Austin office of the U.S. Trustee serves Austin and Waco Divisions of the Western District of Texas.

*See Southern District for Regional Office (Houston) of Region 7 U.S. Trustee Program.*

**Assistant U.S. Trustee: Henry G. Hobbs**
Phone: 512-916-5328
henry.g.hobbs@usdoj.gov
Bankruptcy Analyst: Brian Henault
Trial Attorney: Deborah A. Bynum
Trial Attorney: Valerie Wenger

## U.S. Trustee's Office
## San Antonio Field Office

615 E. Houston St., Room 533
San Antonio, TX 78205-2055
Phone: 210-472-4640
Fax: 210-472-4649

The San Antonio office of the U.S.Trustee serves San Antonio, El Paso and Midland Divisions of the Western District of Texas.

**Assistant U.S. Trustee: Nancy Ratchford**
Phone: 210-472-4640, ext. 223
nancy.ratchford@usdoj.gov

**Bankruptcy Analyst: Michael R. Buckner**
Phone: 210-472-4640, ext. 227
michael.r.buckner@usdoj.gov

**Trial Attorney: Kevin M. Epstein**
Phone: 210-472-4640, ext. 225
kevin.m.epstein@usdoj.gov

**Trial Attorney: Jim Rose**
Phone: 210-472-4640, ext. 228
james.rose@usdoj.gov

# U.S. ATTORNEY'S OFFICES

## Eastern District
www.usdoj.gov/usao/txe/

**U.S. Attorney: John M. Bales**
350 Magnolia St., Suite 150
Beaumont, TX 77701
Phone: 409-839-2538
Fax: 409-839-2550

**Lufkin Office Chief: (Vacant)**
**Contact: Matt Quinn in Beaumont Office**
415 S. 1st St., Suite 201
Lufkin, TX 75901
Phone: 936-639-4003
Fax: 936-639-4033

**Plano Office Chief: Kevin McClendon**
101 E. Park Blvd., Suite 500
Plano, TX 75074
Phone: 972-509-1201
Fax: 972-509-1209

**Sherman Office Chief: Maureen Smith**
600 E. Taylor St., Suite 2000
Sherman, TX 75090
Phone: 903-868-9454
Fax: 903-868-2792

**Texarkana Office Chief: Jim Middleton**
500 N. Stateline Ave., Suite 402
Texarkana, TX 75501
Phone: 903-590-1400
Fax: 903-792-5164

**Tyler Office Chief: Jim Middleton**
110 N. College Ave., Suite 700
Tyler, TX 75702-0204
Phone: 903-590-1400
Fax: 903-590-1439

## Northern District
www.usdoj.gov/usao/txn/

**U.S. Attorney (Acting): John R. Parker**
1100 Commerce St., Third Floor
Dallas, TX 75242
Phone: 214-659-8600

**Amarillo Office**
500 S. Taylor St., Suite 300, LB 238
Amarillo, TX 79101-2446
Phone: 806-324-2356

**Fort Worth Office**
801 Cherry St., Unit 4, Suite 1700
Fort Worth, TX 76102-6882
Phone: 817-252-5200

**Lubbock Office**
1205 Texas Ave., Suite 700
Lubbock, TX 79401-40024
Phone: 806-472-7351

## Southern District
www.usdoj.gov/usao/txs/

**U.S. Attorney: Kenneth Magidson**
1000 Louisiana, Suite 2300
Houston, TX 77002
Phone: 713-567-9000
Fax: 713-718-3300
Assistant U.S. Attorney (Civil): Keith Wyatt
Assistant U.S. Attorney (Criminal): Bryan Best

**Brownsville Office AUSA-in-Charge: Rick Lara**
600 E. Harrison, Suite 201
Brownsville, TX 78520-5106
Phone: 956-548-2554
Fax: 956-548-2711

**Corpus Christi/Victoria Office AUSA-in-Charge: Julie Hanson**
800 N. Shoreline, Suite 500
Corpus Christi, TX 78401
Phone: 361-888-3111
Fax: 361-888-3200

**Laredo Office AUSA-in-Charge: Jose A Moreno**
11204 McPherson Rd., Suite 100-A
Laredo, TX 78045
Phone: 956-723-6523

**McAllen Office AUSA-in-Charge: James Sturgis**
1701 W. Highway 83, Suite 600
McAllen, TX 78501-5160
Phone: 956-618-8010
Fax: 956-618-8009

## Western District
www.usdoj.gov/usao/txw/

**San Antonio (Main) Office**
601 N.W. Loop 410, Suite 600
San Antonio, TX 78216-5597
Phone: 210-384-7100
Fax: 210-384-7105

**U.S. Attorney (Acting): Richard L. Durbin, Jr.**
First Assistant U.S. Attorney: Addie Cote
Assistant U.S. Attorney (Civil): John Paniszczyn
Assistant U.S. Attorney (Criminal): Margaret Leachman

**Alpine Office Chief: Jay Miller**
2500 N. Highway 118, Suite 200
Alpine, TX 79830
Phone: 432-837-7332
Fax: 432-837-7449

**Austin Office Chief: Ashley Hoff**
816 Congress Ave., Suite 1000
Austin, TX 78701
Phone: 512-916-5858
Fax: 512-916-5854

**Del Rio Office Chief: Patrick Burke**
111 E. Broadway, Suite 300
Del Rio, TX 78840
Phone: 830-703-2025
Fax: 830-703-2030

**El Paso Office Chief: Jose Luis Gonzalez**
700 E. San Antonio Ave., Suite 200
El Paso, TX 79901
Phone: 915-534-6884
Fax: 915-534-6024

**Midland Office Chief: William Lewis**
400 W. Illinois St., Suite 1200
Midland, TX 79701
Phone: 432-686-4110
Fax: 432-686-4131

**Pecos Office Chief: Jay Miller**
410 S. Cedar, Room 225
Pecos, TX 79772
Phone: 432-445-4343
Fax: 432-445-2225

**Waco Office Chief: Mark Frazier**
800 Franklin Ave., Suite 280
Waco, TX 76701
Phone: 254-750-1580
Fax: 254-750-1599

# FEDERAL PUBLIC DEFENDER'S OFFICES

## Eastern District
txe.fd.org

**Tyler Division**
**Public Defender: Patrick Black**
110 N. College, Ste 1122
Tyler, TX 75702
Phone: 903-531-9233
Fax: 903-531-9625

**Beaumont Division**
350 Magnolia, Ste 117
Beaumont, TX 77701
Phone: 409-839-2608
Fax: 409-839-2610

**Sherman Division**
600 Taylor St., Ste 4000
Sherman, TX 75090
Phone: 903-892-4448
Fax: 903-892-4808

**Frisco Branch**
7460 Warren Pkwy., Ste 270
Frisco, TX 75034
Phone: 469-362-8506
Fax: 469-362-6010

## Northern District
txn.fd.org

**Dallas Office**
**Public Defender: Jason D. Hawkins**
525 Griffin St., Suite 629
Dallas, TX 75202
Phone: 214-767-2746
Fax: 214-767-2886

**Amarillo Office**
500 S. Taylor, Suite 110
Amarillo, TX 79101
Phone: 806-324-2370
Fax: 806-324-2372

**Fort Worth Office**
819 Taylor St., Room 9A10
Fort Worth, TX 76102
Phone: 817-978-2753
Fax: 817-978-2757

**Lubbock Office**
1205 Texas Ave., Room 506
Lubbock, TX 79401
Phone: 806-472-7236
Fax: 806-472-7241

## Southern District
www.fpdsdot.org

**Houston Office**
**Public Defender: Marjorie A. Meyers**
440 Louisiana St., Suite 1350
Houston, TX 77002-1669
Phone: 713-718-4600
Fax: 713-718-4610

**Brownsville Office**
600 E. Harrison, Room 102

Brownsville, TX 78520-7119
Phone: 956-548-2573
Fax: 956-548-2674

**Corpus Christi Office**
606 N. Carancahua St., Suite 401
Corpus Christi, TX 78401-0697
Phone: 361-888-3532
Fax: 361-888-3534

**Laredo Office**
1202 Houston St.
Laredo, TX 78040-8018
Phone: 956-753-5313
Fax: 956-753-5317

**McAllen Office**
1701 W. Business Hwy 83, Suite 405
McAllen, TX 78501-5178
Phone: 956-630-2995
Fax: 956-631-8647

## Western District
txw.fd.org

**San Antonio (Main) Office**
**Public Defender: Maureen Scott Franco**
727 E. César E. Chávez Blvd., Suite B-207
San Antonio, TX 78206-1205
Phone: 210-472-6700
Fax: 210-472-4454

**Alpine Office**
108 N. 10th St.
Alpine, TX 79830-5915
Phone: 432-837-5598
Fax: 432-837-9023

**Austin Office**
504 Lavaca St., Ste 960
Austin, TX 78701-2860
Phone: 512-916-5025
Fax: 512-916-5035

**Del Rio Office**
2205 Veterans Blvd., Suite A2
Del Rio, TX 78840-3141
Phone: 830-703-2040
Fax: 830-703-2047

**El Paso Office**
700 E. San Antonio St., Suite D-401
El Paso, TX 79901-7020
Phone: 915-534-6525
Fax: 915-534-6534

# U.S. PROBATION OFFICES

## Eastern District

www.txep.uscourts.gov

**Chief Probation Officer: Shane Ferguson**
211 W. Ferguson, Suite 224
Tyler, TX 75702-7222
Phone: 903-590-1330
Deputy Chief Probation Officer: Myra Kirkwood
Phone: 469-304-4927

**Tyler Supervision Office**
1700 SE Loop 323, Suite 340
Tyler, TX 75701
Phone: 903-566-9790

**Beaumont Office / Supervision Office**
300 Willow St., Room 327
Beaumont, TX 77701-2216
Phone: 409-839-2558

**Lufkin Office**
104 N. 3rd, Room 110
Lufkin, TX 75901
Phone: 936-632-9004

**Plano Office**
500 N. Central Expy., Room 220
Plano, TX 75074
Phone: 972-578-9696

**Sherman Office**
200 N. Travis, Suite 100
Sherman, TX 75090
Phone: 903-893-7706

**Texarkana Office**
500 N. State Line, Room 205
Texarkana, TX 71854-5960
Phone: 903-794-4515

## Northern District

www.txnp.uscourts.gov

**Chief Probation Officer: Misti Westendorff**
1100 Commerce St., Room 1329
Dallas, TX 75242-1391

Phone: 214-753-2500
Fax: 214-753-2570

**Abilene Office**
341 Pine St., Room 2320
Abilene, TX 79601-5928
Phone: 325-676-4111
Fax: 325-676-1936

**Amarillo Office**
205 E. Fifth St., Room 120
Amarillo, TX 79101-1559
Phone: 806-324-2351
Fax: 806-324-2125

**Arlington Office**
2501 Avenue J, Suite 111
Arlington, TX 76006-6182
Phone: 817-649-2577
Fax: 817-649-5954

**Fort Worth Office**
501 W. 10th St., Room 406
Fort Worth, TX 76102-3639
Phone: 817-978-3633
Fax: 817-978-3726

**Lubbock Office**
1205 Texas Ave., Room 106
Lubbock, TX 79401-4001
Phone: 806-472-7001
Fax: 806-472-7018

**San Angelo Office**
33 E. Twohig St., Suite 106-B
San Angelo, TX 76903-6451
Phone: 325-653-8432
Fax: 325-655-9051

**Wichita Falls Office**
1000 Lamar St., Room 309
Wichita Falls, TX 76301-3430
Phone: 940-723-8696
Fax: 940-723-7347

## Southern District

www.txs.uscourts.gov/probation/

**Chief Probation Officer (Acting): Sean Harmon**
515 Rusk Ave., Suite 2301
Houston, TX 77002
Phone: 713-250-5266
Fax: 713-250-5092

**Brownsville Office**
600 E. Harrison, Suite 103
Brownsville, TX 78520-5263
Phone: 956-548-2522

**Corpus Christi Office**
1133 N. Shoreline Blvd., Suite 124
Corpus Christi, TX 78401
Phone: 361-888-3145

**Galveston Office**
601 25th St., Room 401
Galveston, TX 77550
Phone: 409-766-3733

**Laredo Office**
1300 Victoria St., Suite 2111
Laredo, TX 78040
Phone: 956-726-2255

**McAllen Office**
1701 W. Business Hwy 83, Suite 729
McAllen, TX 78501
Phone: 956-618-8035

**Victoria Office**
312 S. Main St., Suite 302
Victoria, TX 77901
Phone: 361-579-6640

# Western District
www.txwp.uscourts.gov/uspo

**Chief Probation Officer: Joe E. Sanchez**
727 E. César E. Chávez Blvd., Suite B-310
San Antonio, TX 78206-1203
Phone: 210-472-6590

**Deputy Chief Probation Officers:**
Suzan Contreras
Gerardo Luna

**Assistant Deputy Chief Probation Officers:**
Victor Calderon
David Natividad

**Alpine Office**
2450 N. Hwy 118

Alpine, TX 79830
Phone: 432-837-3578
Fax: 432-837-7435
**Supervising Probation Officer:**
Michael McDougall

**Austin Office**
501 West Fifth St., Suite 2100
Austin, TX 78701-3822
Phone: 512-916-5761
Fax: 512-916-5766
**Supervising Probation Officers:**
Rick Golden
Lonnie Hellums
Dwayne Jones

**Del Rio Office**
111 E. Broadway, Suite 200
Del Rio, TX 78840
Phone: 830-703-2089
Fax: 830-703-2092
**Supervising Probation Officers:**
Romero Cruz
Darren Kohut
David Merzier
Sylvia Nowlin
Diane Rodriguez

**El Paso Office**
700 E. San Antonio Ave., Suite 500
El Paso, TX 79901-7020
Phone: 915-585-6500
Fax: 915-585-6521
**Supervising Probation Officers:**
Juan Campos
Isabel Carrillo
George Castro
Adele Galante (Retiring in December 2016)
Enrique Lopez
Otis Martin
David C. Trejo
Angelica Vega
Luis Luevano
Tony Glover

**Fort Hood Office**
Bldg. 5794, Tank Destroyer Blvd.
Fort Hood, TX 76544-6252
Phone: 254-668-6136
**Supervising Probation Officers:**
Brenda Frazier
Diane Thomas

**STATE AND FEDERAL COURTS AND AGENCIES**

**Midland Office**
100 E. Wall St., Suite P111
Midland, TX 79701-5243
Phone: 432-686-4060
Fax: 432-686-4065
**Supervising Probation Officers:**
Barbara Arreguy
Oswaldo Hinojos

**Pecos Office**
410 S. Cedar St.
Pecos, TX 79772
Phone: 432-445-2971
Fax: 432-445-7284
**Supervising Probation Officer:**
Karrie Bragg

**Temple Office**
1005 Marlandwood, Suite 113
Temple, TX 76502
Phone: 254-778-7204
Fax: 254-778-1789
**Supervising Probation Officer:**
Gregory C. Robinson

**Waco Office**
800 Franklin Ave., Room 100
Waco, TX 76701-1254
Phone: 254-750-1550
Fax: 254-750-1560
**Supervising Probation Officers:**
LaDonna Reyna
Gregory C. Robinson
David Russell

# FEDERAL BUREAU OF INVESTIGATION

FBI Headquarters
935 Pennsylvania Ave, NW
Washington, D.C. 20535
Phone: 202-324-3000

**Dallas Office Special Agent in Charge:**
**Thomas M. Class, Sr.**
One Justice Way
Dallas, TX 75220
Phone: 972-559-5000
Fax: 972-559-5600
fbi.dallas@ic.fbi.gov
Website: fbi.gov/dallas

**El Paso Office Special Agent in Charge:**
**Douglas Lindquist**
660 S. Mesa Hills Dr., Ste 3000
El Paso, TX 79912-5533
Phone: 915-832-5000
Fax: 915-832-5259
Website: fbi.gov/elpaso

**Houston Office Special Agent in Charge:**
**Perrye K. Turner**
1 Justice Park Dr.
Houston, TX 77092
Phone: 713-693-5000
Fax: 713-936-8999
houston.texas@ic.fbi.gov
Website: fbi.gov/houston

**San Antonio Office Special Agent in Charge:**
**Christopher Combs**
5740 University Heights Blvd.
San Antonio, TX 78249
Phone: 210-225-6741
Fax: 210-650-6153
sanantonio@ic.fbi.gov
Website: fbi.gov/sanantonio

# U.S. SECURITIES AND EXCHANGE COMMISSION

**Fort Worth District Director:**
**Shamoil Shipchandler**
801 Cherry St., Unit 18
Fort Worth, TX 76102
Phone: 817-978-3821
dfw@sec.gov

# DRUG ENFORCEMENT ADMINISTRATION

www.justice.gov/dea

**Dallas Division Special Agent in Charge (Acting):**
**Craig M. Wiles**
10160 Technology Blvd. E
Dallas, TX 75220
Phone: 214-366-6900

**El Paso Division Special Agent in Charge:**
**Will R. Glaspy**
660 S. Mesa Hills Dr., Suite 2000

El Paso, TX 79912
Phone: 915-832-6000

**Houston Division Special Agent in Charge:**
**Joseph M. Arabit**
1433 West Loop South, Ste 600
Houston, TX 77027-9506
Phone: 713-693-3000

# SOCIAL SECURITY
# ADMINISTRATION
www.ssa.gov/dallas

Serving Arkansas, Louisiana, New Mexico,
Oklahoma and Texas

**Region VI Commissioner: Sheila Everett**
1301 Young St. Room 500
Dallas, TX 75202
Phone: 214-767-4207
Fax: 214-767-4259

**Region VI Administrative Law**
Judge Joan Parks-Saunders
Phone: 214-767-9401
Fax: 214-767-9407
joan.parks-saunders@ssa.gov

# EXECUTIVE OFFICE FOR
# IMMIGRATION REVIEW
www.usdoj.gov/eoir
Forms: www.usdoj.gov/eoir/formspage.htm

**Dallas Immigration Court**
Court Administrator: Barbara Baker
1100 Commerce St., Suite 1060
Dallas, TX 75242
Phone: 214-767-1814

**Office of Legislative and Public Affairs**
703-305-0289
pao.eoir@usdoj.gov

**JUDGES**
Daniel Weiss
Xiomara Davis-Gumbs
R. Wayne Kimball
James Nugent
Richard R. Ozmun

**Deitrich H. Sims**
**El Paso Immigration Court**
Court Administrator: Theresa N. Baeza
700 E. San Antonio Ave., Suite 750
El Paso, TX 79901
Phone: 915-534-6020

**JUDGES**
Robert S. Hough
Thomas Roepke
**El Paso Service Processing Center**
8915 Montana Ave., Ste 100
El Paso, TX 79925
Phone: 915-771-1600

**JUDGES**
William L. Abbott
Guadalupe Gonzalez
Sunita Mahtabsar
Stephen Ruhle
**Harlingen Immigration Court**
Court Administrator: Celeste G. Garza
2009 W. Jefferson Ave., Ste 300
Harlingen, TX 78550
Phone: 956-427-8580

**JUDGES**
Howard E. Achtsam
David Ayala
Eleazar Tovar

**Houston Immigration Court**
Court Administrator: Melba Bennett
600 Jefferson, Ste 900
Houston, TX 77002
Phone: 713-718-3870

**JUDGES**
Chris A. Brisack
Mimi S. Yam
Clarease Rankin-Yates
Monique Harris
Nimmo Bhugat

**Houston Service Processing Center**
Court Administrator: Mark Russelburg
5520 Greens Rd.
Houston, TX 77032
Phone: 281-594-5600

**JUDGES**
Saul Greenstein
Lisa Luis
Richard Walton

STATE AND FEDERAL COURTS AND AGENCIES

**Pearsall Immigration Court**
Court Administrator: Marion Hicks
566 Veterans Dr.
Pearsall, TX 78061
Phone: 210-368-5700

**JUDGES**
Meredith B. Tyrakoski
Daniel J. Santander
**Port Isabel Processing Center**
Court Administrator: Celeste G. Garza
27991 Buena Vista Blvd.
Los Fresnos, TX 78566
Phone: 956-547-1789

**JUDGES**
Keith Hunsucker
Robert Powell
Morris Onyewuchi
**San Antonio Immigration Court**
Court Administrator: Daniel Ponce de Leon
800 Dolorosa, Suite 300
San Antonio, TX 78207
Phone: 210-472-6637

**JUDGES**
Margaret D. Burkhart
Gary Burkholder
Anibal D. Martinez
Glenn P. McPhaul

# U.S. CITIZENSHIP AND IMMIGRATION SERVICES

INS Customer Service: 1-800-375-5283
www.uscis.gov
ICE Public Affairs: 202-732-4242
Office of General Counsel: 202-732-5000

**Dallas Field Office**
125 E. John Carpenter Fwy., Ste 500
Irving, TX 75062

**El Paso Field Office**
11541 Montana Ave., Suite 0
El Paso, TX 79936

**Harlingen Field Office**
1717 Zoy St.
Harlingen, TX 78552

**Houston Field Office**
126 Northpoint Dr., Room 2020
Houston TX 77060

**San Antonio Field Office**
8940 Fourwinds Dr., Room 5045
San Antonio, TX 78239

# U.S. CUSTOMS SERVICE

## Customs Management Centers

**Houston Field Operations Office**
Director: Judson Murdoch
2323 S. Shepherd St., Ste 1300
Houston, TX 77019
Phone: 713-387-7200
Fax: 713-387-7303

**Laredo Field Operations Office**
Director: David Higgerson
109 Shiloh Dr., Ste 300
Laredo, TX 78045
Phone: 956-753-1700
Fax: 956-753-1754

**El Paso Field Operations Office**
Director: Hector Mancha
9400 Viscount Blvd., Ste 104
El Paso, TX 79925
Phone: 915-633-7300, ext. 100
Fax: 915-633-7392

# STATE ADMINISTRATIVE JUDICIAL REGIONS

## Region One
www.txcourts.gov/1ajr

Counties Served: Anderson, Bowie, Camp,
Cass, Cherokee, Collin, Dallas, Delta,
Ellis, Fannin, Franklin, Grayson, Gregg,

Harrison, Henderson, Hopkins, Houston, Hunt, Kaufman, Lamar, Marion, Morris, Nacogdoches, Panola, Rains, Red River, Rockwall, Rusk, Shelby, Smith, Titus, Upshur, Van Zandt and Wood.

**Presiding Judge Mary Murphy**
133 N. Riverfront Blvd., LB 50
Dallas, TX 75207
Phone: 214-653-2943
Fax: 214-653-2957
mmurphy@firstadmin.com
Office Manager: Candy Shiver
cshiver@firstadmin.com
Staff Attorney: Alisa Frame
alisa.frame@firstadmin.com

## Region Two
www.mctx.org/courts/second_administrative_judicial_region
Counties Served: Angelina, Bastrop, Brazoria, Brazos, Burleson, Chambers, Fort Bend, Freestone, Galveston, Grimes, Hardin, Harris, Jasper, Jefferson, Lee, Leon, Liberty, Limestone, Madison, Matagorda, Montgomery, Newton, Orange, Polk, Robertson, Sabine, San Augustine, San Jacinto, Trinity, Tyler, Walker, Waller, Washington and Wharton.

**Presiding Judge Olen Underwood**
301 N. Thompson, Suite 102
Conroe TX 77301
Phone: 936-538-8176
Fax: 936-538-8167
Administrative Assistant: Rebecca Brite
Administrative Assistant: Melanie Sipes
melanie.sipes@mctx.org

## Region Three
www.txcourts.gov/3ajr

Counties Served: Austin, Bell, Blanco, Bosque, Burnet, Caldwell, Colorado, Comal, Comanche, Coryell, Falls, Fayette, Gonzales, Guadalupe, Hamilton, Hays, Hill, Lampasas, Lavaca, Llano, McLennan, Milam, Navarro, San Saba, Travis and Williamson.
**Presiding Judge Billy Ray Stubblefield**

405 S. MLK Blvd., Box 9
Georgetown, TX 78626
Phone: 512-943-3777
Fax: 512-943-3767
presidingjudge3@wilco.org
Administrative Assistant: Brenda Wilburn

## Region Four
www.txcourts.gov/4ajr

Counties Served: Aransas, Atascosa, Bee, Bexar, Calhoun, De Witt, Dimmit, Frio, Goliad, Jackson, Karnes, La Salle, Live Oak, Maverick, McMullen, Refugio, San Patricio, Victoria, Webb, Wilson, Zapata and Zavala.

**Presiding Judge David Peeples**
100 Dolorosa, Room 4.08
San Antonio, TX 78205
Phone: 210-335-3954
Fax: 210-335-3955
Administrative Assistant: Leslie Bochniak
lmbochniak@aol.com

## Region Five
www.txcourts.gov/5ajr

Counties Served: Brooks, Cameron, Duval, Hidalgo, Jim Hogg, Jim Wells, Kenedy, Kleberg, Nueces, Starr and Willacy.

**Presiding Judge J. Missy Medary**
200 N. Almond St.
Alice, TX 78332
Phone: 361-668-5766
Fax: 512-367-5788
Administrative Assistants:
JoAnna Gutierrez and Emily L. Jirovec
fifth.region@yahoo.com

## Region Six
www.txcourts.gov/6ajr

Counties Served: Bandera, Brewster, Crockett, Culberson, Edwards, El Paso, Gillespie, Hudspeth, Jeff Davis, Kendall, Kerr, Kimble, Kinney, Mason, McCulloch, Medina, Menard, Pecos, Presidio, Reagan, Real, Sutton, Terrell, Upton, Uvalde and Val Verde.
**Presiding Judge Stephen B. Ables**

700 Main St., 2nd Floor
Kerrville, TX 78028
Phone: 830-459-4300
Fax: 830-792-2294
Administrative Assistant: Becky Henderson
beckyh@co.kerr.tx.us

## Region Seven
www.txcourts.gov/7ajr

Counties Served: Andrews, Borden, Brown, Callahan, Coke, Coleman, Concho, Crane, Dawson, Ector, Fisher, Gaines, Garza, Glasscock, Haskell, Howard, Irion, Jones, Kent, Loving, Lynn, Martin, Midland, Mills, Mitchell, Nolan, Reeves, Runnels, Schleicher, Scurry, Shackleford, Sterling, Stonewall, Taylor, Throckmorton, Tom Green, Ward and Winkler.

**Presiding Judge Dean Rucker**
500 N. Loraine St., Suite 502
Midland, TX 79701-4557
Phone: 432-688-4370
Fax: 432-688-4933
Administrative Assistant: JoAnn Gonzalez

## Region Eight
www.txcourts.gov/8ajr

Counties Served: Archer, Clay, Cooke, Denton, Eastland, Erath, Hood, Jack, Johnson, Montague, Palo Pinto, Parker, Somervell, Stephens, Tarrant, Wichita, Wise and Young.

**Presiding Judge David L. Evans**
401 W. Belknap, 5th Floor
Fort Worth, TX 76196-1148
Phone: 817-884-1558
Fax: 817-884-1560
Administrative Assistant: Tracy Kemp
8thadmin@8thjudicialregion.com

## Region Nine
www.txcourts.gov/9ajr

Counties Served: Armstrong, Bailey, Baylor, Briscoe, Carson, Castro, Childress, Cochran, Collingsworth, Cottle, Crosby, Dallam, Deaf Smith, Dickens, Donley, Floyd, Foard, Gray, Hale, Hall, Hansford, Hardeman, Hartley,

Hemphill, Hockley, Hutchinson, King, Knox, Lamb, Lipscomb, Lubbock, Moore, Motley, Ochiltree, Oldham, Parmer, Potter, Randall, Roberts, Sherman, Swisher, Terry, Wheeler, Wilbarger and Yoakum.

**Presiding Judge Kelly G. Moore**
500 W. Main, Room 302W
Brownfield, TX 79316
Phone: 806-637-1329
Administrative Assistant: Debbi Miller
dmiller@terrycounty.org

# STATE APPELLATE COURTS

# TEXAS SUPREME COURT

201 W. 14th, Room 104
Austin, TX 78701
www.txcourts.gov/supreme

**Clerk: Blake Hawthorne**
P.O. Box 12248
Austin, TX 78711
Phone: 512-463-1312
Fax: 512-463-1365
blake.hawthorne@txcourts.gov
Chief Deputy Clerk: Claudia Jenks
Administrative Assistant: Nadine Schneider

**General Counsel: Nina Hess Hsu**
Phone: 512-475-0938

**Staff Attorney/Public Information: Osler McCarthy**
Phone: 512-463-1441
osler.mccarthy@txcourts.gov

**JUSTICES**
**Place 1: Chief Justice Nathan L. Hecht**
Phone: 512-463-1348
**Place 2: Don R. Willett**
Phone: 512-463-1344
**Place 3: Debra Lehrmann**
Phone: 512-463-1320
**Place 4: John Phillip Devine**
Phone: 512-463-1316
**Place 5: Paul W. Green**
Phone: 512-463-1328
**Place 6: Jeff Brown**
Phone: 512-463-3494

Place 7: Jeffrey S. Boyd
Phone: 512-463-1332
Place 8: Phillip W. Johnson
Phone: 512-463-1336
Place 9: Eva Guzman
Phone: 512-463-1340

# COURT OF CRIMINAL APPEALS

www.txcourts.gov/cca
201 W. 14th, Room 106
Austin, TX 78701

Clerk: Abel Acosta
Phone: 512-463-1551
Fax: 512-463-7061
abel.acosta@txcourts.gov
Chief Deputy Clerks:
John Brown and Kelley Reyes
General Counsel: Sian Schilhab
Phone: 512-463-1597
Supervising Attorney: Michael Stauffacher
Phone: 512-936-1631
Staff Attorney: Kathy Schneider
Phone: 512-936-1627

Presiding Judge Sharon Keller
Phone: 512-463-1590
JUDGES
Place 2: Lawrence E. Meyers
Phone: 512-463-1580
Place 3: Cheryl Johnson
Phone: 512-463-1560
Place 4: Michael E. Keasler
Phone: 512-463-1555
Place 5: Barbara Hervey
Phone: 512-463-1575
Place 6: Elsa Alcala
Phone: 512-463-1585
Place 7: Bert Richardson
Phone: 512-463-1565
Place 8: Kevin P. Yeary
Phone: 512-463-1595
Place 9: David Newell
Phone: 512-463-1570

# STATE COURTS OF APPEALS

## 1st Court of Appeals

301 Fannin
Houston, TX 77002

www.txcourts.gov/1stcoa

Counties Served: Austin, Brazoria, Chambers, Colorado, Fort Bend, Galveston, Grimes, Harris, Waller and Washington.

Clerk: Christopher A. Prine
Phone: 713-274-2700
Chief Staff Attorney: Janet Williams

Chief Justice: Sherry Radack

JUSTICES (IN ORDER OF SENIORITY)
Terry Jennings
Evelyn Keyes
Laura Carter Higley
Jane Bland
Michael C. Massengale
Harvey G. Brown
Rebeca A. Huddle
Russell Lloyd

## 2nd Court of Appeals

401 W. Belknap, Suite 9000
Fort Worth, TX 79196
www.txcourts.gov/2ndcoa
Counties Served: Archer, Clay, Cooke, Denton, Hood, Jack, Montague, Parker, Tarrant, Wichita, Wise and Young.

Clerk: Debra Spisak
Phone: 817-884-1900
Fax: 817-884-1932
debra.spisak@txcourts.gov
Chief Staff Attorney: Lisa M. West

Chief Justice: Terrie Livingston

JUSTICES
Lee Ann Dauphinot
Anne L. Gardner
Sue Walker
Bill Meier
Lee Gabriel
Bonnie Sudderth

## 3rd Court of Appeals

www.txcourts.gov/3rdcoa
209 W. 14th St., Room 101
Austin, TX 78701

Mailing address:
P.O. Box 12547
Austin, TX 78711
Counties Served: Bastrop, Bell, Blanco, Burnet, Caldwell, Coke, Comal, Concho,

**STATE AND FEDERAL COURTS AND AGENCIES**

Fayette, Hays, Irion, Lampasas, Lee, Llano, McCulloch, Milam, Mills, Runnels, San Saba, Schleicher, Sterling, Tom Green, Travis and Williamson.

**Clerk: Jeffrey D. Kyle**
Phone: 512-463-1733
Fax: 512-463-1685
clerk@3rdcoa.courts.state.tx.us

**Chief Justice: Jeff L. Rose**

**JUSTICES**
Cindy Olson Bourland
Melissa Goodwin
Scott K. Field
Bob Pemberton
David Puryear

## 4th Court of Appeals

300 Dolorosa, Suite 3200
San Antonio, TX 78205-3037
www.txcourts.gov/4thcoa
Counties Served: Atascosa, Bandera, Bexar, Brooks, Dimmit, Duval, Edwards, Frio, Gillespie, Guadalupe, Jim Hogg, Jim Wells, Karnes, Kendall, Kerr, Kimble, Kinney, La Salle, Mason, Maverick, McMullen, Medina, Menard, Real, Starr, Sutton, Uvalde, Val Verde, Webb, Wilson, Zapata and Zavala.

**Clerk: Keith Hottle**
Phone: 210-335-2635
Fax: 210-335-2762
keith.hottle@courts.state.tx.us
Chief Staff Attorney: Wendy Martinez

**Chief Justice: Sandee Bryan Marion**
Phone: 210-335-2629

**JUSTICES (IN ORDER OF SENIORITY)**
Karen Angelini
Marialyn Barnard
Rebeca C. Martinez
Patricia O. Alvarez
Luz Elena D. Chapa
Jason Pulliam

## 5th Court of Appeals

600 Commerce St., Suite 200
Dallas, TX 75202-4658
www.txcourts.gov/5thcoa
Counties Served: Collin, Dallas, Grayson, Hunt, Kaufman, and Rockwall.

**Clerk: Lisa Matz**
Phone: 214-712-3450
Fax: 214-745-1083
theclerk@5th.txcourts.gov
Business Administrator: Gayle Humpa
Phone: 214-712-3434
gayle.humpa@5th.txcourts.gov
General Counsel: Cliffie Wesson
Phone: 214-712-3420

**Chief Justice: Carolyn Wright**
Phone: 214-712-3400

**JUSTICES**
David Bridges
Phone: 214-712-3412
Molly Francis
Phone: 214-712-3411
Douglas S. Lang
Phone: 214-712-3402
Elizabeth Lang-Miers
Phone: 214-712-3403
Robert M. Fillmore
Lana Myers
David Evans
David Lewis
Ada Brown
Craig Stoddart
Bill Whitehill
David Schenck

## 6th Court of Appeals

100 N. State Line Ave.,# 20
Texarkana, TX 75501
www.txcourts.gov/6thcoa

Counties Served: Bowie, Camp, Cass, Delta, Fannin, Franklin, Gregg, Harrison, Hopkins, Hunt, Lamar, Marion, Morris, Panola, Red River, Rusk, Titus, Upshur and Wood.

**Clerk: Debbie Autrey**
Phone: 903-798-3046
Fax: 903-798-3034
debbie.autrey@txcourts.gov
Deputy Clerk for Civil Cases: Kim Robinson
Phone: 903-798-3046
Deputy Clerk for Criminal Cases: Molly Pate
Phone: 903-798-3047
Chief Staff Attorney: Kristi McCasland
kristi.mccasland@txcourts.gov

**Chief Justice: Josh R. Morriss, III**
**JUSTICES**
Bailey C. Moseley
Ralph K. Burgess

## 7th Court of Appeals

501 S. Filmore, Suite 2-A
Amarillo, TX 79101-2449
www.txcourts.gov/7thcoa

Mailing Address:
P.O. Box 9540
Amarillo, TX 79105-9540

Counties Served: Armstrong, Bailey, Briscoe, Carson, Castro, Childress, Cochran, Collingsworth, Cottle, Crosby, Dallam, Deaf Smith, Dickens, Donley, Floyd, Foard, Garza, Gray, Hale, Hall, Hansford, Hardeman, Hartley, Hemphill, Hockley, Hutchinson, Kent, King, Lamb, Lipscomb, Lubbock, Lynn, Moore, Motley, Ochiltree, Oldham, Parmer, Potter, Randall, Roberts, Sherman, Swisher, Terry, Wheeler, Wilbarger and Yoakum.

**Clerk: Vivian Long**
Phone: 806-342-2650
Fax: 806-342-2675
vivian.long@txcourts.gov
Chief Deputy Clerk: Rhonda Silverman
Deputy Clerks:
Donna Artis and Donalee Gibson

**Chief Justice: Brian Quinn**

**JUSTICES**
**James T. Campbell**
**Mackey K. Hancock**
**Patrick A. Pirtle**

## 8th Court of Appeals

500 E. San Antonio Ave., Suite 1203
El Paso, TX 79901-2408
www.txcourts.gov/8thcoa

Counties Served: Andrews, Brewster, Crane, Crockett, Culberson, El Paso, Hudspeth, Jeff Davis, Loving, Pecos, Presidio, Reagan, Reeves, Terrell, Upton, Ward and Winkler.

**Clerk: Denise Pacheco**
Phone: 915-546-2240
Fax: 915-546-2252
Chief Staff Attorney: Kay D. Waters

**Chief Justice: Ann Crawford McClure**
**JUSTICES**
**Yvonne T. Rodriguez**
**Steven L. Hughes**

## 9th Court of Appeals

1001 Pearl St., Suite 330
Beaumont, TX 77701-3552
www.txcourts.gov/9thcoa

Counties Served: Hardin, Jasper, Jefferson, Liberty, Montgomery, Newton, Orange, Polk, San Jacinto and Tyler.

**Clerk: Carol Anne Harley**
Phone: 409-835-8402
Fax: 409-835-8497
Chief Staff Attorney: Leslie Saia
Phone: 409-835-8402

**Chief Justice: Steve McKeithen**
Phone: 409-835-8405

**JUSTICES**
**Hollis Horton, III**
Phone: 409-835-8458
**Leanne Johnson**
Phone: 409-835-8404
**Charles A. Kreger**
Phone: 409-835-8403

## 10th Court of Appeals

501 Washington Ave., Room 415
Waco, TX 76701
www.txcourts.gov/10thcoa

Counties Served: Bosque, Brazos, Burleson, Coryell, Ellis, Falls, Freestone, Hamilton, Hill, Johnson, Leon, Limestone, Madison, McLennan, Navarro, Robertson, Somervell and Walker.

**Clerk: Sharri Roessler**
Phone: 254-757-5200
Fax: 254-757-2822
sharri.roessler@txcourts.gov

**Chief Justice: Tom Gray**
tom.gray@txcourts.gov

**JUSTICES**
**Judge Rex Davis**
**Judge Al Scoggins**

## 11th Court of Appeals

100 W. Main St., Suite 300
Eastland, TX 76448
www.txcourts.gov/11thcoa
Mailing Address:
P.O. Box 271
Eastland, TX 76448-0271

Counties Served: Baylor, Borden, Brown, Callahan, Coleman, Comanche, Dawson, Eastland, Ector, Erath, Fisher, Gaines, Glasscock, Haskell, Howard, Jones, Knox, Martin, Midland, Mitchell, Nolan, Palo Pinto, Scurry, Shackelford, Stephens, Stonewall, Taylor and Throckmorton.

**Clerk: Sherry Williamson**
Phone: 254-629-2638
Fax: 254-629-2191
sherry.williamson@txcourts.gov
Chief Staff Attorney: Jill Stephens

**Chief Justice: Jim R. Wright**

**JUSTICES**
John M. Bailey
Mike Willson

## 12th Court of Appeals

1517 W. Front, Suite 354
Tyler, TX 75702
www.txcourts.gov/12thcoa

Counties Served: Anderson, Angelina, Cherokee, Gregg, Henderson, Houston, Nacogdoches, Rains, Rusk, Sabine, San Augustine, Shelby, Smith, Trinity, Upshur, Van Zandt and Wood.

**Clerk: Pam Estes**
Phone: 903-593-8471
Fax: 903-593-2193

**Chief Justice: James T. Worthen**

**JUSTICES**
Brian Hoyle
Greg Neeley

## 13th Court of Appeals
www.txcourts.gov/13thcoa

Corpus Christi Address:
901 Leopard, 10th Floor
Corpus Christi, TX 78401

Edinburg Address:
100 E. Cano, 5th Floor
Edinburg, TX 78539

Counties Served: Aransas, Bee, Calhoun, Cameron, De Witt, Goliad, Gonzales, Hidalgo, Jackson, Kenedy, Kleberg, Lavaca, Live Oak, Matagorda, Nueces, Refugio, San Patricio, Victoria, Wharton and Willacy.

**Clerk: Dorian E. Ramirez**
Phone: 361-888-0416 (Corpus Christi)
Fax: 361-888-0794 (Corpus Christi)
Phone: 956-318-2405 (Edinburg)
Fax: 956-318-2403 (Edinburg)
13thcoaclerks@txcourts.gov
Chief Staff Attorney: Cecile Foy Gsanger

**Chief Justice: Rogelio Valdez**

**JUSTICES**
**Gina M. Benavides**
Phone: 956-318-2409
**Dori Contreras Garza**
Phone: 956-318-2879
**Nora Longoria**
Phone: 956-318-2414
**Gregory T. Perkes**
Phone: 361-888-0608
**Nelda V. Rodriguez**
Phone: 361-888-0605

## 14th Court of Appeals

301 Fannin St., Room 245
Houston, TX 77002
www.txcourts.gov/14thcoa

Counties served: Austin, Brazoria, Chambers, Colorado, Fort Bend, Galveston, Grimes, Harris, Waller and Washington.

**Clerk: Christopher A. Prine**
Phone: 713-274-2800
Chief Staff Attorney: Nina Indelicato

**Chief Justice: Kem Thompson Frost**

**JUSTICES (IN ORDER OF SENIORITY)**
Sr. William J. Boyce
Tracy Christopher
Martha Hill Jamison
Sharon McCally
J. Brett Busby
John Donovan
Marc W. Brown
Ken Wise

## STATE, DISTRICT AND COUNTY COURTS

# ANDERSON COUNTY

Seat: Palestine

500 N. Church St.
Palestine, TX 75801
www.co.anderson.tx.us

**District: Janice Staples**
Room 18
Phone: 903-723-7412
Fax: 903-723-7491
E-mail: jstaples@co.anderson.tx.us

**District Attorney: Allyson Mitchell**
Phone: 903-723-7400
Fax: 903-723-7818
E-mail: amitchell@co.anderson.tx.us
Administrative Assistant: Billie Yates
Phone: 903-723-7455
E-mail: byates@co.anderson.tx.us

**3rd District Court**
**Judge Mark A. Calhoon**
Phone: 903-723-7415
Court Coordinator: Tina Teetz
E-mail: tteetz@co.anderson.tx.us
Court Reporter: Brandi Ray

**87th District Court**
**Judge Deborah Oakes Evans** sits as scheduled.
*Please see Freestone County.*

**349th District Court**
**Judge Pam Foster Fletcher**
Phone: 903-723-7415
Fax: 903-723-7803
Court Coordinator: Tina Teetz
E-mail: tteetz@co.anderson.tx.us
Court Reporter: Misty McAdams
E-mail: mcadamsreporting@windstream.net

**369th District Court**
**Judge Bascom W. Bentley, III**
Phone: 903-723-7415
Fax: 903-723-7803
Court Coordinator: Tina Teetz
E-mail: tteetz@co.anderson.tx.us
Court Reporter: Nancy Adams

**County Clerk: Mark Staples**
Room 10
Phone: 903-723-7432
Fax: 903-723-4625
E-mail: mstaples@co.anderson.tx.us

**County Judge: Robert Johnston**
703 N. Mallard St., Suite 101
Palestine, TX 75801
Phone: 903-723-7406
Fax: 903-723-7494
Administrative Assistant: Lesa Lambright

**County Court at Law**
**Judge Jeff Doran**
Phone: 903-723-7469
Fax: 903-723-7814
Court Coordinator: Elizabeth Attaway
Court Reporter: Sammye Bennett

# ANDREWS COUNTY

Seat: Andrews

201 N. Main St.
Andrews, TX 79714
www.co.andrews.tx.us

**District Clerk: Cynthia Jones**
Room 102
Phone: 432-524-1417
E-mail: ccollingsworth@co.andrews.tx.us

**District and County Attorney: Timothy J. Mason**
121 NW Avenue A
Andrews, TX 79714
Phone: 432-524-1405
Fax: 432-524-5839
E-mail: tmason@co.andrews.tx.us

**109th District Court**
**Judge Martin B. Muncy**
Room 201
Phone: 432-524-1419
E-mail: mbmuncy@co.andrews.tx.us
Court Coordinator: Earlene Broyles
E-mail: ebroyles@co.andrews.tx.us
Court Reporter: Diane Pattillo

County Clerk: Kenda Heckler
P.O. Box 727
Andrews, TX 79714-0727
Phone: 432-524-1426
E-mail: kheckler@co.andrews.tx.us

County Judge: Richard H. Dolgener
Room 104
Phone: 432-524-1401
Fax: 432-524-1470
E-mail: rdolgener@co.andrews.tx.us
Court Administrator: Nancy Dildine
E-mail: ndildine@co.andrews.tx.us

# ANGELINA COUNTY

Seat: Lufkin

215 E. Lufkin Ave.
Lufkin, TX 75902
www.angelinacounty.net

District Clerk: Reba Squyres
Room 102
Phone: 936-634-4312
Fax: 936-634-5915

District Attorney: Art Bauereiss
P.O. Box 908
Lufkin, TX 75902-0908
Phone: 936-632-5090
Fax: 936-637-2818
E-mail: abauereiss@angelinacounty.net

159th District Court
Judge Paul E. White
Room 210
Phone: 936-639-3913
Fax: 936-639-3917
E-mail: pwhite@angelinacounty.net
Court Coordinator: Glenda Taylor
Court Reporter: Whitney Harry
Bailiff: Paul Love

217th District Court
Judge Robert K. Inselmann, Jr.
Room 210
Phone: 936-637-0217
Fax: 936-639-3917
E-mail: binselmann@angelinacounty.net
Court Coordinator: Robin Lowe
Court Reporter: Terri Davis
Bailiff: Johnny Purvis
Phone: 936-637-0217

County Clerk: Amy Fincher
P.O. Box 908
Lufkin, TX 75902-0908
Phone: 936-634-8339
Fax: 936-634-8460
E-mail: afincher@angelinacounty.net

County Attorney: Ed C. Jones
P.O. Box 1845
Lufkin, TX 75902-1845
Phone: 936-639-3929
Fax: 936-639-3905
E-mail: ejones@angelinacounty.net

County Judge: Wes Suiter
P.O. Box 908
Lufkin, TX 75902
Phone: 936-634-5413
Fax: 936-637-7452
E-mail: wsuiter@angelinacounty.net
Administrative Assistant: Sallie Alexander

County Court at Law No. 1
Judge Joe Lee Register
2nd Floor
Phone: 936-639-2204
Fax: 936-639-2673
E-mail: jregister@angelinacounty.net
Court Coordinator (Civil): Linda L. Berry
Phone: 936-671-4069
E-mail: lberry@angelinacounty.net
Court Coordinator (Criminal): Lana Toll
Phone: 936-671-4070
E-mail: ltoll@angelinacounty.net
Court Reporter: Wendy Wilkerson
Phone: 936-671-4072
Bailiff: Alan Poe

County Court at Law No. 2
Judge Derek C. Flournoy
2nd Floor
Phone: 936-634-8984
Fax: 936-634-8145
E-mail: dflournoy@angelinacounty.net
Court Coordinator: Monica Ibarra
E-mail: mibarra@angelinacounty.net
Assistant Court Coordinator: Crystal Brent
E-mail: cbrent@angelinacounty.net
Court Reporter: Elizabeth Murphy
Bailiff: Maxine Willmon Bailey

STATE, DISTRICT AND COUNTY COURTS

# ARANSAS COUNTY

Seat: Rockport

301 N. Live Oak St.
Rockport, TX 78382
www.aransascountytx.gov

**District Clerk: Pam Heard**
Phone: 361-790-0128
Fax: 361-790-5211
E-mail: pheard@aransascounty.org

**36th District Court**
**Judge Starr B. Bauer** sits as scheduled.
*Please see San Patricio County.*

**156th District Court**
**Judge Patrick L. Flanigan** sits as scheduled.
*Please see San Patricio County.*

**343rd District Court**
**Judge Janna K. Whatley** sits as scheduled.
*Please see San Patricio County.*

**County Clerk: Valerie Amason**
Phone: 361-790-0122
Fax: 361-790-0119
E-mail: vamason@aransascounty.org

**County Attorney: Kristen Barnebey**
Phone: 361-790-0114
Fax: 361-790-0199
E-mail: kbarnebey@aransascounty.org

**County Judge: C.H. "Burt" Mills, Jr.**
Phone: 361-790-0100
Fax: 361-727-2043
E-mail: thecountyjudge@aransascounty.org
Administrative Assistant: Linda Garcia

**County Court at Law**
**Judge Richard P. Bianchi**
Phone: 361-790-0138
E-mail: rbianchi@aransascounty.org
Court Coordinator: Ruby Price

# ARCHER COUNTY

Seat: Archer City

100 S. Center St.
Archer City, TX 76351
www.co.archer.tx.us

**District Clerk: Lori Rutledge**
P.O. Box 815
Archer City, TX 76351-0815
Phone: 940-574-4615
Fax: 940-574-2432

**District Attorney: Paige Williams**
*Please see Montague County.*

**97th District Court**
**Judge Jack A. McGaughey** sits as scheduled.
*Please see Clay County.*

## County Court
100 S. Center, 2nd Floor
Archer City, TX 76351

**County Clerk: Karren Winter**
P.O. Box 427
Archer City, TX 76351
Phone: 940-574-3033 or 940-574-4302
Fax: 940-574-2876

**County Attorney: David A. Levy**
P.O. Box 1186
Archer City, TX 76351
Phone: 940-574-4724
Fax: 940-574-2230

**County Judge: Randall C. Jackson**
P.O. Box 458
Archer City, TX 76351
Phone: 940-574-4811
Fax: 940-574-2581

# ARMSTRONG COUNTY

Seat: Claude

101 Trice St.
Claude, TX 79019
www.co.armstrong.tx.us

**District and County Clerk: Tawnee Blodgett**
P.O. Box 309
Claude, TX 79019-0309
Phone: 806-226-2081
Fax: 806-226-5301

**District Attorney: Randall C. Sims**
*Please see Potter County.*

**STATE, DISTRICT AND COUNTY COURTS**

**47th District Court**
**Judge Dan Schaap** sits as scheduled.
*Please see Potter County.*

**County Judge: Hugh Reed**
P.O. Box 189
Claude, TX 79019-0189
Phone: 806-226-3221
Fax: 806-226-2030
Court Coordinator: June Adcock

# ATASCOSA COUNTY

Seat: Jourdanton

One Courthouse Circle Dr.
Jourdanton, TX 78026
www.atascosacountytexas.net

**District Clerk: Margaret E. Littleton**
Suite 4-B
Phone: 830-769-3011
Fax: 830-769-1332
E-mail: mlittleton@atascosacountytexas.gov

**District Attorney: Rene M. Peña**
1327 3rd St.
Floresville, TX 78114
Phone: 830-393-2200
Fax: 830-393-2205
E-mail: DA81st@swbell.net
Office Manager: Terry Reyes

**81st District Court**
**Judge Donna S. Rayes**
Suite 206
Phone: 830-769-3750
Fax: 830-769-2841
Court Coordinator (Civil): Heather Fischer
Court Coordinator (Criminal): De'Ann Belicek
Court Reporter: Richie Gentry
Phone: 830-769-3750
Bailiff: Norma Jordan
E-mail: 665@asco-tx.org

**218th District Court**
**Judge Russell Wilson** sits three or four times
every month.
*Please see Karnes County.*

**County Clerk: Diane Gonzales**
Suite 102
Phone: 830-767-2511
Fax: 830-769-1021
E-mail: countyclerk@atascosacountytexas.gov

**County Attorney: Lucinda Vickers**
Suite 3-B
Phone: 830-769-3573
Fax: 830-769-2757
E-mail: lucinda.vickers@acao-tx.org

**County Judge: Robert L. Hurley**
Suite 101
Phone: 830-769-3093
Fax: 830-769-2349
E-mail: countyjudge@ @atascosacountytexas.gov
Administrative Assistant: Jeanne B. Israel

**County Court at Law**
**Judge Lynn Ellison**
Suite 205
Phone: 830-769-4232
Fax: 830-769-4239
Court Coordinator: Margie Ripple

# AUSTIN COUNTY

Seat: Bellville

One E. Main St.
Bellville, TX 77418-1598
www.austincounty.com

**District Clerk: Sue Murphy**
Phone: 979-865-5911, ext. 2257
Fax: 979-865-8350
E-mail: smurphy@austincounty.com

**District Attorney: Travis J. Koehn**
Phone: 979-865-5933
Fax: 979-865-5828
E-mail: travis.koehn@austincounty.com

**155th District Court**
**Judge Jeff R. Steinhauser** sits as scheduled.
*Please see Fayette County.*

**County Clerk: Carrie Gregor**
Phone: 979-865-5911, ext. 2240
Fax: 979-865-0336
E-mail: countyc@austincounty.com

**County Judge: Tim Lapham**
Phone: 979-865-5911, ext. 2224
Fax: 979-865-8786
E-mail: tlapham@austincounty.com

County Court at Law
**Judge Daniel W. Leedy**
Phone: 979-865-5911, ext. 2260
Fax: 979-865-8350
Court Coordinator: Diana Parker
E-mail: ccl@austincounty.com

# BAILEY COUNTY

Seat: Muleshoe

300 S. First St.
Muleshoe, TX 79347-3621
www.co.bailey.tx.us

**District Clerk: Elaine Parker**
Phone: 806-272-3165
Fax: 806-272-3124

**District Attorney: Kathryn H. Gurley**
*Please see Parmer County.*

**287th District Court**
**Judge Gordon H. Green**
Phone: 806-272-5460
Fax: 806-272-3124

**County Clerk: Robin Dickerson**
Phone: 806-272-3044
Fax: 806-272-3538

**County Attorney: Jackie R. Claborn II**
Phone: 806-272-4205

**County Judge: Sherri Harrison**
Phone: 806-272-3077
Administrative Assistant: Rosie Silva

# BANDERA COUNTY

Seat: Bandera

Bandera County Justice Center
3360 State Hwy. 173 North
Bandera, TX 78003
www.banderacounty.org

**District Clerk: Tammy Kneuper**
P.O. Box 2688
Bandera, TX 78003-2688
Phone: 830-796-4606

Fax: 830-796-8499
E-mail: districtclerk@banderacounty.org

**District Attorney: Scott Monroe**
*Please see Kerr County.*

**198th District Court**
**Judge M. Rex Emerson** sits as scheduled.
*Please see Kerr County.*

**County Clerk: Candy Wheeler**
P.O. Box 823
Bandera, TX 78003-0823
Phone: 830-796-3332
Fax: 830-796-8323
E-mail: candyw@indian-creek.net

**County Attorney: Janna I. Lindig**
P.O. Box 656
Bandera, TX 78003
Phone: 830-796-4075
Fax: 830-796-8218

**County Judge: Richard A. Evans**
P.O. Box 877
Bandera, TX 78003-0877
Phone: 830-796-3781
Fax: 830-796-4210
E-mail: bandcojdg@indian-creek.net
Administrative Assistant: Marcia Short

# BASTROP COUNTY

Seat: Bastrop

804 Pecan St.
Bastrop, TX 78602
www.co.bastrop.tx.us

**District Clerk: Sarah Loucks**
P.O. Box 770
Bastrop, TX 78602
Phone: 512-332-7244
Fax: 512-332-7249

**District Attorney: Bryan Goertz**
Phone: 512-581-7125
Fax: 512-581-7133

**21st District Court**
**Judge Carson Campbell** sits as scheduled.
*Please see Washington County.*

**STATE, DISTRICT AND COUNTY COURTS**

**335th District Court**
**Judge Reva L. Towslee-Corbett** sits as scheduled.
*Please see Burleson County.*

**423rd District Court**
**Judge Christopher D. Duggan**
Phone: 512-581-4037
Fax: 512-581-4038
Civil Court Coordinator: Deborah Shirocky
Criminal Court Coordinator: Andrea Partida
Court Reporter: Michele Fritsche
Phone: 512-581-4239

**County Clerk: Rose Pietsch**
P.O. Box 577
Bastrop, TX 78602
Phone: 512-332-7234
Fax: 512-332-7241

**County Judge: Paul Pape**
Phone: 512-332-7201
Fax: 512-581-7103
E-mail: paul.pape@co.bastrop.tx.us
Executive Assistant: Randi Fishbeck
E-mail: randi.fishbeck@co.bastrop.tx.us
Administrative Assistant: Lyndsey Schroeder
E-mail: lyndsey.schroeder@co.bastrop.tx.us

**County Court at Law**
**Judge Benton Eskew**
Phone: 512-581-4277
Fax: 512-332-7291
Court Coordinator: Jennifer Ensinger
E-mail: jennifer.ensinger@co.bastrop.tx.us
Court Reporter: Angela Freeman
Phone: 512-281-4040
E-mail: angela.freeman@co.bastrop.tx.us

## BAYLOR COUNTY

Seat: Seymour

101 S. Washington St.
Seymour, TX 76380-2566

**District and County Clerk: Chris Jakubicek**
Phone: 940-889-3322
Fax: 940-889-4300
E-mail: bcclerk@srcaccess.net

**District Attorney: David W. Hajek**
P.O. Box 508

Seymour, TX 76380
Phone: 940-889-2852
Fax: 940-888-3036

**50th District Court**
**Judge Bobby D. Burnett** sits as scheduled.
*Please see Cottle County.*

**County Attorney: Jennifer Habert-Dick**
P.O. Box 9
Seymour, TX 76380
Phone: 940-889-5140
Fax: 940-889-3196

**County Judge: Rusty Stafford**
119 E. McLain
Seymour, TX 76380
Phone: 940-889-3553
Fax: 940-889-8856

## BEE COUNTY

Seat: Beeville

105 W. Corpus Christi St.
Beeville, TX 78102
www.co.bee.tx.us

**District Clerk: Zenaida Silva**
Room 304
Phone: 361-621-1562
Fax: 361-492-5984
E-mail: zenaida.silva@co.bee.tx.us

**156th Judicial District Attorney: Jose Luis Aliseda, Jr.**
111 S. St. Mary's St., Suite 203
Beeville, TX 78102
Phone: 361-358-1007
Fax: 361-358-0505

**36th District Court**
**Judge Starr B. Bauer** sits as scheduled.
*Please see San Patricio County.*

**156th District Court**
**Judge Patrick L. Flanigan** sits as scheduled.
*Please see San Patricio County.*

**343rd District Court**
**Judge Janna K. Whatley** sits as scheduled.
*Please see San Patricio County.*

**County Clerk: Mirella Escamilla Davis**
Room 108

Phone: 361-621-1557
Fax: 361-492-5985

**County Attorney: Michael Knight**
113 S. St. Mary's St.
Beeville, TX 78102
Phone: 361-621-1550, option 6
Fax: 361-362-3208
Administrative Assistant: Ashley Maisel

**County Judge: Stephanie Silvas**
Room 109
Phone: 361-621-1550, option 4
Fax: 361-492-5980
E-mail: stephanie.silvas@co.bee.tx.us
Administrative Assistant: Candy Estrada

# BELL COUNTY

Seat: Belton

1201 Huey Rd.
Belton, TX 76513
www.bellcountytx.com

**District Clerk: Joanna Staton**
P.O. Box 909
Belton, TX 76513-0909
Phone: 254-933-5197
Fax: 254-933-5292

**District Attorney: Henry Garza**
P.O. Box 540
Belton, TX 76513-0540
Phone: 254-933-5215
Fax: 254-933-5238

**27th District Court**
**Judge John Gauntt**
Phone: 254-933-5261
Court Coordinator: Jessica Bridge
Court Reporter: Gayla May
Phone: 254-933-5270
Bailiff: Paul McCoy

**146th District Court**
**Judge Jack Jones**
Phone: 254-933-6737
Court Coordinator: Stacy Dunivent
Court Reporter: Teresa Alexander
Phone: 254-933-5267
Bailiff: Pete Eirosius

**169th District Court**
**Judge Gorden G. Adams**
Phone: 254-933-5265
Fax: 254-933-5933
Court Coordinator: Gwenda Thompson
Court Reporter: Carolynn Weber
Phone: 254-933-5269
Bailiff: Julia Helems

**264th District Court**
**Judge Martha J. Trudo**
Phone: 254-933-5245
E-mail: martha.trudo@co.bell.tx.us
Court Coordinator: Debra Severson
Phone: 254-933-5245
Court Reporter: Betty Young
Phone: 254-933-5268
Bailiff: Donnie Hill

**426th District Court**
**Judge Fancy Jezek**
Phone: 254-933-5246
Court Coordinator: Velva Johnson
Court Reporter: Peggy Morris
Phone: 254-933-5788
Bailiff: Dan Rolf

# COUNTY COURT
Bell County Justice Complex
1201 Huey Rd.
Belton, TX 76513

**County Clerk: Shelley Coston**
P.O. Box 480
Belton, TX 76513-0480
Phone: 254-933-5160
Fax: 254-933-5176
E-mail: shelley.coston@co.bell.tx.us
Chief Deputy: Diana Barnard
Phone: 254-933-5169

**County Attorney: James E. Nichols**
P.O. Box 1127
Belton, TX 76513-1127
Phone: 254-933-5135
Fax: 254-933-5150

**County Judge: Jon H. Burrows**
P.O. Box 768
Belton, TX 76513
Phone: 254-933-5105
Fax: 254-933-5179
E-mail: jon.burrows@co.bell.tx.us
Administrative Assistant: Gloria Ramos

**County Court at Law No. 1**
**Judge Jeanne Parker**
P.O. Box 781
Belton, TX 76513
Phone: 254-933-5473
Fax: 254-933-5705
E-mail: jeanne.parker@co.bell.tx.us
Court Coordinator: Sharon Pruitt
Phone: 254-933-5473
Court Reporter: Terry Johnston
Phone: 254-933-5129
Bailiff: Robert Koblosh

**County Court at Law No. 2**
**Judge John Mischtian**
P.O. Box 485
Belton, TX 76513
Phone: 254-933-5125
Fax: 254-933-5256
E-mail: john.mischtian@co.bell.tx.us
Court Coordinator: Connie Taylor
Phone: 254-933-5180
Court Reporter: Shannon Adler
Phone: 254-933-5385
Bailiff: Spike Weaver

**County Court at Law No. 3**
**Judge Rebecca DePew**
P.O. Box 365
Belton, TX 76513
Phone: 254-933-5791 or 254-933-5999
Fax: 254-933-5792
Court Coordinator: Connie Tyler
Phone: 254-933-5180
Judicial Assistants:
Tracy Kneese and Becky Ray
Court Reporter: Biesty Mock Cliftston
Phone: 254-933-5790
Bailiff: Felix Gutierrez

# BEXAR COUNTY

Seat: San Antonio

101 W. Nueva
San Antonio, TX 78205-3028
www.co.bexar.tx.us

**District Clerk: Donna Kay McKinney**
Suite 217
Phone: 210-335-2113
Fax: 210-335-3424
E-mail: donna.mckinney@bexar.org
Chief Deputy: Brady Satcher

**District Attorney: Nicholas La Hood**
7th Floor
Phone: 210-335-2311
Fax: 210-335-2884
E-mail: nlahood@bexar.org

## Civil District Courts
100 Dolorosa
San Antonio, TX 78205

**Civil District Administrator: Gary W. Hutton**
3rd Floor
Phone: 210-335-2300
Fax: 210-335-2843

**37th District Court**
**Judge Michael Mery**
4th Floor
Phone: 210-335-2515
Fax: 210-335-0595
Court Clerk: Jesse Mesa
E-mail: clerk37@bexar.org
Court Reporter: Rhonda Hogan
Bailiff: Charles Pena

**45th District Court**
**Judge Stephani Walsh**
4th Floor
Phone: 210-335-2507
Fax: 210-335-1317
Court Clerk: Rene Charles
E-mail: clerk45@bexar.org
Court Reporter: Judy Stewart
Phone: 210-771-7732
E-mail: jaystwt@aol.com
Bailiff: Hebel Sanoguet, Jr.
Phone: 210-335-3106

**57th District Court**
**Judge Antonia "Toni" Arteaga**
4th Floor
Phone: 210-335-2531
Fax: 210-335-3592
Court Clerk: Jessica Zapata
Court Reporter: Mary Martinez-Wilson
Phone: 210-335-1602
Bailiff: Steve Carpenter

**73rd District Court**
**Judge David A. Canales**
2nd Floor
Phone: 210-335-2523

Fax: 210-335-1008
Court Clerk: Roxanne Huron
E-mail: clerk73@bexar.org
Court Reporter: Luis Duran, Jr.
Phone: 210-335-2518
Bailiff: Sheila Sorola

**131st District Court**
**Judge John D. Gabriel**
4th Floor
Phone: 210-335-2521
Fax: 210-335-2092
Court Clerk: Cynthia Flores
Court Reporter: Letitia Montivias
Phone: 210-335-2057
Bailiff: David Breig

**150th District Court**
**Judge Renee Yanta**
2nd Floor
Phone: 210-335-2533
Fax: 210-335-3264
Court Clerk: Shirley Myers
Court Reporter: Victoria Gonzalez
Phone: 210-335-2570
Bailiff: Michael Flowers

**166th District Court**
**Judge Laura Salinas**
5th Floor
Phone: 210-335-2501
Fax: 210-335-0594
Court Clerk: Richard Flores
E-mail: clerk166@bexar.org
Court Reporter: Debra Jimenez
Phone: 210-335-1236
Bailiff: Charles Lopez

**224th District Court**
**Judge Kathleen Stryker**
2nd Floor
Phone: 210-335-2132
Fax: 210-335-2833
Court Clerk: Barbara Segovia
Court Reporter: Mary Helen Vargas
Phone: 210-335-2138
Bailiff: Jose Valasquez

**225th District Court**
**Judge Peter Sakai**
2nd Floor
Phone: 210-335-2233
Fax: 210-335-3950

Court Clerk: Jennifer Brazil
Court Reporter: Cindy Hyatt
Bailiff: Margo Rendon

**285th District Court**
**Judge Richard E. Price**
2nd Floor
Phone: 210-335-2086
Fax: 210-335-0868
Court Clerk: Denise R. Chavez
Court Reporter: Mary Berry
Phone: 210-335-2289
Bailiff: Adam H. Hernandez, Jr.

**288th District Court**
**Judge Solomon J. Casseb, III**
4th Floor
Phone: 210-335-2663
Fax: 210-335-0593
Court Clerk: Eddie Pichardo
Court Reporter: Kayleen Rivera
Phone: 210-335-1345
Bailiff: Sly Rapier, III

**407th District Court**
**Judge Karen Pozza**
4th Floor
Phone: 210-335-2462
Fax: 210-335-1217
Court Clerk: Mary Velasquez
Court Reporter: Tracy Ray Plummer
Phone: 210-335-2895
Bailiff: Larry Contreras

**408th District Court**
**Judge Larry Noll**
3rd Floor
Phone: 210-335-2831
Fax: 210-335-3042
Court Clerk: Mary Becerra-Cruz
Court Reporter: Craig Carter
Phone: 210-335-2786
Bailiff: Michael Helton

**438th District Court**
**Judge Gloria Saldana**
4th Floor
Phone: 210-335-0448
Fax: 210-335-1535
Court Clerk: Maria Perez
Court Reporter: Judy Mata
Phone: 210-335-1531
Bailiff: Elizabeth Villanueva

**STATE, DISTRICT AND COUNTY COURTS**

# Criminal District Courts

300 Dolorosa St.
San Antonio, TX 78205

**General Administrative Counsel for the Criminal District Court: Melissa Barlow Fischer**
101 W. Nueva, Suite 301
San Antonio, TX 78205
Phone: 210-335-3474
Fax: 210-335-2252
E-mail: mfischer@bexar.org

**Criminal Magistrate Judge: Andrew W. Carruthers**
100 Dolorosa St
3rd Floor
San Antonio TX, 78205
Phone: 210-335-2901
Fax: 210-335-2790
Court Coordinator: Angela Martinez
Phone: 210-335-0546
Court Reporter: Roxie Peña
Court Clerks: Rebecca Leija and Hector Riojas
Phone: 210-335-2902
Bailiffs: Issac Cantero and John Howard

**144th District Court**
**Judge Lorina Rummel**
2nd Floor
Phone: 210-335-2511
Fax: 210-335-2503
Court Coordinator: Martha Stiles
Phone: 210-335-2174
Court Reporter: Kay Gittinger
Phone: 210-335-1106
Bailiff: Martin Gamez

**175th District Court**
**Judge Mary Roman**
4th Floor
Phone: 210-335-2527
Fax: 210-335-2793
Court Coordinator: Denise Sauceda
Phone: 210-335-2569
Court Reporter: Monica Crawford
Phone: 210-335-2529
Court Clerks: Cassandra Longoria and Janie Gonzales
Bailiff: Mel Delgado

**186th District Court**
**Judge Jefferson Moore**
3rd Floor
Phone: 210-335-2505
Fax: 210-335-2509
Court Coordinator: Richard Burch
Phone: 210-335-2424
Court Reporter: Debbie Doolittle
Court Clerks: Donnie Gonzalez and Cynthia Gomez
Bailiffs: Joe Hernandez and Steven Perez

**187th District Court**
**Judge Steven Hilbig**
2nd Floor
Phone: 210-335-2517
Fax: 210-335-2540
Court Coordinator: Laurie Smith
Phone: 210-335-2242
Court Reporter: Bettina Williams
Phone: 210-335-2175
Bailiff: Raul Medellin

**226th District Court**
**Judge Sid L. Harle**
2nd Floor
Phone: 210-335-2446
Fax: 210-335-2551
Court Coordinator: Rachel Rushton
Phone: 210-335-2421
Court Reporter: Bob Hogan
Phone: 210-335-2690
Court Clerk: Rene Benavidas
Bailiff: John Little

**227th District Court**
**Judge Kevin M. O'Connell**
2nd Floor
Phone: 210-335-2304
Fax: 210-335-2574
Court Coordinator: Lisa Solis
Phone: 210-335-2307
Court Reporter: Lisa Ramos
Phone: 210-335-2535
Bailiffs: Rudy Dominguez and Albert Perez

**290th District Court**
**Judge Melisa Skinner**
4th Floor
Phone: 210-335-2696
Fax: 210-335-2648
Court Coordinator: Lance Aldridge
Phone: 210-335-2588
Court Reporter: Marybeth Sasala
Phone: 210-335-1236

Court Clerks: Ashley Chavez and
Sarah Veredja
Bailiffs: Margie Miranda and Nick Reyna

**379th District Court**
**Judge Ron Rangel**
4th Floor
Phone: 210-335-2911
Fax: 210-335-2472
Court Coordinator: Tricia Austin
Phone: 210-335-2906
Court Clerks: Liz Garcia and Yvette Polendo
Court Reporter: Rachel Young
Phone: 210-335-2914
Bailiffs: Joe Gaska and Richard Villareal

**399th District Court**
**Judge Ray J. Olivarri**
1st Floor
Phone: 210-335-3667
Fax: 210-335-3888
Court Coordinator: Laura Castillo
Phone: 210-335-3792
Court Reporter: Sachiko Nagao
Phone: 210-833-3749

**437th District Court**
**Judge Lori Valenzuela**
3rd Floor
Phone: 210-335-2711
Fax: 210-335-2183
Court Coordinator: Natalia Contreras
Phone: 210-335-1383
Court Reporter: Linda Herendez
Court Clerks: Jackie Cade and Lidia Gamez
Bailiff: Saul Guajardo

**Felony Drug Court**
**Judge: Ernie Glenn**
Phone: 210-335-3063
Court Coordinator: Diana Zamarron

# JUVENILE DISTRICT COURTS
235 E. Mitchell St.
San Antonio, TX 78210

**General Administrative Counsel—Juvenile District Courts: Laura Angelini**
Phone: 210-335-1128
Fax: 210-335-7540

**289th District Court**
**Judge Daphne Previti Austin**
600 Mission Rd.

San Antonio, TX 78210
Phone: 210-335-1185
Fax: 210-335-1174
Court Coordinator: Patricia Alvarez
Court Reporter: Kensie Benoit
Bailiff: Joe Maldonado

**386th District Court**
**Judge Laura Parker**
Phone: 210-335-1169
Fax: 210-335-1159
Court Coordinator: Roland Huerta
Phone: 210-335-1155
Court Reporter: Heather Collins
Phone: 210-531-1155
Court Clerks: Eliva Gonzalez and
Sylvia Stewart
Bailiffs: Maricela Montoya and
Jesse De La Cruz

**436th District Court**
**Judge Lisa K. Jarrett**
600 Mission Road
San Antonio, TX 78210
Phone: 210-335-1194
Fax: 210-335-7685
Court Coordinator: Jessie Alvarez
Court Reporter: Holly Dietert
Court Clerks: Joshua Gutierrez
and Julian Torres
Bailiff: Chrissy Perez

# CHILDREN'S COURT
100 Dolorosa St.
San Antonio, TX 78205

**Associate Judge: Charles Montemayor**
Room 3.06
Phone: 210-335-2768
Fax: 210-335-2286
E-mail: cmontemayor@bexar.org
Court Coordinator: Melissa Mendiola
E-mail: melissa.mendiola@bexar.org
Phone: 210-325-2825
Court Clerk: Bianca Garza
Phone: 210-335-2768
E-mail: courtclerks306@bexar.org
Court Reporter: David Zarete
E-mail: dzarete@bexar.org
Bailiff: Pedro Barrera

**Associate Judge: Richard Garcia**
Room 3.07

STATE, DISTRICT AND COUNTY COURTS

Phone: 210-335-2768
Fax: 210-335-3481
E-mail: rich.garcia@bexar.org
Court Coordinator: Rebeca Snodgrass
E-mail: rebeca.snodgrass@bexar.org
Court Clerk: Victor Alvarez
E-mail: courtclerk307@bexar.org
Court Reporter: Angie Jimenez
E-mail: angie.jiminez@bexar.org
Bailiff: Joe Correino

**Associate Judge - Child Support: Eric J. Rodriguez**
Room 4.11
Phone: 210-335-2725
Fax: 210-335-2041
Court Coordinator: Priscilla Carrasco
Phone: 210-335-3915
Court Clerk: Selestina Carrizales
Bailiff: Terry Henderson

**Associate Judge - Child Support: Nick Catoe**
Room 1.20
Phone: 210-335-2706
Fax: 210-335-3900
Court Coordinator: Denise Garza
Court Clerk: Edward Mireles
Bailiff: Sherman Harrison

## PROBATE COURTS
100 Dolorosa St.
San Antonio, TX 78205

**Probate Court No. 1**
**Judge Kelly Cross**
Room 123
Phone: 210-335-2670
Fax: 210-335-3998
Court Clerk: Connie Perez
Staff Attorney: Art Rossi
Phone: 210-335-2647
Court Reporter: Cheryl Hester
Phone: 210-335-2359
Bailiff: Tom Beasley

**Associate Judge: Oscar Kazen**
Phone: 210-335-0507

**Probate Court No. 2**
**Judge Tom Rickhoff**
Room 117
Phone: 210-335-2546
Fax: 210-335-2029
Court Coordinator: Samantha Guerra
Phone: 210-335-2190

Staff Attorney: Martin Collins
Phone: 210-335-0490
Court Reporter: Veronica Bowles
Phone: 210-335-2466
Court Clerk: Teresa Guerra
Court Investigator: Sue Bean
Phone: 210-335-2279
Bailiff: Eddie Maldonado

## COUNTY COURTS
100 Dolorosa St.
San Antonio, TX 78205

*Civil Central Filing 210-335-2231*

**County Clerk: Gerard C. "Gerry" Rickhoff**
Suite 104
Phone: 210-335-2216
Fax: 210-335-2197

**County Judge: Nelson W. Wolff**
101 W. Nueva, 10th Floor
San Antonio, TX 78205
Phone: 210-335-2626
Fax: 210-335-2926
Administrative Assistant: Linda Guajardo
Phone: 210-335-1326
E-mail: lguajardo@bexar.org

**County Court Administrator: Dianne Garcia**
101 W. Nueva, 3rd Floor
San Antonio, TX 78205
Phone: 210-335-2115
Fax: 210-335-2935

**County Court at Law No. 1**
**Judge John D. Fleming**
300 Dolorosa St., 1st Floor
San Antonio, TX 78205
Phone: 210-335-2571
Fax: 210-335-3211
Court Coordinator: Deborah Orosco
Phone: 210-335-2019
Court Clerk: Ruby Martinez
Court Reporter: Gloria Recio
Phone: 210-335-2572
Bailiff: Emeel Hernandez

**County Court at Law No. 2**
**Judge Jason Wolff**
300 Dolorosa St., 4th Floor
San Antonio, TX 78205
Phone: 210-335-2573
Fax: 210-335-2649
Court Coordinator: Jake Grohman
Phone: 210-335-2842

Court Reporter: Edna Casanova
Phone: 210-335-2079
Bailiff: George Mata

**County Court at Law No. 3**
**Judge David J. Rodriguez**
3rd Floor
Phone: 210-335-2575
Fax: 210-335-3945
Court Coordinator: Norma Perez-Cavazos
Phone: 210-335-2948
Court Clerk: Justin Longoria
Court Reporter: Kay Counseller
Phone: 210-335-2578
Bailiff: Lee Lopez

**County Court at Law No. 4**
**Judge Jason Garrahan**
300 Dolorosa St., 2nd Floor
San Antonio, TX 78205
Phone: 210-335-2426
Fax: 210-335-2088
Court Coordinator: Jane Esteves
Phone: 210-335-2401
Court Reporter: Lisa Ward
Phone: 210-335-3929

**County Court at Law No. 5**
**Judge John A. Longoria**
300 Dolorosa St., 4th Floor
San Antonio, TX 78205
Phone: 210-335-2549
Fax: 210-335-3212
Court Coordinator: Pattie Garcia
Phone: 210-335-2172
Court Reporter: Lecha Cavazos
Phone: 210-335-1192

**County Court at Law No. 6**
**Judge Wayne Christian**
300 Dolorosa, 2nd Floor
San Antonio, TX 78205
Phone: 210-335-2156
Fax: 210-335-2275
Court Coordinator: Pat Benavides
Phone: 210-335-2182
Court Reporter: Mike Stachowitz
Phone: 210-335-1605
Bailiff: Jack Glava

**County Court at Law No. 7**
**Judge Eugenia "Genie" Wright**
300 Dolorosa St., 3rd Floor
San Antonio, TX 78205
Phone: 210-335-2002

Fax: 210-335-3158
Court Coordinator: Jerry McCarty
Phone: 210-335-2032
Court Reporter: Paula Cloud
Phone: 210-335-2004
Bailiff: Lisa Piñeda

**County Court at Law No. 8**
**Judge Celeste Brown**
300 Dolorosa St., 1st Floor
San Antonio, TX 78205
Phone: 210-335-2005
Fax: 210-335-0539
Court Coordinator: Alex Chavez
Phone: 210-335-2006
Court Clerks: Monica Avila and Audra Rodriguez
Court Reporter: Christina Galloway
Phone: 210-335-2759
Bailiff: Fred Mendoza

**County Court at Law No. 9**
**Judge Walden Shelton**
300 Dolorosa St., 4th Floor
San Antonio, TX 78205
Phone: 210-335-2008
Fax: 210-335-3958
Court Coordinator: Gina Rios
Phone: 210-335-2009
Court Reporter: Lori Bryant
Phone: 210-335-2425
Bailiff: Rudy Weresch

**County Court at Law No. 10**
**Judge Karen Crouch**
3rd Floor
Phone: 210-335-2947
Fax: 210-335-2908
Court Coordinator: Mario Llano
Phone: 210-335-2948
Court Clerk: Alma Patiño
Court Reporter: Brooke Wagner
Phone: 210-335-2955
Bailiff: Ruth Hernendez

**County Court at Law No. 11**
**Judge Tommy Stolhandske**
300 Dolorosa St., 1st Floor
San Antonio, TX 78205
Phone: 210-335-2023
Fax: 210-335-2040
Court Coordinator: Amy Castaño
Phone: 210-335-2025
Court Reporter: Rosie Ibarra
Phone: 210-335-2024

**STATE, DISTRICT AND COUNTY COURTS**

**County Court at Law No. 12**
**Judge Scott Roberts**
300 Dolorosa St., 2nd Floor
San Antonio, TX 78205
Phone: 210-335-2750
Fax: 210-335-3047
Court Coordinator: Susie Cantu
Phone: 210-335-2894
Court Clerks: Linda Flores and
Tanisha Gaines
Court Reporter: Tonya Thompson
Phone: 210-335-2781
Bailiff: Steve Keefe

**County Court at Law No. 13**
**Judge Crystal Chandler**
300 Dolorosa St., 3rd Floor
San Antonio, TX 78205
Phone: 210-335-2625
Fax: 210-335-1639
Court Coordinator: Justin Clark
Phone: 210-335-1637
Court Reporter: Kandy K. Halley
Phone: 210-335-1638

**County Court at Law No. 14**
**Judge Susan Skinner**
300 Dolorosa St., 2nd Floor
San Antonio, TX 78205
Phone: 210-335-1670
Fax: 210-335-6475
Court Coordinator: Diana Martinez
Phone: 210-335-1671
Court Clerk: Kryselda Talamantes
Court Reporter: Kimberly Rice-Lobello
Phone: 210-335-1673
Bailiff: Wendall Morris

**County Court at Law No. 15**
**Judge Robert Behvens**
300 Dolorosa St., 4th Floor
San Antonio, TX 78205
Phone: 210-335-1245
Fax: 210-335-1344
Court Coordinator: Kathy Plate
Phone: 210-335-1621w
Court Reporter: Melissa Snells
Phone: 210-335-0823

## BLANCO COUNTY

Seat: Johnson City

101 E. Pecan Dr.
Johnson City, TX 78636
www.co.blanco.tx.us

**District Clerk: Debby Elsbury**
P.O. Box 382
Johnson City, TX 78636-0382
Phone: 830-868-0973
Fax: 830-868-2084
E-mail: districtclerk@co.blanco.tx.us

**District Attorney: Wiley B. "Sonny" McAfee**
*Please see Llano County.*

**33rd District Court**
**Judge J. Allan Garrett** sits as scheduled.
*Please see Burnet County.*

**424th District Court**
**Judge Evan Stubbs** sits as scheduled.
*Please see Burnet County.*

**County Clerk: Laura Walla**
P.O. Box 65
Johnson City, TX 78636-0065
Phone: 830-868-7357
Fax: 830-868-4158
E-mail: countyclerk@co.blanco.tx.us

**County Attorney: David Allen Hall**
P.O. Box 471
Johnson City, TX 78636
Phone: 830-868-4447
Fax: 830-868-7417
E-mail: coatty@co.blanco.tx.us

**County Judge: Brett Bray**
P.O. Box 471
Johnson City, TX 78636-0471
Phone: 830-868-4266
Fax: 830-868-9112
E-mail: cojudge@co.blanco.tx.us
Administrative Assistant: Kathy Strickland

## BORDEN COUNTY

Seat: Gail

117 E. Wasson St.
Gail, TX 79738
www.co.borden.tx.us

**District and County Clerk: Jana Underwood**
P.O. Box 124
Gail, TX 79738
Phone: 806-756-4312
Fax: 806-756-4324
E-mail: bordenco@poka.com

**District Attorney: Ben R. Smith**
*Please see Scurry County.*

**132nd District Court**
**Judge Ernie B. Armstrong** sits once a month.
*Please see Scurry County.*

**County Attorney: Marlo Holbrooks**
P.O. Box 156
Gail, TX 79738
Phone: 806-756-4351
E-mail: marlo.holbrooks@co.borden.tx.us

**County Judge: Ross D. Sharp**
P.O. Box 156
Gail, TX 79738
Phone: 806-756-4391
Fax: 806-756-4405
Administrative Assistant: Connie Stipe

# BOSQUE COUNTY

Seat: Meridian

110 S. Main St.
Meridian, TX 76665
www.bosquecounty.us

**District Clerk: Juanita Miller**
P.O. Box 674
Meridian, TX 76665
Phone: 254-435-2334
E-mail: d_clerk@bosquecounty.us

**District Attorney: B. J. Shepherd**
P.O. Box 368
Meridian, TX 76665
Phone: 254-435-2994
Fax: 254-435-2952

**220th District Court**
**Judge Phil Robertson**
Phone: 254-435-6626
Fax: 254-435-9163
Court Coordinator: Linda Meinkowsky
Court Reporter: Don McDonald
Phone: 254-386-1281

**County Clerk: Tabatha Ferguson**
P.O. Box 617
Meridian, TX 76665
Phone: 254-435-2201
Fax: 254-435-2152
E-mail: county_clerk@bosquecounty.us

**County Attorney: Natalie Koehler**
P.O. Box 215
Meridian, TX 76665
Phone: 254-435-2186
Fax: 254-435-2026
E-mail: koehler@bosquecounty.us

**County Court at Law**
**Judge David B. Christian**
P.O. Box 496
Meridian, TX 76665-0496
Phone: 254-435-6601
Fax: 254-435-9966

**County Judge: Dewey Ratliff**
P.O. Box 647
Meridian, TX 76665-0647
Phone: 254-435-2382, ext. 6
Fax: 254-435-2152
Administrative Assistant: Jimmie Lou Lewis

# BOWIE COUNTY

Seat: New Boston

710 James Bowie Dr.
New Boston, TX 75570
www.co.bowie.tx.us

**District Clerk: Billy Fox**
Phone: 903-628-6775
Fax: 903-628-6761
Chief Deputy: Jill Harrington

**District Attorney: Jerry D. Rochelle**
601 Main St.
Texarkana, TX 75501
Phone: 903-735-4800
Fax: 903-735-4819

**5th District Court**
**Judge William W. Miller, Jr.**
Phone: 903-798-3527
Fax: 903-798-3301
Court Coordinator: Becky Sorsby
Court Reporter: Leslie Bates

**STATE, DISTRICT AND COUNTY COURTS**

**102nd District Court**
**Judge Bobby Lockhart, Jr.**
100 N. State Line Ave. Box 10
Texarkana, TX 75501
Phone: 903-798-3527
Fax: 903-798-3301
Court Coordinator: Becky Sorsby
Court Reporter: Melanie Harris
Phone: 903-798-3527

**202nd District Court**
**Judge Leon Pesek, Jr.**
100 N. State Line Ave. Box 10
Texarkana, TX 75501
Phone: 903-628-6771
Fax: 903-628-2217
Court Coordinator: Deborah Nield
Phone: 903-628-6771
Court Reporter: Camille Warren

**County Clerk: Tina Petty**
Phone: 903-628-6742
Fax: 903-628-6729
E-mail: tina.petty@txkusa.org
Chief Deputy: Denise Thornburg
E-mail: denise.thornburg@txkusa.org

**County Judge: James M. Carlow**
Phone: 903-628-6718
Fax: 903-628-6719
E-mail: countyjudge@txkusa.org
Administrative Assistant: Doborah Lann
E-mail: dlann@txkusa.org

**County Court at Law**
**Judge Jeff M. Addison**
Phone: 903-628-6835
Fax: 903-628-2217
Court Coordinator: Sherri Tutt
E-mail: tutt@txkusa.org
Court Reporter: Deanne Adkins
Bailiff: Clyde Shipp

# BRAZORIA COUNTY

Seat: Angleton

111 E. Locust St.
Angleton, TX 77515
www.brazoria-county.com

**District Clerk: Rhonda Barchak**
Suite 500

Phone: 979-864-1316
www.brazoria-county.com/dclerk

**District Attorney: Jeri Yenne**
Suite 408A
Phone: 979-864-1230
Fax: 979-864-1525

**23rd District Court**
**Judge Ben Hardin**
Suite 405
Phone: 979-864-1205
Fax: 979-849-7514
Court Coordinator: Susan Miller
Court Reporter: Donna Reed
Phone: 979-864-1796
Bailiff: Melvin Anders

**149th District Court**
**Judge Terri Holder**
Suite 214-A
Phone: 979-864-1261
Fax: 979-864-1061
Court Coordinator: Tammy Brooks
Court Reporter: Robin Rios
Phone: 979-864-1483
Bailiff: Glen Whisemant

**239th District Court**
**Judge Patrick E. Sebesta**
Suite 310-A
Phone: 979-864-1256
Fax: 979-864-1056
Court Coordinator: Debbie Selleck
Court Reporter: Ida Salinas
Phone: 979-864-1258
Bailiff: Joe Lipscomb

**300th District Court**
**Judge Kenneth R. Hufstetler**
Suite 403
Phone: 979-864-1227
Fax: 979-864-1226
Court Coordinator: Deana Lycka
E-mail: deanal@brazoria-county.com
Court Reporter: Renee Rape
Phone: 979-864-1229
Bailiff: Ruben Vela and Vann Kent

**412th District Court**
**Judge Ed Denman**
Suite 201
Phone: 979-864-1915
Fax: 979-864-1918
Court Coordinator: Linda Kellogg

Court Administrator Criminal: Denise Demon
Phone: 979-864-1263
Court Reporter: Jill Friedrichs
Phone: 979-864-1917
Bailiff: Ali Soeks

**County Clerk: Joyce Hudman**
Suite 200
Phone: 979-864-1355
Fax: 979-864-1358

**County Judge: L.M. Matt Sebesta, Jr.**
Suite 102
Phone: 979-388-1200
Fax: 979-849-4655
E-mail: joek@brazoria-county.com
Administrative Assistant: Cathy Hughes

**County Court at Law No. 1 and Probate Court**
**Judge Jerri Lee Mills**
Suite 207-A
Phone: 979-864-1260
Fax: 979-864-1474
Court Coordinator: Ann Bradley
Court Reporter: Sherri Stadter
Phone: 979-864-1608

**County Court at Law No. 2 and Probate Court**
**Judge Marc Holder**
Suite 300
Phone: 979-864-1571
Fax: 979-864-1047
Court Coordinator: Donna Northsworthy
Court Reporter: Sara Caldwell
Phone: 979-864-1573

**County Court at Law No. 3 and Probate Court**
**Judge Jeremy Warren**
Suite 321-A
Phone: 979-864-1603
Fax: 979-864-1607
Court Coordinator: Kellie Fisk
Court Reporter: Minnie Cadena

**County Court at Law No. 4 and Probate Court**
**Judge Lori Rickert**
Suite 203
Phone: 979-864-1980
Fax: 979-864-1981
Court Coordinator: Jaye Blaha
Court Reporter: Becky Serrato
Phone: 979-864-1982
Bailiff: Larry Moore

# BRAZOS COUNTY

Seat: Bryan

300 E. 26th St.
Bryan, TX 77803-5360
www.co.brazos.tx.us

**District Clerk: Marc Hamlin**
Suite 1200
Phone: 979-361-4230
Fax: 979-361-0197
E-mail: mhamlin@co.brazos.tx.us

**District Attorney: Jarvis Parsons**
Suite 310
Phone: 979-361-4320
Fax: 979-361-4368
E-mail: jparsons@brazoscountytx.gov

**85th District Court**
**Judge Kyle Hawthorne**
Suite 225
Phone: 979-361-4270
Fax: 979-361-4276
E-mail: khawthorne@brazoscountytx.gov
Court Coordinator: Kristie Evans
E-mail: kevans@brazoscountytx.gov
Phone: 979-361-4271
Court Reporter: Paula Frederick
Phone: 979-361-4272
Bailiff: Steve Tyler

**272nd District Court**
**Judge Travis B. Bryan, III**
Suite 207
Phone: 979-361-4219
Fax: 979-361-4517
E-mail: tbryan@brazoscountytx.gov
Court Coordinator: Lisa Parker
E-mail: lparker@brazoscountytx.gov
Court Reporter: Denise Phillips
Phone: 979-361-4220
Court Reporter: Kaetheryne Kyriell
Phone: 936-443-3312
Bailiff: Ernie Montoya

**361st District Court**
**Judge Steve Smith**
Suite 309
Phone: 979-361-4380
Fax: 979-361-4385
E-mail: ssmith@brazoscountytx.gov

STATE, DISTRICT AND COUNTY COURTS

Court Coordinator: Tiffany Chambers
Phone: 979-361-4384
Court Reporter: Wendy Kirby
Phone: 979-361-4381
Bailiff: Patrick Massey

**County Clerk: Karen McQueen**
Suite 120
Phone: 979-361-4124
Fax: 979-361-4125
E-mail: kmcqueen@brazoscountytx.gov

**County Attorney: Rod Anderson**
Suite 1300
Phone: 979-361-4300
Fax: 979-361-4357
E-mail: randerson@brazoscountytx.gov

**County Judge: Duane Peters**
200 S. Texas Ave, Suite 332
Bryan, TX 77803
Phone: 979-361-4102
Fax: 979-361-4503
E-mail: dpeters@co.brazos.tx.us
Administrative Assistant: Bethany Jones

**County Court at Law No. 1**
**Judge Amanda S. Matzke**
Suite 211
Phone: 979-361-4250
Court Coordinator: Tiffany Newton

**County Court at Law No. 2**
**Judge Jim Locke**
Suite 214
Phone: 979-361-4260
Fax: 979-361-4514
Court Coordinator: Sharon Rose
Phone: 979-361-4261

**Child Support Associate Court**
**Judge Lisa Hubacek**
Suite 202
Phone: 979-361-4494
Court Coordinator: Linda Turner
Phone: 979-361-4261

**Family Law Associate Court**
**Judge Cindy Miller**
Suite 202
Phone: 979-361-4683
Fax: 979-361-4684
Court Coordinator: Abbie Reid

**Felony Associate Court**
**Judge Glynis Gore**
Suite 202
Phone: 979-361-4683
Fax: 979-361-4684

**Misdemeanor Associate Court**
**Judge Dana Zachary**
Suite 203
Phone: 979-361-4540
Court Coordinator: Lisa Paradis

# BREWSTER COUNTY

Seat: Alpine

201 W. Ave. E
Alpine, TX 79830
www.co.brewster.tx.us

**District Clerk: Jo Ann Salgado**
P. O. Box 1024
Alpine, TX 79831
Phone: 432-837-6216
Fax: 432-837-6217
E-mail: joann.salgado@co.brewster.tx.us

**District Attorney: Rod Ponton**
*Please see Pecos County.*

**394th District Court**
**Judge Roy B. Ferguson**
P.O. Box 1410
Alpine, TX 79831-1410
Phone: 432-837-5831
E-mail: 394th.jud.dist.court@gmail.com
Court Coordinator: Elizabeth Pimm
Court Reporter: Patricia Reid
P.O. Box 1438
Alpine, TX 79831-1410
Phone: 432-294-1293

**County Clerk: Berta Rios-Martinez**
P.O. Box 119
Alpine, TX 79831-0119
Phone: 432-837-3366
Fax: 432-837-6217
E-mail: bmartinez@co.brewster.tx.us

**County Attorney: Steve Houston**
107 W. Ave. E, Suite 7

Alpine, TX 79830
Phone: 432-837-3520
Fax: 432-837-7393
E-mail: countyattorney@co.brewster.tx.us

**County Judge: Eleazar R. Cano**
P.O. Box 1630
Alpine, TX 79831-1630
Phone: 432-837-2412
Fax: 432-837-1127
E-mail: eleazar.cano@co.brewster.tx.us
Administrative Assistant: Julie Morton
Secretary: Susan Bentley

# BRISCOE COUNTY

Seat: Silverton

415 Main St.
Silverton, TX 79257
www.co.briscoe.tx.us

**District and County Clerk: Bena Hester**
P.O. Box 555
Silverton, TX 79257
Phone: 806-823-2134
Fax: 806-823-2076
E-mail: coclerk@midplains.coop

**District Attorney: Becky McPherson**
*Please see Floyd County.*

**110th District Court**
**Judge William P. Smith** sits the first Tuesday of the month.
*Please see Floyd County.*

**County Attorney: Emily Teegardin**
P.O. Box 119
Silverton, TX 79257
Phone: 806-823-2132
Fax: 806-823-2076
E-mail: emilytlaw@gmail.com

**County Judge: Wayne Nance**
P.O. Box 153
Silverton, TX 79257
Phone: 806-823-2131
Fax: 806-823-2359
E-mail: bcjudge@midplains.coop

# BROOKS COUNTY

Seat: Falfurrias
100 E. Miller St.
Falfurrias, TX 78355
www.co.brooks.tx.us

**District Clerk: Noe Guerra, Jr.**
P.O. Box 534
Falfurrias, TX 78355
Phone: 361-325-5604, ext. 6
E-mail: nguerra@co.brooks.tx.us

**District Attorney: Carlos Omar Garcia**
*Please see Jim Wells County.*

**79th District Court**
**Judge Richard C. Terrell** sits as scheduled.
*Please see Jim Wells County.*

**County Clerk: Frutoso "Pepe" Garza**
P.O. Box 427
Falfurrias, TX 78355-0427
Phone: 361-325-5604, ext. 3
Fax: 361-325-4944
E-mail: fgarza@co.brooks.tx.us

**County Attorney: Homer Mora**
P.O. Box 557
Falfurrias, TX 78355
Phone: 361-325-5604, ext. 2
Fax: 361-325-3777
E-mail: hmora@co.brooks.tx.us

**County Judge: Imelda Barrera**
P.O. Box 515
Falfurrias, TX 78355-0515
Phone: 361-325-5604, ext. 1
Fax: 361-325-5369
E-mail: ibarrera@co.brooks.tx.us
Administrative Assistant: Sylvia Hinojosa
E-mail: shinojosa@co.brooks.tx.us

# BROWN COUNTY

Seat: Brownwood

200 S. Broadway St.
Brownwood, TX 76801
www.browncountytx.org

**District Clerk: Cheryl Jones**
Phone: 325-646-5514

Fax:325-646-0878
E-mail: cheryl.jones@browncountytx.org

**District Attorney: Michael Murray**
Phone: 325-646-0444, ext. 15
Fax: 325-643-4053
E-mail: districtattorney@browncountytx.org
Assistant District Attorney: Elisha Bird
E-mail: daassistant1@browncountytx.org
Assistant District Attorney: Chris Brown
Phone: 325-646-0444, ext. 14
E-mail: daassistant2@browncountytx.org
Assistant District Attorney: Christina Nelson

**35th District Court**
**Judge Stephen Ellis**
Phone: 325-646-1987
Fax: 325-643-6396
E-mail: steve.ellis@browncountytx.org
Court Coordinator: Jennifer Aaron
Phone: 325-646-1987, ext. 201
E-mail: jennifer.aaron@browncountytx.org
Court Reporter: Cristi Escobar
Phone: 325-646-4057
Bailiffs: Ricky Beluin and Dennis Watson

**County Clerk: Sharon Ferguson**
Phone: 325-643-2594
E-mail: sharon.ferguson@browncountytx.org

**County Attorney: Shane Britton**
Phone: 325-646-7431, ext. 19
Fax: 325-643-4053
E-mail: coatty@browncountytx.org

**County Judge: Ernest "Ray" West, III**
Phone: 325-643-2828
Fax: 325-646-7013
E-mail: ray.west@browncountytx.org
Court Coordinator: Jayme Joyner
E-mail: jayme.joyner@browncountytx.org
Court Reporter: Tom Hale

**County Court at Law**
**Judge Sam Moss**
E-mail: sam.moss@browncountytx.org
Phone: 325-646-5859
Fax: 325-646-5980
Court Coordinator: Amanda Bundick
E-mail: amanda.bundick@browncountytx.org
Court Reporter: Nannell Mooney
E-mail: nannellmooneycsr@hotmail.com

# BURLESON COUNTY

Seat: Caldwell

100 W. Buck St.
Caldwell, TX 77836
www.co.burleson.tx.us

**District Clerk: Dana Fritsche**
Suite 303
Phone: 979-567-2336
E-mail: dfritsche@burlesoncounty.org

**District Attorney: Julie Renken**
*Please see Washington County.*

**21st District Court**
**Judge Carson Campbell** sits twice a month.
*Please see Washington County.*

**335th District Court**
**Judge Reva L. Towslee-Corbett**
Suite 411
Phone: 979-567-2335
Fax: 979-567-2382
Court Coordinator: Cindy See
Phone: 979-567-2361
Court Reporter: Holly Schulz
Phone: 979-567-3583

**County Clerk: Anna L. Schielack**
Suite 203
Phone: 979-567-2329
Fax: 979-567-2376

**County Attorney: Joseph J. Skrivanek, III**
Suite 201C
Phone: 979-567-2340
Fax: 979-567-2373

**County Judge: Mike Sutherland**
Suite 306
Phone: 979-567-2333
Fax: 979-567-2372
Court Coordinator and Administrative
Assistant: Karen Bolt

# BURNET COUNTY

Seat: Burnet

North Annex
1701 E. Polk St.
Burnet, TX 78611-3136
www.burnetcountytexas.org

**District Clerk: Casie Walker**
Suite 90
Phone: 512-756-5450
E-mail: district.clerk@burnetcountytexas.org

**District Attorney: Wiley B. "Sonny" McAfee**
*Please see Llano County.*

**33rd District Court**
**Judge J. Allan Garrett**
Phone: 512-756-5436
E-mail: judge33@dcourttexas.org
Court Coordinator: Lisa Bell
Phone: 512-715-5219
E-mail: coordinator33@dcourt.org
Court Reporter: Stephanie Larsen
Phone: 512-715-5238

**424th District Court**
**Judge Evan Stubbs**
Phone: 512-756-5438
E-mail: 424distjudge@dcourttexas.org
Court Coordinator: Jennifer Bunting
E-mail: 424 coordinator @dcourttexas.org
Court Reporter: Jennifer Fest
Phone: 512-715-5238

## County Court
220 S. Pierce St.
Burnet, TX 78611-3136

**County Clerk: Janet F. Parker**
1st Floor
Phone: 512-756-5406
Fax: 512-756-5410
E-mail: ctyclk@burnetcountytexas.org

**County Attorney: Eddie Arredondo**
Phone: 512-756-5476
Fax: 512-756-9290

**County Judge: James Oakley**
Phone: 512-756-5400
Fax: 512-715-5217

E-mail: countyjudge@burnetcountytexas.org
Court Coordinator: Jeanne Emerson
Phone: 512-715-5276
E-mail: comcrt@burnetcountytexas.org
Court Reporter: Vicki Kanewske
Bailiff: Bruce Morgan

**County Court at Law**
**Judge Linda Bayless**
Suite 206
Phone: 512-715-5245
Fax: 512-715-5226
Court Coordinator: Erica Gambrell
Court Reporter: Vicki Kanewske
Bailiff: Bruce Morgan

# CALDWELL COUNTY

Seat: Lockhart

1703 S. Colorado
Lockhart, TX 78644
www.co.caldwell.tx.us

**District Clerk: Tina M. Freeman**
Box 3
Phone: 512-398-1806
Fax: 512-398-1805
Chief Deputy: Janet Caddell

**District Attorney: Fred Weber**
P.O. Box 869
Lockhart, TX 78644
Phone: 512-398-1811, ext. 210
Fax: 512-398-1814

**22nd District Court**
**Judge R. Bruce Boyer** sits as scheduled.
*Please see Hays County.*

**207th District Court**
**Judge Jack H. Robison** sits as scheduled.
*Please see Comal County.*

**421st District Court**
**Judge Todd A. Blomerth**
Phone: 512-398-1839
Court Coordinator: Monica Malaer
Phone: 512-398-1807
Court Reporter: Sheri Linder
Bailiff: John Juarez

**STATE, DISTRICT AND COUNTY COURTS**

## County Court
1703 S. Colorado
Lockhart, TX 78644

**County Clerk: Carol Holcomb**
Box 1
Phone: 512-398-1824
Fax: 512-398-9925

**County Judge: Ken Schawe**
110 S. Main St., 2nd Floor
Lockhart, TX 78644
Phone: 512-398-1808
Fax: 512-898-1828
Email: k.schawe@co.caldwell.tx.us
Executive Assistant: Karen Sphar
Email: karen.sphar@co.caldwell.tx.us

**County Court at Law**
**Judge Edward L. Jarrett**
Box 11
Phone: 512-398-6527
Fax: 512-668-4962
Court Reporter: Leigh Hagg

# CALHOUN COUNTY

Seat: Port Lavaca

211 S. Ann St.
Port Lavaca, TX 77979
www.calhouncotx.org

**District Clerk: Pamela Martin Hartgrove**
2nd Floor
Phone: 361-553-4630
Fax: 361-553-4637

*Note: Clerks do record searches over the phone.*

**District Attorney: Dan W. Heard**
P.O. Box 1001
Port Lavaca, TX 77979-1001
Phone: 361-553-4422
Fax: 361-553-4421

**24th District Court**
Judge Jack W. Marr sits as scheduled.
*Please see Victoria County.*

**135th District Court**
Judge K. Stephen Williams sits as scheduled.
*Please see Victoria County.*

**267th District Court**
**Judge Juergen "Skipper" Koetter** sits as scheduled.
*Please see Victoria County.*
*Note: Hon. Koetter will retire on 3/4/16.*
*Gov. Abbot to appoint new judge.*

**County Clerk: Anna M. Goodman**
Phone: 361-553-4411
Fax: 361-553-4420
E-mail: anna.goodman@calhoucotx.org

**County Judge: Michael J. Pfeifer**
3rd Floor
Phone: 361-553-4600
Fax: 361-553-4444
E-mail: calhoun@tisd.net
Administrative Assistant: Susan Riley
E-mail: susan.riley@calhouncotx.org

**County Court at Law**
**Judge Alex R. Hernandez**
2nd Floor
Phone: 361-553-4640
Court Coordinator: Toi Dowell

# CALLAHAN COUNTY

Seat: Baird

100 W. 4th St.
Baird, TX 79504
www.callahancounty.org

**District Clerk: Amber Tinsley**
Suite 300
Phone: 325-854-5825
Fax: 325-854-5826
E-mail: amber.tinsley@callahancounty.org

**District and County Attorney: Shane Deel**
Suite 202
Phone: 325-854-5810
Fax: 325-854-5811
E-mail: shane.deel@callahancounty.org

**42nd District Court**
Judge John W. Weeks sits every other Thursday.
*Please see Taylor County.*

**County Clerk: Donna Bell**
Suite 104

Phone: 325-854-5815
Fax: 325-854-5816
E-mail: donna.bell@callahancounty.org

**County Judge: Roger Corn**
Suite 200
Phone: 325-854-5805
Fax: 325-854-5806
E-mail: roger.corn@callahancounty.org
Administrative Assistant: Brandy Kirkland
E-mail: brandy.kirkland@callahancounty.org

# CAMERON COUNTY

Seat: Brownsville

974 E. Harrison St.
Brownsville, TX 78520
www.co.cameron.tx.us

**District Clerk: Erica Garza**
Phone: 956-544-0838
Fax: 956-544-0841
E-mail: egarza@co.cameron.tx.us
Chief Deputy: Ricardo Cornejo
E-mail: rcornejo@co.cameron.tx.us

**District Attorney: Luis V. Saenz**
Phone: 956-544-0849
Fax: 956-544-0869

**103rd District Court**
**Judge Janet L. Leal**
3rd Floor
Phone: 956-544-0844
Fax: 956-548-9581
Court Coordinator: Lorraine Perez
E-mail: lorraine.perez@co.cameron.tx.us
Court Clerk: Teddy Garza
E-mail: teodula.garza@co.cameron.tx.us
Court Administrator: Maria G. Cortina
E-mail: mary.cortina@co.cameron.tx.us
Court Reporter: Judith A. Kraus
Phone: 956-544-0844
Bailiff: Jose Garza

**107th District Court**
**Judge Benjamin Euresti, Jr.**
3rd Floor
Phone: 956-544-0845
Fax: 956-544-0841
Court Coordinator: Elva Olivo
E-mail: eolivo@co.cameron.tx.us

Court Clerk: Carolina Ostos
E-mail: costos@co.cameron.tx.us
Court Administrator: Dalila Esquivel
E-mail: desquivel@co.cameron.tx.us
Court Reporter: Sue C. Saenz
Phone: 956-550-1470
Bailiff: Issac Cantu, Jr.

**138th District Court**
**Judge Auturo C. Nelson**
3rd Floor
Phone: 956-544-0877
Court Coordinator: Irma P. Gilman
E-mail: irma.gilman@co.cameron.tx.us
Court Clerk: Janet Lopez
E-mail: jlopez@co.cameron.tx.us
Court Administrator: Raul Martinez, Jr.
E-mail: raul.martinez@co.cameron.tx.us
Court Reporter: Michelle Cardenas
Phone: 956-550-1489
Bailiff: Joel Garcia

**197th District Court**
**Judge Migdalia Lopez**
3rd Floor
Phone: 956-574-8150
Fax: 956-574-8128
Court Coordinator: Jessica Carrizales
E-mail: jccarrizales@co.cameron.tx.us
Court Clerk: Jesus Cantu
Court Administrator: Nora N. Anderson
E-mail: nnanderson@co.cameron.tx.us
Court Reporter: Kary Richardson
Phone: 956-544-0874
Bailiff: Sergio Alaniz

**357th District Court**
**Judge Juan A. Magallanes**
1st Floor
Phone: 956-548-9522
Fax: 956-548-9545
Court Coordinator: Estela Salas
E-mail: esalas@co.cameron.tx.us
Court Clerk: Brenda Garcia-Ramirez
E-mail: bgarcia2@co.cameron.tx.us
Court Administrator: Norma Solis
E-mail: nsolis@co.cameron.tx.us
Court Reporter: Cynthia Garza
Phone: 956-548-9524
Bailiff: Joe Polendo

**404th District Court**
**Judge Elia Cornejo Lopez**
3rd Floor
Phone: 956-544-0837

Fax: 956-548-9569
Court Coordinator: Frankie Olivo
E-mail: frankie.olivo@co.cameron.tx.us
Court Clerk: Celso Amaro
E-mail: celso.amaro@co.cameron.tx.us
Court Administrator: Davis Rojas
E-mail: david.rojas@co.cameron.tx.us
Court Reporter: Gay Richey
Bailiff: Roland Martinez

**444th District Court**
**Judge David Sanchez**
1st Floor
Phone: 956-547-7034
Court Coordinator: Marisol Loya
E-mail: mrloya2@co.cameron.tx.us
Court Clerk: Ezequiel Zepeda
E-mail: ezepeda2@co.cameron.tx.us
Court Administrator: Priscilla Guajardo
E-mail: priscilla.guajardo@co.cameron.tx.us
Court Reporter: Corinna Garcia
Bailiff: Moises Rivera

**445th District Court**
**Judge René E. De Cass**
2nd Floor
Phone: 956-547-7070
Court Coordinator: Blanca Hinojosa
E-mail: blanca.hinojosa@co.cameron.tx.us
Court Clerk: Christina Tusa
E-mail: christina.tusa@ co.cameron.tx.us
Court Administrator: Sugey Muñiz
E-mail: sugey.munez@co.cameron.tx.us
Court Reporter: Rachel Kram
Bailiff: Henry Hernandez

## County Court
974 E. Harrison
Brownsville, TX 78520

**County Clerk: Sylvia G. Perez**
P.O. Box 2178
Brownsville, TX 78522
Phone: 956-544-0815
Fax: 956-544-0813
Chief Deputy: Sandra Sanchez

**County Judge: Pete Sepulveda, Jr.**
1100 E. Monroe St., 2nd Floor
Brownsville, TX 78520
Phone: 956-544-0830
Fax: 956-544-0801
E-mail: pete.sepulveda@co.cameron.tx.us

**County Court at Law No. 1**
**Judge Arturo McDonald, Jr.**
Phone: 956-544-0855
Fax: 956-548-9542
Court Coordinator: Mike Sanchez
E-mail: miguel.sanchez@co.cameron.tx.us
Court Administrator: Brenda Cantu
E-mail: brenda.cantu@co.cameron.tx.us
Court Reporter: Randall Simpson
Court Clerk: Patricia Candela
E-mail: patricia.candela@co.cameron.tx.us
Bailiff: Janet Shears

**County Court at Law No. 2**
**Judge Laura L. Betancourt**
Phone: 956-544-0856
Fax: 956-504-3678
Court Coordinator: Karla Leal
Email: karla.leal@co.cameron.tx.us
Court Administrator: Perla Diaz
E-mail: perla.diaz@co.cameron.tx.us
Court Reporter: Roel Rodriguez
Records Coordinator: Thomas Quintero
Bailiff: Jose Luis Salinas

**County Court at Law No. 3**
**Judge David Gonzales, III**
Phone: 956-574-8136
Fax: 956-574-8140
Court Coordinator: Laura Perez
E-mail: lpperez@co.cameron.tx.us
Court Administrator: Nelly Sanchez
E-mail: nsanchez@co.cameron.tx.us
Court Reporter: Cindy Carranza
Records Coordinator: Sandra Forno
Email: sandra.forno2@co.cameron.tx.us
Bailiff: Leo Fredo Peña

## CAMP COUNTY

Seat: Pittsburg

126 Church St.
Pittsburg, TX 75686
www.co.camp.tx.us

**District Clerk: Teresa Bockmon**
Room 204
Phone: 903-856-3221
Fax: 903-856-0560
E-mail: campcountydistrict1@yahoo.com

**District Attorney: Charles C. Bailey**
*Please see Titus County.*

**76th District Court**
**Judge Danny Woodson**
*Please see Titus County.*

**276th District Court**
**Judge Robert Rolston**
*Please see Morris County.*

**County Clerk: Elaine Young**
Room 102
Phone: 903-856-2731
Fax: 903-856-6112

**County Attorney: Angela Hammonds**
P.O. Box 126
Pittsburg, TX 75686-0970
Phone: 903-856-2409
Fax: 903-856-5278

**County Judge: Thomas Cravey**
Room 303
Phone: 903-856-3845
Fax: 903-856-2309
Administrative Assistant: Barbara Devine

# CARSON COUNTY

Seat: Panhandle

501 Main St.
Panhandle, TX 79068
www.co.carson.tx.us

**District and County Clerk: Celeste Bichsel**
P.O. Box 487
Panhandle, TX 79068
Phone: 806-537-3873
Fax: 806-537-3623

**District Attorney: Luke Inman**
*Please see Donley County.*

**100th District Court**
**Judge Stuart Messer** sits every five weeks.
*Please see Childress County.*

**County Attorney: Scott Sherwood**
P.O. Box 947
Panhandle, TX 79068
Phone: 806-537-3591
Fax: 806-537-3592

**County Judge: Don Looten**
P.O. Box 369
Panhandle, TX 79068-0369
Phone: 806-537-3622
Fax: 806-537-2244
Administrative Assistant: Vanessa Watkins

# CASS COUNTY

Seat: Linden

604 State Highway 8 North
Linden, TX 75563
www.co.cass.tx.us

**District Clerk: Jamie Albertson**
P.O. Box 510
Linden, TX 75563-0510
Phone: 903-756-7514
Fax: 903-756-5253

**District Attorney: Randal Lee**
P.O. Box 839
Linden, TX 75563-0839
Phone: 903-756-7541
Fax: 903-756-3210

**5th District Court**
**Judge William W. Miller, Jr.** sits as scheduled.
*Please see Bowie County.*

**County Clerk: Jamie A. O'Rand**
100 E. Houston St.
Linden, TX 75563
Phone: 903-756-5071
Fax: 903-756-8057
E-mail: orand.countyclerk@casscountytx.org

**County Judge: Becky Wilbanks**
P.O. Box 825
Linden, TX 75563
Phone: 903-756-5181
Fax: 903-756-5732
E-mail: casscojudge@gmail.com
Administrative Assistant: Shanon Brown
E-mail: countyjudge.assistant@gmail.com

**County Court at Law**
**Judge Donald W. Dowd**
P.O. Box 510
Linden, TX 75563
Phone: 903-756-7515
Fax: 903-756-3033

STATE, DISTRICT AND COUNTY COURTS

Court Coodinator: Tina Hamilton
Court Reporter: Jackie Smith
Bailiff: Bill Lawrence

# CASTRO COUNTY

Seat: Dimmitt

100 E. Bedford St.
Dimmitt, TX 79027
www.co.castro.tx.us

**District and County Clerk: JoAnna Blanco**
Room 101
Phone: 806-647-3338
Fax: 806-647-5438
E-mail: jbclerk@castrocounty.org

**District and County Attorney: Shalyn Hamlin**
Room 213
Phone: 806-647-4445
Fax: 806-647-2089

**64th District Court**
**Judge Robert W. Kinkaid, Jr.** sits every other Thursday.
*Please see Hale County.*

**242nd District Court**
**Judge Kregg Hukill** sits every other Thursday.
*Please see Hale County.*

**County Judge: Carroll Gerber**
Room 111
Phone: 806-647-4451
Fax: 806-647-4403
Administrative Assistant: Veronica Pacheco

# CHAMBERS COUNTY

Seat: Anahuac

404 Washington Ave.
Anahuac, TX 77514
www.co.chambers.tx.us

**District Clerk: Patti L. Henry**
P.O. Box NN
Anahuac, TX 77514
Phone: 409-267-2432
Fax: 409-267-8209
E-mail: districtclerk@co.chambers.tx.us

**District Attorney: Cheryl Lieck**
P.O. Box 1409
Anahuac, TX 77514
Phone: 409-267-2680
Fax: 409-267-3105

**253rd District Court**
**Judge Chap B. Cain, III** sits as scheduled.
*Please see Liberty County.*

**344th District Court**
**Judge Randy McDonald**
P.O. Box 490
Anahuac, TX 77514
Phone: 409-267-2429
Fax: 409-267-4363
Court Coordinators: Tonya Hunt
Court Reporter: Teri Daigle
Bailiff: John Feist

**County Clerk: Heather Hawthorne**
P.O. Box 728
Anahuac, TX 77514
Phone: 409-267-2418
Fax: 409-267-8405
E-mail: hhawthorne@co.chambers.tx.us
Chief Deputy Clerk: Robin Edmonds
Chief Clerk (Civil): Melinda Rhame
Chief Clerk (Criminal): Sheri Hemphill

**County Attorney: Scott Peal**
P.O. Box 1200
Anahuac, TX 77514
Phone: 409-267-2411
Fax: 409-267-8296

**County Judge: Jimmy Sylvia**
P.O. Box 939
Anahuac, TX 77514
Phone: 409-267-2440
Fax: 409-267-4453
E-mail: jsylvia@co.chambers.tx.us
Administrative Assistant: Lauren Van Deventer

# CHEROKEE COUNTY

Seat: Rusk

135 S. Main St.
Rusk, TX 75785
www.co.cherokee.tx.us

**District Clerk: Janet Gates**
2nd Floor
Phone: 903-683-4533
Fax: 903-683-2971
E-mail: distclerk@cocherokee.org

**District Attorney: Rachel L. Patton**
P.O. Box 450
Rusk, TX 75785-0450
Phone: 903-683-2573
Fax: 903-683-2309

**2nd District Court**
**Judge Dwight Phifer**
P.O. Box 287
Rusk, TX 75785-0287
Phone: 903-683-2236
Fax: 903-683-2238
Court Coordinator: Mary Monkress
Court Reporter: Cathe Dickson
Bailiff: John Page

**369th District Court**
**Judge Bascom W. Bentley, III** sits the first half of
each month.
*Please see Anderson County.*

**County Clerk: Laverne Lusk**
Phone: 903-683-2350
Fax: 903-683-2457

**County Attorney: Dana Norris Young**
P.O. Box 320
Rusk, TX 75785
Phone: 903-683-2423
Fax: 903-683-5931

**County Judge: Chris Davis**
Phone: 903-683-2324
Fax: 903-683-2393
Administrative Assistant: Peggy Cornelius

**County Court at Law**
**Judge Janice Stone**
Phone: 903-683-6497
Fax: 903-683-2961
Court Coordinators: Letty Herrington and
Karla Kellerman

# CHILDRESS COUNTY

Seat: Childress

100 Ave. E. NW
Childress, TX 79201
www.co.childress.tx.us

**District and County Clerk: Barbara Spitzer**
Courthouse Box 4
Phone: 940-937-6143
Fax: 940-937-3708
E-mail: childressclerks@gmail.com

**District Attorney: Luke Inman**
*Please see Donley County.*

**100th District Court**
**Judge Stuart Messer**
P.O. Box 887
Phone: 806-874-0122
Fax: 806-874-5146
Court Coordinator: Tammy Brinson
Court Reporter: Krista Smith
Constable: Daniel Hernandez

**County Attorney: Gregory Buckley**
Courthouse Box 2
Phone: 940-937-6158
Fax: 940-937-3226
Administrative Assistant: Brandi Manuel

**County Judge: Jay Mayden**
Courthouse Box 1
Phone: 940-937-2221
Fax: 940-937-0166
E-mail: childresscojudge@childresstexas.net
Administrative Assistant: Kim Jones

# CLAY COUNTY

Seat: Henrietta

100 N. Bridge St.
Henrietta, TX 76365-2898
www.co.clay.tx.us

**District Clerk: Dan Slagle**
P.O. Box 568
Henrietta, TX 76365-0568
Phone: 940-538-4561
Fax: 940-538-0147

**District Attorney: Paige Williams**
*Please see Montague County.*

**97th District Court**
**Judge Jack A. McGaughey**
P.O. Box 167
Montague, TX 76251
Phone: 940-894-2066
Fax: 940-894-2560
www.97thdistrictcourt.com
Court Coordinator: Linda Burleson
Court Reporter: Betty Sanders

**County Clerk: Sasha Kelton**
P.O. Box 548
Henrietta, TX 76365-0548
Phone: 940-538-4631
Fax: 940-264-4160

**County Attorney: Seth Slagle**
111 S. Main St.
Henrietta, TX 76365
Phone: 940-538-0533
Fax: 940-538-5567

**County Judge: Kenneth E. Liggett**
214 N. Main
Henrietta, TX 76365
Phone: 940-538-4651
Fax: 940-538-5597
E-mail: ccjudge@claycountytx.com

# COCHRAN COUNTY

Seat: Morton

100 N. Main St.
Morton, TX 79346
www.co.cochran.tx.us

**District and County Clerk: Shanna Dewbre**
Room 102
Phone: 806-266-5450
Fax: 806-266-9027
E-mail: shanna.dewbre@co.cochran.tx.us

**District Attorney: Christopher E. Dennis**
*Please see Hockley County.*

**286th District Court**
**Judge Pat Phelan** sits two to three times a
month.
*Please see Hockley County.*

**County Attorney: J. C. Adams, Jr.**
109-A W. Washington Ave.
Morton, TX 79346
Phone: 806-266-8661
Fax: 806-266-5583

**County Judge: James S. Henry**
Room 105
Phone: 806-266-5508
Fax: 806-266-9027
E-mail: psherry@co.cochran.tx.us

# COKE COUNTY

Seat: Robert Lee

13 E. 7th St.
Robert Lee, TX 76945
www.co.coke.tx.us

**District and County Clerk: Mary Grim**
Phone: 325-453-2631
Fax: 325-453-2650
E-mail: marylgclerk@juno.com

**District Attorney: Allison Palmer**
*Please see Tom Green County.*

**51st District Court**
**Judge Barbara L. Walther** sits once a month.
*Please see Tom Green County.*

**County Attorney: Nancy Arthur**
P.O. Box 55
Robert Lee, TX 76945
Phone: 325-453-2712

**County Judge: Roy Blair**
Phone: 325-453-2641
Fax: 325-453-2157
E-mail: roy.blair@co.coke.tx.us
Administrative Assistant: Lorrie Martin

# COLEMAN COUNTY

Seat: Coleman

100 Live Oak St.
Coleman, TX 76834
www.co.coleman.tx.us

**District Clerk: Margie Mayo**
Suite 201
Phone: 325-625-2568
E-mail: dclerk@webaccess.net

**District Attorney: Heath Hemphill**
114 W. Live Oak
Coleman, TX 76834-0835
Phone: 325-625-1316
Fax: 325-625-1325

**42nd District Court**
**Judge John W. Weeks** sits every other
Thursday.
*Please see Taylor County.*

**County Clerk: Stacey Mendoza**
Suite 105
Phone: 325-625-2889
E-mail: cclerk@web-access.net

**County Attorney: Joe Lee Rose**
107 West St.
Coleman, TX 76834
Phone: 325-625-3731
Fax: 325-625-1724
E-mail: joelaw44@verizon.net

**County Judge: Belly Bledsoe**
Suite 102
Phone: 325-625-4218
E-mail: county.judge@yahoo.com

# COLLIN COUNTY

Seat: McKinney

2100 Bloomdale Rd.
McKinney, TX 75071
www.co.collin.tx.us

**District Clerk: Yoon Kim**
Suite 12132
Phone: 972-548-4320
Fax: 972-548-4697

**District Attorney: Greg Willis**
Suite 100
Phone: 972-548-4323
Fax: 214-491-4860
Administrative Assistant: Della Bryant

# District Courts

**199th District Court**
**Judge Angela Tucker**
Suite 10030
Phone: 972-548-4415
Court Coordinator: Leila Olivarri
E-mail: lolivarri@co.collin.tx.us
Court Reporter: Sheri Vecera
Phone: 972-548-4412
E-mail: svecera@co.collin.tx.us
Bailiff: Bryon Wetzel
Phone: 972-548-4452
E-mail: bwetzel@co.collin.tx.us

**219th District Court**
**Judge Scott J. Becker**
Suite 20132
Phone: 972-548-4402
E-mail: 219@co.collin.tx.us
Web: www.219thcourt.com
Court Coordinator: Amy Munger
Phone: 972-548-4662
E-mail: amunger@co.collin.tx.us
Court Reporter: Indu Bailey
Phone: 972-548-4405
E-mail: ibailey@co.collin.tx.us
Bailiff: Brian Seals
Phone: 972-548-4403
E-mail: bseals@co.collin.tx.us

**296th District Court**
**Judge John R. Roach, Jr.**
Suite 20012
Phone: 972-548-4409
E-mail: 296@co.collin.tx.us
Court Coordinator: Vacant
Court Reporter: Jan Dugger
Phone: 972-548-4407
Bailiff: Tommy Purtle
Phone: 972-548-4410

**366th District Court**
**Judge Ray Wheless**
Suite 30146
Phone: 972-548-4570
Court Coordinator: Todd Hill
E-mail: thill@co.collin.tx.us
Court Reporter: Antoinette Varela
Phone: 972-548-4572
E-mail: avarela@co.collin.tx.us
Bailiff: Keri Toye
Phone: 972-548-4571
E-mail: ktoye@co.collin.tx.us

**STATE, DISTRICT AND COUNTY COURTS**

**380th District Court**
**Judge Benjamin N. Smith**
Suite 30132
Phone: 972-548-4762
Court Coordinator: Amy Cabala
E-mail: acabala@co.collin.tx.us
Court Reporter: Karla Kimbrell
Phone: 972-548-4661
E-mail: kkimbrell@co.collin.tx.us
Bailiff: Luke Eichner
Phone: 972-548-4738
E-mail: leichner@co.collin.tx.us

**401st District Court**
**Judge Mark J. Rusch**
Suite 30030
Phone: 972-548-4241
Court Coordinator: Kim Quillin
E-mail: kquillin@co.collin.tx.us
Court Reporter: Kim Tinsley
Phone: 972-548-4247
E-mail: ktinsley@co.collin.tx.us
Bailiff: Ralph Evans
Phone: 972-548-4248
E-mail: revans2@co.collin.tx.us

**416th District Court**
**Judge Chris Oldner**
Suite 20030
Phone: 972-548-4520
Court Coordinator: Susan Caver
E-mail: scaver@co.collin.tx.us
Court Reporter: Susan Maienschein
Phone: 972-548-4579
E-mail: smaienschein@co.collin.tx.us
Bailiff: Ben Sherrin
Phone: 972-548-4529
E-mail: bsherrin@co.collin.tx.us

**417th District Court**
**Judge Cynthia Wheless**
Suite 30290
Phone: 972-548-4658
E-mail: 417@co.collin.tx.us
Court Coordinator: Angel Marksberry
E-mail: amarksberry@co.collin.tx.us
Court Reporter: Kathy Bounds
Phone: 972-548-4274
E-mail: kbounds@co.collin.tx.us
Bailiff: Rick Willey
Phone: 972-548-4685

**429th District Court**
**Judge Jill Willis**
Suite 30290

Phone: 972-547-5720
Court Coordinator: Joanna Smith
E-mail: jcsmith@co.collin.tx.us
Court Reporter: Shawn Gant
Phone: 972-547-5723
E-mail: sgant@co.collin.tx.us
Bailiff: Darryl Smith
Phone: 972-547-5721
E-mail: dsmith@co.collin.tx.us

**469th District Court**
**Judge Piper McCraw**
Suite 30014
Phone: 972-548-5660
Court Coordinator: Shannon Reynolds
E-mail: sreynolds@co.collin.tx.us
Court Reporter: Stephanie Hunn
Phone: 972-548-5663
E-mail: shunn@co.collin.tx.us
Bailiff: Shane Capps
Phone: 972-548-5661
E-mail: mcapps@co.collin.tx.us

**470th District Court**
**Judge Emily Miskel**
Suite 20146
Phone: 972-548-5670
E-mail: 470@co.collin.tx.us
Court Coordinator: Mallory Maddox
E-mail: mmaddox@co.collin.tx.us
Court Reporter: Tanner Feast
E-mail: tfeast@co.collin.tx.us
Bailiff: Kristoffer Lea
E-mail: klea@co.collin.tx.us

# Probate Court
2100 Bloomdale Rd.
McKinney, TX 75071

**Probate Court**
**Judge Weldon Copeland**
Suite 12010
Phone: 972-548-3810
Court Administrator: Patrice Eubanks-Mora

# County Courts
2100 Bloomdale Rd.
McKinney, TX 75071

**County Clerk: Stacey Kemp**
2300 Bloomdale Rd., Suite 2106
McKinney, TX 75071
Phone: 972-548-4185
Fax: 972-547-5731
E-mail: ctyclerks@co.collin.tx.us

**County Judge: Keith Self**
2300 Bloomdale Rd., Suite 4192
McKinney, TX 75071
Phone: 972-548-4635
Fax: 972-548-4699
E-mail: keith.self@co.collin.tx.us
Administrative Assistant: Nicole Gillespie

**County Court at Law Administrator: Kim Quillin**
Suite 12165
Phone: 972-548-6430
Fax: 972-548-6433
E-mail: cclclerks@co.collin.tx.us
E-Filing: texfile_cclclerks@co.collin.tx.us

**County Court at Law No. 1**
**Judge Corinne Mason**
Suite 20364
Phone: 972-548-3860
Court Coordinator: Adri Starnes
E-mail: astarnes@co.collin.tx.us
Court Reporter: Thomas Mullins
Phone: 972-548-3866
E-mail: tmullins@co.collin.tx.us
Bailiff: David Moore
Phone: 972-548-3863
E-mail: dmoore@co.collin.tx.us

**County Court at Law No. 2**
**Judge Barnett Walker**
Suite 10344
Phone: 972-548-3820
Fax: 972-548-3828
Court Coordinator: Lisa Todd
E-mail: ltodd@co.collin.tx.us
Court Reporter: Kristen Kopp
Phone: 972-548-3823
E-mail: kkopp@co.collin.tx.us
Bailiff: Danny Jones
Phone: 972-548-3824
E-mail: djones@co.collin.tx.us

**County Court at Law No. 3**
**Judge Lance Baxter**
Suite 10256
Phone: 972-548-3695
Court Coordinator: Mindy Quint
E-mail: mquint@co.collin.tx.us
Court Reporter: Denise Condron
Phone: 972-548-3834
E-mail: dcondran@co.collin.tx.us
Bailiff: Chad Humphrey
Phone: 972-548-3833
E-mail: chumphrey@co.collin.tx.us

**County Court at Law No. 4**
**Judge David Rippel**
Suite 10374
Phone: 972-548-3840
Fax: 972-548-3844
Court Coordinator: Darla Wright
Court Reporter: Claudia Webb
Phone: 972-548-3847
E-mail: cwebb2@co.collin.tx.us
Bailiff: Marvin Rousseau
Phone: 972-548-3843
E-mail: jrousseau@co.collin.tx.us

**County Court at Law No. 5**
**Judge Dan Wilson**
Suite 20382
Phone: 972-548-3850
Fax: 972-548-3855
Court Coordinator: Twyla Caton
E-mail: tcaton@co.collin.tx.us
Court Reporter: Crystal Cannon
Phone: 972-548-3854
E-mail: ccannon@co.collin.tx.us
Bailiff: Billy Powell
Phone: 972-548-3853

**County Court at Law No. 6**
**Judge Jay A. Bender**
Suite 30354
Phone: 972-547-1850
Fax: 972-547-1855
Court Coordinator: Stephanie Ables
E-mail: sables@co.collin.tx.us
Court Reporter: Jennifer Corley
Phone: 972-547-1853
E-mail: jcorley@co.collin.tx.us
Bailiff: Charles Gilbert
Phone: 972-547-1852
E-mail: cgilbert@co.collin.tx.us

**County Court at Law No. 7**
**Visiting Judge Keith Dean**
Suite 30372
Phone: 972-548-5680
Court Coordinator: J'net Chambers
E-mail: jchambers@co.collin.tx.us
Court Reporter: Denise Carrillo
E-mail: dcarrillo@co.collin.tx.us
Bailiff: Jordan Webb
Phone: 972-548-5681
E-mail: jwebb@co.collin.tx.us

**STATE, DISTRICT AND COUNTY COURTS**

# COLLINGSWORTH COUNTY

Seat: Wellington

800 West Ave., Box 10
Wellington, TX 79095
www.co.collingsworth.tx.us

**District and County Clerk: Jackie Johnson**
Phone: 806-447-2408
Fax: 806-447-2409

**District Attorney: Luke Inman**
*Please see Donley County.*

**100th District Court**
**Judge Stuart Messer** sits once a month.
*Please see Childress County.*

**County Attorney: G. Keith Davis**
Phone: 806-447-2518
Fax: 806-447-2519

**County Judge: John James**
2nd Floor
Phone: 806-447-5408
Fax: 806-447-5418
Administrative Assistant: Sherideen Thomas

# COLORADO COUNTY

Seat: Columbus

400 Spring St.
Columbus, TX 78934
www.co.colorado.tx.us

**District Clerk: Linda Holman**
Suite 103
Phone: 979-732-2536
Fax: 979-732-2591
E-mail: linda.holman@co.colorado.tx.us

**25th District Court**
**Judge William D. Old, III** sits as scheduled.
*Please see Guadalupe County.*

**2nd 25th District Court**
**Judge W. C. "Bud" Kirkendall** sits as scheduled.
*Please see Guadalupe County.*

**County Clerk: Kimberly Menke**
318 Spring St., Suite 103
Columbus, TX 78934
Phone: 979-732-2155
Fax: 979-732-8852
E-mail: kimberly.menke@co.colorado.tx.us

**County Attorney: Jay Johannes**
Suite 204
Phone: 979-732-8203
Fax: 979-732-9115
E-mail: jay.johannes@co.colorado.tx.us

**County Judge: Ty Prause**
Suite 107
Phone: 979-732-2604
Fax: 979-732-9389
E-mail: ty.prause@co.colorado.tx.us

# COMAL COUNTY

Seat: New Braunfels

150 N. Seguin Ave.
New Braunfels, TX 78130
www.co.comal.tx.us

**District Clerk: Heather N. Kellar**
Suite 304
Phone: 830-221-1250, ext. 1160
Fax: 830-608-2006
E-mail: kellah@co.comal.tx.us

**District Attorney: Jennifer Tharp**
Suite 307
Phone: 830-221-1300
Fax: 830-608-2008
E-mail: tharpj@co.comal.tx.us

**22nd District Court**
**Judge R. Bruce Boyer** sits as scheduled.
*Please see Hays County.*

**207th District Court**
**Judge Jack H. Robison**
Suite 317
Phone: 830-221-1270
Fax: 830-608-2030
Court Coordinator (Civil): Savannah Maurer
Court Coordinator (Criminal): Jeanie Vill
Court Administrator: Steve Thomas
Court Reporter: Mary Scopas
Phone: 830-620-5566
Bailiffs: Adam Vargas and Nick Reininger

STATE, DISTRICT AND COUNTY COURTS

**274th District Court**
**Judge Gary L. Steel** sits as scheduled.
*Please see Guadalupe County.*

**433rd District Court**
**Judge Dibrell "Dib" Waldrip**
Suite 317
Phone: 830-221-1270
Fax: 830-608-2030
E-mail: waldrip@co.comal.tx.us
Court Coordinator: Savannah Maurer
Court Administrator: Steve Thomas
Court Reporter: Cindy Cummings
Phone: 830-620-5566
Bailiffs: Adam Vargas and Nick Reininger

## County Court
199 Main Plaza
New Braunfels, TX 78130

**County Clerk: Bobbie Koepp**
150 N. Seguin, Suite 1234
New Braunfels, TX 78130
Phone: 830-221-1230
Fax: 830-620-3410

**County Judge: Sherman Krause**
Phone: 830-221-1105
Fax: 830-608-2026
E-mail: krause@co.comal.tx.us
Administrative Assistant: Laurie Koehler

**County Court at Law No. 1**
**Judge Randy C. Gray**
Phone: 830-221-1180, ext. 1
Fax: 830-620-3424
E-mail: cclbrc@co.comal.tx.us
Court Coordinator: Kim Damuth
Court Reporter: Carolyn Burkland
Bailiff: Will Reed

**County Court at Law No. 2**
**Judge Charles A. Stephens, II**
150 N. Seguin Ave., Suite 301
New Braunfels, TX 78130
Phone: 830-221-1180, ext. 2
Fax: 830-620-0465
Court Coordinator: Ashley Evans
Court Reporter: Dana Dance
Bailiff: Preston Davis

# COMANCHE COUNTY

Seat: Comanche

101 W. Central Ave.
Comanche, TX 76442
www.comanchecountytexas.net

**District Clerk: Brenda Dickey**
P.O. Box 206
Comanche, TX 76442
Phone: 325-356-2342
Fax: 325-356-2150

**District Attorney: B.J. Shepherd**
*Please see Bosque County.*

**220th District Court**
**Judge Phil Robertson** sits every Tuesday and Thursday.
*Please see Bosque County.*

**County Clerk: Ruby Lesley**
Phone: 325-356-2655
Fax: 325-356-5764

**County Judge: James R. Arthur**
Phone: 325-356-2466
Fax: 356-356-3710
E-mail: ccjsw047@gmail.com
Court Coordinator: Sherry Ward

# CONCHO COUNTY

Seat: Paint Rock

152 N. Roberts
Paint Rock, TX 76866
www.co.concho.tx.us

**District and County Clerk: Phyllis F. Lovell**
P.O. Box 98
Paint Rock, TX 76866-0098
Phone: 325-732-4322
Fax: 325-732-2040
E-mail: p.lovell@co.concho.tx.us

**District Attorney: George E. McCrea**
*Please see Tom Green County.*

**119th District Court**
**Judge Garland "Ben" Woodward** sits twice a month.
*Please see Tom Green County.*

County Attorney: Bill Campbell
P.O. Box 236
Paint Rock, TX 76866
Phone: 325-732-4315

County Judge: David Dillard
P.O. Box 158
Paint Rock, TX 76866-0158
Phone: 325-732-4321

# COOKE COUNTY

Seat: Gainesville

101 S. Dixon St.
Gainesville, TX 76240-4796
www.co.cooke.tx.us

District Clerk: Susan Hughes
Room 207
Phone: 940-668-5450
Fax: 940-668-5476

District Attorney: Janice L. Warder
Phone: 940-668-5466
Fax: 940-668-5499

235th District Court
Judge Janelle M. Haverkamp
Phone: 940-668-5401
Fax: 940-668-5476
Court Coordinator: Jan Brazelton
Court Reporter: Teresa Ward
Phone: 940-668-5485
Bailiff: Daniel Barthold

County Clerk: Rebecca Lawson
101 S. Dixon St.
Gainesville, TX 76240
Phone: 940-668-5420
Fax: 940-668-5486

County Attorney: Edmund Zielinski
101 S. Dixon St.
Gainesville, TX 76240
Phone: 940-668-5459
Fax: 940-668-5444

County Judge: Jason Brinkley
101 S. Dixon St.
Gainesville, TX 76240
Phone: 940-668-5435
Fax: 940-668-5440
Court Administrator: Rheta Gilmer

County Court at Law
Judge John Morris
101 S. Dixon St., Room 108
Gainesville, TX 76240
Phone: 940-668-5470
Fax: 940-668-5477
Court Coordinator: Brandy Hammond
Court Reporter: Traci Reynolds
Phone: 940-668-5446
Bailiffs: Mike Krebs, Daniel Barthold and Ryan Walker

# CORYELL COUNTY

Seat: Gatesville

620 E. Main St.
Gatesville, TX 76528
www.coryellcounty.org

District Clerk: Janice Gray
P.O. Box 4
Gatesville, TX 76528
Phone: 254-865-5911, ext. 2277
Fax: 254-865-5064
E-mail: district_clerk@coryellcounty.org

District Attorney: Dusty Boyd
P.O. Box 919
Gatesville, TX 76528
Phone: 254-865-5911, ext. 2267
Fax: 254-865-5147
E-mail: district_attorney@coryellcounty.org

52nd District Court
Judge Trent D. Farrell
P.O. Box 19
Gatesville, TX 76528
Phone: 254-865-5911, ext. 2242
Fax: 254-865-6143
Court Coordinator: Laurie Morse
Assistant Court Coordinator: Jan Hall
Court Reporter: Jeannye Skinner
Bailiff: Bill Sullivan

County Clerk: Barbara Simpson
P.O. Box 237
Gatesville, TX 76528
Phone: 254-865-5911, ext. 2278
Fax: 254-865-8631
E-mail: county_clerk@coryellcounty.org

County Attorney: Brandon Belt
210 S. 7th St.
Gatesville, TX 76528
Phone: 254-865-5911, ext. 2301
Fax: 254-865-9080
E-mail: county_attorney@coryellcounty.org

County Judge: John E. Firth
800 E. Main St., Suite A
Gatesville, TX 76528
Phone: 254-865-5911, ext. 2222
Fax: 254-865-2040
E-mail: county_judge@coryellcounty.org
Administrative Assistant: Jean Morrison
Phone: 254-865-5911, ext. 2221
E-mail: cojudge_asst@coryellcounty.org

County Court at Law
Judge John Lee
Phone: 254-865-5911, ext. 2227
Fax: 254-864-8631
Court Coordinator and Reporter: Barbara Burson
E-mail: ccl_coordinator@coryellcounty.org

# COTTLE COUNTY

Seat: Paducah

Ninth and Richards Streets
Paducah, TX 79248
www.co.cottle.tx.us

District and County Clerk: Vickey Wederski
P.O. Box 717
Paducah, TX 79248
Phone: 806-492-3823
Fax: 806-492-2625

District Attorney: David W. Hajek
*Please see Baylor County.*

50th District Court
Judge Bobby D. Burnett
P.O. Box 1127
Seymour, TX 76380
Phone: 940-889-6912
Fax: 940-889-6918
Court Administrator: Robin Smajstrla

County Attorney: John Richards
P.O. Box 909
Paducah, TX 79248
Phone: 806-492-3340
Fax: 806-492-2032

County Judge: Karl Holloway
P.O. Box 729
Paducah, TX 79248
Phone: 806-492-3613
Fax: 806-492-2032
Secretary: Laura Slover

# CRANE COUNTY

Seat: Crane

201 W. Sixth St.
Crane, TX 79731
www.co.crane.tx.us

District and County Clerk: Judy Crawford
P.O. Box 578
Crane, TX 79731-0578
Phone: 432-558-3581
Fax: 432-558-1148
E-mail: judy.crawford@co.crane.tx.us

District Attorney: Dorothy Holguin
*Please see Winkler County.*

109th District Court
Judge Martin B. Muncy sits every two weeks.
*Please see Andrews County.*

County Attorney: Susan Loyless
Room 102
Phone: 432-558-1102
Fax: 432-558-1188
E-mail: susan.loyless@co.crane.tx.us
Administrative Assistant: Susan Cadena
E-mail: susan.cadena@co.crane.tx.us

County Judge: John Farmer
Room 102
Phone: 432-558-1100
Fax: 432-558-1188
E-mail: john.farmer@co.crane.tx.us

# CROCKETT COUNTY

Seat: Ozona

907 Avenue D
Ozona, TX 76943
www.co.crockett.tx.us

**District and County Clerk: Ninfa Preddy**
P.O. Drawer C
Ozona, TX 76943
Phone: 325-392-2022
Fax: 325-392-3742
Chief Deputy: Ana Knaack

**District Attorney: Laurie K. English**
*Please see Pecos County.*

**112th District Court**
**Judge Pedro Gomez, Jr.**
P.O. Drawer C
Ozona, TX 76943
Phone: 325-392-5225
E-mail: 112court@wcc.net
Court Administrator: Becky Lumbreras
Court Reporter: Corina Lozano
Phone: 409-771-2562

**County Attorney: Jody K. Upham**
P.O. Box 4150
Ozona, TX 76943
Phone: 325-392-3920
Fax: 325-392-2207

**County Judge: Fred Deaton**
P.O. Box 1857
Ozona, TX 76943-1857
Phone: 325-392-2965
Fax: 325-392-2391
Court Coordinator: Lorena Renteria

# CROSBY COUNTY

Seat: Crosbyton

201 W. Aspen St.
Crosbyton, TX 79322
www.co.crosby.tx.us

**District Clerk: Shari Smith**
Suite 207
Phone: 806-675-2071
Fax: 806-675-2433

**District and County Attorney: Michael Sales**
Suite 106
Phone: 806-675-2062
Fax: 806-675-7053

**72nd District Court**
**Judge Ruben G. Reyes** sits as scheduled.
*Please see Lubbock County.*

**County Clerk: Tammy Marshall**
Suite 102
Phone: 806-675-2334
Fax: 806-675-2980

**County Judge: David Wigley**
Suite 208
Phone: 806-675-2011
Fax: 806-675-2403

# CULBERSON COUNTY

Seat: Van Horn

300 LaCaverna Dr.
Van Horn, TX 79855
www.co.culberson.tx.us

**District and County Clerk: Linda McDonald**
P.O. Box 158
Van Horn, TX 79855
Phone: 432-283-2058
Fax: 432-283-2091
E-mail: lindas199@hotmail.com

**District Attorney: Jaime Esparza**
*Please see El Paso County.*

**205th District Court**
**Judge Francisco X. Dominguez** sits every other month, every 3rd Thursday of that month.
*Please see El Paso County.*

**394th District Court**
**Judge Roy B. Ferguson** sits once a month.
*Please see Brewster County.*

**County Attorney: Stephen Mitchell**
P.O. Box 276
Van Horn, TX 79855
Phone: 432-283-2391
Fax: 432-283-9234
Administrative Assistant: Rosario Yglecias

**County Judge: Carlos Urias**
P.O. Box 927
Van Horn, TX 79855
Phone: 432-283-2059
Fax: 432-283-9234
Administrative Assistant: Adrian Hinojos

# DALLAM COUNTY

Seat: Dalhart

414 Denver St.
Dalhart, TX 79022
www.dallam.org/county

**District and County Clerk: Terri Banks**
P.O. Box 1352
Dalhart, TX 79022
Phone: 806-244-4751
Fax: 806-244-3751
E-mail: clerk@dallam.org

**District Attorney: David M. Green**
*Please see Moore County.*

**69th District Court**
**Judge Ron E. Enns** sits as scheduled.
*Please see Moore County.*

**County Attorney: Jon King**
418 Denrock
Dalhart, TX 79022
Phone: 806-244-5711
E-mail: attorney@dallam.org

**County Judge: Wes Ritchey**
Suite 301
Phone: 806-244-2450
Fax: 806-244-2252
E-mail: daljudge@dallam.org
Administrative Assistant: Libby Caviness

# DALLAS COUNTY

*Civil process desk    ext.* [handwritten annotation] *6848* [handwritten]

Seat: Dallas

600 Commerce St.
Dallas, TX 75202
www.dallascounty.org

**District Clerk: Felicia Pitre**
Suite 103
Phone: 214-653-7149
E-mail: felicia.pitre@dallascounty.org
Electronic Filing Coordinators: Bernita Jefferson and Candice Taylor
Phone: 214-653-7230, ext. 7240

**District Attorney: Susan Hawk**

133 N. Industrial Blvd., LB 19
Dallas, TX 75207-4313
Phone: 214-653-3600
Fax: 214-653-5774
Web: www.dallasda.com

## Civil District Courts
600 Commerce St.
Dallas, TX 75202
www.dallascourts.com

**14th District Court**
**Judge Eric V. Moyé**
5th Floor
Phone: 214-653-6000
Fax: 214-653-6001
Court Coordinator: Bonnie V. Rivera
E-mail: brivera@dallascourts.org
Chief Clerk: Terri Kilgore *— to set hearings* [handwritten]
Phone: 214-653-7337
Court Reporter: Diane Robert
Phone: 214-653-7298
Bailiff: Dennis West

**Associate Judge: Monica Purdy**
6th Floor
Phone: 214-653-6043
E-mail: mpurdy@dallascourts.org

**44th District Court**
**Judge Bonnie L. Goldstein**
5th Floor
Phone: 214-653-6996
Court Coordinator: Jonathan McKinnon
E-mail: jmckinnon@dallascourts.org
Chief Clerk: Carolyn Taylor
Phone: 214-653-7427
Court Reporter: David Lang Ford
Phone: 214-653-7395
Bailiff: Kenneth Vance

**Associate Judge: Monica Purdy**
6th Floor
Phone: 214-653-6043
E-mail: mpurdy@dallascourts.org

**68th District Court**
**Judge Martin Hoffman**
5th Floor
Phone: 214-653-6510
Fax: 214-653-7569
Court Coordinator: ~~Kim Jones~~ *Rhonda* [handwritten]
E-mail: ~~kjones~~@dallascourts.org
Chief Clerk: Veronica Vaughn

Phone: 214-653-7536
Court Reporter: Antoinette Reagor
Phone: 214-653-7158
Bailiff: Nancy Bettes

**Associate Judge: Monica Purdy**
6th Floor
Phone: 214-653-6043
E-mail: mpurdy@dallascourts.org

**95th District Court**
**Judge Ken Molberg**
6th Floor
Phone: 214-653-6361
Fax: 214-653-7991
Court Coordinator: Karin Alonzo
E-mail: kalonzo@dallascourts.org
Chief Clerk: Phillip White
Phone: 214-653-6603
Court Reporter: Deana Rosuse
Phone: 214-653-6747
Bailiff: Robert Crocker

**Associate Judge: Sheryl McFarlin**
6th Floor, Aux. Court 6C
Phone 214-653-6167
E-mail: smcfarlin@dallascourts.org

**101st District Court**
**Judge Staci Williams**
6th Floor
Phone: 214-653-6937
Fax: 214-653-6145
E-mail: 101court@dallascounty.org
Court Coordinator: LaFonda Sims
E-mail: isims@dallascourts.org
Chief Clerk: Kimberly Ferguson
Phone: 214-653-7256
Court Reporter: David Roy
Phone: 214-653-6608
Bailiff: Vacant

**Associate Judge: Monica Purdy**
6th Floor
Phone: 214-653-6043
E-mail: mpurdy@dallascourts.org

**116th District Court**
**Judge Tonya Parker**
6th Floor
Phone: 214-653-6015
Court Coordinator: Shirl Townsend
E-mail: stownsend@dallascourts.org
Chief Clerk: Rosemary De La Cerda
Phone: 214-653-7446

Court Reporter: Renee Carroll
Phone: 214-653-7159
Bailiff: Paul Beckwith

*rcarroll@swbell.net*

**Associate Judge: Sheryl McFarlin**
6th Floor, Aux. Court 6C
Phone 214-653-6167
E-mail: smcfarlin@dallascourts.org

**134th District Court**
**Judge Dale Tillery**
6th Floor
Phone: 214-653-6995
Fax: 214-653-6988
Court Coordinator: Francine Ly
E-mail: fly@dallascourts.org
Chief Clerk: Leslie Richardson
Phone: 214-653-7546
Court Reporter: Vielica Dobbins
Bailiff: Phillip Fisher
Phone: 214-653-6798

**Associate Judge: Monica Purdy**
6th Floor
Phone: 214-653-6043
E-mail: mpurdy@dallascourts.org

**160th District Court**
**Judge Jim Jordan**
6th Floor
Phone: 214-653-7273
Court Coordinator: Stephanie Bacon
E-mail: sbacon@dallascourts.org
Chief Clerk: Debora Clark
Phone: 214-653-7271
Court Reporter: Sharron Rankin
Phone: 214-653-6938
Bailiff: Tom Chism

**Associate Judge: Sheryl McFarlin**
6th Floor, Aux. Court 6C
Phone 214-653-6167
E-mail: smcfarlin@dallascourts.org

**162nd District Court**
**Judge Phyllis Lister Brown**
7th Floor
Phone: 214-653-7348
Fax: 214-653-7195
Court Coordinator: Melinda Thomas
E-mail: mthomas@dallascourts.org
Chief Clerk: Nicholas Zaragoza
Phone: 214-653-7156
Court Reporter: Sheretta Martin
Phone: 214-653-6260
Bailiff: Bob Grant

**Associate Judge: Monica Purdy**
6th Floor
Phone: 214-653-6043
E-mail: mpurdy@dallascourts.org

**191st District Court**
**Judge Gena Slaughter**
7th Floor
Phone: 214-653-6609
Court Coordinator: Marsha Sweet
E-mail: msweet@dallascourts.org
Chief Clerk: Margaret Thomas
Phone: 214-653-7117
Court Reporter: Melba Wright
Phone: 214-653-7146
Bailiff: Melissa Bates

**Associate Judge: Monica Purdy**
6th Floor
Phone: 214-653-6043
E-mail: mpurdy@dallascourts.org

**192nd District Court**
**Judge Craig Smith**
7th Floor
Phone: 214-653-7709
Fax: 214-653-7719
Court Coordinator: Bertha Moore
E-mail: bmoore@dallascourts.org
Chief Clerk: Rhonda Burks
Phone: 214-653-7748
Court Reporter: Tenesa Shaw
Phone: 214-653-7766
Bailiff: Don George

**Associate Judge: Sheryl McFarlin**
6th Floor, Aux. Court 6C
Phone 214-653-6167
E-mail: smcfarlin@dallascourts.org

**193rd District Court**
**Judge Carl Ginsberg**
8th Floor
Phone: 214-653-6998
Court Coordinator: Richard Guy
E-mail: rguy@dallascourts.org
Chief Clerk: Nikita Mosley
Phone: 214-653-7791
Court Reporter: Stephanie Moses
Phone: 214-653-7178
Bailiff: Vacant

**Associate Judge: Monica Purdy**
6th Floor
Phone: 214-653-6043
E-mail: mpurdy@dallascourts.org

**298th District Court**
**Judge Emily G. Tobolowsky**
8th Floor
Phone: 214-653-6781
Court Coordinator: Carolyn Dupree-Brown
E-mail: cbrown@dallascourts.org
Chief Clerk: Cassandra Walker — for hearings
Phone: 214-653-6779
Fax: 214-653-7155
Court Reporter: Marcey Poeckes
Phone: 214-653-6782
Bailiff: Lennie Carpenter

**Associate Judge: Monica Purdy**
6th Floor
Phone: 214-653-6043
E-mail: mpurdy@dallascourts.org

**Tax Court and Visiting Judge**
**Judge M. Kent Sims**
600 Commerce, 6th Floor
Dallas, TX 75202
Phone: 214-653-6061
Court Coordinator: Barbara Gomez
E-mail: bgomez@dallascounty.org
Chief Clerk: Jordan Haynie
Land Bank Clerk: Matthew Little
Phone: 214-653-6062
Court Reporter: Heidi Darst
Phone: 214-653-6629

# Criminal District Courts
133 N. Riverfront Blvd.
Dallas, TX 75207-4313

**Court Manager: Dana Nixon**
2nd Floor — A4, LB4
Phone: 214-653-5723

**Criminal District Court No. 1 - (H)**
**Judge Robert Burns**
LB 38, 6th Floor
Phone: 214-653-5900
Fax: 214-653-5927
Court Coordinator: Myran Gasc
Phone: 214-653-5902
E-mail: myrna.gasc@dallascounty.org
Chief Clerk: Deidre Gill
Court Reporter: Crystal Jones
Phone: 214-653-5903

**Criminal District Court No. 2 - (I)**
**Judge Don Adams**
LB 39, 7th Floor

Phone: 214-653-5910
Fax: 214-761-1319
Court Coordinator: Lupe Mercado
Phone: 214-653-5912
E-mail: lmercado@dallascounty.org
Chief Clerk: Emma Torrez
Court Reporter: Velma Loza
Phone: 214-653-5913

**Criminal District Court No. 3 - (J)**
**Judge Gracie Lewis**
LB 40, 6th Floor
Phone: 214-653-5920
Fax: 214-712-3080
Court Coordinator: LaMonica Littles
Phone: 214-653-5922
E-mail: llittles@dallascounty.org
Chief Clerk: Chad Hamill
Court Reporter: Kim Xavier
Phone: 214-653-5923
Bailiff: Kelvin Krump

**Criminal District Court No. 4 - (K)**
**Judge Dominique Collins**
LB 41, 6th Floor
Phone: 214-653-5932
Fax: 214-712-5015
Court Coordinator: Cornelius Jennings
E-mail: cjennings@dallascounty.org
Chief Clerk: Melissa Hardy
Court Reporter: Charon Evans
Phone: 214-653-5933
Bailiff: Vacant

**Criminal District Court No. 5 - (L)**
**Judge Carter Thompson**
LB 42, 5th Floor
Phone: 214-653-5940
Fax: 214-653-2836
Court Coordinator: Doris Irvin
Phone: 214-653-5942
E-mail: dirvin@dallascounty.org
Chief Clerk: Rosa Castillo
Court Reporter: Victoria Franklin
Phone: 214-653-5943
Bailiff: Vacant

**Criminal District Court No. 6 - (X)**
**Judge Jeanine Howard**
LB 11, 6th Floor
Phone: 972-739-3920
Fax: 214-875-2342
Court Coordinator: Jerry Barker
E-mail: jbarker@dallascounty.org
Phone: 972-739-3910

Court Clerk: Denise Johnson
Court Reporter: Cherie Williams
Phone: 972-739-3912
Bailiffs: Shane Chaddick and Jeffrey Fallwell

**Criminal District Court No. 7 - (Y)**
**Judge Elizabeth Frizell**
LB 54
Phone: 972-739-3915
Fax: 972-739-3917
Court Coordinator: Shronda Davis
E-mail: shronda.davis@dallascounty.org
Phone: 972-739-3905
Court Clerk: Tina Cooper
Court Reporter: Vacant
Phone: 972-739-3906

**194th District Court - (M)**
**Judge Ernest White**
LB 26, 7th Floor
Phone: 214-653-5800
Fax: 214-875-2487
Court Coordinator: Lawrence Stokes
E-mail: lstokes@dallascounty.org
Phone: 214-653-5802
Chief Clerk: Donna O'Neal
Court Reporter: Belinda Baraka
Phone: 214-653-5803
Bailiff: John Robinson

**195th District Court - (N)**
**Judge Fred Tinsley**
LB 27, 7th Floor
Phone: 214-653-5810
Fax: 214-653-5770
Court Coordinator: Claire Foster
E-mail: cmfoster@dallascounty.org
Phone: 214-653-5812
Chief Clerk: Sandra Minter
Court Reporter: Sandy Hughes
Phone: 214-653-5813
Bailiffs: Michael Jones and Kathy Mathis

**203rd District Court - (P)**
**Judge Teresa Hawthorne**
LB 28, 7th Floor
Phone: 214-653-5820
Fax: 214-653-2896
Court Coordinator: Yolanda Baker
E-mail: ybaker@dallascounty.org
Phone: 214-653-5822
Chief Clerk: Sumetra Rayson
Court Reporter: Lisabeth Kellett
Phone: 214-653-5823
Bailiffs: Chequita Coleman and David Miller

**STATE, DISTRICT AND COUNTY COURTS**

**204th District Court - (Q)**
**Judge Tammy Kemp**
LB 29, 7th Floor
Phone: 214-653-5830
Fax: 214-653-5997
Court Coordinator: Helen Wihelm
E-mail: helen.wihelm@dallascounty.org
Phone: 214-653-5832
Chief Clerk: Toya Goings
Court Reporter: Kendra Thibodeaux
Phone: 214-653-5833
Bailiff: Vacant

**265th District Court - (R)**
**Judge Jennifer Bennett**
LB 30, 6th Floor
Phone: 214-653-5840
Court Coordinator: Sharon Johnson
Phone: 214-653-5842
Fax: 214-653-5846
E-mail: sajohnson@dallascounty.org
Chief Clerk: Erika West
Court Reporter: Joseph Phillips
Phone: 214-653-5843

**282nd District Court - (S)**
**Judge Amber Givens-Davis**
LB 32, 5th Floor
Phone: 214-653-5850
Fax: 214-653-5771
Court Coordinator: Morgan Edwards
Phone: 214-653-5852
E-mail: morgan.edwards@dallascounty.org
Chief Clerk: Barbie Barton
Court Reporter: Patricia Holt
Phone: 214-653-5853

**283rd District Court - (T)**
**Judge Rick Magnis**
LB 33, 6th Floor
Phone: 214-653-5860
Fax: 214-653-5684
Court Coordinator: Kissi Jones
Phone: 214-653-5862
E-mail: kdjones@dallascounty.org
Chief Clerk: Shera Linscome
Court Reporter: Mary Snider
Phone: 214-653-5863
Bailiff: Vacant

**291st District Court - (U)**
**Judge Stephanie Mitchell**
LB 34, 7th Floor
Phone: 214-653-5870
Fax: 214-653-2768

Court Coordinator: Jeanette Hollingsworth
Phone: 214-653-5872
E-mail: jeanette.hollingsworth@dallascounty.org
Chief Clerk: Susan Sam
Court Reporter: Sasha Brooks
Phone: 214-653-5873
Bailiff: Vacant

**292nd District Court - (V)**
**Judge Brandon Birmingham**
LB 35, 6th Floor
Phone: 214-653-5880
Fax: 214-653-2861
Court Coordinator: Jessica Esparza Ramirez
Phone: 214-653-5882
E-mail: jessica.esparza@dallascounty.org
Chief Clerk: Sandra Manter
Court Reporter: Peri Wood
Phone: 214-653-5883
Bailiffs: Corey Martin and Christopher Neboh

**363rd District Court - (W)**
**Judge Tracy Holmes**
LB 36, 5th Floor
Phone: 214-653-5894
Fax: 214-653-5614
E-mail: tholmes@dallascounty.org
Court Coordinator: Deborah Baily
Phone: 214-653-5892
E-mail: deborah.bailey@dallascounty.org
Chief Clerk: Mikeshia Allen
Phone: 214-653-5890
Court Reporter: Darline LaBar
Phone: 214-653-5893
Bailiff: Robert Meek

# Family District Courts
600 Commerce St.
Dallas, TX 75202

**254th District Court**
**Judge Susan Rankin**
3rd Floor
Phone: 214-653-6136
Court Coordinator: Michele Morneau
Phone: 214-653-6741
E-mail: mmorneau@dallascounty.org
Chief Clerk: Paul Eagles
Court Reporter: Tanner Feast
Phone: 214-653-6602
E-mail: tfeast@dallascounty.org
Bailiff: Catherine Addison

STATE, DISTRICT AND COUNTY COURTS

Associate Judge: Don Turner
Phone: 214-653-6753
E-mail: donald.turner@dallascounty.org

**255th District Court**
**Judge Kim Cooks**
4th Floor
Phone: 214-653-6159
Court Coordinator: Deborah Nelson
Phone: 214-653-6154
E-mail: deborah.nelson@dallascounty.org
Chief Clerk: Donna Hall
Court Reporter: Joie Rivera
Phone: 214-653-6520

Associate Judge: Scott Beauchamp

**256th District Court**
**Judge David Lopez**
4th Floor
Phone: 214-653-6410
Fax: 214-653-6267
Court Coordinator: Cathy Sanchez
E-mail: cathy.sanchez@dallascounty.org
Chief Clerk: Jesse Rangel
Phone: 214-653-6449
Court Reporter: Glenda Finkley
Phone: 214-653-6452
Bailiff: Wolf Duran

Associate Judge: Regina Moore
Phone: 214-653-6993

**301st District Court**
**Judge Mary Brown**
3rd Floor
Phone: 214-653-7385
Court Coordinator: Catherine Nicholson
Phone: 214-653-7407
E-mail: cnicholson@dallascounty.org
Chief Clerk: Kristy Serrano
Court Reporter: Shantel Beheler
Phone: 214-653-7408
E-mail: sbeheler@dallascounty.org
Bailiff: Torance Clemens

Associate Judge: C. Andrew Ten Eyck
Phone: 214-653-7385

**302nd District Court**
**Judge Tena Callahan**
4th Floor
Phone: 214-653-7375
Fax: 214-653-6131
Court Coordinator: Twyla Weatherford

Phone: 214-653-6189
E-mail: twyla.weatherford@dallascounty.org
Chief Clerk: Barbara Barton
Court Reporter: Elizabeth Neve Griffin
Phone: 214-653-7489
Bailiff: Tom Chisem

Associate Judge: Christine Collie
Phone: 214-653-6992

**303rd District Court**
**Judge Dennise Garcia**
4th Floor
Phone: 214-653-7611
Fax: 214-653-7990
Court Coordinator: Linda Manning
Phone: 214-653-6186
E-mail: lmanning@dallascounty.org
Chief Clerk: Zelda Ridge
E-mail zridge@dallascounty.org
Court Reporter: Donna Kindle
Bailiff: Mary Ann Smith

Associate Judge: Graciela Olvera
Phone: 214-653-6690

**330th District Court**
**Judge Andrea Plumlee**
3rd Floor
Phone: 214-653-7208
Court Coordinator: Rita Bartley
Phone: 214-653-6188
E-mail: rbartley@dallascounty.org
Chief Clerk: Adrenna James
Court Reporter: Francheska Duffey
Phone: 214-653-7450
E-mail: fduffey@dallascounty.org
Bailiff: Kathleen Castillo

Associate Judge: Danielle Diaz
Phone: 214-653-6156
E-mail: danielle.diaz@dallascounty.org

# Juvenile District Courts
2600 Lone Star Dr.
Dallas, TX 75212-6307

**304th District Court**
**Judge Andrea Martin**
3rd Floor
Phone: 214-698-4330
Fax: 214-698-5553
Court Coordinator: Temecca Carter
Phone: 214-698-4936

E-mail: temecca.carter@dallascounty.org
Chief Clerk: Aurora Miranda
Phone: 214-698-4914
Court Reporter: Marty Grant
Phone: 214-698-4952
Bailiff: Dwane Shinpaugh
Phone: 214-698-4921

**Associate Judge: Alice Rodriguez**

**305th District Court**
**Judge Cheryl Lee Shannon**
3rd Floor
Phone: 214-698-4924
Fax: 214-698-4494
Court Coordinator: Tracie Broadnax
Chief Clerk: Patricia Lara
Phone: 214-698-4330
Court Reporter: Pamela Sumler
Phone: 214-698-4951

**Associate Judge: Derrick Morrison**

## Probate Courts
509 Main St.
Dallas, TX 75202

**Probate Manager: Vickie Dean**
Phone: 214-653-7099
Assistant Manager: Diamond Stinson

**Probate Court No. 1**
**Judge Brenda Hull Thompson**
2nd Floor
Phone: 214-653-7236
Fax: 214-653-6002
Administrator: Beth Miller
Docket Assistant: Amanda Wennberg
Auditor: Paula Pittman
Phone: 214-653-7238
Assistant Auditors: Miguel Hernandez and
Christopher Johnson
Court Reporter: Jackie Galindo
Phone: 214-653-6066
Bailiff: Natanya Wilson

**Probate Court No. 2**
**Judge Ingrid M. Warren**
2nd Floor
Phone: 214-653-7138
Fax: 214-875-2569
Administrator: Emily Glidewell
Docket Assistant: Theresa Sims
Auditor: Melanie Baloga

Assistant Auditors: Julie Dodd and Charles
Holmes
Court Reporter: Terri Etekochay
Phone: 214-653-6837
Bailiff: Jerry Bocker

**Probate Court No. 3**
**Judge Margaret Jones-Johnson**
2nd Floor
Phone: 214-653-6813
Administrator: Z. Lewis
Docket Assistant: Elizabeth Laviz-Roberson
Auditor: Matt Ellis
Assistant Auditor: Caesar Nguyen
Court Reporter: Charletta Breed
Phone: 214-653-7828
Bailiff: Michael Lewis
Phone: 214-653-6166

**Associate Judge: John Peyton, Jr.**
Phone: 214-653-7456

**Associate Judge: Lincoln J. Monroe**
Phone: 214-653-7404
E-mail: lincoln.monroe@dallascounty.org

## County Court

**County Clerk: John F. Warren**
509 Main St., Suite 300
Dallas, TX 75202
Phone: 214-653-7099
Fax: 214-653-7176

**County Judge: Clay Jenkins**
411 Elm St.
Dallas, TX 75202-3513
Phone: 214-653-7949
Fax: 214-653-6586
Office Manager: Ruby Blum

## County Courts at Law
600 Commerce St.
Dallas, TX 75202
www.dallascounty.org

**County Court at Law No. 1**
**Judge D'Metria Benson**
5th Floor
Phone: 214-653-7556
Court Coordinator: Seth Little
Phone: 214-653-6581
Chief Clerk: Tasha Hicks-Young

**STATE, DISTRICT AND COUNTY COURTS**

Court Reporter: Cathye Moreno
Phone: 214-653-7496
Bailiff: Danny Moore
Phone: 214-653-6525

**County Court at Law No. 2**
**Judge King Fifer**
5th Floor
Phone: 214-653-7366
Court Coordinator: Laura Nutting
Phone: 214-653-7365
Chief Clerk: Michael Intharansy
Assistant Clerk: Kanetta Menford
Court Reporter: Lanetta Williams
Phone: 214-653-7497

**County Court at Law No. 3**
**Judge Sally Montgomery**
5th Floor
Phone: 214-653-7595
Court Coordinator: Stefanie Evans
Phone: 214-653-6394
Chief Clerk: Daniel Yzagurre
Court Reporter: Janet Wright
Phone: 214-653-7831
Bailiff: John Allen

**County Court at Law No. 4**
**Judge Ken Tapscott**
5th Floor
Phone: 214-653-7466
Court Coordinator: Cathy Moran
Phone: 214-653-7345
Chief Clerk: Jodi Deal
Court Reporter: Coral Hough
Phone: 214-653-7468
Bailiffs: David Bonham and Hollis Edwards

**County Court at Law No. 5**
**Judge Mark Greenberg**
5th Floor
Phone: 214-653-6441
Court Coordinator: Sandra Humphrey
Phone: 214-653-6503
Chief Clerk: Veronica Harris
Court Reporter: Vickie L. Ogden
Phone: 214-653-6443
Bailiff: Johnny Click

## County Criminal Courts
133 N. Riverfront Blvd.
Dallas, TX 75207-4313

County Criminal Courts Manager: "Pat" Patricia
Johnson
2nd Floor
Phone: 214-653-5721
Fax: 214-653-5777

**County Criminal Court No. 1**
**Judge Dan Patterson**
LB 14, 3rd Floor
Phone: 214-653-5600
E-mail: dpatterson@dallascounty.org
Court Coordinator: Barbara Campbell
Phone: 214-653-5605
Chief Clerk: Stella Bravo
Court Reporter: Vickie Tuck
Phone: 214-653-5606
Bailiff: Doris Broughton

**County Criminal Court No. 2**
**Judge Julia Hayes**
LB 15, 3rd Floor
Phone: 214-653-5615
Fax: 214-653-5777
E-mail: julia.hayes@dallascounty.org
Court Coordinator: Teresa Curry
E-mail: tcurry@dallascounty.org
Chief Clerk: Roxanne Gong
Phone: 214-653-5610
Court Reporter: Lettie Hernandez
Phone: 214-653-5616
Bailiff: Larry Kirchner

**County Criminal Court No. 3**
**Judge Doug Skemp**
LB 16, 3rd Floor
Phone: 214-653-5620
Court Coordinator: Sheria Mathis
Phone: 214-653-5625
E-mail: sheria.mathis@dallascounty.org
Chief Clerk: Roxanne Ebert
Court Reporter: Pam Sweeney
Phone: 214-653-5626
Bailiff: James Madison

**County Criminal Court No. 4**
**Judge Nancy C. Mulder**
LB 17, 3rd Floor
Phone: 214-653-5630
Court Coordinator: Marcia Waters
E-mail: marcia.waters@dallascounty.org
Phone: 214-653-5635
Chief Clerk: Vacant
Court Reporter: Marissa Garza
Phone: 214-653-5636
Bailiff: Cliendall Lewis

**County Criminal Court No. 5**
**Judge Lisa Green**
LB 18, 3rd Floor
Phone: 214-653-5640
Court Coordinator: Naidja Taylor
E-mail: naidja.taylor@dallascounty.org
Chief Clerk: Vanessa Hardeman
Court Reporter: Robin Benton
Phone: 214-653-5646
Bailiff: Raymond T. Williams

**County Criminal Court No. 6**
**Judge Angela M. King**
LB 20, 3rd Floor
Phone: 214-653-5650
Court Coordinator: Ann Cruz
E-mail: acruz@dallascounty.org
Phone: 214-653-5655
Chief Clerk: Danielle Reagor
Court Reporter: Trisha Phillips
Phone: 214-653-5656
Bailiff: Greg Fischer

**County Criminal Court No. 7**
**Judge Elizabeth H. Crowder**
LB 21, 4th Floor
Phone: 214-653-5660
Court Coordinator: Susan Vahala
Phone: 214-653-5665
E-mail: svahala@dallascounty.org
Chief Clerk: Jennifer Skinner
Court Reporter: Trashuna Salaam
Phone: 214-653-5666

**County Criminal Court No. 8**
**Judge Tina Yoo Clinton**
LB 22, 4th Floor
Phone: 214-653-5670
Court Coordinator: Beth Doyle
E-mail: bdoyle@dallascounty.org
Phone: 214-653-5675
Chief Clerk: Jennifer Skinner
Court Reporter: Sharyl Zeno
Phone: 214-653-5676
Bailiff: Micky Elliott

**County Criminal Court No. 9**
**Judge Peggy Hoffman**
LB 23, 4th Floor
Phone: 214-653-5680
Court Coordinator: Diane Hawkins
Phone: 214-653-5685
E-mail: mhawkins@dallascounty.org

Chief Clerk: Danyelle Reigor
Court Reporter: Sandi Morelan
Phone: 214-653-5686
Bailiff: Joe Martinez

**County Criminal Court No. 10**
**Judge Roberto Cañas, Jr.**
LB 10, 4th Floor
Phone: 214-653-5690
Court Coordinator: Terri Neal
Phone: 214-653-5695
E-mail: tneal@dallascounty.org
Chief Clerk: Renae Seeger
Court Reporter: Sharina Fowler
Phone: 214-653-5696
Bailiff: David Vines

**County Criminal Court No. 11**
**Judge Shequitta Kelly**
LB 48, 4th Floor
Phone: 214-712-5068
Court Coordinator: Jacobe Graham
Phone: 214-712-5077
E-mail: jacobe.graham@dallascounty.org
Chief Clerk: Renae Seeger
Court Reporter: Estrella Pineda
Phone: 214-712-5078
Bailiff: Mike Jones

**Criminal Court of Appeals No. 1**
**Judge Kristin Wade**
LB 9, 3rd Floor
Phone: 214-653-5700
Court Coordinator: Tania Robinson
Phone: 214-653-5705
E-mail: trobinson@dallascounty.org
Court Clerk: Elisa Cedillo
Phone: 214-653-5606
Bailiff: Raymond Davis

**Criminal Court of Appeal No. 2**
**Judge Jeffrey Rosenfield**
LB 10, 3rd Floor
Phone: 214-653-5710
Court Coordinator: Judy Williams
Phone: 214-653-5715
E-mail: juwilliams@dallascounty.org
Chief Clerk: Vanessa Hardeman
Court Reporter: Terri Jones
Phone: 214-653-5716

**STATE, DISTRICT AND COUNTY COURTS**

# DAWSON COUNTY

Seat: Lamesa

400 S. First St.
Lamesa, TX 79331
www.co.dawson.tx.us

**District Clerk: Pam Huse**
P.O. Box 1268
Lamesa TX 79331-1268
Phone: 806-872-7373
Fax: 806-872-9513
E-mail: pamhuse@windstream.net

**District Attorney: Michael Munk**
P.O. Box 1124
Lamesa, TX 79331-0008
Phone: 806-872-2259
Fax: 806-872-3174
E-mail: michael.munk@co.dawson.tx.us

**106th District Court**
**Judge Carter T. Schildknecht**
P.O. Box 1268
Lamesa, TX 79331-1268
Phone: 806-872-3740
Fax: 806-872-7810
E-mail: djudge@co.dawson.tx.us
Court Administrator: Jana Furlow
Court Reporter: J'Lyn Sauseda

**County Clerk: Gloria Vera**
P.O. Box 1268
Lamesa, TX 79331-1268
Phone: 806-872-3778
Fax: 806-872-2473
Email: gvera@co.dawson.tx.us

**County Attorney: Steven B. Payson**
P.O. Box 1268
Lamesa, TX 79331-1268
Phone: 806-872-3310
Fax: 806-872-0494
Email: spayson@co.dawson.tx.us

**County Judge: Foy O'Brien**
P.O. Box 1268
Lamesa, TX 79331-1268
Phone: 806-872-7544
Fax: 806-872-7496
Email: fobrien@co.dawson.tx.us

# DEAF SMITH COUNTY

Seat: Hereford

235 E. 3rd St.
Hereford, TX 79045-5593
www.co.deaf-smith.tx.us

**District Clerk: Elaine Gerber**
Room 304
Phone: 806-364-3901
Fax: 806-363-7007
E-mail: egerber@deafsmithcounty.texas.gov

**District Attorney: Jim English**
Room 401
Phone: 806-364-3700
Fax: 806-363-7039
E-mail: jenglish@deafsmithcounty.texas.gov

**222nd District Court**
**Judge Roland Saul**
Room 305
Phone: 806-364-7222
Fax: 806-363-7011
E-mail: rsaul@deafsmithcounty.texas.gov
Court Coordinator: Gloria Ellis
Court Reporter: Tracy McCall

**County Clerk: Imelda DeLaCerda**
Room 203
Phone: 806-363-7077
Fax: 806-363-7023
E-mail: idelacerda@deafsmithcounty.texas.gov

**County Judge: D.J. Wagner**
Room 201
Phone: 806-363-7000
Fax: 806-363-7022
E-mail: dwagner@deafsmithcounty.texas.gov
Administrative Assistant: Becky Silva

# DELTA COUNTY

Seat: Cooper

200 W. Dallas Ave.
Cooper, TX 75432
www.co.delta.tx.us

New Web site in the works:
www.deltacountytx.com

**District and County Clerk: Jane Jones**
Phone: 903-395-4400, ext. 222
Fax: 903-395-4260
E-mail: deltaclerk@deltacountytx.com

**District Attorney: Will Ramsay**
*Please see Hopkins County.*

**8th District Court**
**Judge Eddie Northcutt** sits as scheduled.
*Please see Hopkins County.*

**62nd District Court**
**Judge Will Biard** sits as scheduled.
*Please see Lamar County.*

**County Attorney: Edgar J. Garrett, Jr.**
Phone: 903-395-4400, ext. 235
Fax: 903-395-2178

**County Judge: Jason Murray**
Phone: 903-395-4400, ext. 226
Fax: 903-395-2178

# DENTON COUNTY

Seat: Denton

1450 E. McKinney St.
Denton, TX 76209
www.dentoncounty.com

**District Clerk: Sherri Adelstein**
P.O. Box 2146
Denton, TX 76202-2146
Phone: 940-349-2200
Phone (Criminal): 940-349-2210
Fax: 940-349-2211
E-mail: sherri.adelstein@dentoncounty.com

**Senior District Court Administrators:**
**Larry Harbour and Sandra Hardy**
3rd Floor
Phone: 940-349-2303 or 940-349-2300

**District Attorney: Paul Johnson**
P.O. Box 2344
Denton, TX 76209
Phone: 940-349-2600
Fax: 940-349-2601
E-mail: dentonda@dentoncounty.com

**16th District Court**
**Judge Sherry Shipman**
3rd Floor
Phone: 940-349-2310
Fax: 940-349-2311
E-mail: sherry.shipman@dentoncounty.com
Court Coordinator: Shannon Davis
E-mail: shannon.davis@dentoncounty.com
Court Reporter: Michael Navarro
Phone: 940-349-2312
E-mail: michael.navarro@dentoncounty.com
Bailiff: William Calvert

**158th District Court**
**Judge Steve Burgess**
3rd Floor
Phone: 940-349-2320
E-mail: steve.burgess@dentoncounty.com
Court Coordinator: Rebecca Hobon
E-mail: rebecca.hobon@dentoncounty.com
Court Reporter: Christi Fuhrmann
Bailiff: Chad Bynum

**211th District Court**
**Judge Brody Shanklin**
2nd Floor
Phone: 940-349-2330
Fax: 940-349-2331
E-mail: brody.shanklin@dentoncounty.com
Court Coordinator: Theresa Portales
E-mail: theresa.portales@dentoncounty.com
Court Reporter: Robert French
Phone: 940-349-2332
Bailiff: Debbie Hunter

**362nd District Court**
**Judge Bruce McFarling**
3rd Floor
Phone: 940-349-2340
Fax: 940-349-2301
E-mail: bruce.mcfarling@dentoncounty.com
Administrator: Melody Carlton
E-mail: melody.carlton@dentoncounty.com
Court Reporter: Molly Bowers
Phone: 940-349-2342
Bailiff: Andrew Hartwell

**367th District Court**
**Judge Margaret Barnes**
3rd Floor
Phone: 940-349-2350
Fax: 940-349-2301
E-mail: margaret.barnes@dentoncounty.com
Administrator: Pamela Smith
E-mail: pam.smith@dentoncounty.com

STATE, DISTRICT AND COUNTY COURTS

Court Reporter: Robin Callaway-Newton
Phone: 940-349-2352
Bailiff: Brad Swaner
Phone: 940-349-2354

**393rd District Court**
**Judge Doug Robison**
4th Floor
Phone: 940-349-2360
Fax: 940-349-2361
Court Coordinator: Carol Pelzel
E-mail: carol.pelzel@dentoncounty.com
Court Reporter: Dawn Green
Phone: 940-349-2363
Bailiff: Barran Stone

**431st District Court**
**Judge Jonathan Bailey**
2nd Floor
Phone: 940-349-4370
E-mail: jonathan.bailey@dentoncounty.com
Court Coordinator: Denise Spalding
E-mail: denise.spalding@dentoncounty.com
Court Reporter: Vacant
Phone: 940-349-4372
Bailiff: Wanda Griffin

**442nd District Court**
**Judge Tiffany Haertling**
2nd Floor
Phone: 940-349-4380
Court Coordinator: Ali Silva
E-mail: ali.silva@dentoncounty.com
Court Reporter: Nicki Garcia
Phone: 940-349-4382
E-mail: niki.garcia@dentoncounty.com
Bailiff: Gwen Weaver

**IV-D Court**
**Associate Judge OCA: Casey Conine**
2nd Floor
Phone: 940-349-2280
Fax: 940-349-2281
Court Coordinator: Casey Nortman

## Probate Court

**Probate Court**
**Judge Bonnie Robison**
2nd Floor
Phone: 940-349-2140
Fax: 940-349-2141
E-mail: bonnie.robison@dentoncounty.com
Trial Court Administrator: Jerome Coleman

E-mail: jerome.coleman@dentoncounty.com
Court Investigator: Carol Dabner
Phone: 940-349-2148
Court Reporter: Wynne "Winnie" Pauly
Phone: 940-349-2142
Bailiff: Stacy Holden

**Associate Judge: David W. Jahn**

## County Court

**County Clerk: Juli Luke**
P.O. Box 2187
Denton, TX 76202
Phone: 940-349-2012
Fax: 940-349-2013
E-mail: juli.luke@dentoncounty.com

**County Judge: Mary Horn**
110 W. Hickory, 2nd Floor
Denton, TX 76201-4168
Phone: 940-349-2820
Fax: 940-349-2821
Administrative Assistant: Kate Lynass
E-mail: kate.lynass@dentoncounty.com

**County Court at Law No. 1 - Juvenile Court**
**Judge Kimberly McCary**
210 S. Woodrow Ln.
Denton, TX 76205
Phone: 940-349-2520
Fax: 940-349-2521
E-mail: kimberly.mccary@dentoncounty.com
Court Administrator: Debra Roan
Phone: 940-349-2526
E-mail: debra.roan@dentoncounty.com
Court Reporter: Mary Bryce
Phone: 940-349-2522
E-mail: mary.bryce@dentoncounty.com
Bailiff: Kemila Haley
Phone: 940-349-2523

**County Court at Law No. 2**
**Judge Robert Ramirez**
4th Floor
Phone: 940-349-2120
Fax: 940-349-2121
Court Administrator: Cassy Miller
E-mail: cassy.miller@dentoncounty.com
Court Reporter: Patricia Lopez
Phone: 940-349-2122
Bailiff: Rick Smith

**County Criminal Court No. 1**
**Judge Jim E. Crouch**
1st Floor
Phone: 940-349-2160
Fax: 940-349-2161
E-mail: jim.crouch@dentoncounty.com
Court Administrator: Sharon Stuckly
E-mail: sharon.stuckly@dentoncounty.com
Court Reporter: Pam Payne
Phone: 940-349-2162
E-mail: pam.payne@dentoncounty.com
Bailiff: Stephen Smith
Phone: 940-349-2163
E-mail: stephen.smith@dentoncounty.com

**County Criminal Court No. 2**
**Judge Virgil Vahlenkamp, Jr.**
1st Floor
Phone: 940-349-2170
Fax: 940-349-2171
E-mail: virgil.vahlenkamp@dentoncounty.com
Court Administrator: Diana Owens
E-mail: diana.owens@dentoncounty.com
Court Reporter: Cori Warren
Phone: 940-349-2172
Bailiff: Vacant

**County Criminal Court No. 3**
**Judge David D. Garcia**
4th Floor
Phone: 940-349-2180
Fax: 940-349-2181
E-mail: david.garcia@dentoncounty.com
Court Administrator: Brenda Mays
E-mail: brenda.mays@dentoncounty.com
Court Reporter: Mellony Ariail
Phone: 940-349-2182
E-mail: mellony.ariail@dentoncounty.com
Bailiff: Travis Giguere
Phone: 940-349-2183
E-mail: travis.giguere@dentoncounty.com

**County Criminal Court No. 4**
**Judge Joe Bridges**
4th Floor
Phone: 940-349-2380
Fax: 940-349-2381
E-mail: joe.bridges@dentoncounty.com
Court Administrator: Bobbie Moore
Phone: 940-349-2100
E-mail: bobbie.moore@dentoncounty.com
Court Reporter: Marsha Bretches
Phone: 940-349-2382
E-mail: marsha.bretches@dentoncounty.com
Bailiff: Bob Hargenrater
E-mail: bob.hargenrater@dentoncounty.com

**County Criminal Court No. 5**
**Judge Coby Waddill**
4th Floor
Phone: 940-349-2190
Fax: 940-349-2181
E-mail: coby.waddill@dentoncounty.com
Court Administrator: Sandra Jones
E-mail: sandra.jones@dentoncounty.com
Court Reporter: Lana Hagenbucher
Phone: 940-349-2192
E-mail: lana.hagenbucher@dentoncounty.com
Bailiff: Sam Bishop
Phone: 940-349-2193
E-mail: sammy.bishop@dentoncounty.com

# DEWITT COUNTY

Seat: Cuero

307 N. Gonzales St.
Cuero, TX 77954
www.co.dewitt.tx.us

**District Clerk: Tabeth Gardner**
307 N. Gonzales St.
Cuero, TX 77954
Phone: 361-275-0931
Fax: 361-275-0934
E-mail: tabeth.gardner@co.dewitt.tx.us

**District Attorney: Michael Sheppard**
Phone: 361-275-2612
Fax: 361-275-3282

**24th District Court**
**Judge Jack W. Marr** sits as scheduled.
*Please see Victoria County.*

**135th District Court**
**Judge K. Stephen Williams** sits as scheduled.
*Please see Victoria County.*

**267th District Court**
**Judge Juergen "Skipper" Koetter** sits as scheduled.
*Please see Victoria County.*
*Note: Hon. Koetter will retire on 3/4/16.*
*Gov. Abbot to appoint new judge.*

**County Clerk: Natalie Carson**
Phone: 361-275-0864
Fax: 361-275-0866
E-mail: natalie.carson@co.dewitt.tx.us

County Attorney: Raymond Reese
Phone: 361-275-0812
Fax: 361-275-0814
E-mail: kim.drozd@co.dewitt.tx.us

County Judge: Daryl Fowler
Phone: 361-275-0916
Fax: 361-275-0919
E-mail: daryl.fowler@co.dewitt.tx.us
Administrative Assistant: Kathy Weischwill

## DICKENS COUNTY

Seat: Dickens

Courthouse Annex
508 Row C
Dickens, TX 79229

District and County Clerk: Becky Hill
P.O. Box 120
Dickens, TX 79229
Phone: 806-623-5531
Fax: 806-623-5240

District Attorney: Becky McPherson
*Please see Floyd County.*

110th District Court
Judge William P. Smith sits once a month.
*Please see Floyd County.*

County Judge: Kevin Brendle
P.O. Box 179
Dickens, TX 79229
Phone: 806-623-5532
Fax: 806-623-5319
E-mail: dcjudge@caprock-spur.com

## DIMMIT COUNTY

Seat: Carrizo Springs

103 N. 5th St.
Carrizo Springs, TX 78834-3161
www.dimmitcounty.org

District Clerk: Maricela G. Gonzalez
Phone: 830-876-4244
Fax: 830-876-4200

District Attorney: Roberto Serna
*Please see Maverick County.*

293rd District Court
Judge Cynthia L. Muniz sits once a month.
*Please see Maverick County.*

365th District Court
Judge Amado Abascal, III sits twice a month.
Also see Maverick County.

County Clerk: Mario Z. Garcia
Phone: 830-876-4238
Fax: 830-876-4205

County Attorney: Daniel M. Gonzalez
Phone: 830-876-4236
Fax: 830-876-4219

County Judge: Francisco G. Ponce
Phone: 830-876-2323, ext. 6
Fax: 830-876-4202

## DONLEY COUNTY

Seat: Clarendon

300 S. Sully St.
Clarendon, TX 79226
www.co.donley.tx.us

District and County Clerk: Fay Vargas
P.O. Drawer U
Clarendon, TX 79226
Phone: 806-874-3436
Fax: 806-874-3351
E-mail: doncoclerk@windstream.net

District Attorney: Luke Inman
800 West Ave., Box 1
Wellington, TX 79095
Phone: 806-477-0055
Fax: 866-238-2738

100th District Court
Judge Stuart Messer sits once a month.
*Please see Childress County.*

County Attorney: Landon Lambert
P.O. Box 876
Clarendon, TX 79226
Phone: 806-874-0216
Fax: 806-874-1847
Email: landonplambert@gmail.com

County Judge: John Howard
P.O. Box 909
Clarendon, TX 79226-0909
Phone: 806-874-3625
Fax: 806-874-1181
E-mail: doncojudge@windstream.net
Administrative Assistant: Rhonda Aveni

## DUVAL COUNTY

Seat: San Diego

400 E. Gravis St.
San Diego, TX 78384
www.co.duval.tx.us

**District Clerk: Richard Barton**
P.O. Drawer 428
San Diego, TX 78384-0428
Phone: 361-279-6239

**District Attorney: Omar Escobar**
P.O. Drawer 1061
San Diego, TX 78384-1061
Phone: 361-279-6220
Fax: 361-279-2646
Assistant: Rumaldo Solis, Jr.

**229th District Court**
**Judge Ana Lisa Garza** sits one week of every month.
*Please see Starr County.*

**County Clerk: Elodia M. Garza**
P.O. Box 248
San Diego, TX 78384
Phone: 361-279-6272
Fax: 361-279-3159

**County Attorney: Baldemar F. Gutierrez**
P.O. Drawer 1076
San Diego, TX 78384
Phone: 361-279-6232
Fax: 361-279-7365

**County Judge: Ricardo Carrillo**
P.O. Box 189
San Diego, TX 78384
Phone: 361-279-6208
Fax: 361-279-3310
Email: ricardo.carrillo@co.duval.tx.us
Court Clerk: Tomasita C. Salinas

## EASTLAND COUNTY

Seat: Eastland

100 W. Main St.
Eastland, TX 76448
www.eastlandcountytexas.com

**District Clerk: Tessa K. Culverhouse**
Suite 206
Phone: 254-629-2664
Fax: 254-629-6070
E-mail: ecdc@eastlandcountytexas.com

**District Attorney: Russell Thomason**
Suite 204
Phone: 254-629-2659
Fax: 254-629-3361

**91st District Court**
**Judge Steven R. Herod**
Suite 302
Phone: 254-629-1797
Fax: 254-629-1558
Court Coordinator: Tonya Orsini
Court Reporter: Patricia Wright

**County Clerk: Cathy Jentho**
Suite 102
Phone: 254-629-1583
Fax: 254-629-8125
E-mail: ecco@eastlandcountytexas.com

**County Judge: Rex Fields**
Suite 203
Phone: 254-629-1263
Fax: 254-629-6090
E-mail: ecjudge@eastlandcountytexas.com
Administrative Assistant: Linda Whetstone

## ECTOR COUNTY

Seat: Odessa

300 N. Grant Ave.
Odessa, TX 79761
www.co.ector.tx.us

**District Clerk: Clarissa Webster**
Room 301
Phone: 432-498-4290
Fax: 432-498-4292
E-mail: clarissa.webster@ectorcountytx.gov

STATE, DISTRICT AND COUNTY COURTS

**District Attorney: Bobby Bland**
Room 305
Phone: 432-498-4230
Fax: 432-498-4293
E-mail: bobby.bland@ectorcountytx.gov

**District Court Administrator: Margarita Salazar**
Room 316
Phone: 432-498-4280
E-mail: margarita.salazar@ectorcountytx.gov

**70th District Court**
**Judge Denn Whalen**
Room 331
Phone: 432-498-4270
Fax: 432-498-4173
E-mail: denn.whalen@ectorcountytx.gov
Court Coordinator: Tina Gurule
Court Reporter: Tina Gregg

**161st District Court**
**Judge John W. Smith**
Room 335
Phone: 432-498-4260
Fax: 432-498-4173
E-mail: john.smith@ectorcountytx.gov
Court Coordinator: Missi Walden
Court Reporter: Joel Rodriguez

**244th District Court**
**Judge James M. Rush**
Room 324
Phone: 432-498-4240
Fax: 432-498-4173
E-mail: james.rush@ectorcountytx.gov
Court Coordinator: Renita Brownlee
Court Reporter: Roger Epps

**358th District Court**
**Judge W. Stacy Trotter**
Room 322
Phone: 432-498-4250
Fax: 432-498-4173
E-mail: stacy.trotter@ectorcountytx.gov
Court Coordinator: Sonia Cortez
Court Reporter: Cindy Nelson

**446th District Court**
**Judge Sara Billingsley**
Room 109
Phone: 432-498-4393
Fax: 432-498-4391
E-mail: sara.billingsley@ectorcountytx.gov
Court Coordinator: Michelle Conn
Court Reporter: Shelley Curtis

**County Clerk: Linda Haney**
Room 111
Phone: 432-498-4130
Fax: 432-498-4177

**County Attorney: Dusty Gallivan**
Room 201
Phone: 432-498-4150
Fax: 432-498-4154

**County Judge: Ron Eckert**
Room 227
Phone: 432-498-4100
Fax: 432-498-4101
Court Administrator: Donna Speed

**County Court at Law No. 1**
**Judge James A. Bobo**
Room 234
Phone: 432-498-4110
Fax: 432-498-4112
Court Coordinator: Deanna Webster
Phone: 432-498-4111

**County Court at Law No. 2**
**Judge Scott Layh**
Room 235
Phone: 432-498-4120
Court Coordinator: Brenda Melson
Court Reporter: Melinda Garriga

# EDWARDS COUNTY

Seat: Rocksprings

400 Main St.
Rocksprings, TX 78880

**District and County Clerk: Olga Lydia Reyes**
P.O. Box 184
Rocksprings, TX 78880-0184
Phone: 830-683-2235
Fax: 830-683-5376
E-mail: clerk@swtexas.net

**District Attorney: Tonya S. Ahlschwede**
*Please see Mason County.*

**452nd District Court**
**Judge Robert R. Hofman** sits once a month.
*Please see Mason County.*

**County Attorney: Allen R. Moody**
P.O. Box 707
Rocksprings, TX 78880
Phone: 830-683-6126
Fax: 830-683-6129
E-mail: moodyoffice@swtexas.net

**County Judge: Souli Asa Shanklin**
P.O. Box 348
Rocksprings, TX 78880
Phone: 830-683-6122
Fax: 830-683-6385
E-mail: countyjudge@swtexas.net

# EL PASO COUNTY

Seat: El Paso

500 E. San Antonio Ave.
El Paso, TX 79901-2489
www.co.el-paso.tx.us

**District Clerk: Norma L. Favela**
Suite 103
Phone: 915-546-2021
Fax: 915-546-8139
E-mail: districtclerk@epcounty.com

**District Attorney: Jaime Esparza**
Room 201
Phone: 915-546-2059
Fax: 915-533-5520
E-mail: daesparza@epcounty.com

## District Courts

**Council of Judges Administration**
**Executive Director: Mike Izquierdo**
Suite 101
Phone 915-546-2143
Fax: 915-546-2019
E-mail: mizquierdo@epcounty.com
Administrator: Martha Bañales
E-mail: mbanales@epcounty.com
Jury Panel Bailiff: Victor Ramirez
E-mail: viramirez@epcounty.com

**Criminal District Court No. 1**
**Judge Diane Navarette**
Room 469
Phone: 915-546-8192
Fax: 915-546-8103

Court Coordinator: Grace Herrera
E-mail: gherrera@epcounty.com
Court Reporter: Angie Morales
E-mail: amorales@epcounty.com
Bailiff: Ruben Garcia

**34th District Court**
**Judge William E. Moody**
Room 905A
Phone: 915-546-2101
Fax: 915-532-8513
E-mail: wmoody@epcounty.com
Court Coordinator: Michelle Nolasco
E-mail: mnolasco@epcounty.com
Court Clerk (Criminal): Briana Serrano
Court Reporter: Laura Akers
E-mail: lakers@epcounty.com
Bailiff: Bobby Holguin
E-mail: bholguin@epcounty.com

**41st District Court**
**Judge Annabell Perez**
Room 1006
Phone: 915-546-2149
Fax: 915-834-8220
Court Coordinator: Norma Head
E-mail: nhead@epcounty.com
Court Reporter: Leticia Perez
E-mail: lperez@epcounty.com
Bailiff: Richard Pantoja
E-mail: rpantoja@epcounty.com

**120th District Court**
**Judge Maria Salas-Mendoza**
Room 605
Phone: 915-546-2103
Fax: 915-546-2069
Court Coordinator: Myrna Hernandez
E-mail: myhernandez@epcounty.com
Court Reporter: Mary Caraveo
E-mail: mcaraveo@epcounty.com
Bailiff: Esteban Anchondo
E-mail: eanchando@epcounty.com

**168th District Court**
**Judge Marcos Lizarraga**
Room 602
Phone: 915-546-2141
Fax: 915-546-2142
Court Coordinator: Robert Vasquez
E-mail: rvasquez@epcounty.com
Court Reporter: Rachel Simons
Bailiff: Kevin Quinn
E-mail: kquinn@epcounty.com

**171st District Court**
**Judge Bonnie Rangel**
Room 601
Phone: 915-546-2100
Fax: 915-546-2114
E-mail: 171Court@epcounty.com
Court Coordinator: Rebecca Gonzalez
E-mail: rgonzalez@epcounty.com
Court Reporter: Anita Garcia
E-mail angarcia@epcounty.com
Bailiff: Richard Salazar
E-mail: rsalazar@epcounty.com

**205th District Court**
**Judge Francisco X. Dominguez**
Room 1002
Phone: 915-546-2107
Fax: 915-546-2013
Court Coordinator: Aurora Molina-Estrade
E-mail: auestrade@epcounty.com
Court Reporter: Jo-Anne Hilverding
E-mail: dlee@epcounty.com
Bailiff: Jorge Estrada
E-mail: joestrada@epcounty.com

**210th District Court**
**Judge Gonzalo Garcia**
Room 1005
Phone: 915-546-2130
Fax: 915-546-2031
Court Coordinator: Sandra Aguirre
E-mail: saguirre@epcounty.com
Court Reporter: Erika Wright
E-mail: ewright@epcounty.com
Bailiff: Jesus Pantoja, Jr.
E-mail: jespantoja@epcounty.com

**243rd District Court**
**Judge Luis Aguilar**
Room 901
Phone: 915-546-2168
Fax: 915-546-8107
Court Coordinator: Lyndia Samigiel
E-mail: lsamigiel@epcounty.com
Court Reporter: Andrea Quezada
E-mail: aquezada@epcounty.com
Bailiff: Raul Perito
E-mail: rperito@epcounty.com

**327th District Court**
**Judge Linda Chew**
Room 606
Phone: 915-546-2032
Fax: 915-546-2131

Court Coordinator: Estela Alarcon
E-mail: ealarcon@epcounty.com
Court Reporter: Rosie Moreno
E-mail: romoreno@epcounty.com
Bailiff: Bert Cervantes
E-mail: lucervantes@epcounty.com

**346th District Court**
**Judge Angelica Juarez Barill**
Room 701
Phone: 915-546-2119
Fax: 915-546-2233
Court Coordinator: Adrian Almeralla
E-mail: adalmeralla@epcounty.com
Court Reporter: Liz Bonney
E-mail: lbonney@epcounty.com
Compliance Officer: Gilberto R. Carrasco
Bailiff: Francisco Hernandez
E-mail: frhernandez@epcounty.com

**384th District Court**
**Judge Patrick M. Garcia**
Room 906
Phone: 915-546-2134
Fax: 915-543-3882
Court Coordinator: Priscilla Fernandes
Court Reporter: Genesis Stephens
E-mail: gstephens@epcounty.com
Bailiff: Rashad Jones
E-mail: rjones@epcounty.com

**409th District Court**
**Judge Sam Medrano, Jr.**
Room 459
Phone: 915-834-8209
Fax: 915-834-8204
Court Coordinator: Aracely Gomez
E-mail: aragomez@epcounty.com
Court Reporter: Natalie Martinez
E-mail: nmartinez@epcounty.com
Bailiff: David Martinez
E-mail: damartinez@epcounty.com

**448th District Court**
**Judge Sergio Enriquez**
Room 404
Phone: 915-543-3893
Fax: 915-834-8263
Court Coordinator: Sandra Gutierrez
Court Reporter: Anita Robles
E-mail: arobles@epcounty.com
Bailiff: Hector Sanchez

## DISTRICT COURTS - FAMILY

**65th Judicial District**
**Judge Yahara Lisa Gutierrez**
Room 1105
Phone: 915-546-2102
Fax: 915-546-8157
E-mail: ylgutierrez@epcounty.com
Court Coordinator: Meyte Escobedo
E-mail: mescobedo@epcounty.com
Court Reporter: Fresita Fonseca
E-mail: ffonseca@epcounty.com
Bailiff: Howard Capshaw
E-mail: hcapshaw@epcounty.com

**383rd District Court**
**Judge Mike Herrera**
Room 1101
Phone: 915-546-2132
Fax: 915-546-2020
E-mail: mherrera@epcounty.com
Court Coordinator: Carmen-Avitia Ortiz
E-mail: cavitia@epcounty.com
Court Reporter: Dalene Malendez
Bailiff: Ray Perez
E-mail: rperez@epcounty.com

**388th District Court**
**Judge Laura Strathmann**
Suite 902
Phone: 915-543-3850
Fax: 915-543-3832
Legal Secretary: Isabel Carrasco
Court Coordinator: Stephanie Clark
Administrative Assistant: David Herrera
Court Reporter: Patricia Madrid
Bailiff: Robert Holguin

## Probate Courts

**Probate Court No. 1**
**Judge Patricia Chew**
Room 803
Phone: 915-546-2161
Fax: 915-875-8527
E-mail: probatecourt@epcounty.com
Court Coordinator: Valerie Olivas
E-mail: volivas@epcounty.com
Court Master: Joseph Strelitz
Guardian Specialist: Sandra Lozano
E-mail: slozano@epcounty.com
Court Reporter: Meryl McCoy
E-mail: mmcoyr@epcounty.com
Court Investigator: Beth Parsons

E-mail: bparsons@epcounty.com
Court Auditor: Gloria Lopez

**Probate Court No. 2**
**Judge Eduardo Gamboa**
Room 422
Phone: 915-546-8183
Fax: 915-875-8530
Court Coordinator: Bea Castillo
E-mail: bcastillo@ epcounty.com
Court Administrator: Robert Ahumada
E-mail: rahumada@epcounty.com
Court Reporter: Camilla Madrid
Court Visitor: Jose Seriana
Court Investigators: Raquel Lauretano and
Alma Calderon
Probate Assistant: Mary Martinez

## County Courts

**County Clerk: Delia Briones**
Room 105
Phone: 915-546-2071
Fax: 915-546-2012
E-mail: debriones@epcounty.com
Chief Deputy: Carol Sagaribay
E-mail: csagaribay@epcounty.com

**County Attorney: Jo Anne Bernal**
Room 503
Phone: 915-546-2050
Fax: 915-546-2133
E-mail: joanne.bernal@epcounty.com

**County Judge: Veronica Escobar**
Room 301
Phone: 915-546-2098
Fax: 915-543-3888
E-mail: countyjudge@epcounty.com
Executive Assistant: Celeste Varela
E-mail: cvarela@epcounty.com
Chief of Staff: Ruben Vogt
E-mail: rvogt@epcounty.com

**Courts at Law Administrator: Flora I. Alarcon**
Room 302
Phone: 915-546-2093
Fax: 915-546-2192
E-mail: falarcon@epcounty.com

**County Court at Law No. 1**
**Judge Ricardo Herrera**
Room 802
Phone: 915-546-2011

Fax: 915-543-3865
Court Coordinator: Vacant
Court Reporter: Della North
E-mail: dnorth@epcounty.com
Bailiff: Chris Solis
E-mail: csolis@epcounty.com

### County Court at Law No. 2
**Judge Julie Gonzalez**
Room 801
Phone: 915-546-2145
Fax: 915-543-3866
Court Coordinator: Mario Delgado
E-mail: mdelgado@epcounty.com
Court Reporter: Diane Williams
E-mail: dwilliams@epcounty.com
Bailiff: Chinh Nguyen
E-mail: cnguyen@epcounty.com

### County Court at Law No. 3
**Judge Javier Alvarez**
Room 1001
Phone: 915-546-2183
Fax: 915-546-2184
E-mail: jalvarez@epcounty.com
Court Coordinator: Georgina Enriquez
E-mail: genriquez@epcounty.com
Court Reporter: Debora L. Lee
E-mail: delee@epcounty.com
Bailiff: Yessenia Quinones

### County Court at Law No. 4
**Judge Alejandro Gonzalez**
Room 805
Phone: 915-546-2190
Fax: 915-546-2191
Court Coordinator: Catherine Quezada
E-mail: cquezada@epcounty.com
Court Reporter: Laura Armendariz
E-mail: laarmendariz@epcounty.com
Bailiff: Carlos Mendoza

### County Court at Law No. 5
**Judge Carlos Villa**
Room 806
Phone: 915-546-2004
Fax: 915-543-3861
Court Coordinator: Patricia Bustamante
E-mail: pbustamente@epcounty.com
Court Reporter: Bertha Prieto
Bailiff: Mike Garcia
E-mail: migarcia@epcounty.com

### County Court at Law No. 6
**Judge M. Sue Kurita**

Room 1106
Phone: 915-543-3868
Fax: 915-543-3830
Court Coordinator: Dolores Gutierrez
E-mail: dgutierrez@epcounty.com
Court Reporter: D'anne Asleson
Bailiff: Isaac Hernandez
E-mail: ishernandez@epcounty.com

### County Court at Law No. 7
**Judge Tom Spieczny**
Room 1201 A
Phone: 915-543-3877
Fax: 915-543-3883
Court Coordinator: Alejandra Ibave
E-mail: aibavo@epcounty.com
Court Reporter: Maria Chavez
Bailiff: Brigitte Ballou
E-mail: bballou@epcounty.com

### County Criminal Court at Law No. 1
**Judge Alma R. Trejo**
Room 706
Phone: 915-834-8241
Fax: 915-834-8285
Court Coordinator: Melanie Ramirez
E-mail: mramirez@epcounty.com
Court Reporter: Mary Ann Marin
E-mail: mamarin@epcounty.com
Bailiff: Edward Rios
E-mail: erios@epcounty.com

### County Criminal Court at Law No. 2
**Judge Robert S. Anchondo**
Room 704
Phone: 915-834-8232
Fax: 915-834-8212
Court Coordinator: Lorena Acosta
E-mail: lacosta@epcounty.com
Court Reporter: Debbie Bradley
E-mail: dbradley@epcounty.com
Bailiff: Mike Stevens
E-mail: mstevens@epcounty.com

### County Criminal Court at Law No. 3
**Judge Carlos Carrasco**
Room 413
Phone: 915-834-8240
Fax: 915-834-8217
Court Coordinator: Margie Hannah
E-mail: mhannah@epcounty.com
Court Reporter: Macielle Sanchez
E-mail: masanchez@epcounty.com
Bailiff: Ralph Tellez
E-mail: ratellez@epcounty.com

**County Criminal Court at Law No. 4**
**Judge Jesus R. Herrera**
Room 702
Phone: 915-834-8248
Fax: 915-834-8274
Court Coordinator: Jesus S. Carreon
E-mail: jecarreon@epcounty.com
Court Reporter: Jason Mestas
Bailiff: Guillermo "Mo" Maldonado
E-mail: gmaldonado@epcounty.com

# ELLIS COUNTY

Seat: Waxahachie

109 S. Jackson
Waxahachie, TX 75165
www.co.ellis.tx.us

**District Clerk: Melanie Reed**
Phone: 972-825-5091
Fax: 972-825-5093
E-mail: melanie.reed@co.ellis.tx.us

**District Attorney: Patrick M. Wilson**
Phone: 972-825-5035
Fax: 972-825-5047

**40th District Court**
**Judge Bob Carroll**
Phone: 972-825-5060
Fax: 972-825-5061
Court Coordinator: Donna Tay
E-mail: donna.tay@co.ellis.tx.us
Court Reporter: Michele McManus
Phone: 972-825-5064
E-mail: michele.mcmanus@co.ellis.tx.us
Bailiffs: Dale Cheek and Anthony Golden

**378th District Court**
**Judge Joe Grubbs**
Phone: 972-825-5014
Fax: 972-825-5010
Court Coordinator: Mimi McBroom
E-mail: mimi.mcbroom@co.ellis.tx.us
Court Reporter: Tricia Thompson
Phone: 972-825-5015
E-mail: tricia.thompson10@yahoo.com

**443rd District Court**
**Judge Cindy Ermatinger**
3rd Floor
Phone: 972-825-5284

Fax: 972-825-5276
Court Coordinator: Olivia Tucker
E-mail: olivia.tucker@co.ellis.tx.us
Court Reporter: Kelly Pelletier

**County Clerk: Cindy Polley**
Phone: 972-825-5070
Fax: 972-825-5075
E-mail: cindy.polley@co.ellis.tx.us

**County Judge: Carol Bush**
101 W. Main St.
Phone: 972-825-5011
Fax: 972-825-5012
E-mail: countyjudge@co.ellis.tx.us
Administrative Assistant: Susan Soros
E-mail: susan.soros@co.ellis.tx.us

**County Court at Law No. 1**
**Judge Jim Chapman**
Phone: 972-825-5255
Fax: 972-825-5256
Court Coordinator: Carla Cobb
E-mail: carla.cobb@co.ellis.tx.us
Court Reporter: Michelle Escobar
E-mail: michelle.escobar@co.ellis.tx.us

**County Court at Law No. 2**
**Judge A. Gene Calvert, Jr.**
Phone: 972-825-5066
Court Coordinator: Patricia Marshall
E-mail: patricia.marshall@co.ellis.tx.us
Court Reporter: Tierney Lilley
E-mail: tierney.lilley@co.ellis.tx.us

# ERATH COUNTY

Seat: Stephenville

112 W. College
Stephenville, TX 76401
www.co.erath.tx.us

**District Clerk: Wanda Pringle**
Phone: 254-965-1486
Fax: 254-965-7156
E-mail: districtclerk@co.erath.tx.us

electronic filings.

**District Attorney: M. Alan Nash**
Phone: 254-965-1462
Fax: 254-965-5543

E-mail: da@co.erath.tx.us
Assistant District Attorney: Jett Smith

**266th District Court**
**Judge Jason Cashon**
Room 114
Phone: 254-965-1485
Fax: 254-965-4287
E-mail: districtcourt@co.erath.tx.us
Court Coordinator: Candy Perry
Court Reporter: Tommy Johnson
Phone: 254-968-1457
Bailiff: Alfonso Campos

**County Clerk: Gwinda Jones**
100 W. Washington
Stephenville, TX 76401
Phone: 254-965-1482
Fax: 254-965-5732
E-mail: countyclerk@co.erath.tx.us

**County Attorney: Lisa Pence**
100 W. Washington
Stephenville, TX 76401
Phone: 254-965-1453
Fax: 254-965-1421
E-mail: coattorney@co.erath.tx.us

**County Judge: Joe Tab Thompson**
100 W. Washington
Stephenville, TX 76401
Phone: 254-965-1452
Fax: 254-965-1466
E-mail: countyjudge@co.erath.tx.us
Administrative Assistant: Micki Bell
E-mail: indigent@co.erath.tx.us

**County Court at Law**
**Judge Blake Thompson**
100 W. Washington
Stephenville, TX 76401
Phone: 254-965-1417
Fax: 254-965-1402
E-mail: courtatlaw@co.erath.tx.us
Court Coordinator: Tonja Hider

## FALLS COUNTY

Seat: Marlin

125 Bridge St.
Marlin, TX 76661

**District Clerk: Christy Wideman**
P.O. Box 229
Marlin, TX 76661-0229
Phone: 254-883-1419
Fax: 254-804-1090

**District Attorney: Kathryn "Jody" Gilliam**
Suite 309
Phone: 254-883-1416
Fax: 254-883-1418

**82nd District Court**
**Judge Robert M. Stem**
P.O. Box 79
Marlin, TX 76661-0075
Phone: 254-883-1421
Fax: 254-883-2260
Court Coordinator: Marsha Rekieta
Court Reporter: Judith G. Werlinger

**County Clerk: Linda Watkins**
P.O. Box 458
Marlin, TX 76661-0458
Phone: 254-883-1408
Fax: 254-883-2260
E-mail: linda.watkins@co.falls.tx.us

**County Judge: Jay T. Elliott**
P.O. Box 458
Marlin, TX 76661-0458
Phone: 254-883-1426
Fax: 254-883-3802
E-mail: jay.t.elliott@co.falls.tx.us
Administrative Assistant: Kelly Szelestey

## FANNIN COUNTY

Seat: Bonham

101 E. Sam Rayburn Dr.
Bonham, TX 75418-4346
www.co.fannin.tx.us

**District Clerk: Nancy Young**
Suite 201
Phone: 903-583-7459
Fax: 903-640-1826
E-mail: njyoung@fanninco.net

**Criminal District Attorney: Richard Glaser**
Suite 301
Phone: 903-583-7448

Fax: 903-583-7682
E-mail: reglaser@fanninco.net
Office Administrator: Butch Henderson
E-mail: bhenderson@fanninco.net

**336th District Court**
**Judge Laurine J. Blake**
Suite 200
Phone: 903-583-2863
Fax: 903-640-1826
Court Coordinator: Sheryl Manis
E-mail: smanis@fanninco.net
Court Reporter: Charla Reamy
E-mail: creamy@fanninco.net
Bailiff: Wayne Shouse
E-mail: wshouse@fanninco.net

**County Clerk: Tammy Biggar**
Suite 102
Phone: 903-583-7486
Fax: 903-640-4241
E-mail: countyclerk@fanninco.net

**County Judge: Creta L. Carter, II**
Suite 101
Phone: 903-583-7455
Fax: 903-583-7811
E-mail: clcarter@fanninco.net
Administrative Assistant: Leah Gibby
E-mail: lgibby@fanninco.net

**County Court at Law**
**Judge Charles Butler**
210 S. Main
Bonham, TX 75418
Phone: 903-583-9258
Fax: 903-583-9283
E-mail: cbutler@fanninco.net
Court Coordinator: Lana Gibbs
E-mail: lgibbs@fanninco.net
Court Reporter: Gale Fiasco
E-mail: gfiasco@fanninco.net
Bailliff: Paul Holt
E-mail: pholt@fanninco.net

# FAYETTE COUNTY

Seat: La Grange

151 N. Washington St.
La Grange, TX 78945
www.co.fayette.tx.us

**District Clerk: Linda Svrcek**
Room 102
Phone: 979-968-3548
Fax: 979-968-2618
E-mail: linda.svreck@co.fayette.tx.us

**District and County Attorney: Peggy Supak**
Room 203
Phone: 979-968-8402
Fax: 979-968-8404

**155th District Court**
**Judge Jeff R. Steinhauser**
Room 201
Phone: 979-968-8500
Fax: 979-966-0799
E-mail: 155disct@co.fayette.tx.us
Court Coordinator: Bethany Zapalac
Court Reporter: Nancy Urbanowicz

**County Clerk: Julie Karstedt**
P.O. Box 59
La Grange, TX 78945
Phone: 979-968-3251
Fax: 979-968-8531
E-mail: julie.karstedt@co.fayette.tx.us

**County Judge: Edward F. Janecka**
Room 301
Phone: 979-968-6469
Fax: 979-968-8621
E-mail: ed.janecka@co.fayette.tx.us
Administrative Assistant: Cassie Austin
E-mail: cassie.austin@co.fayette.tx.us

# FISHER COUNTY

Seat: Roby

112 N. Concho St.
Roby, TX 79543
www.co.fisher.tx.us

**District Clerk: Tammy Haley**
P.O. Box 88
Roby, TX 79543-0088
Phone: 325-776-2279
Fax: 325-776-3253

**District Attorney: Ann Reed**
*Please see Nolan County.*
E-mail: gcmorgan52@yahoo.com

County Judge: Marty Lucke
Room 105
Phone: 806-983-4905
Fax: 806-983-4939
Court Coordinator: Nikki Seymour
Phone: 806-983-4906
E-mail: countycourt077@gmail.com

# FLOYD COUNTY

Seat: Floydada

105 S. Main St.
Floydada, TX 79235

District Clerk: Patty Davenport
Room 207
Phone: 806-983-4923
Fax: 806-983-4938

District Attorney: Becky McPherson
Room 205
Phone: 806-983-2197
Fax: 806-983-2400

110th District Court
Judge William P. Smith
Room 204
Phone: 806-983-3384
Fax: 806-983-3796
Court Coordinator: Caitlin Stephens
Court Reporter: Terri Wyatt
Phone: 806-271-4387

County Clerk: Ginger Morgan
Room 101
Phone: 806-983-4900
Fax: 806-983-4921
E-mail: gcmorgan52@yahoo.com

County Judge: Marty Lucke
Room 105
Phone: 806-983-4905
Fax: 806-983-4939
Court Coordinator: Nikki Seymour
Phone: 806-983-4906
E-mail: countycourt077@gmail.com

# FOARD COUNTY

Seat: Crowell

101 S. Main St.
Crowell, TX 79227

District and County Clerk: Debra Hopkins
P.O. Box 539
Crowell, TX 79227-0539
Phone: 940-684-1365
Fax: 940-684-1918

District Attorney: John S. Heatly
*Please see Wilbarger County.*

46th District Court
Judge Dan M. Bird sits as scheduled.
*Please see Wilbarger County.*

County Attorney: Marshall Capps
Phone: 940-684-1450
Fax: 940-684-1458

County Judge: Mark Christopher
P.O. Box 660
Crowell, TX 79227
Phone: 940-684-1424
Administrative Assistant: Cheryl Branch

# FORT BEND COUNTY

Seat: Richmond
1422 Euqene Heimann Cir.
Richmond, TX 77469
www.fortbendcountytx.gov

District Clerk: Annie R. Elliott
301 Jackson Street
Richmond, TX 77469
Phone: 281-341-4515
Fax: 281-341-4519
E-mail: annie.elliot@fortbendcountytx.gov
District Attorney: John F. Healey, Jr.
301 Jackson St.
Richmond, TX 77469
Phone: 281-341-4460
Fax: 281-341-4440

## District Courts

240th District Court
Judge Chad Bridges
Phone: 281-341-8600
Fax: 281-341-8604
Court Coordinator: Sheila Shifferly
Court Reporter: Elizabeth Wittu
Phone: 281-341-8601
Bailiff: John Gutierrez
Associate Judge: Stuti Patel

Phone: 281-341-4457
Fax: 281-341-4546
Court Coordinator: Rachel Crisler
E-mail: rachel.crisler@fortbendcountytx.gov
Bailiff: Kenny Nipps

**268th District Court**
**Judge Brady G. Elliott**
Phone: 281-341-8610
Fax: 281-341-8614
Court Coordinator: Monica Struve
Court Reporter: Mindy Hall
Phone: 281-341-8611
Bailiff: David Lopez

**Associate Judge: John M. Hawkins**
Phone: 281-341-4547
Court Coordinator: Rachel Crisler
Fax: 281-341-4546
Bailiff: Mitch Davila
Phone: 281-238-2019

**328th District Court**
**Judge Ronald R. Pope**
Phone: 281-341-4406
Fax: 281-341-4426
E-mail: 328th@fortbendcountytx.gov
Court Coordinator: Sue Anne Pitcock
Court Reporter: Sylvia Thompson
Phone: 281-341-4407
Bailiff: Rudy Parisi
Phone: 281-341-3933

**Associate Judge: Walter Armatys**
Phone: 281-341-3347
Bailiff: Roger Thomson

**387th District Court**
**Judge Brenda Mullinix**
Phone: 281-238-3290
Fax: 281-238-3289
Court Coordinator: Allyson N. Stephens
allysonstephens@fortbendcountytx.gov
Court Reporter: Laurin Rainer
laurin.rainer@fortbendcountytx.gov
Phone: 281-238-3291
Bailiff: Eddie Powell
Phone: 281-344-3962
eddie.powell@fortbendcountytx.gov

**Associate Judge: David Perwin**
Phone: 281-238-3290
Bailiff: Kendrick Randon
kendrick.randon@fortbendcountytx.gov

**400th District Court**
**Judge Maggie Jaramillo**

Phone: 281-341-4422
Fax: 281-344-3928
E-mail: 400dc@fortbendcountytx.gov
Court Coordinator: Gabriela Mindieta
E-mail: mindigab@fortbendcountytx.gov
Court Reporter: Karen Rothman
Phone: 281-341-4421
E-mail: rothmkar@fortbendcountytx.gov
Bailiff: Scott Rodriguez

**Associate Judge: Stuti Patel**
Phone: 281-341-4457

**434th District Court**
**Judge James H. Shoemake**
Phone: 281-633-7653
Court Coordinator: Susan Delatore
E-mail: delatsus@fortbendcountytx.gov
Court Reporter: Karen Wollsey
Bailiff: Noel Gonzales

**Associate Judge: John M. Hawkins**
Phone: 281-341-4457
Bailiff: Mitch Davila

**Drug Court**
**Judge Ross Sears**
Phone: 281-341-4424

## County Courts
301 Jackson St.
Richmond, TX 77469

**County Clerk: Laura Richard**
Suite 101
Phone: 281-341-8685
Fax (Civil/Probate): 281-341-4520
Fax (Misdemeanor/Juvenile): 281-341-8681
E-mail: cclerk@fortbendcountytx.gov

**County Judge: Robert E. Hebert**
401 Jackson St.
Richmond, TX 77469
Phone: 281-341-8608
Fax: 281-341-8609
E-mail: hebertb@fortbendcountytx.gov
Executive Assistant: Ann Werlean
E-mail: werleann@fortbendcountytx.gov

**County Court at Law No. 1**
**Judge Christopher G. Morales**
Phone: 281-633-7415
Fax: 281-633-7414
Court Coordinator: Regina G. Green
Court Reporter: Stephanie A. Webb
E-mail: webbstep@fortbendcountytx.gov
Phone: 281-633-7416
Bailiff: Jacob Wilson

Phone: 281-633-7411
Probate Auditor: Sandra H. Lesley
Phone: 281-633-7413

**County Court at Law No. 2**
**Judge Jefferey McMeans**
Suite 323
Phone: 281-341-4446
Fax: 281-341-4456
Court Coordinator: Candi Hooper
E-mail: candi.hooper@fortbendcountytx.gov
Court Reporter: Kelly Kelly
Phone: 281-341-4447
E-mail: kelly.kelly@fortbendcountytx.gov
Probate Auditor: Brenda Michalik
Phone: 281-341-4443
E-mail: brenda.michalik@fortbendcountytx.gov
Bailiff: Chris Garcia
Phone: 281-341-4448

**County Court at Law No. 3**
**Judge Susan G. Lowery**
Phone: 281-341-4430
Fax: 281-344-3918
Court Coordinator: LInda Avila
Phone: 281-341-4429
E-mail: lavila@fortbendcountytx.gov
Court Reporter: Robin Rosen
Phone: 281-344-3915
Probate Auditor: Benny Charles
Phone: 281-344-3912
Bailiff: Daniel Limas
Phone: 281-344-3924

**County Court at Law No. 4**
**Judge R. H. "Sandy" Bielstein**
Phone: 281-238-1995
Fax: 281-238-3370
Court Coordinator: Jenica G. Salazar
E-mail: jenica.salazar@fortbendcountytx.gov
Court Reporter: Roger Adair
Phone: 281-238-3298
Probation Auditor: Kymberly McMorries
Phone: 281-238-3297
E-mail: kymberly.mcmorries@fortbendcountytx.gov
Bailiff: Dale Kelly
Phone: 281-238-3278

# FRANKLIN COUNTY

Seat: Mount Vernon

208 Highway 37 S.
Mount Vernon, TX 75457

**District Clerk: Ellen Jaggers**
P.O. Box 750
Mount Vernon, TX 75457-0750
Phone: 903-537-8337
Fax: 903-537-8338
E-mail: ejaggers@co.franklin.tx.us

**District Attorney: Will Ramsay**
*Please see Hopkins County.*

**8th District Court**
**Judge Eddie Northcutt** sits as scheduled.
*Please see Hopkins County.*

**62nd District Court**
**Judge Will Biard** sits as scheduled.
*Please see Lamar County.*

**County Clerk: Betty Crane**
200 N. Kaufman St.
Mount Vernon, TX 75457
Phone: 903-537-2342, ext. 2
Fax: 903-537-2962
E-mail: bcrane@co.franklin.tx.us

**County Attorney: Gene Stump**
Phone: 903-537-2342, ext. 4
Fax: 903-537-2418

**County Judge: Scott Lee**
Phone: 903-537-2342, ext. 6
Fax: 903-537-2418
E-mail: slee@co.franklin.tx.us
Administrative Assistant: Katie Stump

# FREESTONE COUNTY

Seat: Fairfield

118 E. Commerce St.
Fairfield, TX 75840
www.co.freestone.tx.us

**District Clerk: Teresa Black**
P.O. Box 722
Fairfield, TX 75840-0722
Phone: 903-389-2534
Fax: 903-389-8421

**District and County Attorney: Christopher Martin**
Room 305
Phone: 903-389-3977
Fax: 903-389-5289

**77th District Court**
**Judge Patrick Simmons**

P.O. Box 722
Fairfield, TX 75840
Phone: 903-389-2534
Court Reporter: Sherry Current
Phone: 254-717-0041
Court Coordinator: Misty Lewis

**87th District Court**
**Judge Deborah Oakes Evans**
P.O. Box 722
Fairfield, TX 75840-0722
Phone: 903-389-4836
Fax: 903-389-8421
Court Coordinator: Misty Lewis
Court Reporter: Ellen Earles
Phone: 903-723-7415
E-mail: earles.ellen@gmail.com

**County Clerk: Linda Jarvis**
P.O. Box 1010
Fairfield, TX 75840
Phone: 903-389-2635
Fax: 903-389-6956

**County Judge: Linda K. Grant**
118 E. Commerce St.
Fairfield, TX 75840
Room 205
Phone: 903-389-3335
Fax: 903-389-3839
Administrative Assistant: Pilar Harris

# FRIO COUNTY

Seat: Pearsall

500 E. San Antonio St.
Pearsall, TX 78061
www.co.frio.tx.us

**District Clerk: Ramona B. Rodriguez**
Suite 8
Phone: 830-334-8073
Fax: 830-334-0047

**District Attorney: Rene M. Peña**
*Please see Atascosa County.*

**81st District Court**
**Judge Donna S. Rayes** sits twice a month.
*Please see Atascosa County.*

**218th District Court**
**Judge Russell Wilson** sits twice a month.
*Please see Karnes County.*

**County Clerk: Angie Tullis**
Suite 6

Phone: 830-334-2214
Fax: 830-334-0021

**County Attorney: Hector M. Lozano**
Suite 1
Phone: 830-334-2162
Fax: 830-334-0015

**County Judge: Arnulfo L. Luna**
Suite 7
Phone: 830-334-2154
Fax: 830-334-0010
Administrative Assistant: Delma Aguirre

# GAINES COUNTY

Seat: Seminole

101 S. Main St.
Seminole, TX 79360
www.co.gaines.tx.us

**District Clerk: Sharon Taylor**
Room 311
Phone: 432-758-4013
Fax: 432-758-4036
E-mail: sharon.taylor@co.gaines.tx.us

**First Deputy: Dee Keener**
E-mail: dee.keener@co.gaines.tx.us

**Second Deputy: Susan Murphree**
E-mail: susan.murphree@co.gaines.tx.us

**District Attorney: Michael Munk**
*Please see Dawson County.*

**106th District Court**
**Judge Carter T. Schildknecht**
*Please see Dawson County.*

**County Clerk: Vicki Phillips**
Room 206
Phone: 432-758-4003
Fax: 432-758-1442

**County Attorney: Joe Nagy**
Phone: 432-758-4001

**County Judge: Tom N. Keyes**
P.O. Box 847
Seminole, TX 79360
Phone: 432-758-5411
Fax: 432-758-4031
Administrative Assistant: Benette McDonald

# GALVESTON COUNTY

Seat: Galveston

600 59th St.
Galveston, TX 77551-4196
www.co.galveston.tx.us

**District Clerk: John D. Kinard**
Suite 4001
Phone: 409-766-2424
Fax: 409-766-2292

**District Attorney: Jack Roady**
Suite 1001
Phone: 409-766-2355
Fax: 409-766-2290

**10th District Court**
**Judge Kerry L. Neves**
Suite 4305
Phone: 409-766-2230
Fax: 409-770-5266
Court Coordinator: Lori Wilson
Court Reporter: Gail Jalufka
Phone: 409-766-2231
Bailiff: Andrea Gradney

**56th District Court**
**Judge Lonnie Cox**
Suite 3204
Phone: 409-766-2226
Fax: 409-770-5264
Court Coordinator: Kay Henson
E-mail: kay.henson@co.galveston.tx.us
Court Reporter: Vacant
Phone: 409-766-2227
Bailiff: Renita Glaze

**122nd District Court**
**Judge John Ellisor**
Suite 4304
Phone: 409-766-2275
Fax: 409-770-6265
Court Coordinator: Becky Hernandez
E-mail: becky.hernandez@co.galveston.tx.us
Court Reporter: Connie Chan
Phone: 409-770-5169
Bailiff: Carl Kelly

**212th District Court**
**Judge Patricia Grady**
Suite 3305
Phone: 409-766-2266
Fax: 409-765-2610
Court Coordinator: JoAnn Fentanes
E-mail: joann.fentanes@co.galveston.tx.us
Court Reporter: Jennifer Hall
Phone: 409-766-2264

Bailiff: Shannon Reyes
Phone: 409-766-1009

**306th District Court — Family Court**
**Judge Anne B. Darring**
Suite 3304
Phone: 409-766-2255
Fax: 409-765-2936
Court Coordinator: Jaclyn Cobb-Chavez
E-mail: jaclyn.cobb-chavez@co.galveston.tx.us
Court Reporter: Mary Kate Piper
E-mail: kate.piper@galveston.tx.us
Phone: 409-766-2254
Bailiff: Bruno Pham-ky
E-mail: bruno.pham-ky@galveston.tx.us
Phone: 409-766-5230

**Associate Judge: Stephen Baker**
Phone: 409-621-7928

**405th District Court**
**Judge Michelle M. Slaughter**
Suite 4204
Phone: 409-765-2688
Fax: 409-765-2689
Court Coordinator: Dana B. Winston
E-mail: dana.winston@co.galveston.tx.us
Court Reporter: Cylena Korkmas
Phone: 409-765-2683
Bailiff: J.L. Campbell

## Probate Court

**Probate Court Judge Kimberly Sullivan**
Suite 2305
Phone: 409-766-2251
Fax: 409-765-3221
Court Coordinator: Christine Welsh
E-mail: christine.welsh@co.galveston.tx.us
Court Administrator: Annaya Martin
Phone: 404-766-2482
E-mail: annaya.martin@co.galveston.tx.us
Court Reporter: John P. Partain
Phone: 409-766-2654
Guardianship Investigator: Debbie Diaz
Phone: 409-770-5188
E-mail: debbie.diaz@co.galveston.tx.us
Auditor: Monica Cavazos
Phone: 409-770-5140
E-mail: monica.cavazos@co.galveston.tx.us
Bailiff: John Gerami
E-mail: john.gerami@co.galveston.tx.us

## County Court

**County Clerk: Dwight D. Sullivan**
P.O. Box 17253
Galveston, TX 77552-7253
Phone: 409-766-2200
Fax: 409-765-3160

County Judge: Mark Henry
722 Moody, 2nd Floor
Galveston, TX 77550
Phone: 409-766-2244
Fax: 409-766-4590
E-mail: mark.henry@co.galveston.tx.us
Chief of Staff: Tyler Drummond
E-mail: tyler.drummond@co.galveston.tx.us
Office Coordinator: Dianna Martinez
E-mail: dianna.martinez@co.galveston.tx.us
Administrative Assistant: Linda Liechty

**County Court at Law No. 1**
**Judge John Grady**
Suite 2304
Phone: 409-766-2233
Fax: 409-765-2945
Court Coordinator: Connie Nolan
Court Reporter: Lynnette "Bitty" Erskine
Phone: 409-766-2235
Bailiff: Karen Bates

**County Court at Law No. 2**
**Judge Barbara E. Roberts**
Suite 2204
Phone: 409-766-2405
Fax: 409-795-3034
Court Coordinator: Jose Mejia
E-mail: jose.mejia@co.galveston.tx.us
Court Reporter: Janna Fowler
Phone: 409-766-2407
E-mail: janna.fowler@co.galveston.tx.us
Bailiff: Jesse Khaled

**County Court at Law No. 3**
**Judge Jack Ewing**
Suite 2205
Phone: 409-621-7920
Fax: 409-765-3154
Court Coordinator: Katherine Bush
Court Reporter: Amri Davison
Phone: 409-621-7921
Bailiff: Ryan Patrick

# GARZA COUNTY

Seat: Post

300 W. Main St.
Post, TX 79356
www.garzacounty.net
**District and County Clerk: Jim Plummer**
P.O. Box 366
Post, TX 79356-0366

Phone: 806-495-4430
Fax: 806-495-4431
E-mail: james.plummer@co.garza.tx.us
**District Attorney: Michael Munk**
*Please see Dawson County.*

**106th District Court**
**Judge Carter T. Schildknecht** sits twice a month.
*Please see Dawson County.*

**County Attorney: Ted Weems**
Phone: 806-495-4440
Fax: 806-495-4496
E-mail: ted.weems@co.garza.tx.us

**County Judge: Lee Norman**
Phone: 806-495-4405
Fax: 806-495-4482
E-mail: lee.norman@co.garza.tx.us

# GILLESPIE COUNTY

Seat: Fredericksburg

101 W. Main St.
Fredericksburg, TX 78624
www.gillespiecounty.org

**District Clerk: Jan Davis**
Phone: 830-997-6517
Fax: 830-992-2613
E-mail: jdavis@gillespiecounty.org

**District Attorney: Bruce E. Curry**
*Please see Kerr County.*

**216th District Court**
**Judge N. Keith Williams** sits as scheduled.
*Please see Kerr County.*
**County Clerk: Mary Lynn Rusche**
Phone: 830-997-6515
Fax: 830-997-9958
E-mail: mlrusche@gillespiecounty.org

**County Attorney: Christopher G. Nevins**
125 W. Main St., Suite L41
Fredericksburg, TX 78624
Phone: 830-990-0675
Fax: 830-992-2615
E-mail: countyattorney@gillespiecounty.org

**County Judge: Mark H. Stroeher**
Phone: 830-997-7502
Fax: 830-992-2608
E-mail: mstroeher@gillespiecounty.org

# GLASSCOCK COUNTY

Seat: Garden City

117 E. Currie
Garden City, TX 79739
www.co.glasscock.tx.us

**District and County Clerk: Rebecca Batla**
P.O. Box 190
Garden City, TX 79739-0190
Phone: 432-354-2371
Fax: 432-354-2616

**District and County Attorney: Hardy L. Wilkerson**
*Please see Howard County.*

**118th District Court**
**Judge Timothy D. Yeats, III** sits as scheduled.
*Please see Howard County.*

**County Judge: Kim Halfmann**
P.O. Box 67
Garden City, TX 79739-0067
Phone: 432-354-2639
Fax: 432-354-2348

# GOLIAD COUNTY

Seat: Goliad

127 N. Courthouse Square
Goliad, TX 77963
www.co.goliad.tx.us

**District and County Clerk: Mary Ellen Flores**
P.O. Box 50
Goliad, TX 77963
Phone: 361-645-3294
Fax: 361-645-3858

**District Attorney: Michael Sheppard**
*Please see DeWitt County.*

**24th District Court**
**Judge Jack W. Marr** sits as scheduled.
*Please see Victoria County.*

**135th District Court**
**Judge K. Stephen Williams** sits as scheduled.
*Please see Victoria County.*

**267th District Court**
**Judge Juergen "Skipper" Koetter** sits as scheduled.
*Please see Victoria County.*
*Note: Hon. Koetter will retire on 3/4/16.*
*Gov. Abbot to appoint new judge.*

**County Attorney: Rob Baiamonte**
P.O. Box 24
Goliad, TX 77963
Phone: 361-645-2184
Fax: 361-645-1711

**County Judge: P.T. (Pat) Calhoun**
P.O. Box 677
Goliad, TX 77963
Phone: 361-645-3337
Fax: 361-645-3474

# GONZALES COUNTY

Seat: Gonzales

414 St. Joseph St.
Gonzales, TX 78629
www.co.gonzales.tx.us

**District Clerk: Janice Sutton**
Suite 300
Phone: 830-672-2326
Fax: 830-672-9313
E-mail: justton@co.gonzales.tx.us

**25th District Court**
**Judge William D. Old, III** sits at least three times a month.
*Please see Guadalupe County.*
**2nd 25th District Court**
**Judge W. C. "Bud" Kirkendall**
*Please see Guadalupe County.*

**County Clerk: Lee Riedel**
1709 Sarah Dewitt Dr.
Gonzales, TX 78629-0077
Phone: 830-672-2801
Fax: 830-672-2636
E-mail: lriedel@co.gonzales.tx.us

**County Attorney: Paul S. Watkins**
With felony responsibilities.
415 St. Louis St.
Gonzales, TX 78629-4029
E-mail: countyattorney@co.gonzales.tx.us
Phone: 830-672-6527
Fax: 830-672-5868

**County Judge: David Bird**
Suite 200
Phone: 830-672-2327
Fax: 830-672-5477
E-mail: countyjudge089@gonzales.tx.us

# GRAY COUNTY

Seat: Pampa

205 N. Russell St.
Pampa, TX 79065
www.co.gray.tx.us

**District Clerk: Jo Mays**
P.O. Box 1139
Pampa, TX 79066-1139
Phone: 806-669-8010
Fax: 806-669-8053
E-mail: jo.mays@graycch.com

**District Attorney: Franklin McDonough**
P.O. Box 1592
Pampa, TX 79066-1592
Phone: 806-669-8035
Fax: 806-669-8050
E-mail: franklin.mcdonough@graycch.com

**31st District Court**
**Judge Steven R. Emmert** sits as scheduled.
*Please see Wheeler County.*

**223rd District Court**
**Judge Phil N. Vanderpool**
P.O. Box 2160
Pampa, TX 79066-2160
Phone: 806-669-8014
E-mail: 223rddistrictcourt@gmail.com
Court Coordinator: Krissie Dudley
E-mail: krissie.dudley@graycch.com
Court Reporter: Karen Morris
Phone: 806-669-8013
Bailiff: Clark Teague

**County Clerk: Susan Winborne**
P.O. Box 1902
Pampa, TX 79066-1902
Phone: 806-669-8004
Fax: 806-669-8054
E-mail: susan.winborne@graycch.com
**County Attorney: Josh Seabourn**
205 N. Russell, Room 202

Pampa, TX 79065
Phone: 806-669-8003
E-mail: josh.seabourn@graycch.com

**County Judge: Richard D. Peet**
Suite 205
Phone: 806-669-8007
E-mail: richard.peet@graycch.com

# GRAYSON COUNTY

Seat: Sherman

200 S. Crockett St.
Sherman, TX 75090
www.co.grayson.tx.us

**District Clerk: Kelly Ashmore**
Suite 120-A
Phone: 903-813-4352
Fax: 903-870-0609
E-mail: kashmore@co.grayson.tx.us

**District Attorney: Joseph D. Brown**
Suite 116A
Phone: 903-813-4361
E-mail: brownj@co.grayson.tx.us

**15th District Court**
**Judge James P. Fallon**
Phone: 903-813-4303
Court Coordinator: Deborah Whitney
E-mail: whitneyd@co.grayson.tx.us
Court Reporter: Janet Kamras
Phone: 903-813-4315
Email: kamrasj@co.grayson.tx.us
Bailiff: Charley Smith
Phone: 903-813-4302

**59th District Court**
**Judge Rayburn "Rim" M. Nall, Jr.**
Phone: 903-813-4305
Court Coordinator: Christie Anderson
E-mail: andersonc@co.grayson.tx.us
Court Reporter: Cindy Bardwell
Phone: 903-813-4314
Bailiff: John Smith
Phone: 903-813-4307

**397th District Court**
**Judge Brian Gary**
Phone: 903-813-4311
Court Coordinator: Jennifer Tusty
E-mail: tustyj@co.grayson.tx.us
Court Reporter: Paula Thomas
Phone: 903-813-4313
Bailiff: Ed Coldin

**County Clerk: Wilma Blackshear-Bush**
100 W. Houston St., Suite 17
Sherman, TX 75090
Phone: 903-813-4335
Fax: 903-870-0829

**County Judge: Bill Magers**
100 W. Houston St., Suite 15
Sherman, TX 75090
Phone: 903-813-4228
Secretary: Julie Lollar

**County Court at Law No. 1**
**Judge James "Corky" Henderson**
Phone: 903-813-4000, ext. 2904
Court Coordinator: Kristi Risner
E-mail: risnerk@co.grayson.tx.us
Court Reporter: Misty Skinner
Phone: 903-813-4380
E-mail: skinnerm@co.grayson.tx.us
Bailiff: Jaimie Hubbard
E-mail: hubbardj@co.grayson.tx.us

**County Court at Law No. 2**
**Judge Carol M. Siebman**
Phone: 903-813-4063
Court Coordinator: Kristi Risner
E-mail: risnerk@co.grayson.tx.us
Court Reporter: Tammy Allen
Phone: 903-813-4339
E-mail: allent@co.grayson.tx.us
Bailiff: J.D. Cook
Phone: 903-813-4000, ext. 4381
E-mail: cookjd@co.grayson.tx.us

# GREGG COUNTY

Seat: Longview

101 E. Methvin St.
Longview, TX 75601
www.co.gregg.tx.us

**District Clerk: Barbara Duncan**
P.O. Box 711
Longview, TX 75606-0711
Phone: 903-237-2663
Fax: 903-236-8474
E-mail: barbara.duncan@co.gregg.tx.us

**District Attorney: Carl Dorrough**
Suite 333
Phone: 903-236-8440
Fax: 903-236-8490

**124th District Court**
**Judge Alfonso Charles**
Suite 447
Phone: 903-236-1765
Fax: 903-236-0747
E-mail: terri.shepherd@co.gregg.tx.us
Court Coordinator: Terri Shepherd
Court Reporter: Tina Campbell

**188th District Court**
**Judge David Brabham**
Suite 408
Phone: 903-237-2588
Fax: 903-236-8603
E-mail: david.brabham@co.gregg.tx.us
Court Coordinator: Dawn Callow
Court Reporter: Grelynn Freeman

**307th District Court**
**Judge James T. Womack**
Suite 463
Phone: 903-237-2534
Fax: 903-234-3150
Court Coordinator: Chastity Baker
E-mail: chastity.baker@co.gregg.tx.us
Court Reporter: Kasi Harris
Phone: 903-234-3154

**County Clerk: Connie Wade**
Suite 200
Phone: 903-236-8430
Fax: 903-237-2574
E-mail: connie.wade@co.gregg.tx.us
Chief Deputy: Gladyce Carver
E-mail: gladyce.carver@co.gregg.tx.us

**County Judge: Bill Stoudt**
Suite 300
Phone: 903-236-8420
Fax: 903-237-2699
Administrative Assistant: Diane Pearson
E-mail: diane.pearson@co.gregg.tx.us

**County Court at Law No. 1**
**Judge Rebecca L. Simpson**
Suite 416
Phone: 903-236-8445
Fax: 903-237-2517
Court Coordinator: Michelle Gilley
E-mail: michelle.gilley@co.gregg.tx.us
Court Reporter: Lisa Frizzell
Phone: 903-237-2518

**County Court at Law No. 2**
**Judge Vincent Dulweber**
Suite 303
Phone: 903-234-3110
Fax: 903-234-3112
Court Coordinator: Wendy Ligon
E-mail: wendy.ligon@co.gregg.tx.us
Court Reporter: Sheryl Bowen
Phone: 903-234-3111

## GRIMES COUNTY

Seat: Anderson

100 Main St.
Anderson, TX 77830
www.co.grimes.tx.us

**District Clerk: Gay Wells**
P.O. Box 234
Anderson, TX 77830-0234
Phone: 936-873-4432
Fax: 936-873-2514

**District Attorney: Tuck M. McLain**
1022 Highway 90
Anderson, TX 77830
Phone: 936-873-4484
Fax: 936-873-2688

**12th District Court**
**Judge Donald L. Kraemer** sits as scheduled.
*Please see Walker County.*

**506th District Court**
**Judge Albert M. McCaig, Jr.** sits as scheduled.
*Please see Waller County.*

**County Clerk: David Pasket**
P.O. Box 209
Anderson, TX 77830-0209
Phone: 936-873-4410
Fax: 936-873-3308

**County Attorney: Jon C. Fultz**
P.O. Box 439
Anderson, TX 77830-0439
Phone: 936-873-6455
Fax: 936-873-2514

**County Judge: Ben Leman**
P.O. Box 160
Anderson, TX 77830-0160
Phone: 936-873-4475
Fax: 936-873-5065
E-mail: ben.leman@co.grimes.tx.us
Administrative Assistant: Michelle Stewart
E-mail: michelle.stewart@co.grimes.tx.us

## GUADALUPE COUNTY

Seat: Seguin

211 W. Court St.
Seguin, TX 78155
www.co.guadalupe.tx.us

**District Clerk: Debi Crow**
Phone: 830-303-4188, ext. 1275
Fax: 830-379-1943
E-mail: debic@co.guadalupe.tx.us
E-file: www.eFilingforTexas.gov

**District Attorney: Heather McMinn**
Phone: 830-303-1922
Fax: 830-303-2137
E-mail: heather.mcminn@co.guadalupe.tx.us

**25th District Court**
**Judge William D. Old, III**
Phone: 830-303-4188, ext. 1265
Fax: 830-379-0633
E-mail: bill.old@co.guadalupe.tx.us
Court Coordinator: Lynn Bothe
E-mail: lynnb@co.guadalupe.tx.us
Court Reporter: Patty Wagner
Phone: 830-303-4188, ext. 1265

**2nd 25th District Court**
**Judge W. C. "Bud" Kirkendall**
Suite 302
Phone: 830-303-4188, ext. 1300
Fax: 830-303-0847
E-mail: wckirkendall@co.guadalupe.tx.us
Court Coordinator: Judy Cadell
E-mail: judy.caddell@co.guadalupe.tx.us
Court Reporter: Phyllis Bush
Phone: 979-562-2877

STATE, DISTRICT AND COUNTY COURTS

**274th District Court**
Judge Gary L. Steel
Room 205
Phone: 830-303-4188, ext. 1273
Fax: 830-379-0633
E-mail: 274juddist@co.guadalupe.tx.us
Court Coordinator: Kim McMahon
E-mail: kimberly.mcmahon@co.guadalupe.tx.us
Court Reporter: Richard Roberts
Phone: 830-228-4634

**County Clerk: Teresa Kiel**
Phone: 830-303-8863
Fax: 830-401-0300
E-mail: tkiel@co.guadalupe.tx.us

**County Attorney: David Willborn**
211 W. Court
Seguin, TX 78155
Phone: 830-303-6130
Fax: 830-379-9491
E-mail: dwillborn@co.guadalupe.tx.us

**County Judge: Kyle Kutscher**
211 W. Court St.
Seguin, TX 78155
Phone: 830-303-4188, ext. 1311
Fax: 830-303-4064
E-mail: kyle.kutscher@co.guadalupe.tx.us
Administrative Assistant: Doreen Luehlfing
Phone: 830-303-4188, ext. 1312

**County Court at Law**
Judge Robin V. Dwyer
211 W. Court
Seguin, TX 78155
Phone: 830-303-8869
Fax: 830-303-5325
Court Coordinator: Karen Nelson
E-mail: knelson@co.guadalupe.tx.us

**County Court at Law No. 2**
Judge William F. Follis, Jr.
211 W. Court
Seguin, TX 78155
Phone: 830-303-8871
Court Coordinator: Kathy Boos
Court Reporter: Stacey Sharron

## HALE COUNTY

Seat: Plainview

225 Broadway St.
Plainview, TX 79072-8050

**District Clerk: Carla Cannon**
Suite 4
Phone: 806-291-5226
Fax: 806-291-5206
E-mail: ccannon@halecounty.org

**District Attorney: Wally Hatch**
Suite 1
Plainview, TX 79072-8050
Phone: 806-291-5241
E-mail: whatch@halecounty.org

**64th District Court**
Judge Robert W. Kinkaid, Jr.
Suite 5
Phone: 806-291-5234
Court Coordinator: Nancy Carter
Court Reporter: Myra Chapa
Phone: 806-291-5233

**242nd District Court**
Judge Kregg Hukill
Suite 3
Phone: 806-291-5254
Court Coordinator: Elsa Carrera
Court Reporter: Holly Craven
Phone: 806-291-5257

**County Clerk: Latrice Kemp**
500 Broadway St., Room 140
Plainview, TX 79072
Phone: 806-291-5261
Fax: 806-291-9810

**County Attorney: Jim Tirey**
500 Broadway St., Room 340
Plainview, TX 79072
Phone: 806-291-5306
Fax: 806-291-5308

**County Judge: Bill Coleman**
500 Broadway St., Room 240
Plainview, TX 79072
Phone: 806-291-5214

## HALL COUNTY

Seat: Memphis

512 W. Main St.
Memphis, TX 79245
www.co.hall.tx.us

**District and County Clerk: Raye Bailey**
Phone: 806-259-2627
Fax: 806-259-5078

**District Attorney: Luke Inman**
*Please see Donley County.*

**100th District Court**
**Judge Stuart Messer** sits every five weeks.
*Please see Childress County.*

**County Attorney: John Deaver**
Phone: 806-259-2651

**County Judge: Ray Powell**
Phone: 806-259-2511
Fax: 806-259-3083

# HAMILTON COUNTY

Seat: Hamilton

102 N. Rice St., Suite 215
Hamilton, TX 76531-1860
www.co.hamilton.tx.us

**District Clerk: Sandy Layhew**
2nd Floor
Phone: 254-386-1240
Fax: 254-386-1242
E-mail: districtclerk@hamiltoncountytx.org

**District Attorney: B. J. Shepherd**
*Please see Bosque County.*

**220th District Court**
**Judge Phil Robertson** sits on Wednesdays.
*Please see Bosque County.*

**County Clerk: Debbie Rudolph**
Suite 107
Phone: 254-386-1205
Fax: 254-386-8727
E-mail: countyclerk@hamiltoncountytx.org

**County Attorney: Mark Henkes**
100 W. Main St.
Hamilton, TX 76531
Phone: 254-386-3217

**County Judge: W. Mark Tynes**
Phone: 254-386-1295
Fax: 254-386-1291

E-mail: countyjudge@hamiltoncountytx.org
Administrative Assistant: Clydell Massingill
Phone: 254-386-1290
E-mail: countyjudgesec@hamiltoncountytx.org

# HANSFORD COUNTY

Seat: Spearman

One NW Courthouse Square
Spearman, TX 79081
www.co.hansford.tx.us

**District and County Clerk: Kim V. Vera**
Phone: 806-659-4110
Fax: 806-659-4168
E-mail: kvera.cdc@co.hansford.tx.us

**District Attorney: Mark Snider**
*Please see Hutchinson County.*

**84th District Court**
**Judge William "Bill" D. Smith**
P.O. Box 3437
Stinnett, TX 79083-3437
Phone: 806-659-4160 or 806-878-4022
Fax: 806-659-4168
Court Coordinator: Jan Lewis
Court Reporter: Debra Martin

**County Attorney: John Hutchison**
P.O. Box 703
Spearman, TX 79081
Phone: 806-659-3703
Fax: 806-659-1035
E-mail: jlhutch@mac.com

**County Judge: Benny D. Wilson**
Phone: 806-659-4100
E-mail: countyjudge@hansfordcountytx.com

# HARDEMAN COUNTY

Seat: Quanah

300 Main
Quanah, TX 79252

**District and County Clerk: Ellen London**
P.O. Box 30
Quanah, TX 79252-0030
Phone: 940-663-2901

Fax: 940-663-5161
E-mail: londonellen@ymail.com

**District Attorney: John S. Heatly**
*Please see Wilbarger County.*

**46th District Court**
**Judge Dan M. Bird** sits as scheduled.
*Please see Wilbarger County.*

**County Attorney: Stanley Watson**
Phone: 940-663-5222
Fax: 940-663-6103

**County Judge: Ronald Ingram**
P.O. Box 30
Quanah, TX 79252
Phone: 940-663-2911
Fax: 940-663-2565
Secretary: Traysha Newsom

# HARDIN COUNTY

Seat: Kountze

300 Monroe St.
Kountze, TX 77625-5994
www.co.hardin.tx.us

**District Clerk: Dana Hogg**
P.O. Box 2997
Kountze, TX 77625-2997
Phone: 409-246-5150
Fax: 409-246-5288

**District Attorney: David Sheffield**
P.O. Box 1409
Kountze, TX 77625-1409
Phone: 409-246-5160
Fax: 409-246-5142

**88th District Court**
**Judge Earl Stover, III**
P.O. Box 607
Kountze, TX 77625-0607
Phone: 409-246-5151
Fax: 409-246-5194
Court Coordinator: Linda Kellum
Court Reporter: Debby McGregor
Phone: 409-246-5153
Bailiff: Billy Paine

**356th District Court**
**Judge Steve Thomas**
P.O. Box 640
Kountze, TX 77625-0640
Phone: 409-246-5155
Fax: 409-246-4700
Court Coordinator: Rita Peterson
Court Reporter: Debbie Walters
Bailiff: Red Cooper

**County Clerk: Glenda Alston**
P.O. Box 38
Kountze, TX 77625
Phone: 409-246-5185
Fax: 409-246-3208
E-mail: hardincountyclerk@co.hardin.tx.us

**County Attorney: Rebecca Walton**
P.O. Box 516
Kountze, TX 77625
Phone: 409-246-5165
Fax: 409-246-4389

**County Judge: Wayne McDaniel**
Phone: 409-246-5120
Fax: 409-246-5195
Legal Assistant: Lora Keefer
Administrative Assistant: Elysia Battista

# HARRIS COUNTY

Seat: Houston

201 Caroline St.
Houston, TX 77002
www.hctx.net

**District Clerk: Chris Daniel**
Suite 420
Phone: 713-755-5734

**District Court Administrator: Clay Bowman**
1201 Franklin St., 7th Floor
Houston, TX 77002
Phone: 713-755-6576
Fax: 713-755-8973
E-mail: clay_bowman@justex.net

**District Attorney: Devon Anderson**
1201 Franklin St., Suite 600
Houston, TX 77002
Phone: 713-755-5800
Fax: 713-755-6865

## Civil District Courts

**11th District Court**
**Judge Mike Miller**
9th Floor
Phone: 713-368-6020
Court Coordinator: Jackie Struss
Phone: 713-368-6025
E-mail: jackie_struss@justex.net
Court Clerk: Gabriela De La Rosa
Court Reporter: Terri Anderson
Phone: 713-368-6030
E-mail: terri_anderson@justex.net
Bailiff: Gail Bonner-Henderson
Phone: 713-368-6028
E-mail: gail.bonner-hender@sheriff.hctx.net

**55th District Court**
**Judge Jeff Shadwick**
9th Floor
Phone: 713-368-6055
Court Coordinator: George Cardenas
Phone: 713-368-6050
E-mail: george_cardenas@justex.net
Court Clerk: Daniel Flores
E-mail: daniel.flores@hcdistrictclerk.com
Assistant Clerk: Tammy Tolman
Court Reporter: Gina Wilburn
Phone: 713-368-6056
E-mail: gina_wilburn@justex.net
Bailiff: Rudy Guillen
Phone: 713-368-6058

**61st District Court**
**Judge Erin Lunceford**
9th Floor
Phone: 713-368-6070
Court Coordinator: Darla Coons
Phone: 713-368-6076
E-mail: darla_coons@justex.net
Lead Clerk: Teresa Kirby
E-mail: teresa_kirby@justex.net
Court Reporter: Jessica Kim
Phone: 713-368-6077
E-mail: jessica_kim@justex.net
Bailiff: Mark Novak
Phone: 713-368-6084
E-mail: mark.novak@sheriff.hctx.net

**80th District Court**
**Judge Larry Weiman**
9th Floor
Phone: 713-368-6100
Trial Coordinator: Sonia Miranda

Phone: 713-368-6098
Senior Clerk: Justin Fitzgerald
Phone: 713-368-6070
E-mail: justin.fitzgerald@hcdistrictclerk.com
Court Clerk: Alex Casares
Court Reporter: Michelle Tucker
Phone: 713-368-6090
Bailiff: Michael Benson
Phone: 713-368-6102

**113th District Court**
**Judge Michael Landrum**
10th Floor
Phone: 713-368-6113
Court Coordinator: Jeff Boyd
Phone: 713-368-6125
E-mail: jeff_boyd@justex.net
Court Clerk: Delton Arnic
Court Reporter: Delicia Struss
Phone: 713-368-6123
E-mail: delicia.struss@justex.net
Bailiff: Karen Lacey
Phone: 713-368-6117

**125th District Court**
**Judge Kyle Carter**
10th Floor
Phone: 713-368-6141
Court Coordinator: Bridget Stanfield
Phone: 713-368-6130
E-mail: bridgett_standfield@justex.net
Court Clerk: Melissa Torres
E-mail: melissa.torres@hcdistrictclerk.com
Assistant Clerk: Bradley Darnell
Court Reporter: Kendra Garcia
Phone: 713-368-6144
E-mail: kendra_garcia@justex.net
Bailiff: Daniel Henning
Phone: 713-368-6137

**127th District Court**
**Judge R. K. Sandill**
10th Floor
Phone: 713-368-6161
Court Coordinator: Donnie Syptak
Phone: 713-368-6166
E-mail: donnie_syptak@justex.net
Court Clerk: Carol Williams
E-mail: carol.williams@hcdistrictclerk.com
Senior Clerk: Shelly Brume
Court Reporter: Susan Saulsberry
E-mail: suzanne_saulsberry@justex.net
Phone: 713-368-6168
Bailiff: Gilbert Valverde
Phone: 713-368-6156

**129th District Court**
**Judge Michael Gomez**
10th Floor
Phone: 713-368-6180
Fax: 713-368-6886
Court Coordinator: Dee Thomas
Phone: 713-368-6177
E-mail: delores_thomas@justex.net
Court Clerk: Jonathan Patton
Assistant Clerk: Bradley Darnell
Court Reporter: Jennifer Philips
Phone: 713-368-6170
Bailiff: Desni Termin
Phone: 713-368-6179

**133rd District Court**
**Judge Jaclanel McFarland**
11th Floor
Phone: 713-368-6200
E-mail: 133court@justex.net
Court Coordinator: Betsy Wall
Phone: 713-368-6195
E-mail: betsy_wall@justex.net
Court Clerk: Evelyn Palmer
Senior Clerk: Jimmy Rodriguez
Court Reporter: Darlene Stein
Phone: 713-368-6204
Bailiff: James Koen
Phone: 713-368-6205

**151st District Court**
**Judge Mike Engelhart**
11th Floor
Phone: 713-368-6222
Court Coordinator: Corina Teniente
Phone: 713-368-6211
E-mail: corina_teniente@justex.net
Court Clerk: Veronica Gonzalez
Senior Clerk: Jimmy Rodriguez
Court Reporter: Carolyn Coronado
Phone: 713-368-6212
Bailiff: Victor C. Johnson
Phone: 713-368-6220

**152nd District Court**
**Judge Robert Schaffer**
11th Floor
Phone: 713-368-6040
Court Coordinator: Nalani Callico
E-mail: nalani_callico@justex.net
Court Clerk: Salene Smith
E-mail: salene.smith@hcdistrictclerk.com
Assistant Court Clerk: Katina Williams
Court Reporter: Cynthia Montalvo
Phone: 713-368-6037

E-mail: cynthiam@justex.net
Bailiff: Stephanie Williams
Phone: 713-368-6807
E-mail: stephanie.williams@sheriff.hctx.net

**157th District Court**
**Judge Randy Wilson**
11th Floor
Phone: 713-368-6230
Court Coordinator: Barbara G. Conley
Phone: 713-368-6240
E-mail: barbara_conley@justex.net
Senior Court Clerk: Lisa Cooper
Court Clerk: Katina Williams
Court Reporter: Sheri Ullrich
Phone: 713-755-6242
Bailiff: Elizabeth Murray
Phone: 713-368-6235

**164th District Court**
**Judge Alexandra Smoots-Hogan**
12th Floor
Phone: 713-368-6264
Court Coordinator: Andy Sanchez
Phone: 713-368-6260
E-mail: andy_sanchez@justex.net
Senior Clerk: Marcella Henderson
Phone: 713-368-6270
Court Clerk: Chanda Williams
Court Reporter: Donna King
Phone: 713-368-6256
Bailiff: Marty Mingo
Phone: 713-755-6267

**165th District Court**
**Judge Debra Ibarra Mayfield**
12th Floor
Phone: 713-368-6270
Court Coordinator: Rick Wilson
Phone: 713-368-6282
E-mail: rick_wilson@justex.net
Senior Clerk: Marcella Henderson
Court Clerk: Beverly Chevalier
Court Reporter: Peggy Hershelman
Phone: 713-368-6275
E-mail: peggy_hershelman@justex.net
Bailiff: Robert Perry
Phone: 713-368-6272

**189th District Court**
**Judge Bill Burke**
12th Floor
Phone: 713-368-6300
Court Coordinator: Cathy Norton
Phone: 713-368-6292

STATE, DISTRICT AND COUNTY COURTS

E-mail: cathy_norton@justex.net
Court Clerk: Arionne McNeal
Assistant Clerk: Deandra Mosley
Court Reporter: Amanda Smothers King
Phone: 713-368-6304
E-mail: amanda_king@justex.net
Bailiff: Pamela Puente
Phone: 713-368-6308

**190th District Court**
**Judge Patricia J. Kerrigan**
12th Floor
Phone: 713-368-6310
Court Coordinator: Lori Codina
Phone: 713-368-6328
E-mail: lori_codina@justex.net
Court Clerk: Arron Sonnier
Court Reporter: My-Thuy Cieslar
Phone: 713-368-6326
E-mail: mythuy_cieslar@justex.net
Bailiff: Rudy Ocampo
Phone: 713-368-6320

**215th District Court**
**Judge Elaine H. Palmer**
13th Floor
Phone: 713-368-6330
Court Coordinator: Patricia Ellis-Griggs
Phone: 713-368-6340
E-mail: tricia_griggs@justex.net
Court Clerk: Jeanette Spencer
Senior Clerk: Joshua J. Bovell
Court Reporter: Cantrece Addison
Phone: 713-368-6335
E-mail: cantrece_addison@justex.net
Bailiff: Dale Troutt
Phone: 713-368-6336

**234th District Court**
**Judge Wesley Ward**
13th Floor
Phone: 713-368-6350
Court Coordinator: Jim Sitgreaves
Phone: 713-368-6351
E-mail: jim_sitgreaves@justex.net
Court Clerk: Lawanda Cornett
Assistant Clerk: Sasha Prince
Court Reporter: Norma Duarte
Phone: 713-368-6354
Bailiff: Ed Nanez
Phone: 713-368-6360

**269th District Court**
**Judge Dan T. Hinde**
13th Floor

Phone: 713-368-6370
Court Coordinator: Alex Garibay
Phone: 713-368-6376
E-mail: alex_garibay@justex.net
Court Clerk: Pam Robicheaux
Senior Clerk: Joshua J. Bovell
Court Reporter: Kathleen Keese
Bailiff: Darrell Anderson
Phone: 713-368-6381

**270th District Court**
**Judge Brent Gamble**
13th Floor
Phone: 713-368-6400
Court Coordinator: Monica Nunez
Phone: 713-368-6405
E-mail: monica_nunez@justex.net
Court Clerk: Sasha Prince
E-mail: sasha.prince@hcdistrictclerk.com
Senior Clerk: Danielle Gutierrez
Court Reporter: Annette Peltier
Phone: 713-368-6409
Bailiff: Pete Martinez
Phone: 713-368-6408

**281st District Court**
**Judge Sylvia A. Matthews**
14th Floor
Phone: 713-368-6430
Court Coordinator: Rick Torres
Phone: 713-368-6442
E-mail: rick_torres@justex.net
Senior Clerk: Daiquiri Roy
E-mail: daiquiri.roy@hcdistrictclerk.com
Court Reporter: Rhonda Armbruster
Phone: 713-368-6440
E-mail: rhonda_armbruster@justex.net
Bailiff: Leatha Colson
Phone: 713-368-6431
E-mail: leatha.colson@sheriff.hctx.net

**295th District Court**
**Judge Caroline E. Baker**
14th Floor
Phone: 713-368-6450
Court Coordinator: Kimberly Self
E-mail: kimberly_self@justex.net
Phone: 713-368-6466
E-mail: jackie_struss@justex.net
Court Clerk: Will Frazier
Court Reporter: Kimberly Kidd
Phone: 713-368-6453
E-mail: kimberly_kidd@justex.net
Bailiff: George Loya
Phone: 713-368-6452
E-mail: george.loya@sheriff.hctx.net

**STATE, DISTRICT AND COUNTY COURTS**

**STATE, DISTRICT AND COUNTY COURTS**

### 333rd District Court
**Judge Joseph J. Halbach, Jr.**
14th Floor
Phone: 713-368-6470
Fax: 713-368-7034
Court Coordinator: Vicki Garcia
Phone: 713-368-6484
E-mail: vicki_garcia@justex.net
Court Clerk: Euniecy Gentry
Court Reporter: Jodi Masera
Phone: 713-368-6485
E-mail: jodi_masera@justex.net
Bailiff: Vacant
Phone: 713-368-6487

### 334th District Court
**Judge Grant Dorfman**
14th Floor
Phone: 713-368-6500
Court Coordinator: Walter Bucko
Phone: 713-368-6492
E-mail: walter_bucko@justex.net
Court Clerk: Danielle Jimenez
E-mail: danielle.jimenez@hcdistrictclerk.com
Assistant Clerk: Davia Ford
Court Reporter: Cynthia Berry
Phone: 713-368-6493
Bailiff: Lloyd Williams
Phone: 713-368-6503

## Criminal District Courts
1201 Franklin St.
Houston, TX 77002

### 174th District Court
**Judge Ruben Guerrero**
19th Floor
Phone: 713-755-6324
Court Coordinator: Diane Madrid
E-mail: diane_madrid@justex.net
Court Clerk: Vivica Mason
Phone: 713-755-6326
Assistant Clerk: Vacant
Process Server: David Melchor
Court Reporter: B.J. Orsack
Court Liaison Officer: Patricia Cisneros
Bailiff: James Turner

### 176th District Court
**Judge Stacey W. Bond**
19th Floor
Phone: 713-755-6328
Fax: 713-368-9211
Court Coordinator: Janet Warner

E-mail: janet_warner@justex.net
Court Clerk: Shannon Charleston
Process Server: Caroline Sawyers
Court Reporter: Judy Fox
Bailiff: Chalmust Allen
Phone: 713-755-6330

### 177th District Court
**Judge Ryan Patrick**
19th Floor
Phone: 713-755-6332
Fax: 713-755-5523
Court Coordinator: Chandra Boyston
Court Clerk: Michelle Roppolo
Court Reporter: Linda Hacker
Process Server: Danny Davis
Phone: 713-755-6335
Court Liaison Officer: Wendell Warren
Bailiff: Edmundo Ojeda
Phone: 713-755-6333

### 178th District Court
**Judge David Mendoza**
19th Floor
Phone: 713-755-6336
Fax: 713-368-9204
Court Coordinator: Mary Leal
E-mail: mary_leal@justex.net
Court Clerk: Nakia Mills
Court Reporter: Carol Castillo
Process Server: Gary Bronikowski
Phone: 713-755-6339
Court Liaison Officer: Pablo Villa
Bailiff: Barry Standley

### 179th District Court
**Judge Kristin M. Guiney**
18th Floor
Phone: 713-755-6340
Fax: 713-368-9224
Court Coordinator: John King
E-mail: john_king@justex.net
Court Clerk: Allison LeDee
Court Reporter: Renee Reagan
Process Server: A.J. Gerac
Court Liaison Officer: Melinda Collins
Bailiff: Valerie Jenkins

### 180th District Court
**Judge Catherine Evans**
18th Floor
Phone: 713-755-6344
Court Coordinator: Annette Manuel
E-mail: annette_manuel@dca.co.harris.tx.us
Court Clerk: Joline Hart

Court Liaison Officer: Jackie Scurry
Phone: 713-755-6347
Court Reporters: Tamra Parks and Kathleen Powers
Process Server: Daniel Arcenaux
Bailiff: G.L. Glover

**182nd District Court**
**Judge Jeannine S. Barr**
18th Floor
Phone: 713-755-6350
Court Coordinator: Diane Hasler
E-mail: diane_hasler@dca.co.harris.tx.us
Court Clerk: Margaret Bolton
Court Reporter: Roxanne Wiltshire
Bailiff: Karen Wood
Phone: 713-368-6350

**183rd District Court**
**Judge Vanessa Velasquez**
18th Floor
Phone: 713-755-6354
Fax: 713-755-755-8918
Court Coordinator: Eloisa Sanchez
E-mail: eloisa_sanchez@justex.net
Court Clerk: Ana Melendez
Phone: 713-755-6356
Court Reporter: Billy Jalufka
Process Server: Paul Gries
Court Liaison Officer: Shawn Ticer
Bailiff: Graviel Hernandez

**184th District Court**
**Judge Jan Krocker**
17th Floor
Phone: 713-755-6358
Court Coordinator: Deberly Ruth
Court Clerk: Joshua Ochoa
Assistant Clerk: Erin Hills
Court Reporter: Cynthia Lee
Process Server: Gary Phillips
Court Liaison Officer: Courtney Allen
Phone: 713-755-0926
Bailiff: Donna Durham

**185th District Court**
**Judge Susan Brown**
17th Floor
Phone: 713-755-6362
Court Coordinator: Sherila Johnson
E-mail: sherila_johnson@justex.net
Court Clerk: Christina Cztinski
Court Reporter: Carrie Logan
Process Server: Carlton Freeney
Court Liaison Officer: David Preston
Bailiff: Stephen McLendon

**208th District Court**
**Judge Denise Collins**
17th Floor
Phone: 713-755-6374
Court Coordinator: Mona Natemeyer
E-mail: mona_natemeyer@justex.net
Senior Court Clerk: Erica Buck
Court Reporter: Cheryl Pierce
Process Server: Thomas Gentry
Bailiff: Terry Smith

**209th District Court**
**Judge Michael T. McSpadden**
17th Floor
Phone: 713-755-6378
Court Coordinator: Kathy Joachim
E-mail: kathy_joachim@justex.net
Court Clerk: Laura Blair Stone
Court Reporter: Valdeane Wainwright
Process Server: Dan Douglas
Bailiff: Jon Ray

**228th District Court**
**Judge Marc C. Carter**
16th Floor
Phone: 713-755-6650
Fax: 713-755-4425
Court Coordinator: Vanessa Guerrero
E-mail: vanessa_guerrero@justex.net
Court Clerk: Jennifer Green
Court Reporter: Lisa Mills
Process Server: Edward Jackson
Bailiff: Lennard Walker

**230th District Court**
**Judge Brad Hart**
16th Floor
Phone: 713-755-6782
Court Coordinator: Quinesha Ross
E-mail: quinesha_ross@justex.net
Court Clerk: Ariel Sanchez
Court Reporter: Trish Matthews
Process Server: John Harton
Bailiff: Carl Culberson

**232nd District Court**
**Judge Mary Lou Keel**
16th Floor
Phone: 713-755-6778
Fax: 713-755-4425
Court Coordinator: Eddie Rodriguez
E-mail: eddie_rodriquez@justex.net
Court Clerk: Kathy Polvadore-Tickle
Court Reporter: Arlene Webb
Process Server: Marcus Clay

STATE, DISTRICT AND COUNTY COURTS

Court Liaison Officer: Ana Sanchez
Bailiff: Michael Perry

**248th District Court**
**Judge Katherine Cabaniss**
16th Floor
Phone: 713-755-7094
Court Coordinator: Genetha Kimbrough
Court Clerk: Carli Garcia
Court Reporter: Louise Steckler
Process Server: Hilbert Nunez
Court Liaison Officer: Mary Reed
Bailiff: David Hernandez

**262nd District Court**
**Judge Denise Bradley**
15th Floor
Phone: 713-755-6961
Court Coordinator: Virgina Almanza-Cerda
E-mail: virgina_almanza@justex.net
Court Clerk: John Meltzer
Court Reporter: Mattie Kimble
Process Server: Forrest Reddick
Phone: 713-755-6964
Court Liaison Officer: Jeannine Hernandez
Bailiff: Tony Kaminski
Phone: 713-755-6963

**263rd District Court**
**Judge Jim Wallace**
15th Floor
Phone: 713-755-6944
Fax: 713-368-9209
Court Coordinator: Erica Thomas-Brice
E-mail: erica_thomas-brice@justex.net
Court Clerk: William Jones
Court Reporter: Marcia Barnett
Process Server: Chad Butcher
Court Liaison Officer: Emilie Pawlowski
Bailiff: Derek Ruffino

**337th District Court**
**Judge Renee Magee**
15th Floor
Phone: 713-755-7746
Court Coordinator: Joseph Debruyn
E-mail: joseph_debruyn@justex.net
Court Clerk: Tom Jones
Phone: 713-755-7748
Court Reporter: Mary Ann Rodriguez
Process Server: Kevin McGehee
Court Liaison Officer: Bernice Armstrong
Phone: 713-755-0851
Bailiff: J.J. Perry

**338th District Court**
**Judge Brock Thomas**
15th Floor
Phone: 713-755-7774
Court Coordinator: Norma Lopez
E-mail: norma_lopez@justex.net
Court Clerk: Dorian Day
Court Reporter: Jill Hamby
Process Server: Carey Beran
Court Liaison Officer: Jacquelyn Wertz
Bailiff: Frank Schillaci

**339th District Court**
**Judge Maria T. Jackson**
14th Floor
Phone: 713-755-7784
Fax: 713-368-9201
Court Coordinator: Cynthia Bates
E-mail: cynthia_bates@justex.net
Court Clerk: Elizabeth Marcano
Court Reporter: Pam Knobloch
Process Server: Marjorie Tayler
Court Liaison Officer: Belinda George
Bailiff: John P. Kelly

**351st District Court**
**Judge Mark K. Ellis**
14th Floor
Phone: 713-755-5620
Court Coordinator: Tramesha Randall
E-mail: tramesha_randall@justex.net
Court Clerk: Cheron Harper
Court Reporter: Toni Goubeaud
Process Server: Kevin Goudeau
Court Liaison Officer: Lillie Jefferson
Bailiff: Joseph Williams

# Family District Courts
201 Caroline St.
Houston, TX 77002-1901

**245th District Court**
**Judge Roy L. Moore**
15th floor
Phone: 713-368-5900
Court Coordinator: Rosie Diaz
E-mail: rosie_diaz@justex.net
Court Clerk: Chandria Hutchison
Assistant Clerk: Sandra McCaian
Court Reporter: Rebecca Hammons
Bailiffs: Tarshia Banks and Troy Byers

**Associate Judge: Jim Cooper**
Phone: 713-368-5900

**246th District Court**
**Judge Charley Prine**
16th Floor
Phone: 713-755-6938
Court Coordinator: Yolanda Harris
Phone: 713-755-1103
E-mail: yolanda_harris@justex.net
Court Clerk: Shanell Collins
Assistant Clerk: Ramon Pickerom
Court Reporter: Chelsea Erickson
Phone: 713-755-1104
Bailiff: K.D. Williams
Phone: 713-755-2351

**Associate Judge: Cheslie Ramos**
Phone: 713-274-4500

**247th District Court**
**Judge John Schmude**
15th floor
Phone: 713-368-6570
Court Coordinator: Pamela Hunt
Phone: 713-368-6572
E-mail: pamela_hunt@justex.com
Assistant Clerk: Ann Rodriguez
Court Clerk: Raven Hubbard
Court Reporter: Phyllis Gonzales
Bailiffs: Wilma Dearman and Mark Theirry

**Associate Judge: Paula Vlahakos**
Court Clerk: Marllee Henderson

**257th District Court**
**Judge Judy Warne**
16th Floor
Phone: 713-274-4560
Court Coordinator: Melissa Parker
Phone: 713-274-4564
E-mail: melissa_parker@justex.net
Court Clerk: Kristel Rubio
Assistant Clerk: Lorena Rubio
Court Reporter: Eunice Tillman
Phone: 713-274-4571
Bailiffs: Janet Johnson and Charles Thompson

**Associate Judge: Deborah Patterson**
Phone: 713-274-4560
Court Reporter: Beverly Ellis

**280th District Court**
**Judge Lynn Bradshaw- Hull**
1200 Congress, 1st Floor
Houston, TX 77002
Phone: 713-274-4680

Court Coordinator: Susan Lindemann
Phone: 713-274-4681
E-mail: susan_lindemann@justex.net
Court Clerk: Maria Barron
Assistant Clerk: Raul Serrano
Court Reporter: Tish Tafolla
Phone: 713-274-4682
Bailiffs: Shannon Gibson and Marcus Moreno
Phone: 713-274-4685

**308th District Court**
**Judge James Lombadino**
8th Floor
Phone: 713-274-4600
Fax: 713-274-4616
Court Coordinator: Norma Ovalle
Senior Court Clerk: Rachel Hardy
Court Reporter: Leticia Salas
Phone: 713-755-4802
Bailiff: Joe Morin

**Associate Judge: David Sydow, Jr.**
Phone: 713-274-4600

**309th District Court**
**Judge Sheri Y. Dean**
16th Floor
Phone: 713-274-4520
Court Coordinator: Madeline Russell
Phone: 713-755-5635
Court Clerk: Sandra Gomez
Assistant Clerk: Patricia Montgomery
Court Reporter: Delores Johnson
Phone: 713-755-4801
Bailiffs: Robenia Bayer-Barthe and Ernest Lee

**Associate Judge: Beverly Malazzo**

**310th District Court**
**Judge Lisa A. Millard**
201 Caroline St., 15th floor
Phone: 713-368-6550
Court Coordinator: Molly Nguyen
E-mail: molly_nguyen@justex.net
Court Clerk: Nidia S. Alberto
Assistant Clerk: Tomas Cruz
Court Reporter: Benjamin Alva
Bailiff: Friedrich W. Harrison

**Associate Judge: Conrad L. Moren**

**311th District Court**
**Judge Alicia K. Franklin-York**

**STATE, DISTRICT AND COUNTY COURTS**

8th Floor
Phone: 713-755-6242
Court Coordinator: Victor Almendarez
Phone: 713-755-4356
Court Clerk: Rochele Howard
Assistant Clerk: Jessica Contreras
Court Reporter: Stephanie Wells
Bailiffs: Eddie Harrold and Charles Smart

**Associate Judge: Meca Walker**

**312th District Court**
**Judge David Farr**
16th Floor
Phone: 713-274-4590
Court Coordinator: Pat Plotkin
E-mail: pat_plotkin@justex.net
Court Clerk: Dawn Hutchings
Assistant Clerk: Shawn Simien
Court Reporter: Barbara Nagji
Bailiffs: Michelle Hoskins and Dwayne Small

**Associate Judge: Eileen Gaffney**
Court Reporter: Kim Weidenhelt

## Juvenile District Courts
1200 Congress St.
Houston, TX 77002
Central Fax: 713-755-8886

**313th District Court**
**Judge Glenn Devlin**
5th Floor
Phone: 713-222-4900
Court Coordinator: Natalie Yates
Phone: 713-222-4905
E-mail: natalie_yates@justex.net
Clerk: Stacey Riley
Court Reporter: Jill Bartek
Bailiff: Dean Hobbs

**Associate Judge: Stephen Newhouse**

**314th District Court**
**Judge John Phillips**
5th Floor
Phone: 713-222-4910
Court Coordinator: Michael Millard
Phone: 713-222-4915
E-mail: michael_millard@justex.net
Court Clerk: Stephanie Castillo
Court Reporter: Julia Rangel
Phone: 713-755-3323
Bailiff: Richard Kovalchulk

**Associate Judge: Kelly Graul**

**315th District Court**
**Judge Michael Schneider**
7th Floor
Phone: 713-222-4950
Court Coordinator: Beverly Bryant
Phone: 713-222-4955
E-mail: beverly_bryant@justex.net
Court Clerk: Zamira Roman
Court Reporter: Cara Skinner
Bailiff: Michael Hutchison

**Associate Judge: Angela E. Ellis**

## Probate Courts
201 Caroline St.
Houston, TX 77002
www.hctx.net/probate

**Probate Director: Jacquelyn Washington**
Phone: 713-755-6460
Assistant Director: Jennifer Cantu
Phone: 713-755-6462

**Probate Court No. 1**
**Judge Loyd Wright**
6th Floor
Phone: 713-368-6700
Fax: 713-368-7300
Court Coordinator: Kimberly Hightower
E-mail: kimberly.hightower@prob.hctx.net
Court Clerk: Marisol Hasting
Assistant Clerk: Toni Williams
Court Reporter: Don Pylant
E-mail: donald.pylant@prob.hctx.net
Guardianship Coordinator: Cres Machicek
Staff Attorney: Susie Rowley
Court Investigator: Anthi Pavlicek
Show Cause Coordinator: Christina Toler
Auditor: Kevin Scott
Assistant Auditor: Betty Hazlewood
Bailiff: Renae Brown

**Associate Judge: Ruth Ann Stiles**
E-mail: ruth.stiles@prob.hctx.net

**Probate Court No. 2**
**Judge Mike Wood**
6th Floor
Phone: 713-368-6710
Fax: 713-368-7150
Court Coordinator: Yolanda Lopez
Court Reporter: Tina White

**STATE, DISTRICT AND COUNTY COURTS**

E-mail: tina.white@prob.hctx.net
Guardianship Coordinator: Marilyn Lewis
E-mail: marilyn.lewis@prob.hctx.net
Court Investigator: Dawn King
Auditor: Shirley A. Weigelt
Assistant Auditor: Debra Slaughter
Bailiff: Chung Gee
E-mail: chung_gee@hctx.net

**Associate Judge: Ann Greene**
E-mail: ann.green@prob.hctx.net

**Probate Court No. 3**
**Judge Rory R. Olsen**
7th Floor
Phone: 713-368-6730
Fax: 713-368-7166
Court Coordinator: Deanise Jagnanan
E-mail: deanise_jagnanan@prob.hctx.net
Assistant Court Coordinator: Renee
Stockwell
Court Reporter: Robin Day
E-mail: robin.kulhanek@prob.hctx.net
Guardianship Coordinator: Brandy
Williamson
Staff Attorney: James Conrad
Court Investigator: Tara Zinn
Assistant Court Investigator: Imani Murigu
Auditor: Javier Cuellar
Bailiff: Holmes Simpson

**Associate Judge: Amy Parson**

**Probate Court No. 4**
**Judge Christine Butts**
7th Floor
Phone: 713-368-6767
Fax: 713-368-7171
E-mail: christine.butts@prob.hctx.net
Court Coordinator: Eileen Harris
Court Clerk: Henry Williams
E-mail: hwilliams@cco.hctx.net
Court Reporter: Hipolita Lopez
Guardianship Coordinator: Sherrie Fox
Court Investigators: Lavern Ashley and Tasia
Dobard
Auditor: Jose L. Martinez
Bailiff: Michael Tillman

**Associate Judge: Clarinda Cornstock**

## County Court
1001 Preston St.
Houston, TX 77002

**County Clerk: Stan Stanart**
201 Caroline, 4th Floor
P.O. Box 1525
Houston, TX 77251-1525
Phone: 713-755-6411
Fax: 713-755-4638
E-mail: ccinfo@cco.hctx.net

**County Attorney: Vince Ryan**
1019 Congress Ave., 15th Floor
Houston, TX 77002-1799
Phone: 713-755-5101
Fax: 713-755-8924

**County Judge: Ed Emmett**
Suite 911
Phone: 713-755-4000
Administrative Assistant: Leanna Abbott
Phone: 713-755-4011
E-mail: leanna.abbott@cjo.hctx.net

## County Civil
## Courts at Law
201 Caroline St.
Houston, TX 77002

**Court Manager: Ed Wells**
1201 Franklin., 7th floor
Phone: 713-755-5394
Fax: 713-755-8931

**County Civil Court at Law No. 1**
**Judge Clyde Leuchtag**
5th Floor
Phone: 713-368-6610
Court Coordinator: Melissa Hammond
Court Clerks: Kayla Meyers and Kelli
Ramirez
Phone: 713-755-6794
Court Reporter: Lettie Witter
Bailiff: Fran Fontenot
Phone: 713-368-6611

**County Civil Court at Law No. 2**
**Judge Theresa Chang**
5th Floor
Phone: 713-368-6640
Court Coordinator: Grace Cantada
Phone: 713-368-6641
Court Clerks: Maria de la Rosa and
Janice Gonzales
Phone: 713-755-6796
Court Reporter: Kevin Bruzewski

Phone: 713-368-6642
Bailiff: Anthony Hemmitt
Phone: 713-368-6644

**County Civil Court at Law No. 3**
**Judge Linda Storey**
5th Floor
Phone: 713-368-6660
Court Coordinator: Dawn McEwen
Court Clerks: Liz Lopez and Kimberly Rojas
Phone: 713-755-1112
Court Reporter: Laura Cutherell
Phone: 713-368-6658
Bailiff: Luchelle McBride
Phone: 713-368-6663

**County Civil Court at Law No. 4**
**Judge Roberta A. Lloyd**
5th Floor
Phone: 713-368-6680
Court Coordinator: Stephanie Baker
Court Clerks: Tonya Garza and Mariela Morales
Court Reporter: Vacant
Bailiff: Joe J. Gonzales

# County Criminal

## Courts at Law
1201 Franklin St.
Houston, TX 77002

**Court Manager: Ed Wells**
7th Floor
Phone: 713-755-5394
Fax: 713-755-8931

**County Criminal Court at Law No. 1**
**Judge Paula Goodhart**
7th Floor
Phone: 713-755-6180
Fax: 713-755-8931
Court Coordinator: Karen Harrison
Court Clerks: Maria Hernandez and Uniquea Morales
Court Liaison: Mona Lewis
Court Reporter: Terri Johnstone
Process Server: Rene Reyes
Bailiff: Bernard Kuzminski

**County Criminal Court at Law No. 2**
**Judge Bill Harmon**
7th Floor
Phone: 713-755-6184

Fax: 713-755-4882
Court Coordinator: Rosario Khalaf
Court Clerks: Umik Allen and Billie Brown
Court Reporter: Ida Garcia
Process Server: Billy Manning
Bailiff: Gina Grahmann
Phone: 713-755-3739

**County Criminal Court at Law No. 3**
**Judge Natalie C. Fleming**
8th Floor
Phone: 713-755-6188
Fax: 713-365-9269
Court Coordinator: Carol Cummings
Court Clerk: Elizabeth Murphy
Court Reporter: Karen Bauer
Process Server: Richard Bailey
Court Liaison Officer: Patricia Davila
Bailiff: Carol Ramirez

**County Criminal Court at Law No. 4**
**Judge John Clinton**
8th Floor
Phone: 713-755-6192
Fax: 713-368-9269
Court Coordinator: Yolanda Florido
Court Clerk: Angela Jerez
Court Reporter: Amanda Fazio
Process Server: Danny Wisdom
Court Liaison Officer: Brenda Clayton
Bailiff: Perry Hannusch

**County Criminal Court at Law No. 5**
**Judge Margaret Stewart Harris**
9th Floor
Phone: 713-755-6196
Fax: 713-368-9268
Court Coordinator: Dolores Phillips
Court Clerks: Erica Castillo and Addam Jordan
Court Reporter: Ramona St. Julian Sonnier
Process Server: Shirley Morrison
Bailiff: Prime Jonesia

**County Criminal Court at Law No. 6**
**Judge Larry Standley**
9th Floor
Phone: 713-755-6200
Fax: 713-755-8931
Court Coordinator: Carmen Vazquez
Court Clerk: Jessica Ordon
Court Reporter: Katelyen Harrelson
Process Server: Roy Pantoja
Court Liaison Officer: Sharelle Lloyd
Bailiff: Roy Pantoja

**County Criminal Court at Law No. 7**
**Judge Pam Derbyshire**
9th Floor
Phone: 713-755-6204
Fax: 713-368-9268
Court Coordinator: Peggy Gunder
Court Clerk: Lawanda Smith
Court Reporter: Vacant
Court Liaison Officer: Olen Manning
Bailiffs: Douglas McNeal and Jerry Vaja

**County Criminal Court at Law No. 8**
**Judge Jay Karahan**
9th Floor
Phone: 713-755-6208
Fax: 713-368-9264
Court Coordinator: Donna Ramos
Court Clerk: Ivone Gomez
Court Reporter: Tiffany Yettes
Process Server: Lisa Martinez
Court Liaison Officer: Larry Uresti
Bailiff: Gary Dean

**County Criminal Court at Law No. 9**
**Judge Analia H. Wilkerson**
10th Floor
Phone: 713-755-6212
Fax: 713-368-9265
Court Coordinator: Sheri Gilbert
Court Clerk: Jairus Jean
Court Reporter: Tavis Jacks
Process Server: Kelvin Casey
Court Liaison Officer: Carmen Sanchez
Bailiff: Reginald Thomas

**County Criminal Court at Law No. 10**
**Judge Dan Spjut**
10th Floor
Phone: 713-755-6216
Fax: 713-368-9265
Court Coordinator: Marvin Rodriguez
Court Clerk: Dana Fernandez
Court Reporter: Vacant
Process Server: Leah Leal
Court Liaison Officer: Cyndi Perez
Bailiffs: Sean Gilbert and Kirk Freddy

**County Criminal Court at Law No. 11**
**Judge Diane Bull**
10th Floor
Phone: 713-755-7780
Fax: 713-368-9267
Court Coordinator: Rachel Ferrel

Court Clerk: Ja'Mae Robinson
Court Reporter: Karen Young
Process Server: Larry Garcia
Court Liaison Officer: Lawrence Mitchell
Bailiff: Paul Prior

**County Criminal Court at Law No. 12**
**Judge Robin Brown**
10th Floor
Phone: 713-755-7738
Fax: 713-368-9267
Court Coordinator: Stephanie Spears
Court Clerk: Talitha Brown
Court Reporter: Laurie Buchanan
Process Server: Devon Desch
Court Liaison Officer: Alexis Walwyn
Bailiff: Bobby Andrews

**County Criminal Court at Law No. 13**
**Judge Don Smyth**
11th Floor
Phone: 713-755-7950
Fax: 713-755-4874
Court Coordinator: Mary Smith
Court Clerk: Dodie Sheffield
Court Reporter: Deanne Bridwell
Process Server: Scott Blankenburg
Court Liaison Officer: Beverly Cox
Bailiff: T.L. Greenwood

**County Criminal Court at Law No. 14**
**Judge Michael R. Fields**
11th Floor
Phone: 713-755-5683
Fax: 713-368-9281
Court Coordinator: Gabriel Montero
Court Clerk: Crystal Kenneston
Court Reporter: Serena Pace
Process Server: Latonya Willrich
Bailiff: William Dorendie

**County Criminal Court at Law No. 15**
**Judge Jean Spradling Hughes**
11th Floor
Phone: 713-755-4760
Fax: 713-755-4874
Court Coordinator: Laura Conte
Court Clerk: Linda Martinez
Court Reporter: Connie Cole
Process Server: William Wilson
Court Liaison Officer: George Townes
Bailiff: Manuel Lopez

STATE, DISTRICT AND COUNTY COURTS

# HARRISON COUNTY

Seat: Marshall

200 W. Houston St.
Marshall, TX 75670
www.harrisoncountytexas.org

**District Clerk: Sherry Griffis**
Suite 234
Phone: 903-935-8409
Fax: 903-927-1918
E-mail: sherryg@co.harrison.tx.us

**District Attorney: Coke Solomon**
P.O. Box 776
Marshall, TX 75671-0776
Phone: 903-935-8408
Fax: 903-938-9312

**71st District Court**
**Judge Brad Morin**
Room 219
Phone: 903-935-8407
Fax: 903-935-9963
E-mail: bradm@co.harrison.tx.us
Court Coordinator: Leslie Hawsey
E-mail: lesliem@co.harrison.tx.us
Court Reporter: Tanya McFarland

**County Clerk: Patsy Cox**
P.O. Box 1365
Marshall, TX 75671
Phone: 903-935-8403
Fax: 903-935-4877
E-mail: patsyc@co.harrison.tx.us

**County Judge: Hugh Taylor**
1 Peter Whetsone Square
Marshall, TX, 75670
Room 314
Phone: 903-935-8401
Fax: 903-935-4853
E-mail: hught@co.harrison.tx.us
Administrative Assistant: Charlene Graff
E-mail: charleneg@co.harrison.tx.us

**County Court at Law**
**Judge Joe Black**
Suite 263
Phone: 903-935-8406
Fax: 903-934-9668

Court Coordinator: Delfina Mays
E-mail: delm@co.harrison.us.tx

# HARTLEY COUNTY

Seat: Channing

900 Main St.
Channing, TX 79018
www.co.hartley.tx.us

**District and County Clerk: Melissa Mead**
P.O. Box 189
Channing, TX 79018-0997
Phone: 806-235-3582
Fax: 806-235-2316
E-mail: melissa.mead@co.hartley.tx.us

**District Attorney: David M. Green**
*Please see Moore County.*

**69th District Court**
**Judge Ron E. Enns** sits two Wednesdays a
month.
*Please see Moore County.*

**County Attorney: Robert Elliot**
Phone: 806-235-2603
Fax: 806-635-5133

**County Judge: Ronnie Gordon**
P.O. Box 69
Channing, TX 79018-9997
Phone: 806-235-3442
Fax: 806-635-5133
E-mail: ronnie.gordon@co.hartley.tx.us

# HASKELL COUNTY

Seat: Haskell

One Avenue D
Haskell, TX 79521
www.co.haskell.tx.us

**District Clerk: Penny Anderson**
P.O. Box 27
Haskell, TX 79521-0027
Phone: 940-864-2030
Fax: 940-864-5616
E-mail: penny.anderson@co.haskell.tx.us

**District Attorney: Michael E. Fouts**
P. O. Box 193
Haskell, TX 79521
Phone: 940-864-2072
Fax: 940-864-3364
E-mail: da@co.haskell.tx.us

**39th District Court**
**Judge Shane Hadaway**
P.O. Box 966
Haskell, TX 79521-0966
Phone: 940-864-2661
Fax: 940-863-4202
E-mail: dj39th@gmail.com
Court Coordinator: Deborah Mayfield
Court Reporter: Sherry Hatley
Phone: 940-742-4207
Bailiff: David Halliburton

**County Clerk: Belia Abila**
P.O. Box 725
Haskell, TX 79521
Phone: 940-864-2451
Fax: 940-864-6164
E-mail: belia.abila@co.haskell.tx.us

**County Attorney: Kristen L. Fouts**
P.O. Box 551
Haskell, TX 79521
Phone: 940-864-2066
Fax: 940-864-5616
E-mail: kfouts@aol.com

**County Judge: David C. Davis**
Phone: 940-864-2851
Fax: 940-864-5722
E-mail: cojudge@co.haskell.tx.us

# HAYS COUNTY

Seat: San Marcos

712 S. Stagecoach Tr.
San Marcos, TX 78666
www.co.hays.tx.us

**District Clerk: Beverly Crumley**
Suite 2211
Phone: 512-393-7660
Fax: 512-393-7674
E-mail: distclerk@co.hays.tx.us

**District Attorney: Wesley Mau**
Phone: 512-393-7600
Fax: 512-393-7619
E-mail: wes.mau@co.hays.tx.us
Office Administrator: Emily S. Sierra
E-mail: emily_sierra@co.hays.tx.us

**22nd District Court**
**Judge R. Bruce Boyer**
Suite 3240
Phone: 512-393-7700
Fax: 512-393-7713
E-mail: djrbb@co.hays.tx.us
Court Administrator (Civil): Valerie DeLeon
Court Administrator (Criminal): Steve Thomas

**207th District Court**
**Judge Jack H. Robison** sits as scheduled.
*Please see Comal County.*

**274th District Court**
**Judge Gary L. Steel** sits as scheduled.
*Please see Guadalupe County.*

**428th District Court**
**Judge William "Bill" Henry**
Suite 3240
Phone: 512-393-7700
Fax: 512-393-7713
E-mail: bill.henry@co.hays.tx.us
Court Coordinator: Steve Thomas
E-mail: steve.thomas@co.hays.tx.us
Court Reporter: Ruby Castellija

**County Clerk: Liz Q. Gonzalez**
Phone: 512-393-7738
Fax: 512-393-7332
E-mail: clerk@co.hays.tx.us

**County Judge: Bert Cobb**
Phone: 512-393-2205
Fax: 512-392-2282
E-mail: bertcobb@co.hays.tx.us
Chief of Staff: Lon Shell
Phone: 512-392-2217
E-mail: lon.shell@co.hays.tx.us
Executive Assistant: Janice Jones
E-mail: janice.jones@co.hays.tx.us

**County Court at Law No. 1**
**Judge Robert Updegrove**
Phone: 512-393-7625
E-mail: rupdegrove@co.hays.tx.us
Court Coordinator: Rene Garner
Court Reporter: Lori Schmid

**County Court at Law No. 2**
**Judge David Glicker**
Phone: 512-393-7625
E-mail: juez@co.hays.tx.us
Court Coordinator: Rene Garner
Court Reporter: Gina May

# HEMPHILL COUNTY

Seat: Canadian

400 Main St.
Canadian, TX 79014

**District and County Clerk: Lisa Johnson**
P.O. Box 867
Canadian, TX 79014-0867
Phone: 806-323-6212
Fax: 806-323-8125

**District Attorney: Franklin McDonough**
*Please see Gray County.*

**31st District Court**
**Judge Steven R. Emmert** sits as scheduled.
*Please see Wheeler County.*

**County Attorney: Ty Sparks**
Phone: 806-323-5521

**County Judge: George Briant**
Phone: 806-323-6521
Fax: 806-323-5271
Administrative Assistant: June Brunson

# HENDERSON COUNTY

Seat: Athens

100 E. Tyler St.
Athens, TX 75751-2561
www.co.henderson.tx.us

**District Clerk: Betty Herriage**
Room 203
Phone: 903-675-6115
Fax: 903-677-7274
E-mail: bherriage@co.henderson.tx.us

**District Attorney: R. Scott McKee**
109 W. Corsicana St., Suite 103
Athens, TX 75751
Phone: 903-675-6100
Fax: 903-675-6196

**3rd District Court**
**Judge Mark A. Calhoon** sits the second or third Monday and Tuesday of every month.
*Please see Anderson County.*

**173rd District Court**
**Judge Dan Moore**
Room 207
Phone: 903-675-6107
Fax: 903-675-6106
Court Coordinator: Patsy Fowler
Court Reporter: Patrick Thurmond
Phone: 903-675-6156
Bailiff: Eric Ward

**392nd District Court**
**Judge Carter W. Tarrance**
109 W. Corsicana St., Suite 101
Athens, TX 75751
Phone: 903-675-6110
Fax: 903-677-7280
Court Coordinator: Janet Richison
Court Reporter: Melanie Oldham
Phone: 903-675-6111
Bailiff: Kelli Warren

**County Clerk: Mary Margaret Wright**
125 N. Praireville St., Room 101
Phone: 903-675-6140
Fax: 903-675-6105

**County Attorney: Clint Davis**
Room 100
Phone: 903-675-6112
Fax: 903-675-6192
Office Manager: Diane Russ

**County Judge: Richard Sanders**
Room 100
Phone: 903-675-6120
Fax: 903-675-6190
Court Coordinator: Renee Oliver

**County Court at Law No. 1**
**Judge Scott Williams**
Room 101
Phone: 903-675-6162
Fax: 903-675-6191
Court Coordinator: Stacey Norman
Court Reporter: Laurie Brown

**County Court at Law No. 2**
**Judge Nancy Perryman**
109 W. Corsicana St., Suite 106
Athens, TX 75751

Phone: 903-676-4010
Fax: 903-676-4013
Court Coordinator: Juli DeMoss
E-mail: jdemoss@co.henderson.tx.us
Court Reporter: Shelly Etheridge
Bailiff: Ron Holder

# HIDALGO COUNTY

Seat: Edinburg

100 N. Closner Blvd.
Edinburg, TX 78539-3523
www.co.hidalgo.tx.us

**District Clerk: Laura Hinojosa**
P.O. Box 87
Edinburg, TX 78540
Phone: 956-318-2200
Fax: 956-318-2251
E-mail: districtclerk@co.hildago.tx.us

**Criminal District Attorney: Ricardo Rodriguez**
3rd Floor
Phone: 956-318-2300
Fax: 956-318-2301

**92nd District Court**
**Judge Luis M. Singleterry**
2nd Floor
Phone: 956-318-2250
Fax: 956-318-2345
Court Coordinator (Civil): Pedro Lobato
Court Coordinator (Criminal): Cecilia Paz
Court Reporter: Julia Aldrette
Bailiff: Jose Hernandez

**93rd District Court**
**Judge Rodolfo Delgado**
2nd Floor
Phone: 956-318-2255
Fax: 956-318-2552
Court Coordinator: Joel Espinoza
Assistant Coordinator: Irma Hinojosa
Court Reporter: Jackie Inks
Phone: 956-318-2257
Bailiff: Alexandria Peña

**139th District Court**
**Judge J. R. "Bobby" Flores**
2nd Floor
Phone: 956-318-2260

Fax: 956-383-7608
Court Coordinator: Sylvia Reyes
Assistant Coordinator: Mary Ramirez
Court Reporter: Jessie Salazar
Phone: 956-318-2263
Bailiff: Jerry Lopez

**206th District Court—MDL Cases**
**Judge Rose Guerra Reyna**
2nd Floor
Phone: 956-318-2265
Fax: 956-318-2005
Court Coordinator: Delma Silva
Assistant Coordinator: Victor Hernandez
MDL Hailstorm Caseworker: Brenda Lopez
Court Reporter: Diana Thash
Phone: 956-318-2267
Bailiff: Margarita Reyes

**275th District Court**
**Judge Juan R. Partida**
1st Floor
Phone: 956-318-2270
Fax: 956-318-2589
Court Coordinator: Gina Alvarez
Phone: 956-318-2271
Assistant Coordinator (Civil): Carilu Lela
Court Reporter: Dalia Robeldo
Phone: 956-318-2272
Bailiff: Jose Alvarez

**332nd District Court**
**Judge Mario E. Ramirez, Jr.**
2nd Floor
Phone: 956-318-2275
Fax: 956-318-2698
Court Coordinator: Tootsie Barrera
Assistant Coordinator: Damian Carranza
Court Reporter: Regina Vasquez
Bailiff: Jose Perez

**370th District Court**
**Judge Noe Gonzalez**
1st Floor
Phone: 956-318-2280
Fax: 956-318-2285
Court Coordinator: Ester Contreras
Assistant Coordinator: Alicia Salinas
Court Reporter: Lisa M. Kinsel
Phone: 956-318-2282
Bailiff: Lazaro Baltarar

**389th District Court**
**Judge Leticia Lopez**
2nd Floor

Phone: 956-318-2080
Fax: 956-318-2084
Court Coordinator: Luisa Pearson
Assistant Coordinator: Ailynn Skinner-Barney
Court Reporter: Gabriella Silva
Bailiff: Vacant

### 398th District Court
**Judge Aida Salinas Flores**
2nd Floor
Phone: 956-318-2470
Fax: 956-318-2475
Court Coordinator: Chris Garces, Jr.
Assistant Coordinator: Ester Cantu
Phone: 956-318-2372
Court Reporter: Shana Lively
Phone: 956-318-2473
Bailiff: Moises Flores, Jr.

### 430th District Court
**Judge Israel Ramon, Jr.**
111 S. 9th
Edinburg, TX 78539
Phone: 956-318-2900
Fax: 956-381-0477
Court Coordinator: Maricela C. Salinas
Assistant Coordinator: Salvdo Padilla
Court Reporter: Velma Arellano
Bailiff: Orando Cantu

### 449th District Court
**Judge Jesus Contreras**
1001 N. Doolittle Rd.
Edinburg, TX 78542
Phone: 956-381-0744
Court Coordinator: Regina Moreno
Phone: 956-381-0744, ext. 6582
E-mail: regina.moreno@co.hidalgo.tx.us
Assistant Coordinator: Eric Pacheco
Phone: 956-381-0744, ext. 6585
E-mail: eric.pacheco@co.hidalgo.tx.us
Court Reporter: Bernette Mathis
Phone: 956-381-0744, ext. 6584
E-mail: bernette.mathis@co.hidalgo.tx.us
Bailiff: Oscar Gonzales
Phone: 956-381-0744, ext. 6581
E-mail: oscar.gonzales@co.hidalgo.tx.us

### County Clerk: Arturo Guajardo, Jr.
P.O. Box 58
Edinburg, TX 78540
Phone: 956-318-2100
Fax: 956-318-2105
Chief Deputy: Annette C. Muniz
Office Manager: Noe Lopez

### County Attorney: Steve Crane
Phone: 956-682-5501

### County Judge: Ramon Garcia
302 W. University
Edinburg, TX 78539
Phone: 956-318-2600
Fax: 956-318-2699

### County Court at Law No. 1
**Judge Rudy Gonzalez**
3rd Floor
Phone: 956-318-2375
Fax: 956-318-2373
Court Administrator: JC Cantu
Court Coordinator: Toni Garcia
Court Reporter: Cindi Cavazos
Bailiff: Albert Cortez

### County Court at Law No. 2
**Judge Jaime J. Palacios**
3rd Floor
Phone: 956-318-2380
Fax: 956-318-2384
Court Coordinator: Maria Elena Banning
Assistant Coordinator: Rhonda Cruz
Court Reporter: Kathryn Roberts
Bailiff: Hector Diaz

### Probate Court
**Judge Homero Garza**
3rd Floor
Phone: 956-318-2385
Fax: 956-318-2387
Court Auditor: Hector Garcia
Court Coordinator: Lydia Barrientes
Assistant Coordinator: Yolanda Hernandez
Court Reporter: Roland P. Quintanilla
Court Investigator: David Marroquin
Bailiff: Melissa Martinez

### County Court at Law No. 4
**Judge Frederico Garza**
3rd Floor
Phone: 956-318-2390
Fax: 956-318-2396
Court Administrator: Aida Ramirez
Court Coordinator: Rachel Segura
Court Reporter: Shantel Zambrano
Bailiff: Rick Lizcano

### County Court at Law No. 5
**Judge Arnoldo Cantu**
2nd Floor
Phone: 956-318-2460

**STATE, DISTRICT AND COUNTY COURTS**

Fax: 956-318-2463
Court Reporter: Evelyn Aguilar
Court Coordinator: Joanna Guerra
Assistant Coordinator: Norma Perez
Bailiff: Albert Delgado

**County Court at Law No. 6**
**Judge Albert Garcia**
2nd Floor
Phone: 956-289-7400
Court Coordinator: Frank Fuentes
Assistant Coordinator: Raquel Nevarez
Court Reporter: Veronica Mayfield-Jones
Bailiff: Cesar Gutierrez

**County Court at Law No. 7**
**Judge Sergio Valdez**
Annex Building
Phone: 956-292-7780
Court Coordinator: Noe Martinez, III
Assistant Coordinator: Yadira Cortinas
Court Reporter: Teresa Navarro
Bailiff: Alex Pinzon

**County Court at Law No. 8**
**Judge Omar Maldonado**
Annex Building
Phone: 956-292-7740
Court Coordinator: Kathy Gonzalez
Assistant Coordinator: Eddie Villanueva
Court Reporter: Don Mielton
Bailiff: Carlos Perez

# HILL COUNTY

Seat: Hillsboro

Hill County Courthouse Square 1
Hillsboro, TX 76645
www.co.hill.tx.us

**District Clerk: Angelia Orr**
P.O. Box 634
Hillsboro, TX 76645-0634
Phone: 254-582-4042
Fax: 254-582-4035
E-mail: districtclerk@co.hill.tx.us

**District Attorney: Mark Pratt**
P.O. Box 400
Hillsboro, TX 76645-0400
Phone: 254-582-4070
Fax: 254-582-4036

**66th District Court**
**Judge Lee Harris**
P.O. Box 284
Hillsboro, TX 76645-0284
Phone: 254-582-4045
Fax: 254-582-4010
Court Coordinator: Jane Hall
Assistant Court Coordinator: Ida Alcala
Court Reporter: Janet McConathy

**County Clerk: Nicole Tanner**
P.O. Box 398
Hillsboro, TX 76645
Phone: 254-582-4030
Fax: 254-582-4003
E-mail: countyclerk@co.hill.tx.us

**County Attorney: David Holmes**
P.O. Box 253
Hillsboro, TX 76645-2353
Phone: 254-582-4047
Fax: 254-582-4013

**County Judge: Justin W. Lewis**
P.O. Box 457
Hillsboro, TX 76645
Phone: 254-582-4020
Fax: 254-582-4028
Court Coordinator: Paula Svacina

**County Court at Law**
**Judge Matt Crain**
P.O. Box 874
Hillsboro, TX 76645
Phone: 254-582-4068
Fax: 254-582-4071
E-mail: courtatlaw@co.hill.tx.us
Court Coordinator: Lori Primm

# HOCKLEY COUNTY

Seat: Levelland

802 Houston St.
Levelland, TX 79336
www.co.hockley.tx.us

**District Clerk: Dennis Price**
Suite 316
Phone: 806-894-8527
Fax: 806-894-3891

*STATE, DISTRICT AND COUNTY COURTS*

**District Attorney: Christopher E. Dennis**
Suite 212
Phone: 806-894-3130
Fax: 806-894-3543

**286th District Court**
**Judge Pat Phelan**
Suite 315
Phone: 806-894-8240
Fax: 806-894-3891
Court Coordinator: Rhonda Bradley
Court Reporter: Annette Goodman
Phone: 806-894-6230
Bailiff: Glen Burton

**County Clerk: Irene Gumula**
Suite 213
Phone: 806-894-3185
Fax: 806-894-6917

**County Attorney: Anna Hord**
Suite 211
Phone: 806-894-5455
Fax: 806-894-3543
E-mail: ahord@hockleycounty.org

**County Judge: Larry D. Sprowls**
Suite 101
Phone: 806-894-6856
Fax: 806-894-6820
Court Coordinator: Sharla Baldridge
E-mail: sbaldridge@hockleycounty.org

## HOOD COUNTY

Seat: Granbury

1200 W. Pearl St.
Granbury, TX 76048
www.co.hood.tx.us

**District Clerk: Tonna Trumble Hitt**
Phone: 817-579-3236
Fax: 817-579-3239
E-mail: ttrumble@co.hood.tx.us

**District Attorney: Robert Christian**
Phone: 817-579-3245
Fax: 817-579-3247
E-mail: rchristian@co.hood.tx.us

**355th District Court**
**Judge Ralph H. Walton, Jr.**

Phone: 817-579-3233
Fax: 817-579-3243
Court Coordinator: Penny Weisend
E-mail: pweisend@co.hood.tx.us
Assistant Court Coordinator: Tricia Walter
Court Reporter: Mike Carlisle
Phone: 817-579-3255
Bailiff: Ron Berryman

**County Clerk: Katie Lang**
P.O. Box 339
Granbury, TX 76048
Phone: 817-579-3222, ext. 5621
Fax: 817-408-3459
E-mail: klang@co.hood.tx.us
Chief Deputy: Dean Armstrong
Phone: 817-579-3222, ext. 5620
E-mail: ldarmstrong@co.hood.tx.us

**County Attorney: Lori Kaspar**
Phone: 817-579-3216
Fax: 817-579-3218 or 817-579-3257

**County Judge: Darrell Cockerham**
100 E. Pearl St.
Granbury, TX 76048
Phone: 817-579-3200
Fax: 817-579-3213
E-mail: dcockerham@co.hood.tx.us
Court Administrator: Beth Stanley
E-mail: bstanley@co.hood.tx.us
Administration Assistant: Mary Sutton
E-mail: msutton@co.hood.tx.us

**County Court at Law**
**Judge Vincent J. Messina**
Phone: 817-408-3480
Fax: 817-408-3483
Court Coordinator: Micky Shearon
Phone: 817-408-3480, ext. 5632
E-mail: mshearon@co.hood.tx.us
Court Reporter: Cheryl Walters
Phone: 817-408-3485
E-mail: csr4hccl@yahoo.com
Bailiff: Steve Mehaffey

## HOPKINS COUNTY

Seat: Sulphur Springs

118 Church St.
Sulphur Springs, TX 75482-2602
www.hopkinscountytx.org

**District Clerk: Cheryl Fulcher**
Phone: 903-438-4081
Fax: 903-438-4114

**District Attorney: Will Ramsay**
110 Main St.
Sulphur Springs, TX 75482
Phone: 903-885-0641
Fax: 903-885-0640

**8th District Court**
**Judge Eddie Northcutt**
Phone: 903-438-4022
Fax: 903-438-4092
Court Coordinator: Regina Collins
Court Reporter: Jana Rushing

**62nd District Court**
**Judge Will Biard**
Phone: 903-737-2434
Court Reporter: Anna Upchurch

**County Clerk: Debbie Shirley**
128 Jefferson St., Suite C
Sulphur Springs, TX 75482
Phone: 903-438-4074
Fax: 903-438-4110
E-mail: cclerk@hopkinscountytx.org

**County Attorney: Dusty Rabe**
128 Jefferson St., Suite B
Sulphur Springs, TX 75482
Phone: 903-438-4017
Fax: 903-438-4016

**County Judge: Robert Newsom**
P.O. Box 288
Sulphur Springs, TX 75483
Phone: 903-438-4006
Fax: 903-438-4007
E-mail: rnewsom@hopkinscountytx.org

**County Court at Law**
**Judge Amy Smith**
P.O. Box 288
Sulphur Springs, TX 75483
Phone: 903-438-4004
Court Coordinator: Elizabeth Vice
Phone: 903-438-4004
E-mail: liz@hopkinscountytx.org

# HOUSTON COUNTY

Seat: Crockett

401 E. Houston Ave.
Crockett, TX 75835
www.co.houston.tx.us

**District Clerk: Carolyn Rains**
Phone: 936-544-3255
Fax: 936-544-9523
E-mail: districtclerk@co.houston.tx.us

**District Attorney: Donna Kaspar**
P.O. Box 1076
Crockett, TX 75835
Phone: 936-544-3255, ext. 245
Fax: 936-544-2790
E-mail: dgordon@co.houston.tx.us

**3rd District Court**
**Judge Mark A. Calhoon** sits the first two weeks
of every month.
*Please see Anderson County.*

**349th District Court**
**Judge Pam Foster Fletcher** sits the last two
weeks of every month.
*Please see Anderson County.*

**County Clerk: Bridget Lamb**
P.O. Box 370
Crockett, TX 75835
Phone: 936-544-3255, ext. 240
Fax: 936-544-1954
E-mail: bridget.lamb@co.houston.tx.us

**County Attorney: Daphne Session**
2nd Floor
Phone: 936-544-3255, ext. 270
Fax: 936-544-9811
E-mail: daphne.session@co.houston.tx.us

**County Judge: Erin Ford**
401 E. Goliad, Ste. 201
Crockett, TX 75835
Phone: 936-544-3255, ext. 221
Fax: 936-544-8053
E-mail: countyjudge@co.houston.tx.us
Administrative Assistant: Jan Pigford
E-mail: jan.pigford@co.houston.tx.us

STATE, DISTRICT AND COUNTY COURTS

County Court at Law
Judge Sarah Tunnell Clark
2nd Floor
Phone: 936-544-3255, ext. 230
Fax: 936-545-9605
Court Coordinator: Terri Meadows
E-mail: terrimeadows02@yahoo.com
Court Reporter: Betty Chenault
Phone: 936-544-3255, ext. 231
Bailiff: Andy Biscamp

# HOWARD COUNTY

Seat: Big Spring

312 Scurry St.
Big Spring, TX 79720
www.co.howard.tx.us

District Clerk: Colleen Barton
Phone: 432-264-2223
Fax: 432-264-2256
E-mail: colleen.barton@howardcountytx.com

District Attorney: Hardy L. Wilkerson
P.O. Drawer 149
Big Spring, TX 79721
Phone: 432-264-2220
Fax: 432-264-2222

118th District Court
Judge Timothy D. Yeats, III
P.O. Box 528
Big Spring, TX 79721-0528
Phone: 432-264-2225
Fax: 432-264-2270
E-mail: timothy.yeats@howardcountytx.com
Court Coordinator: Sherry Newsom
Court Reporter: Karen Freeman
Phone: 432-264-2225

## County Court
300 Main St.
Big Spring, TX 79720

County Clerk: Donna Wright
P.O. Box 1468
Big Spring, TX 79721-1468
Phone: 432-264-2213
Fax: 432-264-2215
E-mail: donna.wright@howardcountytx.com

County Attorney: Joshua Hamby
P.O. Box 2096
Big Spring, TX 79721
Phone: 432-264-2205
Fax: 432-264-2206

County Judge: Kathryn Wiseman
Room 207
Phone: 432-264-2202
Fax: 432-264-2206
E-mail: kathryn.wiseman@howardcountytx.com

# HUDSPETH COUNTY

Seat: Sierra Blanca

109 Millican
Sierra Blanca, TX 79851
www.co.hudspeth.tx.us

District and County Clerk: Virginia Doyal
P.O. Box 58
Sierra Blanca, TX 79851-0058
Phone: 915-369-2301
Fax: 915-369-0055
E-mail: hudspethcountyclerk@outlook.com

District Attorney: Jaime Esparza
*Please see El Paso County.*

205th District Court
Judge Fransisco X. Dominguez sits every other month.
*Please see El Paso County.*

394th District Court
Judge Roy B. Ferguson sits as scheduled.
*Please see Brewster County.*

County Attorney: C. R. "Kit" Bramblett
P.O. Box 221528
El Paso, TX 79913
Phone: 915-833-2144
Fax: 915-833-2517

County Judge: Mike Doyal
P.O. Box 68
Sierra Blanca, TX 79851
Phone: 915-369-2321
Fax: 915-369-2361
E-mail: doyal_mike@yahoo.com
Secretary: Alejandra Marquez

STATE, DISTRICT AND COUNTY COURTS

# HUNT COUNTY

Seat: Greenville

2507 Lee St.
Greenville, TX 75401
www.huntcounty.net

**District Clerk: Stacey Landrum**
P.O. Box 1437
Greenville, TX 75403-1437
Phone: 903-408-4172
Chief Deputy: Susan Spradling

**District Attorney: Noble D. Walker**
P.O. Box 441
Greenville, TX 75403-0441
Phone: 903-408-4180
Fax: 903-408-4296

**196th District Court**
**Judge Andrew Bench**
P.O. Box 1097
Greenville, TX 75403-1097
Phone: 903-408-4190
Court Coordinator: Julie Deary
Court Reporter: Edwin Walker
Bailiff: Daniel Uzialko

**354th District Court**
**Judge Richard Beacom**
P.O. Box 1097
Greenville, TX 75403-1097
Phone: 903-408-4194
Court Coordinator: Donna Meeks
Court Reporter: Julie Vrooman
Bailiff: Benny Brothers

**County Clerk: Jennifer Lindenzweig**
P.O. Box 1316
Greenville, TX 75403-1316
Phone: 903-408-4130
Fax: 903-408-4287

**County Attorney: Joel Littlefield**
P.O. Box 1097
Greenville, TX 75403
Phone: 903-408-4112
Fax: 903-408-4297

**County Judge: John Horn**
P.O. Box 1097
Greenville, TX 75403-1097

Phone: 903-408-4146
Fax: 903-408-4299
E-mail: cojudge@huntcounty.net
Administrative Assistant: Amanda Blakenship

**County Court at Law No. 1**
**Judge Timothy Linden**
P.O. Box 1097
Greenville, TX 75403-1097
Phone: 903-408-4200
Court Coordinator: Cathy Stroud
Court Reporter: Cher Perry
Bailiff: Eric Huggins

**County Court at Law No. 2**
**Judge F. Duncan Thomas**
P.O. Box 1097
Greenville, TX 75403-1097
Phone: 903-408-4234
Court Coordinator: Debra Mason
Court Reporter: Shannon Head
Bailiff: Janie Hammargren

# HUTCHINSON COUNTY

Seat: Stinnett

500 Main St.
Stinnett, TX 79083
www.co.hutchinson.tx.us

**District Clerk: Robin Stroud**
P.O. Box 580
Stinnett, TX 79083
Phone: 806-878-4017
Fax: 806-878-4042
E-mail: rstroud@hutchinsoncnty.com

**District Attorney: Mark Snider**
P.O. Box 3431
Stinnett, TX 79083-3431
Phone: 806-878-4036
Fax: 806-878-4038
E-mail: 84thdamark@hutchinsoncnty.com

**84th District Court**
**Judge William "Bill" D. Smith** sits every Wednesday.
*Please see Hansford County.*

**316th District Court**
**Judge James M. Mosley**

P.O. Box 1181
Stinnett, TX 79083-1181
Phone: 806-878-4019
Fax: 806-878-4023
Court Coordinator: Kimi Lantelme
Court Reporter: Lavonna Stater

**County Clerk: Jan Barnes**
P.O. Box 1186
Stinnett, TX 79083-1186
Phone: 806-878-4002
Fax: 806-878-3497
E-mail: jbarnes@hutchinsoncnty.com

**County Attorney: Michael Milner**
1400 Veta, Suite 108
Borger, TX 79007
Phone: 806-273-0134
Fax: 806-273-0123

**County Judge: Faye Blanks**
P.O. Box 790
Stinnett, TX 79083-0790
Phone: 806-878-4000
Fax: 806-878-4048
E-mail: judgeblanks@hutchinsoncnty,com
Administrative Assistant: Hallie Throckmorton

# IRION COUNTY

Seat: Mertzon

209 N. Parkview Ave.
Mertzon, TX 76941
www.co.irion.tx.us

**District and County Clerk: Molly Criner**
P.O. Box 736
Mertzon, TX 76941-0736
Phone: 325-835-2421
Fax: 325-835-7941
E-mail: irionclerk@gmail.com

**District Attorney: Allison Palmer**
*Please see Tom Green County.*

**51st District Court**
**Judge Barbara L. Walther** sits once a month.
*Please see Tom Green County.*

**County Attorney: Kenneth Greer, Jr.**
P.O. Box 907

Mertzon, TX 76941-0907
Phone: 325-835-7101
Fax: 325-835-2008

**County Judge: Tom Aiken**
P.O. Box 770
Mertzon, TX 76941-0770
Phone: 325-835-4361
Fax: 325-835-2008
Administrative Assistant: Debbie McMahon

# JACK COUNTY

Seat: Jacksboro

100 N. Main St.
Jacksboro, TX 76458
www.jackcounty.org

**District Clerk: Tracie Pippin**
Phone: 940-567-2141
Fax: 940-567-2696
E-mail: districtclerk@jackcounty.org

**District Attorney: Greg Lowery**
*Please see Wise County.*

**271st District Court**
**Judge John H. Fostel** sits as scheduled.
*Please see Wise County.*

**County Clerk: Janice Robinson**
Phone: 940-567-2111
Fax: 940-567-6441
E-mail: jrobinson@jackcounty.org

**County Attorney: M. Brad Dixon**
Phone: 940-567-3321
Fax: 940-567-6306
E-mail: mbdixon@jackcounty.org

**County Judge: Mitchell G. Davenport**
Phone: 940-567-2241
Administrative Assistant: Debra Tillery
Fax: 940-567-5502

# JACKSON COUNTY

Seat: Edna

115 W. Main St.

Edna, TX 77957-2793
www.co.jackson.tx.us

**District Clerk: Sharon Mathis**
Room 203
Phone: 361-782-3812
Fax: 361-782-3056
E-mail: s.mathis@co.jackson.tx.us

**District and County Attorney: Robert E. Bell**
Room 205
Phone: 361-782-7170
Fax: 361-782-3730

**24th District Court**
**Judge Jack W. Marr** sits as scheduled.
*Please see Victoria County.*

**135th District Court**
**Judge K. Stephen Williams** sits as scheduled.
*Please see Victoria County.*

**267th District Court**
**Judge Juergen "Skipper" Koetter** sits as
scheduled.
*Please see Victoria County.*
*Note: Hon. Koetter will retire on 3/4/16.*
*Gov. Abbot to appoint new judge.*

**County Clerk: Barbara Earl**
Room 101
Phone: 361-782-3563
Fax: 361-782-3132
E-mail: b.earl@co.jackson.tx.us

**County Judge: Dennis Simons**
Room 207
Phone: 361-782-2352
Fax: 361-782-5253
E-mail: d.simons@co.jackson.tx.us
Administrative Assistant: Michele Matejek
E-mail: m.matejek@co.jackson.tx.us

# JASPER COUNTY

Seat: Jasper

121 N. Austin St.
Jasper, TX 75951
www.co.jasper.tx.us

**District Clerk: Kathy Kent**
Room 202

Phone: 409-384-2721
Fax: 409-383-7501

**District and County Attorney: Steve Hollis**
Suite 101
Phone: 409-384-4362
Fax: 409-384-1309

**1st District Court**
**Judge Craig Mixson**
Room 205
Phone: 409-384-3792
Fax: 409-384-9722
Court Coordinator: Sharon Miller
Phone: 409-384-9570
Court Reporter: Donnece Foster
Phone: 409-489-9728
Bailiff: Sammy Ruggles

**1A District Court**
**Judge Delinda Gibbs-Walker**
Room 204
Phone: 409-384-5474
Fax: 409-384-9722
Court Coordinator: Sharon Miller
Phone: 409-384-9570
Court Reporter: Shelly Stephenson
Phone: 409-386-0881
Bailiff: Sammy Ruggles

**County Clerk: Debbie Newman**
P.O. Box 2070
Jasper, TX 75951
Phone: 409-384-2632
Fax: 409-384-7198
E-mail: debbie.newman@co.jasper.tx.us

**County Judge: Mark Allen**
Room 106
Phone: 409-384-2612
Fax: 409-384-9745
E-mail: mark.allen@co.jasper.tx.us

# JEFF DAVIS COUNTY

Seat: Fort Davis

100 Court Ave.
Fort Davis, TX 79734
www.co.jeff-davis.tx.us

**District and County Clerk: Jennifer Wright**
P.O. Box 398

Fort Davis, TX 79734
Phone: 432-426-3251
Fax: 432-426-3760

**District Attorney: Rod Ponton**
*Please see Pecos County.*

**394th District Court**
**Judge Roy B. Ferguson** sits once a month.
*Please see Brewster County.*

**County Attorney: Teresa Todd**
P.O. Box 1642
Fort Davis, TX 79734
Phone: 432-426-4434

**County Judge: Jeannette Duer**
P.O. Box 836
Fort Davis, TX 79734
Phone: 432-426-3968

# JEFFERSON COUNTY

Seat: Beaumont

1001 Pearl St.
Beaumont, TX 77701
www.co.jefferson.tx.us

**District Clerk: Jamie Smith**
Room 203
Phone: 409-835-8580
Fax: 409-835-8527

**District Attorney: Bob Wortham**
3rd floor
Beaumont, TX 77704-2553
Phone: 409-835-8550
Fax: 409-835-8573

## Civil District Courts
1001 Pearl St.
Beaumont, TX 77701

**58th District Court**
**Judge W. Kent Walston**
Phone: 409-835-8434
Fax: 409-835-8552
Court Coordinator: Sydney Moreau
E-mail: smoreau@co.jefferson.tx.us
Court Reporter: Anita Seegers
E-mail: aseegers@co.jefferson.tx.us
Phone: 409-835-8529
Bailiff: Charley Anderson

**60th District Court**
**Judge Gary Sanderson**
Phone: 409-835-8472
Fax: 409-784-5849
Court Coordinator: Cathy Dollinger
E-mail: cdollinger@co.jefferson.tx.us
Court Reporter: Cecilia Gower
Phone: 409-835-8409
Bailiff: Beverly Redmon
E-mail: bredmon@co.jefferson.tx.us

**136th District Court**
**Judge Milton G. Shuffield**
1085 Pearl St.
Beaumont, TX 77701
Phone: 409-835-8481
Fax: 409-784-5814
Court Coordinator: Michelle LaBrie
E-mail: 136thclerk@co.jefferson.tx.us
Court Reporter: Kayla Calamia
Phone: 409-835-8514
Bailiff: Stanley Hatcher
E-mail: shatcher@co.jefferson.tx.us

**172nd District Court**
**Judge Donald J. Floyd**
1001 Pearl St.
Beaumont, TX 77701
Phone: 409-835-8485
Fax: 409-784-5929
Court Coordinator: Donna Henry
E-mail: dhenry@co.jefferson.tx.us
Court Reporter: Holly Giffin
Phone: 409-839-2344
E-mail: hgiffin@co.jefferson.tx.us
Bailiff: dwain Pierre

## Criminal District Courts
1001 Pearl St.
Beaumont, TX 77701

**252nd District Court**
**Judge Raquel West**
Phone: 409-835-8597
Fax: 409-835-8656
Court Coordinator: Patrisha Kloefkorn
Court Clerk: Dolly McPhillips
E-mail: dmcphillips@co.jefferson.tx.us
Court Reporter: Summer Tanner
Phone: 409-835-8637
E-mail stanner@co.jefferson.tx.us
Bailiff: Lennie Hawthorne
Phone: 409-835-5786

**Criminal District Court**
**Judge John Stevens**
Phone: 409-835-8432
Fax: 409-835-8766
Court Coordinator: Kellie Holmes
Phone: 409-835-8433
E-mail: holmes@co.jefferson.tx.us
Court Coordinator: Lacy Simon
E-mail: lsimon@co.jefferson.tx.us
Court Reporter: Rene Muholland
Phone: 409-835-8410
Bailiff: Dennis Boteler

**Drug Impact Court**
**Judge Larry Gist**
215 Franklin St.
Beaumont, TX 77701
Phone: 409-835-8506
Court Coordinator: Susan Beck
E-mail: sbeck@co.jefferson.tx.us
Court Clerk: Christy DeRoven
E-mail: cderoven@co.jefferson.tx.us
Court Reporter: Kim Broussard
Bailiff: J.D. Bivins

## Family District Courts
1149 Pearl St.
Beaumont, TX 77701

**279th District Court**
**Judge Randy Shelton**
Phone: 409-835-8655
Fax: 409-835-8764
Court Coordinator: Renee Murrell
E-mail: rbouse@co.jefferson.tx.us
Court Reporter: Angie Morman
E-mail: amorman@co.jefferson.tx.us
Bailiff: Ronnie Guidry

**317th District Court**
**Judge Larry Thorne**
Phone: 409-835-8588
Fax: 409-839-2376
Court Coordinator: Susie O'Quinn
E-mail: soquinn@co.jefferson.tx.us
Court Reporter: Tracey Burk
Bailiff: Julie Pantallion

## County Courts

**County Clerk: Carolyn L. Guidry**
P.O. Box 1151
Beaumont, TX 77701
Phone: 409-835-8475

Fax: 409-839-2394
Chief Deputy: Theresa Goodness

**County Judge: Jeff Branick**
1149 Pearl St., 4th floor
Beaumont, TX 77704-4025
Phone: 409-835-8466
Fax: 409-839-2311
E-mail: jbranick@co.jefferson.tx.us
Administrative Secretary: Loma George

**County Court at Law No. 1**
**Judge Gerald W. Eddins**
1149 Pearl St.
Beaumont, TX 77701
Phone: 409-835-8470
Court Coordinator: Effie Keffer
E-mail: ekeffer@co.jefferson.tx.us
Court Reporter: Veronica Wimberly
Bailiff: Derrick Copes

**County Court at Law No. 2**
**Judge Cory Crenshaw**
Phone: 409-835-8429
Court Coordinator: Melanie Smith
E-mail: msmith@co.jefferson.tx.us
Court Coordinator: Tina Benoit
Phone: 409-835-8607
E-mail: tbenoit@co.jefferson.tx.us
Court Reporter: Elizabeth Parks
E-mail: lparks@co.jefferson.tx.us
Bailiff: Doug Boyd

**County Court at Law No. 3**
**Judge Clint M. Woods**
Phone: 409-835-8698
Court Coordinator: Calista Collins
Phone: 409-835-8407
Court Coordinator: Cynthia Jackson
E-mail: cjackson@co.jefferson.tx.us
E-mail: ccollins@co.jefferson.tx.us
Court Reporter: Brandi Sewell
Phone: 409-835-8491
Bailiff: Robert W. Compton

## JIM HOGG COUNTY

Seat: Hebbronville

102 E. Tilley St.
Hebbronville, TX 78361
www.jimhoggcounty.net

**STATE, DISTRICT AND COUNTY COURTS**

**District and County Clerk: Zonia G. Morales**
P.O. Box 878
Hebbronville, TX 78361
Phone: 361-527-4031
Fax: 361-527-5843
E-mail: zonia.morales@co.jim-hogg.tx.us

**District Attorney: Omar Escobar**
P.O. Box 340
Hebbronville, TX 78361-0340
Phone: 361-527-4056
Fax: 361-527-5832

**229th District Court**
**Judge Ana Lisa Garza** sits once a month.
*Please see Starr County.*

**County Attorney: Rodolfo V. Gutierrez**
P.O. Box 729
Hebbronville, TX 78361
Phone: 361-527-3425

**County Judge: Humberto Gonzalez**
P.O. Box 729
Hebbronville, TX 78361
Phone: 361-527-3015
Fax: 361-527-5800
E-mail: hgonzalez@co.jim-hogg.tx.us

# JIM WELLS COUNTY

Seat: Alice

200 N. Almond St.
Alice, TX 78332
www.co.jim-wells.tx.us

**District Clerk: R. David Guerrero**
P.O. Drawer 2219
Alice, TX 78333
Phone: 361-668-5717
Fax: 361-668-5732
E-mail: rdavidguerrero@sbcglobal.net
Chief Deputy: Delfi Flores

**District Attorney: Carlos Omar Garcia**
P.O. Drawer 3157
Alice, TX 78333-3157
Phone: 361-668-5716
Fax: 361-668-9974

**79th District Court**
**Judge Richard C. Terrell**
P.O. Box 3080
Alice, TX 78333-1375
Phone: 361-668-5718
Fax: 361-668-8240
Court Coordinator: Carol Salinas
Court Reporter: Sonia Treviño
Bailiff: J. Mario Guerra

**County Clerk: J.C. Perez, III**
P.O. Box 1459
Alice, TX 78333
Phone: 361-668-5702
Fax: 361-661-1372

**County Attorney: Jesusa Sanchez-Vera**
Phone: 361-668-5700
Fax: 361-668-5768

**County Judge: Pedro Treviño, Jr.**
Phone: 361-668-5706
Fax: 361-668-8671

**County Court at Law**
**Judge Michael V. Garcia**
Phone: 361-668-5895
Bailiff: George A. Saenz

# JOHNSON COUNTY

Seat: Cleburne

204 S. Buffalo Ave.
Cleburne, TX 76033
www.johnsoncountytx.org

**District Clerk: David R. Lloyd**
P.O. Box 495
Cleburne, TX 76033-0495
Phone: 817-556-6839
Fax: 817-556-6120
E-mail: jcdc@johnsoncountytx.org

**District Attorney: Dale S. Hanna**
Suite 209
Phone: 817-556-6802, ext. 1104
Fax: 817-556-6816

**18th District Court**
**Judge John E. Neill**
Suite 304
Phone: 817-556-6820

Fax: 817-556-6831
Court Coordinator (Civil): Sharon Powell
Phone: 817-556-6193
E-mail: sharonp@johnsoncountytx.org
Court Coordinator (Criminal): Joy Penney
Court Reporter: Renee Hall
Phone: 817-556-6822
Bailiff: Rudy Luna

**249th District Court**
**Judge D. Wayne Bridewell**
Suite 208
Phone: 817-556-6825
Fax: 817-556-6849
Court Coordinator (Civil): Gina Horton
Court Coordinator (Criminal): Rachel Bleth
Phone: 817-556-6830
Court Reporter: LuAnn Gill
Phone: 817-556-6829
Bailiff: Danny Green

**413th District Court**
**Judge William C. Bosworth, Jr.**
Suite 207
Phone: 817-556-6040
Fax: 817-556-6043
Court Coordinator (Civil): Kori Evertt
Court Coordinator (Criminal): Cindy Miller
Phone: 817-556-6870
Court Reporter: Pamela Waits
Phone: 817-556-6041
Bailiff: Darby Tucker

**County Clerk: Becky Ivey**
Suite 407
Phone: 817-556-6321
Fax: 817-556-6170
E-mail: becky@johnsoncountytx.org

**County Attorney: Bill Moore**
Suite 410
Phone: 817-556-6330
Fax: 817-556-6331

**County Judge: Roger O. Harmon**
2 N. Main St.
Cleburne, TX 76033
Phone: 817-556-6360
Fax: 817-556-6359
E-mail: countyjudge@johnsoncountytx.org
Administrative Assistant: Alison Hitchcock

**County Court at Law No. 1**
**Judge Robert B. Mayfield, III**
Suite 408

Phone: 817-556-6353
Fax: 817-556-6399
Court Coordinator (Civil): Amy Finley
Court Coordinator (Criminal): Reba Henry
Phone: 817-556-6357
Court Reporter: Tracie Miller
Phone: 817-556-6358
Bailiff: Kelley Carter
Phone: 817-556-6355
Probate Auditor: Iryna Spangler
Phone: 817-556-6874

**County Court at Law No. 2**
**Judge F. Steven McClure**
Suite 409
Phone: 817-556-6395
Fax: 817-556-6190
E-mail: courtatlaw2@johnsoncountytx.org
Court Coordinator (Civil): Paula Cribbs
Phone: 817-556-6397, ext. 1353
Court Coordinator (Criminal): Maralyn Wheeler
Phone: 817-556-6397, ext. 1352
Court Reporter: Karen Jones
Phone: 817-556-6396
Probate Auditor: Iryna Spangler
Phone: 817-556-6574
Bailiff: Will Keeton
Phone: 817-556-6344

# JONES COUNTY

Seat: Anson

12th and Commercial St.
Anson, TX 79501
www.co.jones.tx.us

**District Clerk: Lacey Hansen**
P.O. Box 308
Anson, TX 79501-0308
Phone: 325-823-3731
Fax: 325-823-3289

**District Attorney: Joe Edd Boaz**
P.O. Box 507
Anson, TX 79501-0507
Phone: 325-823-2742
Fax: 325-823-2322

**259th District Court**
**Judge Brooks H. Hagler**
P.O. Box 429

STATE, DISTRICT AND COUNTY COURTS

Anson, TX 79501-0429
Phone: 325-823-2721
Fax: 325-823-4200
Court Coordinator Santa Franco
Court Reporter: Michelle Lopez
Phone: 325-823-2721

**County Clerk: LeeAnn Jennings**
P.O. Box 552
Anson, TX 79501-0552
Phone: 325-823-3762
Fax: 325-823-3979

**County Attorney: Chad Cowan**
P.O. Box 68
Anson, TX 79501-0068
Phone: 325-823-3771
Fax: 325-823-4223

**County Judge: Dale Spurgin**
P.O. Box 148
Anson, TX 79501-0148
Phone: 325-823-3741
Fax: 325-823-4223
Administrative Assistant: Alecia Hanson

# KARNES COUNTY

Seat: Karnes City

210 W. Calvert Ave.
Karnes City, TX 78118-2930
www.co.karnes.tx.us

**District Clerk: Denise Rodriguez**
210 W. Calvert St., Suite 180
Karnes City, TX 78118
Phone: 830-780-3065 | 830-780-2562
Fax: 830-780-3227
E-mail: denise.rodriguez@co.karnes.tx.us

**District Attorney: René M. Peña**
*Please see Atascosa County.*

**81st District Court**
**Judge Donna S. Rayes** sits once a month.
*Please see Atascosa County.*

**218th District Court**
**Judge Russell Wilson**
210 W. Calvert Ave., Suite 152
Phone: 830-780-3089
Fax: 830-780-3227 or 830-769-2841

Court Coordinator (Civil): Heather Fischer
Court Coordinator (Criminal): Deane Belicek
Phone: 830-769-3750
Court Reporter: Steve Turner
Phone: 830-569-8500

**County Clerk: Carol Swize**
Phone: 830-780-3938
Fax: 830-780-4576

**County Attorney: Herb Hancock**
Phone: 830-780-3736
Fax: 830-780-4790
**County Judge: Walter R. Long, Jr.**
Phone: 830-780-3732
Fax: 830-780-4538
E-mail: walter.long@co.karnes.tx.us
Administrative Assistant: Mary Lozano

# KAUFMAN COUNTY

Seat: Kaufman

100 W. Mulberry St.
Kaufman, TX 75142
www.kaufmancounty.net

**District Clerk: Rhonda Hughey**
2nd Floor
Phone: 972-932-4331, ext. 1274

**District Attorney: Erleigh Norville-Wiley**
Phone: 972-932-4331, ext. 1260
Fax: 972-932-0357

**86th District Court**
**Judge Casey Blair**
Phone: 972-932-0251
Fax: 972-932-7626
Court Coordinator: Katie Griffin
Court Reporter: Elizabeth Woods
Phone: 972-932-0253

**422nd District Court**
**Judge B. Michael Chitty**
Phone: 972-932-0257
Fax: 972-932-8067
Court Coordinator: Jennifer Surratt
Court Reporter: Donna Gehl
Phone: 972-932-0258
Bailiff: Gaylen Weir
Phone: 972-932-4331, ext. 1157

County Clerk: Laura A. Hughes
Phone: 972-932-4331, ext. 1200
Fax: 972-962-8018

County Judge: James Bruce Wood, Sr.
Phone: 972-932-4331, ext. 1218
Fax: 972-932-1368

County Court at Law No. 1
Judge Dennis P. Jones
Phone: 972-932-4331, ext. 1211
Fax: 972-932-0505
Court Coordinator: Lindy Wood
Phone: 972-932-0212
Court Reporter: Scott Smith
Phone: 972-932-0214
Bailiff: Teresa Smith
Phone: 972-932-0213

County Court at Law No. 2
Judge Bobbie Rich
Phone: 972-932-4331, ext. 1255
Fax: 972-932-0755
Court Coordinator: Bailey McCormick
Phone: 972-932-0255
Court Reporter: Sherry Hooper
Phone: 972-932-4331, ext. 1155
Bailiff: Gaylen Weir
Phone: 972-932-0114

# KENDALL COUNTY

Seat: Boerne

201 E. San Antonio St.
Boerne, TX 78006
www.co.kendall.tx.us

District Clerk: Susan Jackson
Suite 201
Phone: 830-249-9343, ext. 260
Fax: 830-249-1763
E-mail: susan.jackson@co.kendall.tx.us

District Attorney: Bruce E. Curry
*Please see Kerr County.*

216th District Court
Judge N. Keith Williams sits one week every
month.
*Please see Kerr County.*

County Clerk: Darlene Herrin
Phone: 830-249-9343, ext. 230
Fax: 830-249-3472
E-mail: darlene.herrin@co.kendall.tx.us

County Attorney: Don Allee
Suite 306
Phone: 830-249-9343, ext. 295
Fax: 830-249-4176
E-mail: don.allee@co.kendall.tx.us

County Judge: Darrell Lux
Phone: 830-249-9343, ext. 213
E-mail: darrell.lux@co.kendall.tx.us
Administrative Assistant: Sally Peters
Phone: 830-336-2881

County Court at Law
Judge William "Bill" Palmer
Phone: 830-249-9343
E-mail: william.palmer@co.kendall.tx.us
Court Reporter: Tami Wolff

# KENEDY COUNTY

Seat: Sarita

151 Mallory St.
Sarita, TX 78385
www.co.kenedy.tx.us

District and County Clerk: Veronica Vela
P.O. Box 227
Sarita, TX 78385-0227
Phone: 361-294-5220
Fax: 361-294-5218
E-mail: vvela@co.kenedy.tx.us

District Attorney: John T. Hubert
*Please see Kleberg County.*

105th District Court
Judge Jack W. Pulcher sits once a month.
*Please see Nueces County.*

County Attorney: Allison Strauss
P.O. Box 202
Sarita, TX 78385
Phone: 361-294-5292
Fax: 361-294-5303

County Judge: Louis Turcotte, III
P.O. Box 37

**STATE, DISTRICT AND COUNTY COURTS**

Sarita, TX 78385
Phone: 361-294-5224
Fax: 361-294-5244
Administrative Assistant: Petrita Hernandez

# KENT COUNTY

Seat: Jayton

101 Main St.
Jayton, TX 79528
www.co.kent.tx.us

**District and County Clerk: Richard C. Harrison**
P.O. Box 9
Jayton, TX 79528
Phone: 806-237-3881
Fax: 806-237-2300

**District Attorney: Micheal E. Fouts**
*Please see Haskell County.*

**39th District Court**
**Judge Shane Hadaway** sits once a month.
*Please see Haskell County.*

**County Attorney: Bill Ballard**
P.O. Box 3
Jayton, TX 79528
Phone: 806-237-3975
Fax: 806-237-2632

**County Judge: Jim C. White**
P.O. Box 6
Jayton, TX 79528-0006
Phone: 806-237-3373
Fax: 806-237-2632

# KERR COUNTY

Seat: Kerrville

700 Main St.
Kerrville, TX 78028
www.co.kerr.tx.us

**District Clerk: Robbin Burlew**
Suite 236
Phone: 830-792-2281
Fax: 830-792-2289

**198th District Attorney: Scott Monroe**
402 Clearwater Paseo, Suite 500
Kerrville, TX 78028-4532
Phone: 830-315-2460
Fax: 830-315-2461

**216th District Attorney: Bruce E. Curry**
200 Earl Garrett St., Suite 202
Kerrville, TX 78028
Phone: 830-896-4744
Fax: 830-896-2620

**198th District Court**
**Judge M. Rex Emerson**
Phone: 830-792-2290
Court Coordinator: Christine McEntyre
Court Reporter: Paula Beaver
Phone: 830-537-4724
Bailiffs: Scott Van Clavern and Albert
Luebano

**216th District Court**
**Judge N. Keith Williams**
Phone: 830-792-2290
Court Coordinator: Christine McEntyre
Court Reporter: Dandy Middleton
Phone: 830-257-5063
Bailiffs: Scott Van Clavern and Albert
Luebano

**County Clerk: Rebecca Bolin**
Suite 122
Phone: 830-792-2255
Fax: 830-792-2274
E-mail: countyclerk@co.kerr.tx.us

**County Attorney: Heather Stebbins**
Suite BA 103
Phone: 830-792-2220
Fax: 830-792-2228

**County Judge: Tom Pollard**
Suite 101
Phone: 830-792-2211
Fax: 830-792-2218
E-mail: cojudge@co.kerr.tx.us
Administrative Assistant: Jody Grinstead
E-mail: jgrinstead@co.kerr.tx.us

**County Court at Law**
**Judge Susan Harris**
Suite 123
Phone: 830-792-2207
Fax: 830-895-3711
E-mail: ccladmin@co.kerr.tx.us

Court Coordinator: Alicia Peña
Court Reporter: Kelly Rode

# KIMBLE COUNTY

Seat: Junction

501 Main St.
Junction, TX 76849-4763
www.co.kimble.tx.us
**District and County Clerk: Haydee Torres**
Phone: 325-446-3353
Fax: 325-446-2986
E-mail: haydee.torres@co.kimble.tx.us

**District Attorney: Tonya S. Ahlschwede**
*Please see Mason County.*

**452nd District Court**
**Judge Robert R. Hoffman** sits once a month.
*Please see Mason County.*

**County Attorney: Allen Ahlschwede**
P.O. Box 46
Phone: 325-446-2378
Fax: 325-446-9427

**County Judge: Delbert R. Roberts**
501 Main St.
Junction, TX 76849-4763
Phone: 325-446-2724
Fax: 325-446-2986
E-mail: delbert.roberts@co.kimble.tx.us

# KING COUNTY

Seat: Guthrie

800 South Baker
Guthrie, TX 79236
www.co.king.tx.us

**District and County Clerk: Jammye D, Timmons**
P.O. Box 135
Guthrie, TX 79236-0135
Phone: 806-596-4412
Fax: 806-596-4664
E-mail: kcdclerk@gmail.com

**District Attorney: David W. Hajek**
*Please see Baylor County.*

**50th District Court**
**Judge Bobby D. Burnett** sits twice a month.
*Please see Cottle County.*

**County Judge: Duane Daniel**
P.O. Box 127
Guthrie, TX 79236-0127
Phone: 806-596-4411
E-mail: kcjudge@caprock-spur.com

# KINNEY COUNTY

Seat: Brackettville

501 Ann St.
Brackettville, TX 78832
www.co.kinney.tx.us

**District and County Clerk: Dora Elia Sandoval**
P.O. Drawer 9
Brackettville, TX 78832-0009
Phone: 830-563-2521
Fax: 830-563-2644
E-mail: kcclerk@hotmail.com

**District Attorney: Fred Hernandez**
*Please see Val Verde County.*

**63rd District Court**
**Judge Enrique Fernandez** sits twice a year and
a six-month term.
*Please see Val Verde County.*

**County Attorney: Robert Adams**
P.O. Box 365
Brackettville, TX 78832-0365
Phone: 830-563-2240

**County Judge: Tully Shahan**
P.O. Box 348
Brackettville, TX 78832
Phone: 830-563-2401
Fax: 830-563-9163
Assistant: Cindy Connell

# KLEBERG COUNTY

Seat: Kingsville

700 E. Kleberg St.
Kingsville, TX 78363
www.co.kleberg.tx.us

**STATE, DISTRICT AND COUNTY COURTS**

**District Clerk: Jennifer Whittington**
P.O. Box 312
Kingsville, TX 78364-0312
Phone: 361-595-8561
Fax: 361-595-8525
E-mail: jwhittington@co.kleberg.tx.us

**District Attorney: John T. Hubert**
P.O. Box 1471
Kingsville, TX 78364-1471
Phone: 361-595-8544
Fax: 361-595-8522
E-mail: johnhubertesq@gmail.com

**105th District Court**
**Judge Jack W. Pulcher** sits as scheduled.
*Please see Nueces County.*

**County Clerk: Stephanie G. Garza**
P.O. Box 1327
Kingsville. TX 78364-1327
Phone: 361-595-8548
Fax: 361-593-1355
E-mail: sgarza@co.kleberg.tx.us

**County Attorney: Kira Talip**
P.O. Box 1411
Kingsville. TX 78364-1411
Phone: 361-595-8583
Fax: 361-595-4726
E-mail: ktalip@co.kleberg.tx.us

**County Judge: Rudy Madrid**
P.O. Box 752
Kingsville, TX 78363-0752
Phone: 361-595-8585
Fax: 361-592-0838
E-mail: rmadrid@co.kleberg.tx.us
Administrative Assistant: Frances Garcia
E-mail: fgarcia@co.kleberg.tx.us

**County Court at Law**
**Judge Pete De La Garza**
P.O. Box 1556
Kingsville, TX 78364-1556
Phone: 361-595-8565
Fax: 361-592-4218
E-mail: aisassi@co.kleberg.tx.us
Court Coordinator: Katherine Madrid

# KNOX COUNTY

Seat: Benjamin

100 W. Cedar St.
Benjamin, TX 79505

**District and County Clerk: Lisa Cypert**
P.O. Box 196
Benjamin, TX 79505-0196
Phone: 940-459-2441
Fax: 940-459-2005

**District Attorney: David W. Hajek**
*Please see Baylor County.*

**50th District Court**
**Judge Bobby D. Burnett** sits twice a month.
*Please see Cottle County.*

**County Judge: Stan Wojcik**
P.O. Box 77
Benjamin, TX 79505
Phone: 940-459-2191
Fax: 940-459-2022
Administrative Assistant: Sheri Warren

# LA SALLE COUNTY

Seat: Cotulla

101 Courthouse Square, Suite 107
Cotulla, TX 78014
www.lasallecountytx.org

**District and County Clerk: Margarita A. Esqueda**
Phone: 830-483-5120
E-mail: margie.esqueda@co.la-salle.tx.us

**District Attorney: René M. Peña**
*Please see Atascosa County.*

**81st District Court**
**Judge Donna S. Rayes** sits once a month.
*Please see Atascosa County.*

**218th District Court**
**Judge Russell Wilson** sits as scheduled.
*Please see Karnes County.*

**County Attorney: Elizabeth Martinez**
Phone: 830-483-5127

STATE, DISTRICT AND COUNTY COURTS

Fax: 830-483-5101
E-mail: elizabeth.martinez@co.la-salle.tx.us

**County Judge: Joel Rodriguez, Jr.**
Phone: 830-483-5139
Fax: 830-483-5110
E-mail: joel.rodriguez@co.la-salle.tx.us

# LAMAR COUNTY

Seat: Paris

119 N. Main St.
Paris, TX 75460
www.co.lamar.tx.us

**District Clerk: Shawntel Golden**
Room 405
Phone: 903-737-2427
Fax: 903-785-4905
E-mail: sgolden@co.lamar.tx.us

**District Attorney: Gary Young**
3rd Floor
Phone: 903-737-2458
Fax: 903-737-2455

**6th District Court**
**Judge Eric Clifford**
2nd Floor
Phone: 903-737-2432
Fax: 903-737-2483
Court Reporter: Terry Spangler
Phone: 903-737-2432
Bailiff: Ron Byers

**62nd District Court**
**Judge Will Biard**
2nd Floor
Phone: 903-438-2434
Fax: 903-737-2483
Court Reporter: Anna Upchurch
Phone: 903-737-2434
Bailiff: Ron Byers

**County Clerk: Russ Towers**
Phone: 903-737-2420
Fax: 903-782-1100
E-mail: countyclerk_lamar_txkm@yahoo.com

**County Judge: M. C. Superville, Jr.**
1st Floor
Phone: 903-737-2411

Fax: 903-785-3858
E-mail: judge_superville@co.lamar.tx.us

**County Court at Law**
**Judge Bill Harris**
4th Floor
Phone: 903-782-1104
Court Reporter: Mary Ann Taylor
Bailiff: Jason Garrett
Phone: 903-782-1103

# LAMB COUNTY

Seat: Littlefield

100 6th Dr.
Littlefield, TX 79339
www.co.lamb.tx.us

**District Clerk: Stephanie Chester**
Room 212
Phone: 806-385-4222, ext. 240
Fax: 806-385-3554
E-mail: 154districtclerk@nts-online.net

**District and County Attorney: Scott A. Say**
Room 111
Phone: 806-385-4222, ext. 208
Fax: 806-385-6485
E-mail: scottsay@nts-online.net
Assistant Attorney: Rickie Redman

**154th District Court**
**Judge Felix Klein**
Room 211
Phone: 806-385-4222, ext. 251
E-mail: 154districtcourt@nts-online.net
Court Coordinator: Jaime Leal

**County Clerk: Tonya Ritchie**
Room 103
Phone: 806-385-4222
Fax: 806-385-6485
E-mail: tonyaritchie@nts-online.net

**County Judge: James M. De Loach**
Room 101
Phone: 806-385-4222, ext. 200
Fax: 806-385-6485
E-mail: jmdeloach@nts-online.net
Administrative Assistant: Cynthia Bussey

# LAMPASAS COUNTY

Seat: Lampasas

409 S. Pecan St.
Lampasas, TX 76550
www.co.lampasas.tx.us

**District Clerk: Terri Cox**
P.O. Box 327
Lampasas, TX 76550-0327
Phone: 512-556-8271, ext. 240
Fax: 512-556-9463

**District and County Attorney: John Greenwood**
P.O. Box 1300
Lampasas, TX 76550-1300
Phone: 512-556-8271
Fax: 512-556-4572

**27th District Court**
**Judge John Gauntt** sits every Friday.
*Please see Bell County.*

**County Clerk: Connie Hartmann**
P.O. Box 347
Lampasas, TX 76550-0347
Phone: 512-556-8271, ext. 204
Fax: 512-556-8966

**County Judge: Wayne Boultinghouse**
P.O. Box 231
Lampasas, TX 76550-0231
Phone: 512-556-8271
Fax: 512-556-8270

# LAVACA COUNTY

Seat: Hallettsville

109 N. LaGrange St.
Hallettsville, TX 77964
www.co.lavaca.tx.us

**District Clerk: Sherry T. Henke**
P.O. Box 306
Hallettsville, TX 77964
Phone: 361-798-2351
Fax: 361-798-5674
E-mail: sherryh@lavacacounty.net

**25th District Court**
**Judge William D. Old, III** sits as scheduled.
*Please see Guadalupe County.*

**2nd 25th District Court**
**Judge W. C. "Bud" Kirkendall** sits as scheduled.
*Please see Guadalupe County.*

**County Clerk: Elizabeth Kouba**
412 N. Texana
Hallettsville, TX 77964
Phone: 361-798-3612
Fax: 361-798-1610

**County Attorney: John Stuart Fryer**
P.O. Box 576
Hallettsville, TX 77964-0576
Phone: 361-798-4757
Fax: 361-798-2816

**County Judge: Tramer J. Woytek**
P.O. Box 243
Hallettsville, TX 77964-0243
Phone: 361-798-2301
Fax: 361-798-5490

# LEE COUNTY

Seat: Giddings

200 S. Main St.
Giddings, TX 78942
www.co.lee.tx.us

**District Clerk: Lisa Teinert**
P.O. Box 176
Giddings, TX 78942
Phone: 979-542-2947
Fax: 979-542-2444
E-mail: lisa.teinert@co.lee.tx.us

**District and County Attorney: Martin Placke**
Room 305
Phone: 979-542-3233
Fax: 979-542-1226

**21st District Court**
**Judge Carson Campbell** sits as scheduled.
*Please see Washington County.*

**335th District Court**
**Judge Reva L. Towslee-Corbett** sits as scheduled.
*Please see Burleson County.*

**County Clerk: Sharon Blasig**
P.O. Box 419
Giddings, TX 78942
Phone: 979-542-3684
Fax: 979-542-2623
E-mail: sharon.blasig@co.lee.tx.us

**County Judge: Paul E. Fischer**
Room 107
Phone: 979-542-3178
Fax: 979-542-2988
E-mail: paul.fischer@co.lee.tx.us
Administrative Assistant: Jessica Graefe
E-mail: jessica.graefe@co.lee.tx.us

## LEON COUNTY

Seat: Centerville

139 E. Main St.
Centerville, TX 75833
www.co.leon.tx.us

**District Clerk: Beverly Wilson**
P.O. Box 39
Centerville, TX 75833
Phone: 903-536-2227
Fax: 903-536-5058

*Note: See District Clerk's Website for Leon County local rules and setting request form.*

**District Attorney: Hope Knight**
155 N. Cass St.
Centerville, TX 75833
Phone: 903-536-7161
Fax: 903-536-8000

**87th District Court**
**Judge Deborah Oakes Evans** sits as scheduled monthly on the 1st Monday and 3rd Friday.
*Please see Freestone County.*

**278th District Court**
**Judge Hal Ridley** sits monthly.
*Please see Walker County.*

**369th District Court**
**Judge Bascom W. Bentley, III** sits monthly.
*Please see Anderson County.*

**County Clerk: Christie Wakefield**
P.O. Box 98

Centerville, TX 75833
Phone: 903-536-2352
Fax: 903-536-7581
E-mail: christie.wakefield@co.leon.tx.us

**County Attorney: James R. Witt**
P.O. Box 429
Centerville, TX 75833
Phone: 903-536-2131
Fax: 903-536-7044
Administrative Assistant: Cassandra Noey

**County Judge: Byron Ryder**
P.O. Box 429
Centerville, TX 75833
Phone: 903-536-2331
Fax: 903-536-7044
Administrative Assistant: Lynda Bradley
E-mail: lynda.bradley@co.leon.tx.us

## LIBERTY COUNTY

Seat: Liberty

1923 Sam Houston St.
Liberty, TX 77575
www.co.liberty.tx.us

**District Clerk: Donna G. Brown**
Room 115
Phone: 936-336-4682
Fax: 936-336-1115

**District Attorney: Logan Pickett**
Phone: 936-336-4609
Fax: 936-336-4644

**75th District Court**
**Judge Mark Morefield**
Room 304
Phone: 936-336-4678
Fax: 936-334-8980
Court Coordinator: Peggy Thrasher
Court Reporter: Cliff Smith
Phone: 936-336-4679
Bailiff: John W. Davis, III

**253rd District Court**
**Judge Chap B. Cain, III**
Room 223
Phone: 936-336-4668
Court Coordinator: Linda Leonard
Court Reporter: Jo Anne Horn

Phone: 936-334-3210
Bailiff: Chadwick D. Elmore
Phone: 936-336-4642

**County Clerk: Paulette Williams**
P.O. Box 369
Liberty, TX 77575
Phone: 936-336-4670
Fax: 936-334-8174
E-mail: coclerk@co.liberty.tx.us

**County Attorney: Wesley Hinch**
Suite 202
Phone: 936-336-4650

**County Judge: Jay Knight**
Room 201
Phone: 936-336-4665
Fax: 936-336-4518
E-mail: cojudge@co.liberty.tx.us
Administrative Assistant: Diane Hartfield

**County Court at Law**
**Judge Thomas Chambers**
Room 222
Phone: 936-336-4662
E-mail: ccal@co.liberty.tx.us
Court Coordinator: Tiffany Slankard
E-mail: tiffany.slankard@co.liberty.tx.us
Court Reporter: Jamie Hudspeth
Bailiff: Robert Harper

# LIMESTONE COUNTY

Seat: Groesbeck

200 W. State St.
Groesbeck, TX 76642
www.co.limestone.tx.us

**District Clerk: Carol Jenkins**
P.O. Box 230
Groesbeck, TX 76642-0230
Phone: 254-729-3206
Fax: 254-729-2960
E-mail: carol.jenkins@limestone.tx.us

**District and County Attorney: William Roy DeFriend**
200 W. State St., Ste. 110
Groesbeck, TX 76642
Phone: 254-729-3814
Fax: 254-729-5699
E-mail: rdefriend@co.limestone.tx.us

**77th District Court**
**Judge Patrick Simmons**
P.O. Box 230
Groesbeck, TX 76642-0230
Phone: 254-729-5705
Fax: 254-729-2960
Court Coordinator: Martha Lynch
E-mail: martha.lynch@co.limestone.tx.us
Court Reporter: Sherry Current

**87th District Court**
**Judge Deborah Oakes Evans** sits as scheduled.
*Please see Freestone County.*

**County Clerk: Peggy Beck**
P.O. Box 350
Groesbeck, TX 76642-0350
Phone: 254-729-5504
Fax: 254-729-2951
E-mail: coclerk@co.limestone.tx.us

**County Judge: Daniel L. Burkeen**
Suite 101
Phone: 254-729-3810
Fax: 254-729-2643
E-mail: daniel.burkeen@co.limestone.tx.us
Administrative Assistant: Lori Moore
E-mail: lori.moore@co.limestone.tx.us

# LIPSCOMB COUNTY

Seat: Lipscomb

101 S. Main St.
Lipscomb, TX 79056
www.co.lipscomb.tx.us

**District and County Clerk: Kim Blau**
P.O. Box 70
Lipscomb, TX 79056-0070
Phone: 806-862-3091
Fax: 806-862-3004

**District Attorney: Franklin McDonough**
*Please see Gray County.*

**31st District Court**
**Judge Steven R. Emmert** sits once a month.
*Please see Wheeler County.*

County Attorney: Matthew Bartosiewicz
Phone: 806-658-4545
Fax: 806-658-4524
E-mail: matt@lemon-lawfirm.com

County Judge: Willis V. Smith
P.O. Box 69
Lipscomb, TX 79056-0069
Phone: 806-862-4131
Fax: 806-864-2603
Administrative Assistant: Nadine Barton

## LIVE OAK COUNTY

Seat: George West

301 Houston St.
George West, TX 78022
www.co.live-oak.tx.us

District Clerk: Melanie Matkin
P.O. Box 440
George West, TX 78022
Phone: 361-449-2733, ext. 1047
Fax: 361-449-2992

District Attorney: Jose Luis Aliseda, Jr.
*Please see Bee County.*

36th District Court
Judge Starr B. Bauer sits as scheduled.
*Please see San Patricio County.*

156th District Court
Judge Patrick L. Flanigan sits as scheduled.
*Please see San Patricio County.*

343rd District Court
Judge Janna K. Whatley sits as scheduled.
*Please see San Patricio County.*

County Clerk: Ida Vasquez
P.O. Box 280
George West, TX 78022
Phone: 361-449-2733, ext. 1080
Fax: 361-449-1616

County Attorney: Gene Chapline
P.O. Box 1588
George West, TX 78022
Phone: 361-449-2733, ext. 1025
Fax: 361-449-9488

County Judge: Jim Huff
P.O. Box 487
George West, TX 78022
Phone: 361-449-2733, ext. 1001
Fax: 361-449-3155

## LLANO COUNTY

Seat: Llano

832 Ford St.
Llano, TX 78643
www.co.llano.tx.us

District Clerk: Joyce Gillow
Phone: 325-247-5036
Fax: 325-248-0492
E-mail: joyce.gillow@co.llano.tx.us

District Attorney: Wiley B. "Sonny" McAfee
P.O. Box 725
Llano, TX 78643-0725
Phone: 325-247-5755
Fax: 325-247-5274

33rd District Court
Judge J. Allan Garrett sits as scheduled.
*Please see Burnet County.*

424th District Court
Judge Evan Stubbs sits as scheduled.
*Please see Burnet County.*

County Clerk: Marci Hadeler
P.O. Box 40
Llano, TX 78643
Phone: 325-247-4455
Fax: 325-247-2406

County Attorney: Rebecca Lange
801 Ford St.
Llano, TX 78643-1919
Phone: 325-247-7733
Fax: 325-247-7737

County Judge: Mary Cunningham
801 Ford St., Room 101
Llano, TX 78643-1919
Phone: 325-247-7730
Fax: 325-247-7732
E-mail: llanocountyjudge@co.llano.tx.us
Administrative Assistant: Jannelle Gray
E-mail: countyjudgeassistant@yahoo.com

# LOVING COUNTY

Seat: Mentone

100 Bell St.
Mentone, TX 79754
www.co.loving.tx.us

**District and County Clerk: Mozelle Carr**
P.O. Box 194
Mentone, TX 79754-0194
Phone: 432-377-2441
Fax: 432-377-2701
E-mail: cclerk@co.loving.tx.us

**District Attorney: Randall W. Reynolds**
*Please see Reeves County.*

**143rd District Court**
**Judge Mike Swanson** sits once a month.
*Please see Ward County.*

**County Legal Advisor: Ed Walton**
101 Metro Dr.
Terrell, TX 75160
Phone: 972-499-4833

**County Judge: Skeet Jones**
P.O. Box 193
Mentone, TX 79754
Phone: 432-377-2362
Fax: 432-377-2701

# LUBBOCK COUNTY

Seat: Lubbock

904 Broadway St.
Lubbock, TX 79408
www.co.lubbock.tx.us

**District Clerk: Barbara Sucsy**
P.O. Box 10536
Lubbock, TX 79408
Phone: 806-775-1310
Automated Menu: 806-775-1623
Fax: 806-775-7992

**Director of Court Administration: Dean Stanzione**
904 Broadway, Suite 325
Lubbock, TX 79408
Phone: 806-775-1355

Fax: 806-775-7996
E-mail: dstanzione@co.lubbock.tx.us
E-mail: webmaster@ co.lubbock.tx.us

**District Attorney: Matt D. Powell**
P.O. Box 10536
Lubbock, TX 79408
Phone: 806-775-1100

**72nd District Court**
**Judge Ruben G. Reyes**
3rd Floor
Phone: 806-775-1041
Court Coordinator: Judy Halford
Court Reporter: Rebecca Duval
Phone: 806-775-1040

**99th District Court**
**Judge William "Bill" C. Sowder**
3rd Floor
Phone: 806-775-1038
Court Coordinator: Sue Faison
Court Reporter: Susan Myatt
Phone: 806-775-1037

**137th District Court**
**Judge John J. McClendon, III**
3rd Floor
Phone: 806-775-1035
Court Coordinator: Audrey Beckham
Court Reporter: Breann Hays
Phone: 806-775-1034

**140th District Court**
**Judge Jim Bob Darnell**
3rd Floor
Phone: 806-775-1032
Court Coordinator: Rhonda Devitt
Court Reporter: Charles Hanshew
Phone: 806-775-1031

**237th District Court**
**Judge Les Hatch**
6th Floor
Phone: 806-775-1027
Court Coordinator: Brandi Loya
Court Reporter: Terri Ramsey
Phone: 806-775-1028
Bailiff: Mike Beckham
Phone: 806-778-1029

**364th District Court**
**Judge William R. Eichman, II**
3rd Floor
Phone: 806-775-1026

Fax: 806-775-7996
Court Coordinator: Angela Younglas
Court Reporter: Janette Bills
Phone: 806-775-1025

**Associate Judge: Stephen L. Johnson**
3rd Floor
Phone: 806-775-1702
Fax: 806-775-7996
Court Coordinator: Shannon Kunkel
Court Reporter: Vicki Laing

**County Clerk: Kelly Pinion**
Room 207
P.O. Box 10536
Lubbock, TX 79408
Phone: 806-775-1076
Fax: 806-775-1660

**County Judge: Thomas Head**
P.O. Box 10536
Lubbock, TX 79408
Phone: 806-775-1679
E-mail: thead@co.lubbock.tx.us

**County Court at Law No. 1**
**Judge Mark Hocker**
4th Floor
Phone: 806-775-1305
Court Coordinator: Lorie Tawney
Court Reporter: Tonya Rennels

**County Court at Law No. 2**
**Judge Drue Farmer**
4th Floor
Phone: 806-775-1301
Court Coordinator: Mary Koontz
Court Reporter: Michelle Malay
Phone: 806-775-1306

**County Court at Law No. 3**
**Judge Judy C. Parker**
Phone: 806-775-1309
Court Coordinator: Dalia Garcia
Court Reporter: Teri Finney
Phone: 806-775-1308

## LYNN COUNTY

Seat: Tahoka

S. First and Main St.
Tahoka, TX 79373
www.co.lynn.tx.us

**District Clerk: Sandra Laws**
P.O. Box 939
Tahoka, TX 79373-0939
Phone: 806-561-4274
Fax: 806-561-4151

**District Attorney: Michael Munk**
*Please see Dawson County.*

**106th District Court**
**Judge Carter T. Schildknecht** sits as scheduled.
*Please see Dawson County.*

**County Clerk: Susan Tipton**
P.O. Box 937
Tahoka, TX 79373-0937
Phone: 806-561-4750
Fax: 806-561-4988

**County Attorney: Rebekah Filley**
P.O. Box 848
Tahoka, TX 79373-0848
Phone: 806-561-5286
Fax: 806-561-5287

**County Judge: Mike Braddock**
P.O. Box 1167
Tahoka, TX 79373-1167
Phone: 806-561-4222
Fax: 806-561-4234

## MADISON COUNTY

Seat: Madisonville

101 W. Main St.
Madisonville, TX 77864
www.co.madison.tx.us

**District Clerk: Rhonda Savage**
Room 226
Phone: 936-241-6212
Fax: 936-349-1893
E-mail: rhonda.savage@madisoncountytx.org

**District and County Attorney: Brian Risinger**
Room 207
Phone: 936-348-7049
Fax: 936-348-7052
E-mail: brian.risinger@madisoncountytx.org

**12th District Court**
**Judge Donald L. Kraemer** sits as scheduled.
*Please see Walker County.*

278th District Court
Judge Hal Ridley sits as scheduled.
*Please see Walker County.*

## County Court
103 W. Trinity
Madisonville, TX 77864

**County Clerk: Susanne Morris**
Room 104
Phone: 936-241-6210
Fax: 936-241-6211
E-mail: susanne.morris@madisoncountytx.org

**County Judge: C.E. McDaniel**
Room 113
Phone: 936-241-6200, ext. 1132
Fax: 936-241-6201
E-mail: ce.mcdaniel@madisoncountytx.org
Administrative Assistant: April Covington
E-mail: april.covington@madisoncountytx.org

## MARION COUNTY

Seat: Jefferson

102 W. Austin St.
Jefferson, TX 75657
www.co.marion.tx.us

**District Clerk: Susan Anderson**
P.O. Box 628
Jefferson, TX 75657
Phone: 903-665-2441
Fax: 903-665-2102
E-mail: susan.anderson@co.marion.tx.us

**District Attorney: Angela Smoak**
Room 201
Phone: 903-665-2611
Fax: 903-665-3348

**115th District Court**
Judge Lauren L. Parish sits in March and September.
*Please see Upshur County.*

**276th District Court**
Judge Robert Rolston sits January, May and August.
*Please see Morris County.*

**County Clerk: Vickie Smith**
Room 206
Phone: 903-665-3971
Fax: 903-665-7936

**County Judge: Lex Jones**
Room 205
Phone: 903-665-3261
Fax: 903-665-8732

## MARTIN COUNTY

Seat: Stanton

301 N. Saint Peter St.
Stanton, TX 79782

**District and County Clerk: Sharon Jones**
P.O. Box 906
Stanton, TX 79782-0906
Phone: 432-756-3412
Fax: 432-607-2212
E-mail: martincounty@crcom.net

**District Attorney: Hardy L. Wilkerson**
*Please see Howard County.*

**118th District Court**
Judge Timothy D. Yeats, III sits once or twice a month.
*Please see Howard County.*

**County Attorney: James Napper**
P.O. Box 1370
Stanton, TX 79782
Phone: 432-756-2838
Fax: 432-756-2992
E-mail: napperlawoffice@gmail.com

**County Judge: Bryan Cox**
P.O. Box 1330
Stanton, TX 79782
Phone: 432-756-2231
Fax: 432-756-2992
Administrative Assistant: Missy Hernandez

## MASON COUNTY

Seat: Mason

201 Fort McKavitt St.
Mason, TX 76856
www.co.mason.tx.us

**District and County Clerk: Pam Beam**
P.O. Box 702
Mason, TX 76856-0702
Phone: 325-347-5253
Fax: 325-347-6868
E-mail: co.dist.clerk@co.mason.tx.us

**District Attorney: Tonya S. Ahlschwede**
P.O. Box 635
Mason, TX 76856
Phone: 325-347-8400
Fax: 325-347-8404

**452nd District Court**
**Judge Robert R. Hofman**
P.O. Box 1580
Mason, TX 76856
Phone: 325-347-0755
Fax: 325-347-0756

**County Attorney: Rebekah Witworth**
P.O. Box 157
Mason, TX 76856
Phone: 325-347-5614

**County Judge: Jerry Bearden**
P.O. Box 1726
Mason, TX 76856
Phone: 325-347-5556
Fax: 325-347-6868

# MATAGORDA COUNTY

Seat: Bay City

1700 Seventh St.
Bay City, TX 77414
www.co.matagorda.tx.us

**District Clerk: Jamie Bludau**
Room 307
Phone: 979-244-7621
E-mail: jamie@co.matagorda.tx.us

**District Attorney: Steven Reis**
Room 325
Phone: 979-244-7657
Fax: 979-245-9409
E-mail: sreis@co.matagorda.tx.us

**23rd District Court**
**Judge Ben Hardin** sits twice a month.
*Please see Brazoria County.*

**130th District Court**
**Judge Craig Estlinbaum**
Room 317
Phone: 979-244-7635
Fax: 979-245-6478
Court Coordinator: Bonnie Carlin
E-mail: bcarlin@co.matagorda.tx.us
Court Reporter: Kaye Rollins
Phone: 979-244-7639
Bailiff: Bill Orton

**County Clerk: Janet Hickl**
Room 202
Phone: 979-244-7680
Fax: 979-244-7688
E-mail: jhickl@co.matagorda.tx.us

**County Attorney: Denise Fortenberry**
Room 305
Phone: 979-244-7645
Fax: 979-244-7647

**County Judge: Nate McDonald**
Room 301
Phone: 979-244-7605
Fax: 979-245-3697

# MAVERICK COUNTY

Seat: Eagle Pass

500 Quarry St.
Eagle Pass, TX 78852
www.co.maverick.tx.us
**District Clerk: Leopoldo Vielma**
Suite 5
Phone: 830-773-2629
Fax: 830-773-4439

**District Attorney: Roberto Serna**
458 Madison St.
Eagle Pass, TX 78852
Phone: 830-773-9268
Fax: 830-773-9379

**293rd District Court**
**Judge Cynthia L. Muniz**
P.O. Box 4360
Eagle Pass, TX 78853
Phone: 830-758-1730
Court Coordinator: Aleida G. Castillo
Court Reporter: Susan Billanueva
Phone: 830-773-0662

**STATE, DISTRICT AND COUNTY COURTS**

**365th District Court**
**Judge Amado Abascal, III**
501 Main Street
Eagle Pass, TX 78852
Phone: 830-773-1151
Fax: 830-757-2720
Court Coordinator (Civil): Debbie Montoya
Court Coordinator (Criminal): Cecy Elizando
Court Coordinator (Family): Melissa Gonzalez
Court Reporter: Patricia Salinas

**County Clerk: Sara Montemayor**
Suite 2
Phone: 830-773-2829
Fax: 830-752-4479
E-mail: sara.montemayor@maverick.tx.us

**County Judge: David Saucedo**
Suite 3
Phone: 830-773-3824
Fax: 830-773-6450
Administrative Assistant: Linda Schmerber
Court Coordinator: Angelica Longoria

# MCCULLOCH COUNTY

Seat: Brady

Courthouse Square
Brady, TX 76825
www.co.mcculloch.tx.us

**District Clerk: Michelle Pitcox**
Room 103
Phone: 325-597-0733, ext. 1
Fax: 325-597-0606
E-mail: michelle.pitcox@co.mcculloch.tx.us

**District Attorney: Tonya S. Ahlschwede**
*Please see Mason County.*

**452nd District Court**
**Judge Robert R. Hofman** sits once a month.
*Please see Mason County.*

**County Clerk: Tina A. Smith**
Phone: 325-597-2400, ext. 2
Fax: 325-597-1731E-mail: mccoclerk1@
verizon.net

**County Attorney: Mark Marshall**
Phone: 325-597-9151

**County Judge: Danny Neal**
Phone: 325-597-0733, ext. 4
Administrative Assistant: Margarita Guiterrez

# MCLENNAN COUNTY

Seat: Waco

501 Washington Ave.
Waco, TX 76701
www.co.mclennan.tx.us

**District Clerk: Jon R. Gimble**
Criminal Courts Phone: 254-757-5054
Civil Courts Phone: 254-757-5057
E-mail: district.clerk@co.mclennan.tx.us
E-filing: www.efiletexas.gov

**District Attorney: Abelino "Abel" Reyna**
Phone: 254-757-5084
Fax: 254-757-5021
Hot Check Department: 254-757-5022

**19th District Court**
**Judge Ralph T. Strother**
Room 303
Phone: 254-757-5081
Fax: 254-759-5683
Court Coordinator: Ellen Watson
Assistant Court Coordinator: Jessica Schrader
Assistant Court Administrator: Michele Flores
Court Reporter: Rachell D. Karr

**54th District Court – Criminal Court**
**Judge Matt Johnson**
Room 305
Phone: 254-757-5051
Fax: 254-757-5002
Court Administrator: Penny Savage
Assistant Court Administrators: Paige Light
and Jessica Ficker
Court Reporters: Rebecca Rivera and
Heather Weiser

**74th District Court**
**Judge Gary Coley, Jr.**
2601 Gholson Rd.
Phone: 254-757-5075
Fax: 254-412-1396
Court Coordinator: Molly Renfroe
Juvenile Court Administrator: Lisa Blakemore
Court Reporter: Melinda Nichols

**170th District Court**
**Judge Jim Meyer**
Room 211
Phone: 254-757-5045
Fax: 254-757-5129
E-mail: 170th@co.mclennan.tx.us
Court Coordinator: Carla Childers
Court Reporter: Suzanne Hanus
Bailiff: Kathleen Daniel

**414th District Court**
**Judge Vicki L. Menard**
Room 307
Phone: 254-757-5053
Fax: 254-759-5620
E-mail: 414th@co.mclennan.tx.us
Court Coordinator: Laura Uptmore
Court Reporter: Teresa Santana
Bailiff: Jeff Anderson

**Associate Criminal District/County**
**Judge Douglas Vigil Bain**
Room 110
Phone: 254-757-5004

**County Court Master: Douglas R. Bergen**
600 Austin Ave.
Waco, TX 76701
Phone: 254-756-6607

**CPS Associate Judge: Nikki Mundkowsky**
Phone: 254-227-4538
Administrator: Marcus Crosby
E-mail: marcus.crosby@txcourts.gov

**County Clerk: J. A. "Andy" Harwell**
P.O. Box 1727
Waco, TX 76703-1727
Phone: 254-757-5078
Fax: 254-757-5146

**County Judge: Scott M. Felton**
P.O. Box 1728
Waco, TX 76703-1728
Phone: 254-757-5049
Administrative Assistant: Regan Copeland

**County Courts at Law Administrator: Leslie**
**Polansky**
Suite 210
Phone: 254-757-5030
Fax: 254-757-5013

**County Court at Law No. 1**
**Judge Mike Freeman**

Phone: 254-757-5030
Court Reporter: Debby Kelley
Phone: 254-757-5034

**County Court at Law No. 2**
**Judge Brad Cates**
2nd Floor
Phone: 254-757-5030
Court Reporter: Kathy McDaniel
Phone: 254-757-5038

# MCMULLEN COUNTY

Seat: Tilden

501 River St.
Tilden, TX 78072

**District and County Clerk: Mattie Sadovsky**
P.O. Box 235
Tilden, TX 78072-0235
Phone: 361-274-3215
Fax: 361-274-3858

**District Attorney: Jose Luis Aliseda, Jr.**
*Please see Bee County.*

**36th District Court**
**Judge Starr B. Bauer**
*Please see San Patricio County.*

**156th District Court**
**Judge Patrick Flanigan**
*Please see San Patricio County.*

**343rd District Court**
**Judge Janna K. Whatley**
*Please see San Patricio County.*

**County Judge: James Teal**
P.O. Box 237
Tilden, TX 78072
Phone: 361-274-3341
Fax: 361-274-3693
Administrative Assistant: Jayne Varga

# MEDINA COUNTY

Seat: Hondo

1100 16th St.
Hondo, TX 78861
www.medinacountytexas.org

**STATE, DISTRICT AND COUNTY COURTS**

**District Clerk: Cindy Fowler**
Room 209
Phone: 830-741-6070
Fax: 830-741-6015

**District Attorney: Daniel J. Kindred**
*Please see Uvalde County.*

**38th District Court**
**Judge Camile G. Dubose** sits as scheduled.
*Please see Uvalde County.*

**County Clerk: Lisa Wernette**
Room 109
Phone: 830-741-6040
Fax: 830-741-6015

**County Attorney: Kim Havel**
Phone: 830-741-6080
Fax: 830-741-6015

**County Judge: Chris Schuchart**
1502 Ave. K, Room 201
Hondo, TX 78861
Phone: 830-741-6020
Fax: 830-741-6025
E-mail: countyjudge@medinacountytexas.org
Court Coordinator: Jennifer Adlong
E-mail: jennifer.adlong@medinacountytexas.org

**County Court at Law**
**Judge Vivian Torres**
Room 203
Phone: 830-741-6060
Fax: 830-741-6064
Court Coordinator: Shanna Curiel
Phone: 830-741-6061
E-mail: shanna.curiel@medinacountytexas.org
Bailiffs: Andy Perez and Joey Tapia

## MENARD COUNTY

Seat: Menard

206 E. San Saba St.
Menard, TX 76859
www.co.menard.tx.us

**District and County Clerk: Ann Kothmann**
P.O. Box 1038
Menard, TX 76859
Phone: 325-396-4682
Fax: 325-396-2047
Deputy Clerk: Rhonda Cox

**District Attorney: Tonya S. Ahlschwede**
*Please see Mason County.*

**452nd District Court**
**Judge Robert R. Hofman** sits twice a month.
*Please see Mason County.*

**County Judge: Richard Cordes**
P.O. Box 1038
Menard, TX 76859-1038
Phone: 325-396-4789
Fax: 325-396-2047

## MIDLAND COUNTY

Seat: Midland
500 N. Loraine
Midland, TX 79701
www.co.midland.tx.us

**District Clerk: Ross Bush**
Suite 301
Phone: 432-688-4500
Fax: 432-688-4934

**District Attorney: Teresa Clingman**
2nd Floor
Phone: 432-688-4411
Fax: 432-688-4938

**142nd District Court**
**Judge George D. Gilles**
10th Floor
Phone: 432-688-4375
Fax: 432-688-4923
Court Coordinator: Ibefel Franco
Court Reporter: Melissa Crooks
Bailiff: Robert Carouth

**238th District Court**
**Judge Elizabeth Byer Leonard**
8th Floor
Phone: 432-688-4380
Fax: 432-688-4933
Court Coordinator: JoAnn Gonzalez
Court Reporter: Ruthie Cox
Bailiff: Mike Stamper

**318th District Court**
**Judge David W. Lindemord**
9th Floor
Phone: 432-688-4390
Fax: 432-688-4924

Court Coordinator: Claire Liddiard
Court Reporter: Laquita Dettman
Bailiff: Kevin Napier

**385th District Court**
**Judge Robin M. Darr**
8th Floor
Phone: 432-688-4385
Fax: 432-688-4935
Court Coordinator: Heather Henderson
Court Reporter: Kelly Allen
Bailiff: Keith Morris

**441st District Court**
**Judge Rodney Satterwhite**
9th Floor
Phone: 432-688-4520
Fax: 432-688-4981
Court Coordinator: Nancy Berdoza
Court Reporter: Monica Lancaster
Bailiff: Greg Travland

**County Clerk: Alison Haley**
4th Floor
Phone: 432-688-4490
Fax: 432-688-4926

**County Attorney: Russell Malm**
Suite 1103
Phone: 432-688-4490
Fax: 432-688-4931
Assistant County Attorneys: Kimberly
Carpenter and Ellen Griffith
Administrative Assistant: Leticia Hernandez

**County Judge: Mike Bradford**
Suite 1100
Phone: 432-688-4310
Fax: 432-688-4988
Administrative Assistant: Jenny Hilton

**County Court at Law No. 1**
**Judge Kyle Peeler**
6th Floor
Phone: 432-688-4460
Fax: 432-688-4929
Court Coordinator: Jessica Montoya
Court Reporter: Trina Finnell

**County Court at Law No. 2**
**Judge Marvin L. Moore**
6th Floor
Phone: 432-688-4460
Fax: 432-688-4929
Court Coordinator: Jessica Montoya
Court Reporter: Karen Tucker

# MILAM COUNTY

Seat: Cameron

102 S. Fannin St.
Cameron, TX 76520

**District Clerk: Karen Berry**
Suite 5
Cameron, TX 76520-0999
Phone: 254-697-7052
Fax: 254-697-7056
E-mail: kberry@milamcounty.net

**District Attorney: W.W. Torrey**
204 N. Central
Cameron, TX 76520
Phone: 254-697-7013
Fax: 254-697-7016

**20th District Court**
**Judge John W. Youngblood**
Suite 4
Phone: 254-697-7010
Court Coordinator: Judy Kopriva
Court Reporter: Angela Ralston

**County Clerk: Barbara Vansa**
107 W. Main St.
Cameron, TX 76520
Phone: 254-697-7049
Fax: 254-697-7055

**County Judge: Dave Barkemeyer**
102 S. Fannin St., Suite 1
Cameron, TX 76520
Phone: 254-697-7000
Fax: 254-697-7002

# MILLS COUNTY

Seat: Goldthwaite

1011 4th Street
Goldthwaite, TX 76844
www.co.mills.tx.us

**District and County Clerk: Carolyn Foster**
P.O. Box 646
Goldthwaite, TX 76844-0646
Phone: 325-648-2711
Fax: 325-648-3251
E-mail: carolyn.foster@co.mills.tx.us

STATE, DISTRICT AND COUNTY COURTS

District Attorney: Michael Murray
200 S. Broadway
Brownwood, TX 76801-3192
Phone: 325-646-0444

**35th District Court**
**Judge Stephen Ellis** sits as scheduled.
*Please see Brown County.*

County Attorney: Gerald Hale
1412 Fisher St.
Goldthwaite, TX 76844
P.O. Box 647
Phone: 325-648-2233

County Judge: Kirkland Fulk
P.O. Box 483
Goldthwaite, TX 76844
Phone: 325-648-2222

# MITCHELL COUNTY

Seat: Colorado City

349 Oak St.
Colorado City, TX 79512

District Clerk: Belinda Blassingame
Room 302
Phone: 325-728-5918
Fax: 325-728-8099
E-mail: bblassingame@co.mitchell.tx.us

District Attorney: Ann Reed
Room 208
Phone: 325-235-8639
Fax: 325-728-8697

**32nd District Court**
**Judge Glen Harrison** sits once a week.
*Please see Nolan County.*

County Clerk: Debby Carlock
Room 103
Phone: 325-728-3481, ext. 620
Fax: 325-728-5322
E-mail: dscarlock@co.mitchell.tx.us

County Attorney: Ty Wood
Room 206
Phone: 325-728-3457, ext. 2
Fax: 325-728-3944
Administrative Assistant: Nicole Naylor

County Judge: Currie Ray Mayo
Room 200
Phone: 325-728-8439
E-mail: r.mayo@co.mitchell.tx.us
Administrative Assistant: Patricia Denson

# MONTAGUE COUNTY

Seat: Montague

101 E. Franklin St.
Montague, TX 76251
www.co.montague.tx.us

District Clerk: Lesia Darden
P.O. Box 155
Montague, TX 76251-0155
Phone: 940-894-2571
Fax: 940-894-2077
E-mail: mdc97@windstream.net

District Attorney: Paige Williams
P.O. Box 55
Montague, TX 76251-0055
Phone: 940-894-6211
Fax: 940-894-6203

**97th District Court**
**Judge Jack A. McGaughey** sits as scheduled.
*Please see Clay County.*

County Clerk: Glenda Henson
P.O. Box 77
Montague, TX 76251-0077
Phone: 940-894-2461
Fax: 940-894-6601
E-mail: mcoclerk@windstream.net

County Attorney: Clay Riddle
P.O. Box 336
Montague, TX 76251-0336
Phone: 940-894-2261
Fax: 940-894-2805

County Judge: Rick Lewis
P.O. Box 475
Montague, TX 76251-0475
Phone: 940-894-2401
Fax: 940-894-3999
Administrative Assistant: Valorie Stout

# MONTGOMERY COUNTY

Seat: Conroe

301 N. Main St.
Conroe, TX 77301
www.mctx.org

**District Clerk: Barbara G. Adamick**
P.O. Box 2985
Conroe, TX 77305
Phone: 936-539-7855
E-mail: barbara.adamick@mctx.org

**District Attorney: Brett Ligon**
207 W. Phillips, 2nd Floor
Conroe, TX 77301
Phone: 936-539-7800
Fax: 936-760-6940

**9th District Court**
**Judge Kelly Case**
207 W. Phillips, Suite 306
Conroe, TX 77301
Phone: 936-539-7866
Fax: 936-788-8381
Court Administrator: Rebecca Templet
E-mail: rebecca.templet@mctx.org
Court Reporter: Rebecca Lewis

**221st District Court**
**Judge Lisa Michalk**
Phone: 936-539-7808
Court Coordinator: Natalie Stelly
Phone: 936-760-6903
E-mail: jennifer.wade@mctx.org
Assistant Court Coordinator: Tonnie Whitney
Court Reporter: Cathy M. Busa
Phone: 936-538-8133
Bailiff: Jackie Mitchell

**284th District Court**
**Judge Cara Wood**
Suite 201
Phone: 936-539-7861
Fax: 936-538-3572
Court Coordinator: Lindsey Karm
E-mail: lindsey.karm@mctx.org
Assistant Court Coordinator: Laurie Watson
Court Administrator: Amanda Whittington
E-mail: amanda.whittington@mctx.org
Court Reporter: Kenneth Cramer
E-mail: kenneth.cramer@mctx.org

Staff Counsel: Rag Johnson
Bailiff: Charlie Thompson

**359th District Court**
**Judge Kathleen A. Hamilton**
207 W. Phillips, Suite 305
Conroe, TX 77301
Phone: 936-539-7900
Fax: 936-538-8187
Court Coordinator (Criminal): Dayna Bass
E-mail: dayna.bass@mctx.org
Court Coordinator (Criminal): Susan Mitchell
E-mail: susan.mitchell@mctx.org
Court Reporter: Darlene Forville
E-mail: darlene.forville@mctx.org
Bailiff: Eddie Holmes

**410th District Court**
**Judge K. Michael Mayes**
Suite 200
Phone: 936-539-7860
Fax: 936-538-8160
Court Coordinator: Vicki Warner
E-mail: vicki.warner@mctx.org
Court Administrator: Cathy Ansley
E-mail: cathy.ansley@mctx.org
Court Reporter: Robin Cooksey
E-mail: robin.cooksey@mctx.org

**418th District Court**
**Judge Tracy A. Gilbert**
Suite 217
Phone: 936-538-3618
Fax: 936-538-3660
Court Coordinator: Timothy Parks
E-mail: timothy.parks@mctx.org
Court Administrator: Kimberly Perry
E-mail: kim.perry@mctx.org
Court Reporter: Christa C. Townes
E-mail: christa.townes@mctx.org

**435th District Court**
**Judge Michael Seiler**
301 N. Thompson, Suite 210
Conroe, TX 77301
Phone: 936-538-3532
Fax: 936-538-3619
Court Coordinator: April Knudsen
E-mail: april.knudsen@mctx.org
Court Reporter: Grey Cheney
Phone: 936-538-3638

**County Clerk: Mark Turnbull**
P.O. Box 959
Conroe, TX 77305-0959

Phone: 936-539-7885
Fax: 936-760-6990
E-mail: mark.turnbull@mctx.org

**County Attorney: J.D. Lambright**
207 W. Phillips, Suite 100
Conroe, TX 77301
Phone: 936-539-7828
Fax: 936-760-6920

**County Judge: Craig Doyal**
501 N. Thompson, Suite 401
Conroe, TX 77301
Phone: 936-539-7812
Fax: 936-760-6919
E-mail: cojudge@mctx.org
Administrative Assistants: Sylvia Olszowy
and Patti Werner

**County Court at Law No. 1**
**Judge Dennis Watson**
210 W. Davis St., Suite 201
Conroe, TX 77301
Phone: 936-539-7831
Fax: 936-538-8090
Court Coordinator: Peggy Inglet
Assistant Court Coordinator: Jessica Lamas
Court Reporter: Gracie Caka
E-mail: gracie.caka@mctx.org
Bailiff: Tammy T. Rowell

**County Court at Law No. 2**
**Judge Claudia Laird**
210 W. Davis St., Suite 300
Conroe, TX 77301
Phone: 936-539-7832
Fax: 936-788-8357
Court Coordinator: Peggy Freeman
E-mail: peggy.freeman@mctx.org
Court Reporter: Martha Koomar
E-mail: martha.koomar@mctx.org
Bailiff: Charles Rivette

**County Court at Law No. 3**
**Judge Patrice McDonald**
Phone: 936-539-7973
Fax: 936-760-6942
Court Administrator: Linda Newlin
E-mail: linda.newlin@mctx.org
Court Reporter: Nancy Eleby

**Associate Judge: Amy Atkinson**
Court Coordinator: Debbie Womack
E-mail: debbie.womack@mctx.org
Court Reporter: Kimberly Holzwarth

**County Court at Law No. 4**
**Judge Mary Ann Turner**
210 W. Davis St., Suite 400
Conroe, TX 77301
Phone: 936-538-8174
Fax: 936-760-6904
Court Coordinator: Therese Pringle
E-mail: therese.pringle@mctx.org
Assistant Court Coordinator: Liz Rubio
Phone: 936-538-3533
E-mail: liz.rubio@mctx.org
Court Reporter: Cassie McCoy
E-mail: cassie.mccoy@mctx.org
Bailiff: Javier Salinas

**County Court at Law No. 5**
**Judge Keith Stewart**
207 W. Phillips, Suite 306
Conroe, TX 77301
Phone: 936-538-3615
Fax: 936-538-3617
Court Coordinator: Barbara Nichols
Phone: 936-538-8004
Assistant Court Clerk: Tina Solomon
Court Reporter: Cherie Reegs
Phone: 936-538-3663
Bailiff: Rodney Vanhowten

# MOORE COUNTY

Seat: Dumas

715 Dumas Ave.
Dumas, TX 79029
www.co.moore.tx.us

**District Clerk: Diane Hoefling**
Room 109
Phone: 806-935-4218
Fax: 806-935-6325
E-mail: dhoefling@moore-tx.us
Chief Deputy: J. Holguin
E-mail: jholguin@moore-tx.us

**District Attorney: David M. Green**
Room 304
Phone: 806-935-5654
Fax: 806-935-5655
E-mail: 69thda@moore-tx.com
Assistant District Attorney: Jessica Edwards
E-mail: 69thada@moore-tx.com
Crime Victim Coordinator E-mail:
69thacvc@moore-tx.com

**STATE, DISTRICT AND COUNTY COURTS**

Office Manager: Suzanne DiPiazza
E-mail: 69thdaadm@moore-tx.com

**69th District Court**
**Judge Ron E. Enns**
Room 302
Phone: 806-935-2700
Fax: 806-935-5500
E-mail: renns@moore-tx.com
Court Coordinator: Shalyn Burritt
Court Reporter: Shelly Burnett

**County Clerk: Brenda McKanna**
Room 107
Phone: 806-935-2009
Fax: 806-935-9004
E-mail: bmckanna@moore-tx.com

**County Attorney: Scott Higginbotham**
Room 208
Phone: 806-935-2407
Fax: 806-935-6690
E-mail: mcatty@moore-tx.com

**County Judge: Rowdy Rhoades**
Room 202
Phone: 806-935-5588
Fax: 806-935-5697
E-mail: judgerhoades@moore-tx.com
Administrative Assistant: Carolyn Moore
E-mail: cmoore@moore-tx.com

**County Court at Law**
**Judge Delwin T. McGee**
Room 206
Phone: 806-935-2440
Fax: 806-935-5102
E-mail: delwinmcgee@moore-tx.com
Court Coordinator: Cathy Burnett
E-mail: cburnett@moore-tx.com
Court Reporter: Sherry Kloos

# MORRIS COUNTY

Seat: Daingerfield

500 Broadnax St.
Daingerfield, TX 75638
www.co.morris.tx.us

**District Clerk: Gwen Ashworth**
Phone: 903-645-2321
Fax: 903-645-3433

**District and County Attorney: Steve Cowan**
Phone: 903-645-2021
Fax: 903-645-7666

**76th District Court**
**Judge Danny Woodson** sits as scheduled.
*Please see Titus County.*

**276th District Court**
**Judge Robert Rolston**
P.O. Box 2224
Mt. Pleasant, TX 75636
Phone: 903-645-3556
Court Reporter: Linda Carroll
Phone: 903-645-2581

**County Clerk: Scott Sartain**
Suite D
Phone: 903-645-3911
Fax: 903-645-4026
E-mail: scott.sartain@co.morris.tx.us

**County Judge: Lynda Munkres**
Phone: 903-645-3691
Fax: 903-645-5729
Administrative Assistant: Sherry Ray

# MOTLEY COUNTY

Seat: Matador

701 Dundee
Matador, TX 79244

**District and County Clerk: Jamie Martin**
P.O. Box 660
Matador, TX 79244
Phone: 806-347-2621
Fax: 806-347-2792
E-mail: jamiem@caprock-spur.com

**District Attorney: Becky McPherson**
*Please see Floyd County.*

**110th District Court**
**Judge William P. Smith** sits once a month.
*Please see Floyd County.*

**County Attorney: Tom Edwards**
P.O. Box 678
Matador, TX 79244
Phone: 806-347-2391
Fax: 806-347-2343

County Judge: James B. "Jim" Meader
P.O. Box 719
Matador, TX 79244
Phone: 806-347-2334
Fax: 806-347-2072
E-mail: mcjudge@yahoo.com

# NACOGDOCHES COUNTY

Seat: Nacogdoches

101 W. Main St.
Nacogdoches, TX 75961
www.co.nacogdoches.tx.us

**District Clerk: Loretta Cammack**
Room 120
Phone: 936-560-7730
Fax: 936-560-7839

**District Attorney: Nicole LoStracco**
Room 250
Phone: 936-560-7766
Fax: 936-560-6036

**145th District Court**
**Judge Campbell Cox, II**
Room 220
Phone: 936-560-7748
Fax: 936-560-7826
Court Coordinator: Pat Littleton
Court Reporter: Candace Parke
Bailiff: Mark Morris

**420th District Court**
**Judge Edwin A. Klein**
Room 210
Phone: 936-560-7848
Fax: 936-560-7899
Court Coordinator: Pamela Sowell
E-mail: pam.sowell@co.nacogdoches.tx.us
Court Reporter: Andrea Simmons
Bailiff: Angela Russell

**County Clerk: June Clifton**
Room 110
Phone: 936-560-7733
Fax: 936-559-5926

**County Attorney: John Fleming**
Room 230
Phone: 936-560-7788

Fax: 936-560-7809

**County Judge: Mike Perry**
Room 170
Phone: 936-560-7755
Fax: 936-560-7841
Administrative Assistant: Shannon Burkley

**County Court at Law**
**Judge Jack Sinz**
Room 240
Phone: 936-560-7744
Fax: 936-560-7830
Court Coordinator: Lisa Patton
Phone: 936-560-7742
Administrative Assistant: Tara Williams
Court Reporter: Gary Harris
Phone: 936-560-7815
Bailiff: Loyal Madden

# NAVARRO COUNTY

Seat: Corsicana

800 N. Main St.
Corsicana, TX 75110
www.co.navarro.tx.us

*Note: We will be moving back the the
courthouse soon*
300 W. Third Street, Corsicana, TX 75110

**District Clerk: Joshua B. Tackett**
P.O. Box 1439
Corsicana, TX 75151-1439
Phone: 903-654-3040
Fax: 903-654-3088

**District Attorney: R. Lowell Thompson**
P.O. Box 1150
Corsicana, TX 75151
Phone: 903-654-3047
Fax: 903-872-6858
Administrative Assistant: Cindy Douglas

**13th District Court**
**Judge James E. Lagomarsino**
P.O. Box 333
Corsicana, TX 75151-0333
Phone: 903-654-3020
Fax: 903-654-2704
E-mail: jlagomarsino@navarrocounty.org
Court Coordinator: Melissa Butler

E-mail: mbutler@navarrocounty.org
Court Reporter: Leslie Kirk
Phone: 903-654-3022
E-mail: lkirk@navarrocounty.org
Bailiff: Calvin Gray

**County Clerk: Sherry Dowd**
P.O. Box 423
Corsicana, TX 75151-0423
Phone: 903-654-3035
Fax: 903-872-7329

**County Judge: H. M. Davenport, Jr.**
Suite 102
Phone: 903-654-3025
Fax: 903-654-0778
Administrative Assistant: Sherlyn Curtis

**County Court at Law**
**Judge Amanda Putman**
Temporary Location:
800 N. Main
Corsicana, TX 75110
Phone: 903-875-3322
Fax: 903-875-3326
Court Coordinator: Courtney Kirk
Court Reporter: Lisa Easley
Phone: 903-875-3323
Bailiff: Johnny Johnson

# NEWTON COUNTY

Seat: Newton

110 Court St.
Newton, TX 75966
www.co.newton.tx.us

**District Clerk: Bree Allen**
P.O. Box 535
Newton, TX 75966
Phone: 409-379-3951
Fax: 409-379-9087
E-mail: bree.allen@co.newton.tx.us

**District Attorney: Courtney Tracy-Ponthier**
P.O. Drawer 36
Newton, TX 75966
Phone: 409-379-8600
Fax: 409-379-8603

**1st District Court**
**Judge Craig Mixson** sits on the third Thursday
of every month.
*Please see Jasper County.*

**1A District Court**
**Judge DeLinda Gibbs-Walker** sits on the first
Thursday of each month.
*Please see Jasper County.*

**County Clerk: Sandra K. Duckworh**
P.O. Box 484
Newton, TX 75966
Phone: 409-379-5341
Fax: 409-379-9049
E-mail: sandra.duckworth@co.newton.tx.us

**County Judge: Truman Dougharty**
110 Court St.
Newton, TX 75966
Phone: 409-379-5691
Fax: 409-379-2107
E-mail: truman.dougharty@co.newton.tx.us
Administrative Assistant: Rosemary Johnson

# NOLAN COUNTY

Seat: Sweetwater

100 E. 3rd St.
Sweetwater, TX 79556
www.co.nolan.tx.us

**District Clerk: Jamie Clem**
Room 200
Phone: 325-235-2111

**District Attorney: Ann Reed**
Room 201
Phone: 325-235-8639
Fax: 325-235-5886

**32nd District Court**
**Judge Glen Harrison**
Room 204
Phone: 325-235-3133
Court Administrator: Becky Stewart

**County Clerk: Patricia McGowan**
Room 108
Phone: 325-235-2462
Fax: 325-235-4635
E-mail: pat.mcgowan@co.nolan.tx.us

**County Attorney: Lisa Peterson**
Room 103
Phone: 325-235-5469
Fax: 325-236-9416

STATE, DISTRICT AND COUNTY COURTS

County Judge: Whitley May
Room 105
Phone: 325-235-2263
Fax: 325-236-9416
Administrative Assistant: Amy Corbell

**County Court at Law**
**Judge David Hall**
Room 107
Phone: 325-235-2353
Fax: 325-236-8098
Court Coordinator: Yvonne Lehnert
Court Reporter: Brenda Valdez

# NUECES COUNTY

Seat: Corpus Christi

901 Leopard St.
Corpus Christi, TX 78401
www.co.nueces.tx.us/courts

**District Clerk: Anne Lorentzen**
P.O. Box 2987
Corpus Christi, TX 78403
Phone: 361-888-0472
Fax: 361-888-0571
E-mail: nueces.districtclerk@co.nueces.tx.us

**District Attorney: Mark Skurka**
Suite 206
Phone: 361-888-0410
Fax: 361-888-0399
E-mail: nueces.districtattorney@co.nueces.tx.us

**28th District Court**
**Judge Nanette Hasette**
Room 803
Phone: 361-888-0506
Court Coordinator: Linda M. Harrison
Court Clerk: Ashley Lerma
Court Reporter: Rebecca Rendon
Phone: 361-888-0636
Bailiff: Herman Cantu

**94th District Court**
**Judge Bobby Galvan**
Room 901
Phone: 361-888-0320
Fax: 361-888-0730
Court Coordinator: Ann Marie Cortez
Court Reporter: Sara Rivera
Phone: 361-888-0658

**105th District Court**
**Judge Jack W. Pulcher**
Room 802
Phone: 361-888-0510
Fax: 361-595-0293
Court Coordinator: Tehrra Whipple
E-mail: twhipple@kcscd.com
Court Manager: Amanda M. De La Cerda
E-mail: amanda.delacerda@kcscd.com
Court Reporter: Maggie Raiford
Phone: 361-888-0640
E-mail: maggie.raiford@kcscd.com
Bailiff: Henry Cantu
E-mail: henry.cantu@kcscd.com

**117th District Court**
**Judge Sandra L. Watts**
Room 904
Phone: 361-888-0436
E-mail: 117district.court@nuecesco.com
Court Coordinator: Lilian Fanning
Court Clerk: Subronze Lucas
Court Reporter: Olivia Oballe-Aguilar
Phone: 361-888-0662
Bailiff: Art Gallegos

**148th District Court**
**Judge Guy Williams**
Room 903
Phone: 361-888-0333
Fax: 361-888-0798
Court Coordinator: Thelma A. Lopez
E-mail: thelma.lopez1@nuecesco.com
Court Clerk: Rey Garcia
Court Reporter: Sandra Chavez
Phone: 361-888-0738
Bailiff: Jimmy Solis

**214th District Court**
**Judge Jose Longoria**
Room 902
Phone: 361-888-0463
Fax: 361-888-0671
E-mail: 214district.court@nuecesco.com
Court Coordinator: Melissa McCollum
Court Clerk: Estella Perez
Court Reporter: Kori Hosek
Auxiliary Court Reporter: Valeria Vargas
Phone: 361-888-0238
Bailiff: Anthony Walls

**319th District Court**
**Judge David Stith**
Room 801
Phone: 361-888-0533

Fax: 361-888-0644
Court Coordinator: Sandra J. Banuelos
Court Clerk: Melinda Molina
Court Reporter: Esther Natividad
Phone: 361-888-0645
Bailiff: John Lorenzi

**347th District Court**
**Judge Missy Medary**
Room 804
Phone: 361-888-0593
E-mail: 347district.court@nuecesco.com
Court Coordinator: Andrew C. Garcia
E-mail: andrew.garcia@nuecesco.com
Court Clerk: Krystla Tamez
Court Reporter: Myra Haney
Phone: 361-888-0379
Bailiff: David Alaniz

**County Clerk: Kara Sands**
P.O. Box 2627
Corpus Christi, TX 78403
Phone: 361-888-0580
Fax: 361-888-0329

**County Attorney: Laura Garza Jimenez**
Suite 207
Phone: 361-888-0391
Fax: 361-888-0577

**County Judge: Samuel Loyd Neal, Jr.**
Room 303
Phone: 361-888-0444
E-mail: loyd.neal@co.nueces.tx.us
Chief Assistant: Claudia Lobell

**County Court at Law No. 1**
**Judge Robert J. Vargas**
Suite 701
Phone: 361-888-0344
E-mail: county.court1@nuecesco.com
Court Coordinator: Mary A. Greses
Court Reporter: Patricia Morales
Phone: 361-888-0252
Bailiff: Arturo Treviño

**County Court at Law No. 2**
**Judge Lisa Gonzales**
Suite 702
Phone: 361-888-0596
Fax: 361-888-0250
E-mail: county.court2@nuecesco.com
Court Coordinators: Elisa Avila and Sandra
Medina
Phone: 361-888-9630

Court Reporter: Otilia Serna
Phone: 361-888-0528
Bailiff: Jerry Cantu
Phone: 361-888-0630

**County Court at Law No. 3**
**Judge Deeanne Galvan**
Suite 703
Phone: 361-888-0466
E-mail: county.court3@nuecesco.com
Court Coordinator: Patricia Resendez
Court Clerk: Robin Caron
Court Reporter: Phyllis Morris
Phone: 361-888-0625
Bailiff: Juan Esqueda

**County Court at Law No. 4**
**Judge Mark H. Woerner**
Suite 704
Phone: 361-888-0237
E-mail: county.court4@nuecesco.com
Court Coordinator: Christina Cadena
Court Clerk: Cathy Morin
Court Reporter: Jessica Ramirez
Phone: 361-888-0724
Bailiff: Raul Salazar

**County Court at Law No. 5**
**Judge Timothy J. McCoy**
2310 Gollihar
Corpus Christi, TX 78415
Phone: 361-561-6056
Fax: 361-561-6142
E-mail: county.court5@nuecesco.com
Court Coordinator: Bernice Perez-Beem
E-mail: bernice.perez-beem@nuecesco.com
Court Clerk: Debora Tamez
Phone: 361-561-6057
Court Reporter: Victoria Ortiz
Phone: 361-561-6063
Bailiff: David Matson
Phone: 361-561-6065

# OCHILTREE COUNTY

Seat: Perryton

511 S. Main St.
Perryton, TX 79070
www.co.ochiltree.tx.us

**District Clerk: Shawn Bogard**
Phone: 806-435-8054
Fax: 806-435-8058

**STATE, DISTRICT AND COUNTY COURTS**

**84th District Court**
Judge William "Bill" D. Smith sits two times a week.
*Please see Hansford County.*

**County Clerk: Stacey Brown**
Phone: 806-435-8039
Fax: 806-435-2081

**County Attorney with Felony Jurisdiction:**
**Barrett Dye**
9 S.E. 5th St.
Perryton, TX 79070
Phone: 806-435-8035
Fax: 806-435-8069

**County Judge: Earl McKinley**
Phone: 806-435-8031
Fax: 806-435-2081

# OLDHAM COUNTY

Seat: Vega

105 S. Main St.
Vega, TX 79092
www.co.oldham.tx.us

**District and County Clerk: Darla Lookingbill**
P.O. Box 360
Vega, TX 79092-0360
Phone: 806-267-2667
Fax: 806-267-2671
E-mail: darla.lookingbill@oldham-county.org

**District and County Attorney: Kent Birdsong**
P.O. Box 698
Vega, TX 79092-0698
Phone: 806-267-2233
Fax: 806-267-2798
E-mail: ocatty@oldham-county.org

**222nd District Court**
Judge Roland Saul sits once a month.
*Please see Deaf Smith County.*

**County Judge: Don R. Allred**
P.O. Box 195
Vega, TX 79092-0187
Phone: 806-267-2607
Fax: 806-267-2671
E-mail: don.allred@oldham-county.org
Secretary: Erica McDowell

# ORANGE COUNTY

Seat: Orange

801 W. Division Ave.
Orange, TX 77630
www.co.orange.tx.us

**District Clerk: Vickie Edgerly**
Phone: 409-882-7825
Fax: 409-882-7083
E-mail: vedgerly@co.orange.tx.us

**District and County Attorney: John D. Kimbrough**
Phone: 409-883-6764
Fax: 409-883-9322
E-mail: jkimbrough@co.orange.tx.us

**128th District Court**
Judge Courtney Arkeen
Phone: 409-882-7085
Fax: 409-670-4101
Court Coordinator: Latouia DuBois
E-mail: lleverett@co.orange.tx.us
Court Reporter: Holli Harrison
Bailiff: James Lucia

**163rd District Court**
Judge Dennis Powell
Phone: 409-882-7090
Fax: 409-882-7824
Court Coordinator: Jennifer Fleming
E-mail: dblalock@co.orange.tx.us
Court Reporter: Sarah Moreland
Bailiff: DeWayne Dahl

**260th District Court**
Judge Buddie J. Hahn
Phone: 409-882-7095
Fax: 409-882-7093
Court Coordinator: Judy Mingle
E-mail: jmingle@co.orange.tx.us
Court Reporter: Kellie Derouen
Bailiff: Brian Bishop

**County Clerk: Brandy Robertson**
Phone: 409-882-7055
Fax: 409-882-7012
E-mail: countyclerk@co.orange.tx.us

**County Judge: Stephen Brint Carlton**
123 S. 6th St.
Orange, TX 77630

**STATE, DISTRICT AND COUNTY COURTS**

Phone: 409-882-7070
Fax: 409-882-7079
Administrative Assistant: Holly Wheeler
E-mail: hwheeler@co.orange.tx.us

**County Court at Law**
**Judge Mandy White-Rogers**
Phone: 409-882-7084
Fax: 409-882-7843
Court Coordinator: Jennifer Ellis
E-mail: jellis@co.orange.tx.us
Court Reporter: Holly Wells
Phone: 409-882-7235
Bailiff: Trish Williams

**County Court at Law No. 2**
**Judge Troy Johnson**
Phone: 409-670-4189
Fax: 409-670-4193
Court Coordinator: Jessica Lupo
E-mail: jlupo@co.orange.tx.us
Court Reporter: Cristy Burnett
Bailiff: Eddie Robertson

# PALO PINTO COUNTY

Seat: Palo Pinto

520 Oak St.
Palo Pinto, TX 76484
www.co.palo-pinto.tx.us

**District Clerk: Janie Glover**
P.O. Box 189
Palo Pinto, TX 76484-0189
Phone: 940-659-1279

**District Attorney: Michael K. Burns**
P.O. Box 340
Palo Pinto, TX 76484-0340
Phone: 940-659-1251
Fax: 940-659-3885

**29th District Court**
**Judge Mike Moore**
P.O. Box 187
Palo Pinto, TX 76484-0187
Phone: 940-659-1274
Fax: 940-659-4113
Court Coordinator: Teresia Greenhaw
Court Reporter: Elizabeth Bourquin

**County Clerk: Janette K. Green**
P.O. Box 219
Palo Pinto, TX 76484
Phone: 940-659-1277
Fax: 844-769-4796
E-mail: janette.green@co.palo-pinto.tx.us

**County Attorney: Phil "Bud" Garrett**
P.O. Box 190
Palo Pinto, TX 76484
Phone: 940-659-1278
Fax: 940-659-4210

**County Judge: David C. Nicklas**
P.O. Box 190
Palo Pinto, TX 76484
Phone: 940-659-1253
Fax: 888-965-1552
E-mail: david.nicklas@co.palo-pinto.tx.us
Court Coordinator: Linda Hunsinger

# PANOLA COUNTY

Seat: Carthage

110 S. Sycamore St.
Carthage, TX 75633
www.co.panola.tx.us

**District Clerk: Debra Johnson**
Room 227
Phone: 903-693-0306
Fax: 903-693-6914
E-mail: debra.johnson@co.panola.tx.us

**District Attorney: Danny B. Davidson**
108 S. Sycamore, Suite 301
Carthage, TX 75633
Phone: 903-693-0310
Fax: 903-693-0368
E-mail: panolada@dctexas.net
Assistant District Attorney: Ken Hill
E-mail: ken.hill@co.panola.tx.us
Assistant District Attorney: Katie Nielsen
E-mail: katie.nielsen@co.panola.tx.us

**123rd District Court**
**Judge Charles C. Dickerson** sits as scheduled.
*Please see Shelby County.*

**County Clerk: Bobbie Davis**
Room 201
Phone: 903-693-0302

**STATE, DISTRICT AND COUNTY COURTS**

Fax: 903-693-0328
E-mail: b.davis@co.panola.tx.us

**County Judge: Lee Ann Jones**
Room 216-A
Phone: 903-693-0391
Fax: 903-693-2726
E-mail: leeann.jones@co.panola.tx.us

**County Court at Law**
**Judge Terry D. Bailey**
108 S. Sycamore St., Suite 300
Carthage, TX 75633
Phone: 903-693-0396
Fax: 903-693-3046
E-mail: terry.bailey@co.panola.tx.us
Court Coordinator: Erin Johnson
Court Reporter: Sherri Murphy
Phone: 903-693-0315
E-mail: sherri.murphy@co.panola.tx.us

# PARKER COUNTY

Seat: Weatherford

1 Courthouse Square
Weatherford, TX 76086
www.parkercountytx.com

**District Clerk: Sharena Gilliland**
117 Fort Worth Hwy.
Weatherford, TX 76086
Phone: 817-598-6114
Fax: 817-598-6131

**District Attorney: Don Schnebly**
117 Fort Worth Hwy.
Weatherford, TX 76086
Phone: 817-598-6124
Fax: 817-599-7628

**43rd District Court**
**Judge Craig Towson**
117 Fort Worth Hwy.
Weatherford, TX 76086
Phone: 817-598-6070
Court Coordinator: JoLene DuBoise
Assistant Coordinator: Julie Hendrick
Phone: 817-598-6069
Court Reporter: Glenna Windell
Bailiff: LeAnn Tyson

**415th District Court**
**Judge Graham Quisenberry**
117 Fort Worth Hwy.
Weatherford, TX 76086
Phone: 817-598-6162
Court Coordinator (Civil): Dawn Ryle
Court Coordinator (Criminal): Sheila Scruggs
Court Reporter: Kim Cherry
Bailiff: Doris Allbritton

**County Clerk: Jeane Brunson**
1112 Santa Fe Dr.
Weatherford, TX 76086
Phone: 817-594-7461

**County Attorney: John Forrest**
118 W. Columbia St.
Weatherford, TX 76086
Phone: 817-594-8409
Fax: 817-594-8414

**County Judge: Mark Riley**
Phone: 817-598-6148
Fax: 817-598-6199
E-mail: judge.riley@parkercountytx.com
Office Manager: Brandy Bissland

**County Court at Law No. 1**
**Judge Jerry Buckner**
1112 Santa Fe Dr.
Weatherford TX 76086
Phone: 817-598-6179
Fax: 817-598-6119
Court Coordinator: Brandy Ochs
E-mail: brandy.ochs@parkercountytx.com
Assistant Court Coordinator: Beverly O'Boyle
E-mail: beverly.oboyle@parkercountytx.com
Court Reporter: Jana Thomas
E-mail: jana.thomas@parkercountytx.com
Bailiff: Cathy Laine
E-mail: cathy.laine@parkercountytx.com

**County Court at Law No. 2**
**Judge Curtis Jenkins**
Phone: 817-598-6195
Court Coordinator: Kierin Johnson
E-mail: kierin.johnson@parkercountytx.com
Assistant Court Coordinator: Robin Girard
E-mail: robin.girard@parkercountytx.com
Court Reporter: Julie Booth
E-mail: julie.booth@parkercountytx.com
Bailiff: Mike Taylor
E-mail: mike.taylor@parkercountytx.com

# PARMER COUNTY

Seat: Farwell

401 Third St.
Farwell, TX 79325
www.co.parmer.tx.us

**District Clerk: Sandra Warren**
P.O. Box 195
Farwell, TX 79325-0195
Phone: 806-481-3419
Fax: 806-481-9416
E-mail: pcdc@parmercounty.net
Chief Deputy: Rose Longley
Deputy: Adrian Ancira

**District Attorney: Kathryn H. Gurley**
P.O. Box 729
Friona, TX 79325-0729
Phone: 806-250-2050
Fax: 806-250-9053

**287th District Court**
**Judge Gordon H. Green** sits on Tuesdays and
Thursdays.
*Please see Bailey County.*

**County Clerk: Gerri Bowers**
P.O. Box 356
Farwell, TX 79325
Phone: 806-481-3691
Fax: 806-481-9548
Deputies: Stacey Lamb

**County Attorney: Jeff W. Actkinson**
P.O. Box 286
Farwell, TX 79325-0286
Phone: 806-481-3361
Fax: 806-481-9060

**County Judge: Trey Ellis**
P.O. Box 506
Farwell, TX 79325
Phone: 806-481-3383
Fax: 806-481-9548
Administrative Assistant: Michelle Agee

# PECOS COUNTY

Seat: Fort Stockton

400 S. Nelson St.

Fort Stockton, TX 79735
www.co.pecos.tx.us/gov.html

**District Clerk: Gayle Henderson**
Phone: 432-336-3503
Fax: 432-336-6437
E-mail: gayle.henderson@co.pecos.tx.us

**83rd District Attorney: Rod Ponton**
Phone: 432-336-3322
Fax: 432-336-8333

**112th District Attorney: Laurie K. English**
Phone: 432-336-6294
Fax: 432-336-3839
E-mail: lke112da@aol.com

**83rd District Court**
**Judge Robert E. Cadena** sits as scheduled.
*Please see Val Verde County.*

**112th District Court**
**Judge Pedro Gomez, Jr.** sits as scheduled.
*Please see Crockett County.*

## County Court
200 S. Nelson St.
Fort Stockton, TX 79735

**County Clerk: Liz Chapman**
200 S. Nelson St.
Fort Stockton, TX 79735
Phone: 432-336-7555
Fax: 432-336-7557
E-mail: liz.chapman@co.pecos.tx.us

**County Attorney: Ori White**
103 W. Callaghan
Fort Stockton, TX 79735
Phone: 432-336-3742
Fax: 432-336-2299
E-mail: pcatty@co.pecos.tx.us

**County Judge: Joe Shuster**
103 W. Callaghan
Fort Stockton, TX 79735
Phone: 432-336-2792
Fax: 432-336-6640
E-mail: judge@co.pecos.tx.us

**County Bailiff: Ron Tucker**
Phone: 432-336-3521
Fax: 432-336-2519

**STATE, DISTRICT AND COUNTY COURTS**

## POLK COUNTY

Seat: Livingston

101 W. Mill St.
Livingston, TX 77351
www.co.polk.tx.us

**District Clerk: Bobby J. Richards**
101 W. Mill St., Suite 216
Livingston, TX 77351
Phone: 936-327-6814
Fax: 936-327-6851
E-mail: districtclerk@co.polk.tx.us

**District Attorney: Lee Hon**
101 west Mill Street, Suite 247
Phone: 936-327-6868
Fax: 936-327-6875

**258th District Court**
**Judge Ernest L. McClendon**
101 W. Mill Street, Suite 286
Phone: 936-327-6847
Fax: 936-327-6881
Court Coordinator: Leona Wiggins
Court Reporter: Krista Strouse
Bailiff: Bernita Langly
E-mail: 258court@co.polk.tx.us

**411th District Court**
**Judge Kaycee L. Jones**
101 W. Mill St., Suite 279
Livingston, TX 77351
Phone: 936-327-6848
Fax: 936-327-6860
E-mail: 411court@co.polk.tx.us
Court Coordinator: Emily Wooten
Court Reporter: Kim Keeler
Bailiff: Van Loggins

**County Clerk: Schelana Hock**
P.O. Drawer 2119
Livingston, TX 77351
Phone: 936-327-6805
Fax: 936-327-6855

**County Judge: Sydney Murphy**
101 W. Church St.
Suite 300
Phone: 936-327-6813
Fax: 936-327-6891

**County Court at Law**
**Judge Tom Brown**
Suite 200
Phone: 936-327-6856
Fax: 936-327-6857
Court Coordinator: Joanna Brown
Court Reporter: Sondra Hensarling

## POTTER COUNTY

Seat: Amarillo

501 S. Fillmore St.
Amarillo, TX 79101
www.co.potter.tx.us

**District Clerk: Caroline Woodburn**
P.O. Box 9570
Amarillo, TX 79105-9570
Phone: 806-379-2300
Fax: 806-372-5061
E-mail: districtclerk@co.potter.tx.us
www.idocket.com

**District Attorney: Randall C. Sims**
Suite 5-A
Phone: 806-379-2325
Fax: 806-379-2823
E-mail: randallsims@co.potter.tx.us

**47th District Court**
**Judge Dan Schaap**
Suite 3-A
Phone: 806-379-2350
Fax: 806-379-6158
Court Coordinator: Amanda Weigle
Court Reporter: Dina Wall
Phone: 806-379-2352
Bailiff: Brad Parker

**108th District Court**
**Judge Doug Woodburn**
Suite 4-A
Phone: 806-379-2355
Fax: 806-379-6517
E-mail: woodburnd@pottercscd.org
Court Reporter: Jana Smith
Phone: 806-379-2357
Bailiffs: Clay Duke and George Williams

**181st District Court**
**Judge John B. Board**
Suite 3-B

Phone: 806-379-2360
Fax: 806-379-2869
E-mail: judgeboard@co.potter.tx.us
Court Coordinator: Carley Snider
E-mail: sniderc@pottercscd.org
Court Reporter: Jodi Goodman
Phone: 806-379-2362
Bailiff: Robert Byrd
Phone: 806-379-2363

**251st District Court**
**Judge Ana E. Estevez**
Suite 4-C
Phone: 806-379-2365
Fax: 806-379-6743
E-mail: aestevez@pottercscd.org
Court Coordinator: Angela Johnson
Court Reporter: Barbara Younger
Phone: 806-379-2367
Bailiff: Daniel Aguirre

**320th District Court – Family Court**
**Judge Don Emerson**
Suite 4-B
Phone: 806-379-2370
Fax: 806-379-6248
E-mail: emersond@pottercscd.org
Court Coordinator: Cindy Davis
Court Reporter: Jill Zimmer
Phone: 806-379-2372
Bailiffs: Gary Johnson and Dennis Horn

**County Clerk: Julie Smith**
P.O. Box 9638
Amarillo, TX 79105-9638
Phone: 806-379-2275
Fax: 806-379-2296
E-mail: countyclerk@co.potter.tx.us

**County Attorney: Scott Brumley**
500 S. Fillmore, Room 301
Amarillo, TX 79101
Phone: 806-379-2255, ext. 6
Fax: 806-379-2267

**County Judge: Nancy Tanner**
500 S. Fillmore, Ste. 103
Amarillo, TX 79101
Phone: 806-379-2250
Fax: 806-379-2446
E-mail: nancytanner@mypottercounty.com
Administrative Assistant: Shannon Barnett
E-mail: shannonbarnett@mypottercounty.com

**County Court at Law No. 1**
**Judge W. F. "Corky" Roberts**
500 S. Fillmore, Room 405
Amarillo, TX 79101-2437
Phone: 806-379-2375
Fax: 806-379-2225
E-mail: robertsc@pottercscd.org
Court Coordinator: Pam Hotchkiss
Court Reporter: Dedra Morgan
Bailiff: Darrell Dewey

**County Court at Law No. 2**
**Judge Pamela Cook Sirmon**
500 S. Fillmore, Room 402
Amarillo, TX 79101-2437
Phone: 806-379-2380
Fax: 806-379-2222
E-mail: sirmonp@pottercscd.org
Court Coordinator: LaDon Kilburn
E-mail: kilburnl@potterscsd.org
Court Reporter: Kim Bayless
E-mail: baylessk@pottercscd.org
Bailiff: Steve Langwell
Phone: 803-379-2383
E-mail: langwells@potterscsd.org

# PRESIDIO COUNTY

Seat: Marfa

320 N. Highland Ave.
Marfa, TX 79843
www.co.presidio.tx.us

**District and County Clerk: Virginia Pallarez**
P.O. Box 789
Marfa, TX 79843
Phone: 432-729-3857 District
Phone: 432-729-4812 County
Fax: 432-729-4313

**District Attorney: Rod Ponton**
*Please see Pecos County.*

**394th District Court**
**Judge Roy B. Ferguson** sits as scheduled.
*Please see Brewster County.*

**County Attorney: John Fowlkes**
Phone: 432-729-3034

**County Judge: Cinderela Guevara**
P.O. Box 606

Marfa, TX 79843-0606
Phone: 432-729-4452
Fax: 432-729-4453
Administrative Assistant: Crystal Funk

# RAINS COUNTY

Seat: Emory

220 W. Quitman St., Suite B
Emory, TX 75440
www.co.rains.tx.us

**District Clerk: Deborah Traylor**
Suite C
Phone: 903-473-5000, ext. 101
Fax: 903-473-5008

**District and County Attorney: Robert Vititow**
Suite D
Phone: 903-473-5000, ext. 115
Fax: 903-473-5085

**8th District Court**
**Judge Eddie Northcutt** sits the first and third
Thursday of every month.
*Please see Hopkins County.*

**354th District Court**
**Judge Richard Beacom** sits the second and
fourth Friday of every month.
*Please see Hunt County.*

**County Clerk: Linda Wallace**
Suite B
Phone: 903-473-5000, ext. 103
Fax: 903-473-5086

**County Judge: Wayne Wolfe**
167 E. Quitman Street, Suite 102
Emory, TX 75440-0158
Phone: 903-473-5000, ext. 119
Fax: 903-473-4298
Administrative Assistant: Kathy Lucas
Phone: 903-473-5000, ext. 120

# RANDALL COUNTY

Seat: Canyon

2309 Russell Long Blvd.
Canyon, TX 79015
www.randallcounty.org

**District Clerk: Jo Carter**
Suite 110
Phone: 806-468-5600
Fax: 806-468-5604
E-mail: districtclerk@randallcounty.org

**District Attorney: James Farren**
Suite 120
Phone: 806-468-5570
Fax: 806-468-5566
E-mail: fwatson@randallcounty.org

**47th District Court**
**Judge Dan Schaap** sits as scheduled.
*Please see Potter County.*

**181st District Court**
**Judge John B. Board** sits as scheduled.
*Please see Potter County.*

**251st District Court**
**Judge Ana E. Estevez** sits as scheduled.
*Please see Potter County.*

**County Clerk: Renee Calhoun**
Suite 101
Phone: 806-468-5505
Fax: 806-468-5509
E-mail: countyclerk@randallcounty.org

**County Judge: Ernie Houdashell**
501 16th St. , Suite 303
Canyon, TX 79015-3850
Phone: 806-468-5500
E-mail: elh@randallcounty.org

**County Court at Law No. 1**
**Judge James W. Anderson**
Suite 132
Canyon, TX 79015-3850
Phone: 806-468-5551
Fax: 806-468-5695
Court Coordinator: Joel Forbis
Court Reporter: Terry Loy
Bailiff: Larry Conner

**County Court at Law No. 2**
**Judge Ronnie Walker**
Suite 130
Phone: 806-468-5670
Fax: 806-468-5671
E-mail: countycourtatlaw2@randallcounty.org
Court Coordinator: Jennifer Watson
Court Reporter: Rebecca Guide
Bailiff: Kevin Comerford

# REAGAN COUNTY

Seat: Big Lake

3rd at Plaza St.
Big Lake, TX 76932

**District and County Clerk: Terri Curry**
P.O. Box 100
Big Lake, TX 76932
Phone: 325-884-2442
Fax: 325-884-1503
E-mail: rcclerk@reagancounty.org

**District Attorney: Laurie K. English**
*Please see Pecos County.*

**112th District Court**
**Judge Pedro Gomez, Jr.** sits as scheduled.
*Please see Crockett County.*

**County Judge: Larry Isom**
P.O. Box 100
Big Lake, TX 76932
Phone: 325-884-2665
Fax: 325-884-1503
E-mail: clerk@reagancounty.org
Administrative Assistant: Jill Mitchell

# REAL COUNTY

Seat: Leakey

101 S. Market
Leakey, TX 78873
www.co.real.tx.us

**District and County Clerk: Bella A. Rubio**
P.O. Box 750
Leakey, TX 78873
Phone: 830-232-5202
Fax: 830-232-6888
E-mail: realcl@hctc.net

**District Attorney: Daniel J. Kindred**
*Please see Uvalde County.*

**38th District Court**
**Judge Camille G. Dubose** sits once a month.
*Please see Uvalde County.*

**County Attorney: Bobby J. Rushing**
P.O. Box 27
Leakey, TX 78873
Phone: 830-232-6461
Fax: 830-232-4898

**County Judge: Garry A. Merritt**
P.O. Box 446
Leakey, TX 78873
Phone: 830-232-5304
Fax: 830-232-6040
E-mail: garry.merritt@co.real.tx.us
Administrative Assistant: Jennifer Killina

# RED RIVER COUNTY

Seat: Clarksville

400 N. Walnut St.
Clarksville, TX 75426
www.co.red-river.tx.us

**District Clerk: Janice Gentry**
Phone: 903-427-3761
Fax: 903-427-1201
E-mail: rrcdcourt@yahoo.com

**District and County Attorney: Val Varley**
Phone: 903-427-2009
Fax: 903-427-5316
E-mail: vvarley@valornet.com

**6th District Court**
**Judge Eric Clifford** sits as scheduled.
*Please see Lamar County.*

**102nd District Court**
**Judge Bobby Lockhart, Jr.** sits as scheduled.
*Please see Bowie County.*

**County Clerk: Shawn Weemes**
200 N. Walnut St.
Clarksville, TX 75426
Phone: 903-427-2401
Fax: 903-427-3589
E-mail: redrivercountyclerk194@yahoo.com

**County Judge: L.D. Williamson**
400 N. Walnut St.
Clarksville, TX 75426
Phone: 903-427-2680
Fax: 903-427-5510
E-mail: redriver001@yahoo.com

**STATE, DISTRICT AND COUNTY COURTS**

## REEVES COUNTY

Seat: Pecos

100 E. 4th St.
Pecos, TX 79772

**District Clerk: Pat Tarin**
P.O. Box 848
Pecos, TX 79772-0848
Phone: 432-445-2714
Fax: 432-445-7455
E-mail: pat.tarin@143.court.state.tx.us

**District Attorney: Randall W. Reynolds**
P.O. Box 2012
Pecos, TX 79772-0150
Phone: 432-445-2010
Fax: 432-445-2015
E-mail: ranrey@pecos.net

**143rd District Court**
**Judge Michael Swanson** sits as scheduled.
*Please see Ward County.*

**County Clerk: Dianne O. Florez**
P.O. Box 867
Pecos, TX 79772-0867
Phone: 432-445-5467
Fax: 432-445-3997

**County Judge: Won J. Bang**
Phone: 432-445-5418
Fax: 432-445-5389
E-mail: judgebang@yahoo.com
Administrative Assistant: Diannie Tercero

**County Court at Law**
**Judge Scott J. Johnson**
P.O. Box 749
Pecos, TX 79772-4035
Phone: 432-445-5497
Fax: 432-445-3147
Court Coordinator: Patricia C. Garcia
Court Reporter: Linda Lester

## REFUGIO COUNTY

Seat: Refugio

808 Commerce St.
Refugio, TX 78377
www.co.refugio.tx.us

**District Clerk: Ruby Garcia**
P.O. Box 736
Refugio, TX 78377
Phone: 361-526-2721
Fax: 361-526-5942

**District Attorney: Michael Sheppard**
*Please see DeWitt County*

**24th District Court**
**Judge Jack W. Marr** sits as scheduled.
*Please see Victoria County.*

**135th District Court**
**Judge K. Stephen Williams** sits as scheduled.
*Please see Victoria County.*

**267th District Court**
**Judge Juergen "Skipper" Koetter** sits as
scheduled.
*Please see Victoria County.*
*Note: Hon. Koetter will retire on 3/4/16.*
*Gov. Abbot to appoint new judge.*

**County Clerk: Ida Ramirez**
P.O. Box 704
Refugio, TX 78377
Phone: 361-526-2233
Fax: 361-526-1325

**County Attorney: Todd P. Steele**
P.O. Box 307
Refugio, TX 78377
Phone: 361-526-4123
Fax: 361-526-1763
E-mail: todd.steele@co.refugio.tx.us

**County Judge: Robert E. Blaschke**
Room 104
Phone: 361-526-4434
Fax: 361-526-5100

## ROBERTS COUNTY

Seat: Miami

300 E. Commerical
Miami, TX 79059

**District and County Clerk: Toni Rankin**
P.O. Box 477
Miami, TX 79059-0477
Phone: 806-868-2341
Fax: 806-868-3381

**District Attorney: Franklin McDonough**
*Please see Gray County.*

**31st District Court**
**Judge Steven R. Emmert** sits once a month.
*Please see Wheeler County.*

**County Attorney: William P. Weiman**
P.O. Box 487
Miami, TX 79059
Phone: 806-868-2019
Fax: 806-868-3381

**County Judge: Rick Tennant**
P.O. Box 478
Miami, TX 79059-0478
Phone: 806-868-3721
Fax: 806-868-3381

# ROBERTSON COUNTY

Seat: Franklin

103 E. Morgan St.
Franklin, TX 77856
www.co.robertson.tx.us

**District Clerk: Barbara W. Axtell**
P.O. Box 250
Franklin, TX 77856-0250
Phone: 979-828-3636
Fax: 979-828-5523

**District and County Attorney: W. Coty Siegert**
P.O. Box 409
Franklin, TX 77856-0409
Phone: 979-828-3205
Fax: 979-828-3300

**82nd District Court**
**Judge Robert M. Stem** sits every Monday.
*Please see Falls County.*

**County Clerk: Kathryn N. Brimhall**
P.O. Box 1029
Franklin, TX 77856
Phone: 979-828-4130
Fax: 979-828-1260

**County Judge: Charles Ellison**
P.O. Box 427
Franklin, TX 77856
Phone: 979-828-3542
Fax: 979-828-2944

# ROCKWALL COUNTY

Seat: Rockwall

1111 E. Yellow Jacket Ln.
Rockwall, TX 75087
www.rockwallcountytexas.com

**District Clerk: Kay McDaniel**
Suite 200
Phone: 972-204-6500
Fax: 972-204-6509

**District Attorney: Kenda Culpepper**
Suite 201
Phone: 972-204-6800
Fax: 972-204-6809

**382nd District Court**
**Judge Brett Hall**
Suite 402
Phone: 972-204-6610
Fax: 972-204-6619
Court Coordinator: Linda Pollard
Assistant Court Coordinator:
Martha Johnson
Court Reporter: Linda A. Kaiser
Bailiff: Randy Leonard

**439th District Court**
**Judge David Rakow**
Suite 401
Phone: 972-204-6630
Fax: 972-204-6639
Court Coordinator: Sharon Larey
Assistant Court Coordinator:
Lynda Robertson
Court Reporter: Barbara Tokuz
Bailiff: Ron Smith

**County Clerk: Shelli Miller**
Suite 100
Phone: 972-204-6300
Fax: 972-204-6309

**County Judge: David Sweet**
101 E. Rusk St., Room 202
Rockwall, TX 75087
Phone: 972-204-6000
Fax: 972-204-6009
Assistant: Felicia Morris

**County Court at Law**
**Judge Brian Williams**
Suite 403
Phone: 972-204-6410
Fax: 972-204-6419
Court Coordinator: Paige Parks
Court Reporter: Debbie Hammon
Bailiff: Pat Hannon

# RUNNELS COUNTY

Seat: Ballinger

613 Courthouse Square
Ballinger, TX 76821
www.co.runnels.tx.us

**District Clerk: Tammy Burleson**
P.O. Box 166
Ballinger, TX 76821-0166
Phone: 325-365-2638
Fax: 325-365-9229

**District Attorney: George E. McCrea**
*Please see Tom Green County.*

**119th District Court**
**Judge Garland "Ben" Woodward**
sits as scheduled.
*Please see Tom Green County.*

**County Clerk: Julia Miller**
613 Hutchings Ave., Room 106
Ballinger, TX 76821
Phone: 325-365-2720
Fax: 325-365-3408

**County Attorney: Kenneth Slimp**
613 Hutchings Ave., Room 102
Ballinger, TX 76821
Phone: 325-365-2337
Fax: 325-365-3408

**County Judge: Barry Hilliard**
**613 Hutchings Ave., Room 103**
Phone: 325-365-2633
Fax: 325-365-3408

# RUSK COUNTY

Seat: Henderson

115 N. Main St.
Henderson, TX 75652
www.co.rusk.tx.us

**District Clerk: Terri P. Willard**
P.O. Box 1687
Henderson, TX 75653-1687
Phone: 903-657-0353
Fax: 903-657-1914

**District and County Attorney: Michael Jimerson**
Suite 302
Phone: 903-657-2265
Fax: 903-657-0329

**4th District Court**
**Judge J. Clay Gossett**
Suite 303
Phone: 903-657-0358
Fax: 903-655-1250
Court Coordinator: Annette Griffin
Court Reporter: Terri Boling

**County Clerk: Trudy McGill**
P.O. Box 758
Henderson, TX 75652-0758
Phone: 903-657-0330
Fax: 903-657-2387
E-mail: trudy.mcgill@co.rusk.tx.us

**County Judge: Joel Hale**
Suite 104
Phone: 903-657-0302
Fax: 903-657-0300
Administrative Assistant: Lucy Smith

**County Court at Law**
**Judge Chad W. Dean**
Phone: 903-657-0344
Fax: 903-657-3378
Administrative Assistant: Rhonda Chapman

# SABINE COUNTY

Seat: Hemphill

280 Main St.
Hemphill, TX 75948

**District Clerk: Lisa Pitre**
P.O. Box 850
Hemphill, TX 75948
Phone: 409-787-2912
Fax: 409-787-2623
Chief Deputy: Tellina Wright

**1st District Court**
Judge Craig Mixson sits on the fourth Friday
of every month and holds court during May
and November.
*Please see Jasper County.*

**23rd District Court**
Judge Charles Mitchell sits on the second
Friday of every month and holds court
during February and September.
*Please see San Augustine County.*

**County Clerk: Janice McDaniel**
P.O. Drawer 580
Hemphill, TX 75948
Phone: 409-787-3786
Fax: 409-787-3795

**County Attorney: Bobby Neal**
P.O. Box 1783
Hemphill, TX 75948
Phone: 409-787-2988
Fax: 409-787-3884

**County Judge: Daryl Melton**
P.O. Box 716
Hemphill, TX 75948
Phone: 409-787-3543
Fax: 409-787-2044
Court Coordinator: Jamie Clark
Phone: 409-787-2889

# SAN AUGUSTINE COUNTY

Seat: San Augustine

100 W. Columbia St.
San Augustine, TX 75972
www.co.san-augustine.tx.us

**District Clerk: Jean Steptoe**
Room 202
Phone: 936-275-2231
Fax: 936-275-2389
E-mail: disclerk@co.san-augustine.tx.us

**District Attorney: Kevin Dutton**
P.O. Box 714
San Augustine, TX 75972
Phone: 936-275-9903
Fax: 936-275-9905
Administrative Assistant: Jeanette Bryan

**1st District Court**
Judge Craig Mixson sits on the fourth Friday of
every month at 1:30 p.m.
*Please see Jasper County.*

**273rd District Court**
Judge Charles R. Mitchell
Room 202
Phone: 936-275-9634
Fax: 936-275-2389
E-mail: mitchell6489@sbcglobal.net
Court Coordinator: Sharon Miller
Phone: 409-384-9570
E-mail: sharon.miller@co.jasper.tx.us
Court Reporter: Julie Lambert
Phone: 936-598-3655

**County Clerk: Margo Noble**
223 N. Harrison
San Augustine, TX 75972
Phone: 936-275-2452
Fax: 936-275-2263

**County Attorney: Wesley Hoyt**
Phone: 936-275-0971
E-mail: sacountyattorney@gmail.com
Secretary: Becky Johnson
E-mail: beckyjsaca@att.net

**County Judge: Samye Johnson**
Room 205
Phone: 936-275-2762
E-mail: countyjudge@co.san-augustine.tx.us
Administrative Assistant: Sandy Jenkins
E-mail: sandy.jenkins@co.san-augustine.tx.us

# SAN JACINTO COUNTY

Seat: Coldspring

One State Highway 150
Coldspring, TX 77331
www.co.san-jacinto.tx.us

**District Clerk: Rebecca "Becky" Capers**
Room 4
Phone: 936-653-2909
Fax: 936-653-4659

**District and County Attorney: Roberth H. Trapp**
Room 21
Phone: 936-653-2601
Fax: 936-653-2143
E-mail: roberth.trapp@co.san-jacinto.tx.us

**258th District Court**
**Judge Ernest L. McClendon.**
*Please see Polk County.*

**411th District Court**
**Judge Kaycee L. Jones**
*Please see Polk County.*

**County Clerk: Dawn Wright**
Room 2
Phone: 936-653-2324
Fax: 936-653-8312

**County Judge: John Lovett**
Room 23
Phone: 936-653-2199
Fax: 936-653-3970
Administrative Assistant: Silvia Haro

# SAN PATRICIO COUNTY

Seat: Sinton

400 W. Sinton St. Room 210
Sinton, TX 78387
www.co.san-patricio.tx.us

**District Clerk: Laura Miller**
Room 210
Phone: 361-364-9377
Fax: 361-364-9477

**District Attorney: Michael E. Welborn**
Phone: 361-364-9390
Fax: 361-364-9490

**36th District Court**
**Judge Starr B. Bauer**
P.O. Box 700
Sinton, TX 78387-0700
Phone: 361-364-9310
Fax: 361-364-9410
Court Coordinator: Nina De La Garza
Court Reporter: Mandi Alvarez

**156th District Court**
**Judge Patrick L. Flanigan**

P.O. Box 700
Sinton, TX 78387
Phone: 361-362-3239 or 361-364-9310
Fax: 361-364-9410
Court Coordinator: Sylvia Mejias
Court Reporter: Katrina Gentry

**343rd District Court**
**Judge Janna K. Whatley**
P.O. Box 700
Sinton, TX 78387-0700
Phone: 361-364-9310
Fax: 361-364-9410
Court Coordinator: Elida DeLeon
Court Reporter: Jennifer Hill
Roving Reporter: Lisa Riley

**County Clerk: Gracie Alaniz-Gonzales**
P.O. Box 578
Sinton, TX 78387-0578
Phone: 361-364-9350
Fax: 361-364-9450

**County Attorney: David H. Aken**
Room 109
Phone: 361-364-9338
Fax: 361-364-9440

**County Judge: Terry Simpson**
Room 108
Phone: 361-364-9301
Fax: 361-364-6118

**County Court at Law**
**Judge Elizabeth Welborn**
Room B-15
Phone: 361-364-9325
Fax: 361-364-9425
Court Coordinator: Tina Buffa

# SAN SABA COUNTY

Seat: San Saba

500 E. Wallace St.
San Saba, TX 76877-0001
www.co.san-saba.tx.us

**District and County Clerk: Kim Wells**
Room 202
Phone: 325-372-3614
Fax: 325-372-6484
E-mail: clerk@co.san-saba.tx.us

District Attorney: Wiley B. "Sonny" McAfee
*Please see Llano County.*

**33rd District Court**
Judge J. Allan Garrett sits as scheduled.
*Please see Burnet County.*

**424th District Court**
Judge Evan Stubbs sits as scheduled.
*Please see Burnet County.*

**County Attorney: Randall Robinson**
Phone: 325-372-3747
E-mail: attorney@co.san-saba.tx.us

**County Judge: Bryon Theodosis**
Phone: 325-372-3635
E-mail: judge@co.san-saba.tx.us
Administrative Assistant: Loren Berryhill
E-mail: adminasst911@co.san-saba.tx.us

# SCHLEICHER COUNTY

Seat: Eldorado

2 N. Divide St.
Eldorado, TX 76936
www.co.schleicher.tx.us

**District and County Clerk: Mary Ann Gonzalez**
P.O. Drawer 580
Eldorado, TX 76936-0580
Phone: 325-853-2833, ext. 2
Fax: 325-853-2768
E-mail: schleicherclerk15@gmail.com

**District Attorney: Allison Palmer**
*Please see Tom Green County.*

**51st District Court**
Judge Barbara L. Walther sits once a month.
*Please see Tom Green County.*

**County Attorney: Clint T. Griffin**
P.O. Box 509
Eldorado, TX 76936
Phone: 325-853-2593
Fax: 325-853-2603

**County Judge: Charlie Bradley**
Courthouse Square Box 536
Eldorado, TX 76936
Phone: 325-853-2766
Fax: 325-853-2603

# SCURRY COUNTY

Seat: Snyder

1806 25th St.
Snyder, TX 79549
www.co.scurry.tx.us

**District Clerk: Candace Jones**
Suite 402
Phone: 325-573-5641
Fax: 325-573-1081
E-mail: scurrydc@co.scurry.tx.us

**District Attorney: Ben R. Smith**
Suite 302
Phone: 325-573-2462
Fax: 325-573-9339
E-mail: 132txda@gmail.com

**132nd District Court**
Judge Ernie B. Armstrong
Suite 404
Phone: 325-573-5371
Fax: 325-573-5867
Court Coordinator: Kayla Phipps
Court Reporter: Terry Hanshew
Phone: 325-573-7766

**County Clerk: Melody Appleton**
Suite 300
Phone: 325-573-5332
Fax: 325-573-7396
E-mail: scurrycoclerk@suddenlinkmail.com

**County Attorney: Michael Hartmann**
Suite 201
Phone: 325-573-7440
Fax: 325-573-1266

**County Judge: Ricky Fritz**
Phone: 325-573-8576
Fax: 325-573-1266
E-mail: scjudge@suddenlinkmail.com
Administrative Assistant: Monica Chandler

# SHACKELFORD COUNTY

Seat: Albany

225 S. Main St.
Albany, TX 76430
www.shackelfordcountytexas.com

**District and County Clerk: Cheri Hawkins**
P.O. Box 2109
Albany, TX 76430
Phone: 325-762-2232, ext. 3
Fax: 325-762-3756

**District Attorney: Joe Edd Boaz**
*Please see Jones County.*

**259th District Court**
**Judge Brooks H. Hagler** sits once a month.
*Please see Jones County.*

**County Attorney: Colton Johnson**
P.O. Box 2619
Albany, TX 76430
325-762-2232, ext. 2

**County Judge: Ross Montgomery**
P.O. Box 2797
Albany, TX 76430
Phone: 325-762-2232, ext. 4
Fax: 325-762-3966

## SHELBY COUNTY

Seat: Center

200 San Augustine St.
Center, TX 75935
www.co.shelby.tx.us

**District Clerk: Lori Oliver**
P.O. Drawer 1953
Center, TX 75935
Phone: 936-598-4164
Fax: 936-598-3323

**District Attorney: Kenneth Florence**
Suite 12
Phone: 936-598-2489
Fax: 936-598-4106

**123rd District Court**
**Judge Charles C. Dickerson**
Room 3 936-598-9928
Phone: 903-598-9928
Fax: 936-591-0984
Court Coordinator: Karen Warr
Court Reporter: Terri Hudson
Phone: 903-693-0315
Bailiff: Walter Shofner

**273rd District Court**
**Judge Charles R. Mitchell**
Room 3
Phone: 936-598-3201
Fax: 936-591-3215
Court Coordinator: Karen Warr
Court Reporter: Julie Lambert
Bailiff: Walter Shofner

**County Clerk: Jennifer Fountain**
124 Austin St.
Center, TX 75935
Phone: 936-598-6361
Fax: 936-598-3701

**County Attorney: Gary W. Rholes**
518 Nacagdoches St.
Center, TX 75935
Phone: 936-598-6100
Fax: 936-598-9184

**County Judge: Allison Harbison**
200 San Augustine St.
Center, TX 75935
Phone: 936-598-3863
Fax: 936-598-3146

## SHERMAN COUNTY

Seat: Stratford

701 N. 3rd St.
Stratford, TX 79084
www.co.sherman.tx.us

**District and County Clerk: Gina Gray**
P.O. Box 270
Stratford, TX 79084
Phone: 806-366-2371
Fax: 806-366-5670
E-mail: gina.jones@co.sherman.tx.us

**District Attorney: David M. Green**
*Please see Moore County.*

**69th District Court**
**Judge Ron E. Enns** sits once a month.
*Please see Moore County.*

**County Attorney: Kimberly Allen**
P.O. Box 986
Stratford, TX 79084
Phone: 806-366-2270
Fax: 803-366-3130

**County Judge: Terri B. Carter**
P.O. Box 165
Stratford, TX 79084
Phone: 806-366-2021
Fax: 806-366-3011
E-mail: cojudge@co.sherman.tx.us
Administrative Assistant: Margaret Ewers

# SMITH COUNTY

Seat: Tyler

100 N. Broadway Ave.
Tyler, TX 75702-7236
www.smith-county.com

**District Clerk: Lois Rogers**
Phone: 903-590-1660
Fax: 903-590-1661
E-mail: lrogers@smith-county.com

**7th District Court**
**Judge Kerry L. Russell**
Phone: 903-590-1640
Fax: 903-590-1641
Court Coordinator (Civil): Terry Cockrum
Phone: 903-590-1643
Court Coordinator (Criminal): Toni White
Phone: 903-590-1642
Court Reporter: Jennifer Lawrence
Phone: 903-590-1647
Bailiff: Rachel Stewart
Phone: 903-590-1646

**114th District Court**
**Judge Christi Kennedy**
2nd Floor
Phone: 903-590-1623
Court Coordinator (Criminal): Tammy Camp-Miller
Court Coordinator (Civil): Lori Farmer
Phone: 903-590-1625
Court Reporter: Cassie Condrey
Phone: 903-590-1628
Bailiff: Consauluea Mass
Phone: 903-590-1622

**241st District Court**
**Judge Jack Skeen, Jr.**
2nd Floor
Phone: 903-590-1634
Fax: 903-590-1631
Court Coordinator (Civil): Denise Langston

Court Coordinator (Crimnal): Amanda Deck
Phone: 903-590-1635
Court Reporter: Christy Humphries
Phone: 903-590-1636
Bailiff: Randy Hiller

**321st District Court**
**Judge Carole Clark**
1st Floor
Phone: 903-590-1601
Fax: 903-590-1606
Court Administrator: Vicki Dunn
Assistant Court Coordinator: Rosie Rogers
Phone: 903-590-1602
Drug Court Coordinator: Susan Oxford
Phone: 903-590-1617
Court Reporter: Kristy Crawford
Phone: 903-590-1603
Bailiff: Leonard Spurling

**County Clerk: Karen Phillips**
200 E. Ferguson, 3rd Floor
Tyler, TX 75702
Phone: 903-590-4672
Fax: 903-590-4689

**County Judge: Joel Baker**
200 E. Ferguson, Suite 304
Tyler, TX 75702
Phone: 903-590-4616
Fax: 903-590-4612
Administrative Assistant: Karen Garner
Court Coordinator: Lynn R. McGinnis
E-mail: lmcginnis@smith-county.com
Mental Health Court Coordinator: Donna Henry
E-mail: dhenry@smith-county.com

**County Court at Law No. 1**
**Judge Jason A. Ellis**
Room 209
Phone: 903-590-1650
Fax: 903-590-1656
Civil Court Coordinator (Civil): Jodi Wich
Court Coordinator (Criminal): Phyllis Duke
Court Reporter: Kim Christopher
Phone: 903-590-1655
Bailiff: India Samuels

**County Court at Law No. 2**
**Judge Randall L. Rogers**
1st Floor
Phone: 903-590-1609
Fax: 903-590-1608
Court Coordinator (Civil): Shavonda Mass

STATE, DISTRICT AND COUNTY COURTS

Phone: 903-590-1611
Court Coordinator (Criminal): Paul Clarkton
Court Reporter: Marcie Powell
Phone: 903-590-1614
Bailiff: Wanda Hunter
Phone: 903-590-1616

**County Court at Law No. 3**
**Judge Floyd T. Getz**
Suite 303
Phone: 903-590-1692
Fax: 903-590-1696
Court Coordinator (Juvenile): Patti Simmons
Court Coordinator (Adult): Laurita Vodak
Phone: 903-590-1691
Court Reporter: Tandrea Baxter
Phone: 903-590-1694
Bailiff: Edward Brown

# SOMERVELL COUNTY

Seat: Glen Rose

201 NE Vernon St.
Glen Rose, TX 76043

**District and County Clerk: Michelle Reynolds**
107 NE Vernon
Glen Rose, TX 76043
Phone: 254-897-4427
Fax: 254-897-3233
E-mail: michelle.reynolds@co.somervell.tx.us

**District Attorney: Dale S. Hanna**
*Please see Johnson County.*

**18th District Court**
**Judge John E. Neill** sits as scheduled.
*Please see Johnson County.*

**249th District Court**
**Judge D. Wayne Bridewell** sits as scheduled.
*Please see Johnson County.*

**County Attorney: Andrew Lucas**
P.O. Box 1335
Glen Rose, TX 76403
Phone: 254-897-2277
Fax: 254-897-2600
E-mail: andrew.lucas@co.somervell.tx.us

**County Judge: Danny L. Chambers**
P.O. Box 851
Glen Rose, TX 76043
Phone: 254-897-2322
Fax: 254-897-7314
E-mail: cojudge@co.somervell.tx.us
Secretary: Pat Patterson

# STARR COUNTY

Seat: Rio Grande City

401 N. Britton Ave.
Rio Grande City, TX 78582-8020

**District Clerk: Eloy R. Garcia**
Suite 304
Phone: 956-716-4800, ext. 8482 or 8485
Fax: 956-487-8493
Chief Deputy: Brendaly Guerrero

**District Attorney: Omar Escobar**
Suite 417
Phone: 956-487-8651
Fax: 956-487-8697
E-mail: starrda03@yahoo.com

**229th District Court**
**Judge Ana Lisa Garza**
Phone: 956-487-2636
Court Coordinator: Ana SaenzAssistant
Court Coordinator: Eduina Guerra
Court Clerks: Elida Duenez and Pauline Galvan
Court Reporter: Ramiro Hernandez
Bailiff: Maria Nellie Gonzalez

**381st District Court**
**Judge Jose Luis Garza**
Phone: 956-487-8664
Fax: 956-487-8493
Court Coordinator (Civil): Bertha Garcia
Court Coordinator (Criminal): Cynthia Fuentes
Court Reporter: Julian Alderette
Bailiff: Ralph Carrera

**County Clerk: Dennis Gonzalez**
Suite 201
Phone: 956-766-4800, ext. 8032
Fax: 956-487-8674
Court Clerk: Stephanie Ortiz
Phone: 956-716-4800

**County Attorney: Victor Canales, Jr.**
Suite 405
Phone: 956-487-8015

**County Judge: Eugenio Falcon Jr.**
100 N. Room 3167
Rio Grande City, TX 78582
Phone: 956-487-8015
Fax: 956-487-8709
E-mail: eloy.vera@co.starr.tx.us
Administrative Assistant: Eugenio Falcon, Jr.

**County Court at Law**
**Judge Romero Molina**
Phone: 956-487-8502
Fax: 956-487-8493
Court Coordinator: Basilio D. Villarreal, IV

# STEPHENS COUNTY

Seat: Breckenridge

200 W. Walker St.
Breckenridge, TX 76424
www.co.stephens.tx.us

**District Clerk: Christie Coapland**
2nd Floor
Phone: 254-559-3151
Fax: 254-559-8127

**District Attorney: Dee Hudson Peavy**
*Please see Young County.*

**90th District Court**
**Judge Stephen E. Bristow** sits as scheduled.
*Please see Young County.*

**County Clerk: Jackie Ensey**
Phone: 254-559-3700
Fax: 254-559-5892

**County Attorney: Gary Trammel**
Phone: 254-559-9091
Fax: 254-559-8127

**County Judge: Gary L. Fuller**
Phone: 254-559-2190
Fax: 254-559-7296

# STERLING COUNTY

Seat: Sterling City

609 Fourth Ave.
Sterling City, TX 76951
www.co.sterling.tx.us

**District and County Clerk: Jerri McCutchen**
P.O. Box 55
Sterling City, TX 76951
Phone: 325-378-5191
Fax: 325-378-3111

**District Attorney: Allison Palmer**
*Please see Tom Green County.*

**51st District Court**
**Judge Barbara L. Walther** sits once a month.
*Please see Tom Green County.*

**County Pro-tem: Trey Poage**
P.O. Box 88
Sterling City, TX 76951
Phone: 325-378-5621

**County Judge: Leslie A. Mackie**
P.O. Box 819
Sterling City, TX 76951-0819
Phone: 325-378-3481

# STONEWALL COUNTY

Seat: Aspermont

128 Town Square Ln.
Aspermont, TX 79502

**District and County Clerk: Holly McLaury**
P.O. Drawer P
Aspermont, TX 79502-0914
Phone: 940-989-2272
Fax:940-988-4001
E-mail: holly.mclaury@stonewallcountytx.org

**District Attorney: Michael E. Fouts**
*Please see Haskell County.*

**39th District Court**
**Judge Shane Hadaway** sits once a month.
*Please see Haskell County.*

**STATE, DISTRICT AND COUNTY COURTS**

County Judge: Ronnie Moorhead
P.O. Box 366
Aspermont, TX 79502-0366
Phone: 940-989-3393
Fax: 940-989-3105
E-mail: countyjudge@stonewallcountytx.org
Secretary: LaTisha Martin

# SUTTON COUNTY

Seat: Sonora

101 N. E. Water St.
Sonora, TX 76950
www.suttoncounty.org

**District and County Clerk: Rachel Chavez Duran**
300 E. Oak St., Suite 3
Sonora, TX 76950
Phone: 325-387-3815
Fax: 325-387-6028
E-mail: clerk@suttoncounty.org

**District Attorney: Laurie K. English**
*Please see Pecos County.*

**112th District Court**
**Judge Pedro Gomez, Jr.** sits once a month.
*Please see Crockett County.*

**County Attorney: David W. Wallace**
P.O. Box 1508
Sonora, TX 76950
Phone: 325-387-6553
Fax: 325-387-6554

**County Judge: Steve Smith**
300 E. Oak St., Suite 4
Sonora, TX 76950
Phone: 325-387-2711
Fax: 325-387-5166
E-mail: s.smith@suttoncounty.org
Secretary: Jessica Rose

# SWISHER COUNTY

Seat: Tulia

119 S. Maxwell Ave.
Tulia, TX 79088
www.co.swisher.tx.us

**District and County Clerk: CJ Chasco**
Phone: 806-995-3294
Fax: 806-995-4121
E-mail: cj.chasco@swisher-tx.net
Web: www.swisherclerk.com

**64th District Court**
**Judge Robert W. Kinkaid, Jr.** sits every other Wednesday, unless special settings.
*Please see Hale County.*

**242nd District Court**
**Judge Kregg Hukill** sits alternating Wednesdays from 64th Judge, unless special settings.
*Please see Hale County.*

**County Attorney: J. Michael Criswell**
Phone: 806-995-3505
Fax: 806-995-1525
E-mail: swisherca@swisher-tx.net
**County Judge: Harold Keeter**
Phone: 806-995-3504
Fax: 806-995-2214
E-mail: harold.keeter@swisher-tx.net
Administrative Assistant: Kathy Cumby
E-mail: kathy.cumby@swisher-tx.net

# TARRANT COUNTY
*e-filing questions 817.212.6953 civil*

Seat: Fort Worth

401 W. Belknap St.
Fort Worth, TX 76196-0220
www.tarrantcounty.com

**District Clerk: Thomas A. Wilder**
Phone Numbers:
Administrative: 817-884-1574
Civil: 817-884-1240
Criminal: 817-884-1342
Family: 817-884-1265
Fax: 817-884-1484

**District Attorney: Sharen Wilson**
Phone: 817-884-1400
Fax: 817-884-3333

## Civil District Courts
100 N. Calhoun
Fort Worth, TX 76196

**17th District Court**
**Judge Melody Wilkinson**
3rd Floor
Phone: 817-884-1460
Fax: 817-884-1372
Court Coordinator: Nancy Bentley
Court Clerk: Daletia Cunningham
Phone: 817-884-1567
Court Reporter: Beana Scobee
Phone: 817-884-1459
Bailiff: Roger Hoyle

**48th District Court**
**Judge David L. Evans**
4th Floor
Phone: 817-884-2690
Fax: 817-884-2384
Court Coordinator: Cori Balderas
Phone: 817-884-2690
Court Clerk: Kathy Bullard
Phone: 817-884-1568
Court Reporter: Micki Smith
Phone: 817-884-1479
Bailiff: Robert Green
Phone: 817-884-1461

**67th District Court**
**Judge Don Cosby**
4th Floor
Phone: 817-884-1452
Court Coordinator: Becky Holland
E-mail: beckyholland@tarrantcounty.com
Court Clerk: Kelly Jones
Phone: 817-884-1569
Court Reporter: Monica Lindstrom
Phone: 817-884-1453

**96th District Court**
**Judge R.H. Wallace Jr.**
4th Floor
Phone: 817-884-1450
Fax: 817-884-3593
Court Coordinator: Marcia Huckaby
Phone: 817-884-2685
Court Clerk: Falicia Salazar
Phone: 817-884-1570
Court Reporter: Reginald Butler
Phone: 817-884-1451
Bailiff: Howard Kotarski

**141st District Court**
**Judge John P. Chupp**
200 E. Weatherford St.
Fort Worth, TX 76916
Phone: 817-884-1992

Fax: 817-884-3593
Court Coordinator: Cydney Grubb
Court Clerk: Yolanda Garza
Phone: 817-884-1588
Court Reporter: Tina Fett
Phone: 817-884-1423
Bailiff: David Bridgewater
Phone: 817-884-1422

**153rd District Court**
**Judge Susan McCoy**
3rd Floor
Phone: 817-884-2691
Court Coordinator: Patricia Cannon
Court Clerk: Tanya Weiss
Phone: 817-884-1592
Court Reporter: Suzanne Berry
Phone: 817-884-1471

**236th District Court**
**Judge Thomas W. Lowe, III**
5th Floor
Phone: 817-884-1709
Fax: 817-212-6801
Court Coordinator: Terri Gallagher
Court Clerk: Kelu Kerr
Phone: 817-884-1585
Court Reporter: Jacci Walker
Phone: 817-884-1127
Bailiff: Kyle Schugart
Phone: 817-884-1797

**342nd District Court**
**Judge Wade Birdwell**
200 E. Weatherford St.
Fort Worth, TX 76916
Phone: 817-884-2710
Court Coordinator: Sheila Jenkins
Court Clerk: Vickie Carter
Phone: 817-884-1594
Court Reporter: Holly Bishop
Phone: 817-884-2712
Bailiff: Leticia Wilbourn
Phone: 817-884-2713

**348th District Court**
**Judge Dana M. Womack**
3rd Floor
Phone: 817-884-2715
Court Coordinator: Pam Krempp
Court Clerk: Juanita Duran
Phone: 817-884-2787
Court Reporter: Annette Bos
Phone: 817-884-1790
Bailiff: Bedford Buckner
Phone: 817-884-3453

**352nd District Court**
**Judge Mark T. Pittman**
4th Floor
Phone: 817-884-2730
Fax: 817-884-2384
Court Coordinator: Linda Blair
E-mail: lblair@tarrantcounty.com
Court Clerk: Lisa Adams
Phone: 817-884-1183
Court Reporter: Monica Willenburg Guzman
Phone: 817-884-2732
E-mail: mguzman@tarrantcounty.com
Bailiff: Michael Higgins
Phone: 817-884-2644
E-mail: mlhiggins@tarrantcounty.com

# Criminal District Courts

**Criminal District Court No. 1**
**Judge Elizabeth Beach**
5th Floor
Phone: 817-884-1351
Fax: 817-884-1191
Court Coordinator: Kachelle Johnson
Phone: 817-884-1255
Court Clerk: LeeAnn Swan
Phone: 817-884-1283
Assistant Court Clerk: Amanda Brazil
Court Reporter: Andrea Reed
Phone: 817-884-2893

**Criminal District Court No. 2**
**Judge Wayne F. Salvant**
6th Floor
Phone: 817-884-1347
Fax: 817-884-1542
Court Coordinator: Dawn Gallagher
Phone: 817-884-1976
Court Clerk: Gail Kueckelhan
Phone: 817-884-1223
Court Reporter: Lorie Naylor
Phone: 817-884-2837
Bailiff: Chris Duron

**Criminal District Court No. 3**
**Judge Robb Catalano**
7th Floor
Phone: 817-884-1356
Fax: 817-884-1404
Court Coordinator: Sheila Finney
Phone: 817-884-1252
Court Clerk: Brittany Bobbitt
Phone: 817-884-1973
Court Reporter: Debbie Edwards

Phone: 817-884-1359
Bailiffs: Daniel Estrada, Angela Jones and John Shelton

**Criminal District Court No. 4**
**Judge Mike Thomas**
8th Floor
Phone: 817-884-1362
Fax: 817-884-3365
Court Coordinator: Dell Morgan
Phone: 817-884-1980
Court Clerk: Candice Monier
Phone: 817-884-1230
Court Reporter: Vacant
Phone: 817-884-2597
Bailiff: Henry Walker

**213th District Court**
**Judge Louis E. Sturns**
5th Floor
Phone: 817-884-1529
Fax: 817-884-1971
Court Coordinator: Tammy Barnes
Phone: 817-884-1977
Court Clerk: Kim Wheeler-Mendoza
Phone: 817-884-1788
Court Reporter: Sheila Walker
Phone: 817-884-1531
Bailiffs: Ricky Camp and Joe Lasater

**297th District Court**
**Judge David Hagerman**
5th Floor
Phone: 817-884-1908
Fax: 817-884-3274
Court Coordinator: Nona McDonald
Phone: 817-884-1256
Court Clerk: Annette Guiterrez
Phone: 817-884-1226
Court Reporter: Valerie K. Allen
Phone: 817-884-2915
Bailiff: Edmund Choice

**371st District Court**
**Judge Mollee Westfall**
5th Floor
Phone: 817-884-2538
Fax: 817-212-7567
Court Coordinator: Pam Cole
Phone: 817-884-2989
Court Clerk: Marisol Bonilla
Court Reporter: Brenda Clark
Phone: 817-884-2895
Bailiff: Randy Banister
Phone: 817-884-2986

**372nd District Court**
**Judge Scott Wisch**
6th Floor
Phone: 817-884-2990
Fax: 817-884-3361
Court Coordinator: Lorrie Parham
Phone: 817-884-2995
Court Clerk: Lisa Carlton
Phone: 817-884-2541
Court Reporter: Karen Smith
Phone: 817-884-2996
Bailiffs: Paul Brinkley, Richard Closner and
Stephen Farrow

**396th District Court**
**Judge George Gallagher**
6th Floor
Phone: 817-884-2768
Fax: 817-850-3361
Court Coordinator: Tommy LaRue
Phone: 817-884-2765
Court Clerk: Maria Lara
Phone: 817-884-2766
Fax: 817-850-2945
Court Reporter: Lisa Morton
Phone: 817-884-2767
Bailiffs: Cary King, Michael Holt and Bryan
Nickelson

**432nd District Court**
**Judge Ruben Gonzalez**
6th Floor
Phone: 817-884-2935
Fax: 817-884-3361
Court Coordinator: Tisha Wills
Court Clerk: Lori Tucker
Court Reporter: Angie Taylor

# Family District Courts
200 E. Weatherford St.
Fort Worth, TX 76196-0240

**231st District Court**
**Judge Jesus Nevarez, Jr.**
5th Floor
Phone: 817-884-3796
Fax: 817-884-3577
Court Coordinator: LeAnn Moore
Phone: 817-884-1580
Court Clerk: Rayne Erwin
Phone: 817-884-1300
Court Reporter: Caroline Stewart
Phone: 817-884-2724
Bailiff: Tom Cleveland

**Associate Judge: Lindsay DeVos**
Phone: 817-884-2756
Bailiff: Juan Gonzalez

**233rd District Court**
**Judge William W. Harris**
5th Floor
Phone: 817-884-1794
Fax: 817-884-2817
Court Coordinator: Leslie Young
Phone: 817-884-2686
Court Clerk: Brittany Terry
Phone: 817-884-1581
Court Reporter: LuAnn Spurrier
Phone: 817-884-1795

**Associate Judge: Diane Haddcock**
Bailiff: Juan Gonzalez
Phone: 817-884-1197

**322nd District Court**
**Judge Nancy Berger**
4th Floor
Phone: 817-884-1427
Court Coordinator: Lindsey Baker
Phone: 817-884-1597
E-mail: lkbaker@tarrantcounty.com
Court Clerk: Alison Harper
Phone: 817-884-1253
Court Reporter: Linda Vera
Phone: 817-884-1428
Bailiff: Edmund Choice

**Associate Judge: James Munford**
Phone: 817-884-3030
Bailiff: Roger Bailey

**323 District Court**
**Judge Timothy Menikos**
2701 Kimbo Rd.
Fort Worth, TX 76111
Phone: 817-838-4600
Fax: 817-838-4633
Court Coordinator: Daniel Beina
Phone: 817-838-4600, ext. 4647
Court Clerk: Donna Zavala
Phone: 817-838-4600, ext. 0653

**Associate Judge: Kim Brown — Juvenile Court**
**Associate Judge: James Teal — Juvenile Court**
**Associate Judge: Ellen Smith — Juvenile Court**

**324th District Court**
**Judge Jerome S. Hennigan**
4th Floor

Phone: 817-884-1432
Court Coordinator: Priscilla Poynor
Court Clerk: April Phillips
Phone: 817-884-2569
Court Reporter: Francis Janezic
Phone: 817-884-1430
Bailiff: David Brock

**Associate Judge: Beth Poulos**
Bailiff: Gina Cundiff
Phone: 817-884-1991

**325th District Court**
**Judge Judith G. Wells**
5th Floor
Phone: 817-884-1587
Fax: 817-884-2701
Court Coordinator: Cheryl Lopez
E-mail: clopez@tarrantcounty.com
Court Clerk: Bill Hahn
Phone: 817-884-2572
Court Reporter: Kirk Moss
Phone: 817-884-1445
Bailiff: Hollis Cate

**Associate Judge: Terry White**
Phone: 817-884-1444
Bailiff: Frances Lambright, Jr.

**360th District Court**
**Judge Michael Sinha**
4th Floor
Phone: 817-884-2708
Fax: 817-844-3360
Court Coordinator: Christy Loveless
Phone: 817-884-2899
Court Clerk: Cheryl Ginunis
Phone: 817-884-1899
Court Reporter: Jennifer Hunter
Phone: 817-884-2722
Bailiff: Jim Albright
Phone: 817-884-2720

**Associate Judge: Cynthia Johns-Mendoza**
Bailiff: Frankie McGill

# Probate Courts
100 W. Weatherford St.
Fort Worth, TX  76196

**Probate Court No. 1**
**Judge Steve M. King**
Room 260A
Phone: 817-884-1200

E-mail: probatecourt1@tarrantcounty.com
Court Coordinator: Heather Beyer
Phone: 817-212-7238
E-mail: hbeyer@tarrantcounty.com
Court Administrator: Mark W. Sullivan
Phone: 817-884-1048
E-mail: msullivan@tarrantcounty.com
Auditor: Livia Barton
Phone: 817-884-1047
E-mail: lbarton@tarrantcounty.com
Court Investigator: Barrie Allen
Phone: 817-884-2189
E-mail: ballen@tarrantcounty.com
Bailiff: Richard A. Floyd
Phone: 817-884-2714
E-mail: rafloyd@tarrantcounty.com

**Associate Judge: Quentin A. McGown**
Phone: 817-212-7037
E-mail: gqmcgown@tarrantcounty.com

**Probate Court No. 2**
**Judge Pat Ferchill**
Room 220A
Phone: 817-884-1415
Court Coordinator: Tina Clay
Court Administrator: Steve Fields
Phone: 817-884-1049
Bailiff: Jay Cannon

**Associate Judge: Lin C. Morrisett**
Phone: 817-884-2794

# County Courts
100 W. Weatherford St.
Fort Worth, TX  76196

**County Clerk: Mary Louise Garcia**
Room 130
Phone: 817-884-1070
Fax: 817-884-3295
E-mail: mlgarcia@tarrantcounty.com

**County Judge: Glen Whitley**
Room 501
Phone: 817-884-1441
Fax: 817-884-2793
E-mail: gwhitley@tarrantcounty.com
Chief of Staff: Tom Stallings

**County Court at Law No. 1**
**Judge Don Pierson**
Room 490
Phone: 817-884-1457

Fax: 817-884-3254
Court Coordinator: Tracey Wood
Phone: 817-884-2761
E-mail: tlwood@tarrantcounty.com
Court Reporter: Becky Partin
Phone: 817-884-1458
Bailiff: James Masulich

**County Court at Law No. 2**
**Judge Jennifer Rymell**
Room 240A
Phone: 817-884-1813
Fax: 817-884-1393
Court Coordinator: D. D. Kuhn
Phone: 817-884-2762
E-mail: dkuhn@tarrantcounty.com
Court Reporter: Traci Johnston
Phone: 817-884-1846
E-mail: tjohnston@tarrantcounty.com
Bailiff: Freddie Wiel
E-mail: lfweil@tarrantcounty.com

**County Court at Law No. 3**
**Judge Mike Hrabal**
Room 290A
Phone: 817-884-1095
Fax: 817-884-2964
Court Coordinator: Carla Philips
Phone: 817-884-1914
Court Reporter: Shari Steen
Phone: 817-884-1916
Bailiff: Ron Pierson

## County Criminal Courts
401 W. Belknap St.
Fort Worth, TX 76196-0236

**County Criminal Court No. 1**
**Judge David E. Cook**
5th Floor
Phone: 817-884-1337
Court Coordinator: Sarah Phillips
Court Clerk: Rene Kuntak
Court Reporter: Patti Richards
Bailiffs: Jackie Burns and Lorenzo Macias

**County Criminal Court No. 2**
**Judge Carey F. Walker**
6th Floor
Phone: 817-884-1338
Fax: 817-850-2356
Court Coordinator: Mary Chaisson
Phone: 817-884-1340
Court Clerk: Arturo De Gallegos

Phone: 817-884-1218
Court Reporter: William Shelton
Bailiffs: Cliff Alcon and Johnny Pettyjohn

**County Criminal Court No. 3**
**Judge Bob McCoy**
7th Floor
Phone: 817-884-1376
Court Coordinator: Rachel Martinez
Phone: 817-884-2595
Court Reporter: Jennifer Bullard
Phone: 817-884-2935
Bailiffs: Shane James and J.R. Rosas

**County Criminal Court No. 4**
**Judge Deborah Nekhom**
5th Floor
Phone: 817-884-1426
Court Coordinator: Signora Lott
Phone: 817-884-2055
E-mail: jplott@tarrantcounty.com
Court Reporter: Michelle Seay
Phone: 817-884-2917
E-mail: mseay@tarrantcounty.com
Bailiffs: Keith Barrett and David Montgomery

**County Criminal Court No. 5**
**Judge Jamie Cummings**
6th Floor
Phone: 817-884-2727
Court Coordinator: Channy Price
Court Reporter: Terry Bradshaw
Phone: 817-884-2728
Bailiff: Bobby Minter

**County Criminal Court No. 6**
**Judge Molly Jones**
8th Floor
Phone: 817-884-2745
Court Coordinator: Carolyn Johnson
Phone: 817-884-2747
Court Reporter: Connie Gilfeather
Bailiffs: Nyla Coleman and
Morris Courtney, Jr.

**County Criminal Court No. 7**
**Judge Cheril Hardy**
8th Floor
Phone: 817-884-2773
Court Coordinator: Georgie Haynes
Phone: 817-884-2969
Court Reporter: Mary Ann Clifton
Phone: 817-884-2776
Bailiff: Bobby Hardin

**STATE, DISTRICT AND COUNTY COURTS**

**County Criminal Court No. 8**
**Judge Charles Vanover**
7th Floor
Phone: 817-884-3400
Court Coordinator: Donna Allen
Phone: 817-884-3403
E-mail: djallen@tarrantcounty.com
Court Reporter: Nancy Hawkins
Phone: 817-884-3402
Bailiffs: Terry Parsons and Michael Sheets

**County Criminal Court No. 9**
**Judge Brent A. Carr**
8th Floor
Phone: 817-884-3410
Court Coordinator: Lori McEndree
Phone: 817-884-3413
Court Reporter: Toni Freeman
Phone: 817-884-3412
Bailiffs: Jeff Baysinger and Sheri Ruben

**County Criminal Court No. 10**
**Judge Phil Sorrells**
6th Floor
Phone: 817-884-3420
Court Coordinator: Jason Peters
Phone: 817-884-3423
Court Reporter: Peggy Ballew
Phone: 817-884-3422
Bailiffs: Maria DeLeon and William Samson

# TAYLOR COUNTY

Seat: Abilene

300 Oak St.
Abilene, TX 79602
www.taylorcountytexas.org

**District Clerk: Patricia Henderson**
Suite 400
Phone: 325-674-1316
Fax: 325-674-1307
E-mail: hendersp@taylorcountytexas.org
Chief Deputy: Tammy Robinson
E-mail: robinsont@taylorcountytexas.org

**District Attorney: James Eidson**
Phone: 325-674-1261
Fax: 325-674-1306

**42nd District Court**
**Judge John W. Weeks**

Suite 401
Phone: 325-674-1314
Fax: 325-674-1256
Court Administrator: Darla Quinney
Court Reporter: Terri Nichols
Phone: 325-674-1258
Bailiff: Terry Odam

**104th District Court**
**Judge Lee Hamilton**
Suite 402
Phone: 325-674-1313
Fax: 325-674-1256
E-mail: hamiltol@taylorcountytexas.org
Court Coordinator: Terry Terry
E-mail: terry@taylorcountytexas.org
Court Reporter: Julie Campbell
Phone: 325-674-1260
Bailiff: Danny Wade

**326th District Court**
**Judge Paul Rotenberry**
Phone: 325-674-1325
Court Coordinator: Lisa Clements
Assistant Court Coordinator: Ann Graham
Court Reporter: Kim Hogan
Bailiff: Rodney Stegall

**Associate Judge: Charles E. Myers**
Phone: 325-674-1310

**Associate Judge: Kenneth Law (IV-D Cases)**
Phone: 325-738-8500

**350th District Court**
**Judge Thomas Wheeler**
Suite 404
Phone: 325-674-1242
Court Coordinator: Wendi S. Pearson
E-mail: pearsonw@taylorcountytexas.org
Court Reporter: Mary K. Ross
Bailiff: Rudy Sayas

**County Clerk: Larry G. Bevill**
Phone: 325-674-1202
Fax: 325-674-1279
E-mail: bevill@taylorcountytexas.org
Chief Deputy: Mendy Wallace
E-mail: wallacem@taylorcountytexas.org
Chief Deputy: Jaime Villarreal
E-mail: villarreal@taylorcountytexas.org

**County Judge: Downing A. Bolls, Jr.**
Phone: 325-674-1235
Fax: 325-674-1365
Court Coordinator: Cindy Sexton

**County Court at Law No. 1**
**Judge Robert Harper**
Suite 500
Phone: 325-674-1323
Fax: 325-738-8528
E-mail: harperr@taylorcountytexas.org
Court Coordinator: Maria Tolentino
Court Reporter: Caroline Kreitler
Bailiff: Harold Sumrall

**County Court at Law No. 2**
**Judge Samuel J. Carroll**
Suite 501
Phone: 325-674-1208
Fax: 325-738-8502
E-mail: rollinsb@taylorcountytexas.org
Court Coordinator: Chris Glasgow
Court Reporter: Caroline Kreitler
Bailiff: Robert Waggener

# TERRELL COUNTY

Seat: Sanderson

105 E. Hackberry
Sanderson, TX 79848
www.co.terrell.tx.us

**District and County Clerk: Martha Allen**
P.O. Drawer 410
Sanderson, TX 79848-0410
Phone: 432-345-2391
Fax: 432-345-2740

**District Attorney: Fred Hernandez**
*Please see Val Verde County.*

**63rd District Court**
**Judge Enrique Fernandez** sits as scheduled.
*Please see Val Verde County.*

**83rd District Court**
**Judge Robert E. Cadena** sits as scheduled.
*Please see Val Verde County.*

**County Attorney: Ken Bellah**
P.O. Box 175
Sanderson, TX 79848
Phone: 432-345-2248
Fax: 432-345-2205

**County Judge: Santiago Flores**
P.O. Box 4810

Sanderson, TX 79848
Phone: 432-345-2421
E-mail: santiago.flores@co.terrell.tx.us

# TERRY COUNTY

Seat: Brownfield

500 W. Main St.
Brownfield, TX 79316
www.co.terry.tx.us

**District Clerk: Paige Lindsey**
Room 209E
Phone: 806-637-4202
Fax: 806-637-1333
E-mail: plindsey@terrycounty.org

**District and County Attorney: Jo'Shae Ferguson-Worley**
Room 208E
Phone: 806-637-4984
Fax: 806-637-4947
E-mail: jworley@terrycounty.org

**121st District Court**
**Judge Kelly G. Moore**
Room 302W
Phone: 806-637-7742
Court Coordinator: Debbi Miller
Phone: 806-637-6958

**County Clerk: Kim Carter**
Room 105
Phone: 806-637-8551
Fax: 806-637-4874
E-mail: kcarter@terrycounty.org

**County Judge: J.D. Butch Wagner**
Room 102
Phone: 806-637-6421
Fax: 806-637-9782
E-mail: jdwagner@terrycounty.org

# THROCKMORTON COUNTY

Seat: Throckmorton

105 N. Minter St.
Throckmorton, TX 76483-0309
www.co.throckmorton.tx.us

**District and County Clerk: Dianna Moore**
P.O. Box 309
Throckmorton, TX 76483
Phone: 940-849-2501
Fax: 940-849-3032
E-mail: throckclerk@gmail.com

**District Attorney: Michael E. Fouts**
*Please see Haskell County.*

**39th District Court**
**Judge Shane Hadaway** sits once a month or as needed.
*Please see Haskell County.*

**County Attorney: Jeff Mathiews**
P.O. Box 452
Throckmorton, TX 76483
Phone: 940-849-0020

**County Judge: W. F. "Trey" Carrington**
P.O. Box 700
Throckmorton, TX 76483
Phone: 940-849-3081
Fax: 940-849-3081
Administrative Assistant: Tina Kavecki

# TITUS COUNTY

Seat: Mount Pleasant

105 W. First St.
Mount Pleasant, TX 75456
www.co.titus.tx.us

**District Clerk: Debra Abston**
P.O. Box 492
Mount Pleasant, TX 75456-0492
Phone: 903-577-6721
Fax: 903-577-6719

**District Attorney: Charles C. Bailey**
P.O. Box 249
Mount Pleasant, TX 75456
Phone: 903-577-6726
Fax: 903-577-6729
E-mail: dacbailey@hotmail.com

**76th District Court**
**Judge Danny Woodson**
P.O. Box 1306
Mount Pleasant, TX 75456
Phone: 903-577-6736
Court Reporter: Cresta LeFeure
Phone: 903-577-6735

**276th District Court**
**Judge Robert Rolston** sits as scheduled.
*Please see Morris County.*

## County Court
100 W. 1st St.
Mount Pleasant, TX 75455

**County Clerk: Joan Newman**
Suite 204
Phone: 903-577-6796
Fax: 903-572-5078
Chief Deputy: Kendra Gray

**County Attorney: John Mark Cobern**
Suite 106
Phone: 903-572-0382
Fax: 903-577-7540
E-mail: tituscountyattorney@gmail.com

**County Judge: Brian P. Lee**
Suite 200
Phone: 903-577-6791
Fax: 903-577-6793
E-mail: titusjudge@gmail.com

# TOM GREEN COUNTY

Seat: San Angelo

112 W. Beauregard Ave.
San Angelo, TX 76903
www.co.tom-green.tx.us

**District Clerk: Sheri Woodfin**
Phone: 325-659-6579
Fax: 325-659-3241
E-mail: sheri.woodfin@co.tom-green.tx.us

**51st District Attorney: Allison Palmer**
124 W. Beauregard Ave.
San Angelo, TX 76903
Phone: 325-659-6583
Fax: 325-658-6831
E-mail: da_web@co.tom-green.tx.us

**119th District Attorney: George E. McCrea**
124 W. Beauregard Ave.
San Angelo, TX 76903
Phone: 325-659-6583
Fax: 325-658-6831
E-mail: da_web@co.tom-green.tx.us

**51st District Court**
**Judge Barbara L. Walther**
2nd Floor
Phone: 325-659-6571
Fax: 325-658-8046
Court Coordinator: Shannon McFarland
Court Reporter: Debbie Harris
Phone: 325-659-6574
Bailiff: Osiel Gamez

**119th District Court**
**Judge Garland "Ben" Woodward**
2nd Floor
Phone: 325-659-6571
Fax: 325-658-8046
Court Coordinator: Belinda Fernandez
Court Reporter: Lori Dobbins
Phone: 325-659-6575
Bailiff: Carey Free

**340th District Court**
**Judge Jay Weatherby**
1st Floor
Phone: 325-659-6571
Fax: 325-658-8046
Court Coordinator: Syliva Noriega
Court Reporter: Cindy Saunders
Phone: 325-659-6573
Bailiff: Alan Hill

**391st District Court**
**Judge Tom Gossett**
2nd Floor
Phone: 325-659-6571
Fax: 325-658-8046
Court Coordinator: Cheryl Torres
Court Reporter: Susan Jett
Phone: 325-695-6456
Bailiff: Bryan Elkin

*[handwritten: Erica Gonzalez ext 316]*

**County Clerk: Elizabeth McGill**
124 W. Beauregard Ave.
San Angelo, TX 76903
Phone: 325-659-6553
Fax: 325-659-3251
E-mail: elizabeth.mcgill@co.tom-green.tx.us

**County Attorney: Chris Taylor**
122 W. Harris Ave.
San Angelo, TX 76903
Phone: 325-659-6562
Fax: 325-655-6430
E-mail: chris.taylor@co.tom-green.tx.us

**County Judge: Steve Floyd**
122 W. Harris Ave.
San Angelo, TX 76903
Phone: 325-653-3318
Fax: 325-659-3258
E-mail: steve.floyd@co.tom-green.tx.us
Court Administrator: Ilma Perez
Court Reporter: Sharla Bredemeyer
Phone: 325-659-6450
Bailiff: Tonia Jennings

**County Court at Law No. 1**
**Judge Ben Nolen**
122 W. Harris Ave.
San Angelo, TX 76903
Phone: 325-659-6473
Fax: 325-659-6457
Court Coordinator: Jose L. Losoya, Jr.
Phone: 325-659-6559
E-mail: joe.losoya@co.tom-green.tx.us
Court Reporter: Sharla Bredemeyer
Phone: 325-659-6450
Bailiff: Mike Freeman
E-mail: mike.freeman@co.tom-green.tx.us

**County Court at Law No. 2**
**Judge Penny A. Roberts**
122 W. Harris Ave.
San Angelo, TX 76903
Phone: 325-658-2495
Fax: 325-659-6458
Court Coordinator: Chanda Hight
Phone: 325-658-2765
E-mail: chanda.hight@co.tom-green.tx.us
Court Coordinator: Ann L. Bailey
E-mail: ann.bailey@co.tom-green.tx.us
Court Reporter: Sharla Bredemeyer
Phone: 325-659-6450
Bailiff: Curtis Williams, Jr.
E-mail: curtis.williamsjr@co.tom-green.tx.us

# TRAVIS COUNTY

Seat: Austin

1000 Guadalupe St.
Austin, TX 78701
www.traviscountytx.gov

**District Clerk: Velva L. Price**
3rd Floor
E-mail: velva.price@traviscountytx.gov
Phone: 512-854-9457
Fax: 512-854-4744

*[sidebar, vertical text]* STATE, DISTRICT AND COUNTY COURTS

**Deputy District Clerk: Chris Dietche**
E-mail: chris.dietche@traviscountytx.gov
Phone: 512-854-9457

**District Attorney: Rosemary Lehmberg**
509 W. 11th St.
Austin, TX 78701
Phone: 512-854-9400
Fax: 512-854-9695

## Civil District Courts
1000 Guadalupe St.
Austin, TX 78701
Central Civil Fax: 512-854-9332

Mailing Address: P.O. Box 1748
Austin, TX 78767

**Court Administrator: Warren Vavra**
Room 435
Phone: 512-854-2484
Fax: 512-854-9174

Family Docket Manager: Jacob Stokes

**53rd District Court**
**Judge Scott H. Jenkins**
Room 421
Phone: 512-854-9308
Court Operations Officer: Tiffaney Gould
Phone: 512-854-7278
E-mail: tiffaney.gould@traviscountytx.gov
Court Clerk: Nancy Rodriguez
Phone: 512-854-5832
Court Reporter: Chavela Crain
Phone: 512-854-9322
Staff Attorney: Elissa Hogan
Phone: 512-854-9366

**98th District Court**
**Judge Rhonda Hurley**
Suite 512
Phone: 512-854-9307
Court Operations Officer: Dorina Cockman
Phone: 512-854-9384
Court Clerk: Steve Salinas
Phone: 512-854-5886
Court Reporter: Patty Day
Phone: 512-854-9629
Staff Attorney: Michelle Roche
Phone: 512-854-7839

**126th District Court**
**Judge Darlene Byrne**

Suite 436
Phone: 512-854-9313
Court Operations Officer: Rene R. Salinas
Phone: 512-854-2484
Court Clerk: Kelly Davis
Phone: 512-854-5887
Court Reporter: Meanette Salgado
Phone: 512-854-7848
Staff Attorney: Katy Gallagher-Parker
Phone: 512-854-4915

**200th District Court**
**Judge Gisela Triana**
Room 508
Phone: 512-854-9306
Court Operations Officer: Diana Capuchino
Phone: 512-854-5838
Court Clerk: Vacant
Court Reporter: LaDelle Abilez
Phone: 512-854-9325
Staff Attorney: James T. Parsons
Phone: 512-854-4916

**201st District Court**
**Judge Amy Clark Meachum**
Suite 314
Phone: 512-854-9305
Court Operations Officer: Vicky Mescher
Phone: 512-854-9319
Court Clerk: Amanda Martinez
Phone: 512-854-5857
Court Reporter: Alicia Racanelli
Phone: 512-854-4028
Staff Attorney: Huette Merrell
Phone: 512-854-9895

**250th District Court**
**Judge Karin Crump**
Suite 500
Phone: 512-854-9312
Court Operations Officer: Grace McGee
Phone: 512-854-4807
Court Clerk: Ifrain "Fino" Alaniz
Phone: 512-854-5800
Court Reporter: Della Rothermel
Phone: 512-854-9321
Staff Attorney: Vasu Behara
Phone: 512-854-9903

**261st District Court**
**Judge Lora J. Livingston**
Suite 308
Phone: 512-854-9309
Court Operations Officer: Mary Jane Lawson
Phone: 512-854-9337

STATE, DISTRICT AND COUNTY COURTS

Court Clerk: Ruben Tamez
Phone: 512-854-5841
Court Reporter: Lasonya Thomas
Phone: 512-854-9331
Staff Attorney: Lindsey Gill
Phone: 512-854-9625

**345th District Court**
**Judge Stephen Yelenosky**
Suite 412
Phone: 512-854-9374
Court Operations Officer: Claire Web
Phone: 512-854-9712
Court Clerk: Patricia "Trish" Winkler
Phone: 512-854-4309
Court Reporter: Albert Alvarez
Phone: 512-854-9373
Staff Attorney: Dana Lewis
Phone: 512-854-9892

**353rd District Court**
**Judge Tim Sulak**
Suite 501
Phone: 512-854-9380
Court Operations Officer: Pam Seger
Phone: 512-854-5852
Court Clerk: Elizabeth Garcia
Phone: 512-854-5852
Court Reporter: Rhonda Watson
Phone: 512-854-9356
Staff Attorney: Megan Johnson
Phone: 512-854-4281

**419th District Court**
**Judge Orlinda Naranjo**
Suite 325
Phone: 512-854-4023
Court Operations Officer: Tammy St. George
Court Clerk: Victoria Chambers
Phone: 512-854-9010
Court Reporter: Dora Canizales
Phone: 512-854-9329
Staff Attorney: Trent Hightower
Phone: 512-854-4029

**Associate Judge: James L. Arth — Family Court**
Suite 506
Phone: 512-854-9300
Court Operations Officer: Charles Upshaw
Phone: 512-854-9457
Court Reporter: Laura Taylor
Phone: 512-854-9054

**Associate Judge: James Andrew Hathcock — Family Court**

Suite 411
Phone: 512-854-9300
Fax: 512-854-9332
Court Clerk: Vacant
Phone: 512-854-5850
Judicial Aide: Laura Gomez
Phone: 512-854-9303
Court Reporter: Angie Hertel
Phone: 512-854-9350
Bailiff: Wilson Andrews
Phone: 512-854-9783

**Associate Judge: Lenoard Saenz — Family Court**
Suite 121
Phone: 512-854-9300
Court Clerk: Vacant
Phone: 512-854-5844
Court Reporter: Shana Wise
Phone: 512-854-9327
Bailiff: Skip Williams
Phone: 512-854-9425

# Criminal District Courts
509 W. 11th St.
Austin, TX 78701

**147th District Court**
**Judge Clifford A. Brown**
7th Floor
Phone: 512-854-9311
Fax: 512-854-6495
Court Coordinator: Jeanette Deleon
Court Clerk: Kay Bennett
Phone: 512-854-9420
Court Reporter: Kimberly Lee
Phone: 512-854-9315
Bailiff: Tyrone Murray
Phone: 512-854-6404

**167th District Court**
**Judge David Wahlberg**
8th Floor
Phone: 512-854-9310
Fax: 512-854-6425
Court Coordinator: Melissa Moreno
Court Clerk: Sonya Underwood
Court Reporter: Shanna Castillo
Phone: 512-854-5804
Deputy: Crig Smith
Phone: 512-854-6404

**299th District Court**
**Judge Karen Sage**

8th Floor
Phone: 512-854-9442
Fax: 512-854-6494
E-mail: 299threst@co.travis.tx.us
Court Coordinator: Lisa McCormick
Court Clerk: Vivian Capello
Court Reporter: Angela Chambers
Phone: 512-854-9353
Bailiff: Craig Smith
Phone: 512-854-9355

**331st District Court**
**Judge David Crain**
9th Floor
Phone: 512-854-9443
Fax: 512-854-9140
Court Clerk: Ana Fraga-Arayo
Judicial Aide: Julie Alvarez
Court Reporter: Raquel Kocher
Phone: 512-854-9357
Court Probation Officer: Roger DeLeon
Bailiff: Sonya Torrez

**390th District Court**
**Judge Julie Kocurek**
7th Floor
Phone: 512-854-4885
Fax: 512-854-4680
Judicial Aide: Virginia Vasquez
Court Reporter: Marti Ruby
Phone: 512-854-4721
Bailiff: Pedro Reyes

**403rd District Court**
**Judge Brenda Kennedy**
6th Floor
Phone: 512-854-9808
Fax: 512-854-4683
Court Coordinator: Kamala White
Phone: 512-854-5811
Court Clerk: Darrell Mansfield
Court Reporter: Roxanne Davenport
Phone: 512-854-9620
Bailiff: Shelby Werner
Phone: 512-854-6448

**427th District Court**
**Judge Jim Coronado**
3rd Floor
Phone: 512-854-3663
Fax: 512-854-2227
Court Coordinator: Jan Cason
Court Clerk: Amber Urrutia
Court Reporter: Ellie Klemens
Phone: 512-854-3667

Bailiff: Tom Maldonado
Phone: 512-854-3665

**Magistrate Court**
**Judge Leon Grizzard**
9th Floor
Phone: 512-854-9099
Fax: 512-854-9140
Court Coordinator: Kerri Keskinen
Court Reporter: Anita Martinez
Phone: 512-854-3639
Bailiff: Martin Estrada
Phone: 512-854-4995

# Probate Court
1000 Guadalupe St., Suite 217
Austin, TX 78701

**Probate Court No. 1**
**Judge Guy Herman**
Phone: 512-854-9258
Fax: 512-854-4418
Court Coordinator: Tanya Scanlon
E-mail: tanya.scanlone@traviscountytx.gov
Court Administrator: Christy Nisbett
Phone: 512-854-9559
Court Reporter: Melissa Voigt
Phone: 512-854-9086
Court Investigator: Tom Ruffer
Phone: 512-854-4978
Staff Attorney: Emily Meisgeier
Phone: 512-854-9283
Guardianship Coordinator: Michael Gianotti
Phone: 512-854-4359
Court Auditor: Alesia Drummer
Phone: 512-854-4358

**Associate Judge: Dan Prashner**
Phone: 512-854-9258

# County Courts

**County Clerk: Dana DeBeauvoir**
P.O. Box 149325
Austin, TX 78714-9325
Phone: 512-854-9188
Fax: 512-854-4526

**County Attorney: David Escamilla**
314 W. 11th St., Suite 300
Austin, TX 78701
Phone: 512-854-9415
Fax: 512-854-9316

County Judge: Sarah Eckhardt
700 Lavaca, Suite 2.300
Austin, TX 78701
Phone: 512-854-9555
Fax: 512-854-9535
E-mail: sara.eckhardt@traviscountytx.org
Executive Assistant: Joe Hon
Phone: 512-854-1123
Chief of Staff: Peter Einhorn
Phone: 512-854-1125

County Court at Law No. 1
Judge Todd Wong
Phone: 512-854-9241
Fax: 512-854-4380
Court Operations Officer: Catherine Jones
Staff Attorney: Lea Downey-Gallatin
Phone: 512-854-4919
Court Reporter: Cathy Mata
Phone: 512-854-9252
Judicial Assistant: Holli Sliter
Phone: 512-854-9645

County Court at Law No. 2
Judge Eric M. Shepperd
Phone: 512-854-9242
Fax: 512-854-4724
Court Operations Officer: Priscila Vallabares
Phone: 512-854-9249
Staff Attorney: Lea Downey Gallatin
Phone: 512-854-4919
Court Reporter: Amanda Anderson
Phone: 512-854-9250
Judicial Assistant: Courtey Lee

County Court at Law No. 3
Judge John Lipscombe
509 W. 11th St., Room 5A312
Austin, TX 78701
Phone: 512-854-9243
Fax: 512-854-4682
Judicial Assistant: Delia Garcia
Court Reporter: Lauren Miller
Phone: 512-854-9247
Office Specialist: Christi Little
Phone: 512-854-3616

County Court at Law No. 4
Judge Mike Denton
509 W. 11th St., Room 3.404
Austin, TX 78701
Phone: 512-854-9896
Fax: 512-854-4887
Judicial Aide: Vicki Padilla
Phone: 512-854-7867

E-mail vicki.padilla@traviccountytx.gov
Court Reporter: Christine Gutierrez
Phone: 512-854-7867
Bailiff: Jesse Ibarra
Phone: 512-854-4884

County Court at Law No. 5
Judge Nancy Honengarten
509 W. 11th St., Room 4.140
Austin, TX 78701
Phone: 512-854-9676
Fax: 512-854-4685
Judicial Aide: Kristen Meitzen
E-mail: kristen.meitzen@traviscountytx.gov
Court Reporter: Karen Vavra
Phone: 512-854-9621
E-mail: karen.vavra@traviscountytx.gov
Probation Officer: Anna Marie DeLaRosa
Phone: 512-854-3510
E-mail: annadelarosa@traviscountytx.gov
Office Specialist and Bailiff: Walter Poston
Phone: 512-854-3632
E-mail: walter.poston@traviscountytx.gov

County Court at Law No. 6
Judge Brandy Mueller
509 W. 11th St., Room 4A312
Austin, TX 78701
Phone: 512-854-9677
Fax: 512-854-4684
E-mail: cc6reset@traviscountytx.gov
Judicial Aide: Jose Becerra
Court Reporter: Suzanne Heard
Phone: 512-854-9622
Bailiff: Dennis Clark
Phone: 512-854-9743

County Court at Law No. 7
Judge Elisabeth A. Earle
509 W. 11th St., Room 6.240
Austin, TX 78701
Phone: 512-854-9679
Fax: 512-854-3793
Judicial Aide: Jennifer Martinez
E-mail: jennifer.martinez@traviscountytx.gov
Court Reporter: Kathy Genung
Phone: 512-854-3792
Bailiff: Chad Cauthen
Phone: 512-854-3791

County Court at Law No. 8
Judge Carlos H. Barrera
5th Floor
Phone: 512-854-7180
Fax: 512-854-7181

Judicial Aide: Marivel Garza
Court Reporter: Elizabeth Davis
Bailiff: Adan Paredes
Phone: 512-854-7182

# TRINITY COUNTY

Seat: Groveton

162 W. First St.
Groveton, TX 75845
www.co.trinity.tx.us

**District Clerk: Kristen Raiford**
P.O. Box 549
Groveton, TX 75845-0548
Phone: 936-642-1118
Fax: 936-642-0002
E-mail: tcdc@co.trinity.tx.us
Administrative Assistants: Kathy Brown and
Lisa Sharp
E-mail: kathy.brown@trinity.tx.us

**District Attorney: Bennie L. Schiro**
P.O. Box 400
Groveton, TX 75845-0400
Phone: 936-642-2401
Fax: 936-642-2040
E-mail: bennie.schiero@co.trinity.tx.us
Legal Assistant: Miranda Howell

**258th District Court**
**Judge Ernest L. McClendon**
101 W. Mill Street, Suite 286
Livingston, TX 77351
Phone: 936-327-6847
Fax: 936-327-6881
E-mail: districtcourt258@livingston.net
Court Coordinator: Leona Wiggins
Court Reporter: Christa Stroust
Bailiff: Tracy Galloway

**411th District Court**
**Judge Kaycee L. Jones** sits twice a month on
Tuesday.
*Please see Polk County.*

**County Clerk: Shasta Bergman**
P.O. Box 456
Groveton, TX 75845-0456
Phone: 936-642-1208
Fax: 936-642-3004
E-mail: shasta.bergman@co.trinity.tx.us

**County Attorney: Joe W. Bell**
P.O. Box 979
Groveton, TX 75845-0979
Phone: 936-642-1725
Fax: 936-642-2362

**County Judge: Steven D. Page**
P.O. Box 457
Groveton, TX 75845-0457
Phone: 936-642-1746
Fax: 936-642-1046
Court Coordinator: Sandra Cole
E-mail: tcj@co.trinity.tx.us

# TYLER COUNTY

Seat: Woodville

100 W. Bluff St.
Woodville, TX 75979-5220
www.co.tyler.tx.us

**District Clerk: Chyrl Pounds**
Room 203
Phone: 409-283-2162

**District Attorney: Lou Ann Cloy**
Phone: 409-283-8136
Fax: 409-283-6128

**1A District Court**
**Judge Delinda Gibbs-Walker** sits the second
Friday of every month.
*Please see Jasper County.*

**88th District Court**
**Judge Earl Stover, III** sits the fourth Monday of
every month and the Thursday before the
fourth Monday.
*Please see Hardin County.*

**County Clerk: Donece Gregory**
116 S. Charlton
Woodville, TX 75979
Phone: 409-283-2281
Fax: 409-283-8049
E-mail: countyclerk.cc@co.tyler.tx.us

**County Judge: Jacques L. Blanchette**
Room 102
Phone: 409-283-2141
Fax: 409-331-0028
E-mail: judge@co.tyler.tx.us

**STATE, DISTRICT AND COUNTY COURTS**

Judicial Assisant: Mary Randel
E-mail: mrandel.cojudge@co.tyler.tx.us

# UPSHUR COUNTY

Seat: Gilmer

100 W. Tyler St.
Gilmer, TX 75644
www.countyofupshur.com

**District Clerk: Karen Bunn**
405 N. Titus St.
Gilmer, TX 75644
Phone: 903-843-5031
Fax: 903-843-3540

**District Attorney: Billy Byrd**
405 N. Titus St.
Gilmer, TX 75644
Phone: 903-843-5513
Fax: 903-843-3661

**115th District Court**
**Judge Lauren L. Parish**
P.O. Box 1052
Gilmer, TX 75644
Phone: 903-843-2836
Fax: 903-843-5109
Court Coordinator: Teena Henson
Court Reporter: Deanna Drennan
Bailiff: Becky Pope

**County Clerk: Terri Ross**
P.O. Box 730
Gilmer, TX 75644
Phone: 903-680-8122
Fax: 903-843-4504
E-mail: terri.ross@countyofupshur.com

**County Judge: Dean Fowler**
P.O. Box 790
Gilmer, TX 75644
Phone: 903-843-4003
Fax: 903-843-0827

# UPTON COUNTY

Seat: Rankin

205 E. 10th St.
Rankin, TX 79778
www.co.upton.tx.us

**District and County Clerk: LaWanda McMurray**
P.O. Box 465
Rankin, TX 79778
Phone: 432-693-2861
Fax: 432-693-2129
E-mail: lmcmurray@co.upton.tx.us

**District Attorney: Laurie K. English**
*Please see Pecos County.*

**112th District Court**
**Judge Pedro Gomez, Jr.** sits as scheduled.
*Please see Crockett County.*

**Court Attorney: Melanie Spratt-Anderson**
P.O. Box 890
Rankin, TX 79778
Phone: 432-693-2222
Fax: 432-693-2243
E-mail: uptonatty@hotmail.com

**County Judge: Bill Eyler**
P.O. Box 482
Rankin, TX 79778
Phone: 432-693-2321
Fax: 432-693-2243
E-mail: cojudge@co.upton.tx.us

# UVALDE COUNTY

Seat: Uvalde

100 N. Getty St.
Uvalde, TX 78801
www.uvaldecounty.com

**District Clerk: Christina J. Ovalle**
Box 15
Phone: 830-278-3918
E-mail: covalle@uvaldecounty.com

**District Attorney: Daniel J. Kindred**
Box 5
Phone: 830-278-2916
Fax: 830-278-4731

**38th District Court**
**Judge Camile G. Dubose**
Box 17
Phone: 830-278-3913
Fax: 830-278-7502
Court Coordinator (Criminal): Lela Ballesteros
E-mail: lela@uvaldecounty.com

Court Coordinator (Civil): Mateo Santos
Phone: 830-741-7146
Fax: 830-741-6015
E-mail: msantos@uvaldecounty.com
Court Reporter: Sherry Gentry
Phone: 830-200-9719
E-mail: rgentry6@gmail.com

**Associate Judge: Kelley Kimble**
Phone: 830-278-8167
Fax: 830-278-3017

**County Clerk: Donna M. Williams**
P.O. Box 284
Uvalde, TX 78802
Phone: 830-278-6614
Fax: 830-278-8692
E-mail: dwilliams@uvaldecounty.com

**County Attorney: John P. Dodson**
318 E. Nopal
Uvalde, TX 78801
Phone: 830-278-6510
Fax: 830-278-6585
E-mail: ucatty@uvaldecounty.com

**County Judge: William R. Mitchell**
#3 Courthouse Square
Uvalde, TX 78801
Phone: 830-278-3216
Fax: 830-278-8703
E-mail: wrmcj@uvaldecounty.com

# VAL VERDE COUNTY

Seat: Del Rio

100 E. Broadway St.
Del Rio, TX 78840

**District Clerk: JoAnn Cervantes**
P.O. Box 1544
Del Rio, TX 78841-1544
Phone: 830-774-7538
Fax: 830-774-7643
E-mail: jcervantes@valverdecounty.org

**District Attorney: Fred Hernandez**
P.O. Box 1405
Del Rio, TX 78841-1405
Phone: 830-775-0505
Fax: 830-775-0352
First Assistant: Roland Andrade

Assistant DA: Omar Fuentes
Border Prosecution Unit Assistant DA:
Gerard Byers

**63rd District Court**
**Judge Enrique Fernandez**
P.O. Drawer 1089
Del Rio, TX 78841-1089
Phone: 830-774-7523
Fax: 830-774-1359
Court Coordinator: Lucy T. Santos
Phone: 830-774-7524
E-mail: lucy_santos@valverdecounty.org
Court Reporter: John Price
Bailiff: Roy Barrera

**83rd District Court**
**Judge Robert E. Cadena**
P.O. Box 1860
Del Rio, TX 78841-1860
Phone: 830-774-7654
Fax: 830-774-7651
E-mail: rcadena@valverdecounty.org
Court Coordinator: Nelva Y. Torres
Court Reporter: Gene Steel
Bailiff: Roy Barrera

# County Court
400 Pecan St.
Del Rio, TX 78840

**County Clerk: Generosa Gracia-Ramon**
P.O. Box 1267
Del Rio, TX 78841-1267
Phone: 830-774-7564
Fax: 830-774-7608
E-mail: gramon@valverdecounty.org
Chief Deputy: Diane Alcala

**County Attorney: Ana Markowski Smith**
Phone: 830-774-7571
Fax: 830-774-1235
First Assistant: David Martinez

**County Judge: Efrain Valdez**
P.O. Box 4250
Del Rio, TX 78841
Phone: 830-774-7501
Fax: 830-775-9406
E-mail: evaldez@valverdecounty.org
Administrative Assistant: Eloy Padilla

**County Court at Law**
**Judge Sergio J. Gonzalez**

P.O. Box 1431
Del Rio, TX 78841-1431
Phone: 830-774-7575
Fax: 830-778-7440
Court Coordinator: Sandra Hernandez
Court Reporter: Patty Abyta
Bailiff: Daniel Reyes

# VAN ZANDT COUNTY

Seat: Canton

121 E. Dallas St.
Canton, TX 75103
www.vanzandtcounty.org

**District Clerk: Karen L. Wilson**
Room 302
Phone: 903-567-6576
Fax: 903-567-1283
E-mail: districtclerk@vanzandtcounty.org

**District Attorney: Chris Martin**
400 S. Buffalo
Canton, TX 75103-1604
Phone: 903-567-4104
Fax: 903-567-6258

**294th District Court**
**Judge Teresa A. Drum**
Room 301
Phone: 903-567-4422
Fax: 903-567-5652
Court Administrator: Kathy Jackson
Court Reporter: Estella Grisham
E-mail: egrisham@vanzandtcounty.org
Bailiff: Linda English

**County Clerk: Pam Pearman**
Room 202
Phone: 903-567-7555
Fax: 903-567-6722
E-mail: ppearman@vanzandtcounty.org

**County Judge: Don Kirkpatrick**
Room 204
Phone: 903-567-4071
Fax: 903-567-7216
Administrative Assistant: Sandy Hill
E-mail: sandy@vanzandtcounty.org

**County Court at Law**
**Judge Randal McDonald**

Phone: 903-567-7988
Fax: 903-567-6854
Court Coordinator: Mary Barker
E-mail: mbarker@vanzandtcounty.org
Court Reporter: Diana Pereria
Bailiff: Greg Ramsey

# VICTORIA COUNTY

Seat: Victoria

115 N. Bridge St.
Victoria, TX 77901
www.vctx.org

**District Clerk: Cathy Stuart**
Room 330
Victoria, TX 77901
Phone: 361-575-0581
Fax: 361-572-5682

**District Attorney: Steve Tyler**
205 N. Bridge St., Suite 301
Victoria, TX 77901
Phone: 361-575-0468
Fax: 361-576-4139

**24th District Court**
**Judge Jack W. Marr**
P.O. Box 1457
Victoria, TX 77903
Phone: 361-575-3172
Court Coordinator: Jackie Gloor
Court Reporter: Marnie Gabrysch
Phone: 361-573-9300

**135th District Court**
**Judge K. Stephen Williams**
Phone: 361-575-2412
Court Coordinator: Jackie Gloor
Court Reporter: Dorinda Norrell
Phone: 361-573-5313

**267th District Court**
**Judge Juergen "Skipper" Koetter**
2nd Floor
Phone: 361-578-1998
Court Coordinator: Jackie Gloor
Court Reporter: Sharon Miori
Phone: 361-578-3806
*Note: Hon. Koetter will retire on 3/4/16.*
*Gov. Abbott to appoint new judge.*

**377th District Court**
**Judge Eli E. Garza**
Phone: 361-578-8756
Court Coordinator: Kim Plummer
Court Reporter: Allison Rother
Phone: 361-576-5876

**County Clerk: Heidi Easley**
P.O. Box 1968
Victoria, TX 77902
Phone: 361-575-1478
Fax: 361-575-6276

**County Judge: Ben Zeller**
101 N. Bridge St., Room 102
Victoria, TX 77901-6544
Phone: 361-575-4558

**County Court at Law No. 1**
**Judge Travis H. Ernst**
Room 203
Phone: 361-575-4550
Court Clerk: Theresa Novosad
Phone: 361-575-1478
Court Coordinator: Becky Wade
Phone: 361-575-1478
Court Reporter: Christy Moya

**County Court at Law No. 2**
**Judge Daniel F. Gilliam**
Phone: 361-575-7195
Court Clerk: Belinda Sepulveda
Phone: 361-575-1478
Court Coordinator: Becky Wade
Court Reporter: Regina Peyton

# WALKER COUNTY

Seat: Huntsville

1100 University Ave.
Huntsville, TX 77340
www.co.walker.tx.us

**District Clerk: Robyn M. Flowers**
Room 209
Phone: 936-436-4972
Fax: 936-436-4973
E-mail: rflowers@co.walker.tx.us

**District Attorney: David P. Weeks**
1036 11th St.
Huntsville, TX 77340

Phone: 936-435-2441
Fax: 936-435-2449

**12th District Court**
**Judge Donald L. Kraemer**
Room 303
Phone: 936-436-4915
Fax: 936-435-8025
Court Coordinator: Becky West
E-mail: bwest@co.walker.tx.us
Court Administrator: Carrol Standley
E-mail: cstandley@co.walker.tx.us
Court Reporter: Jackie Mills

**278th District Court**
**Judge Hal Ridley**
Suite 202
Phone: 936-436-4916
Fax: 936-436-4917
Court Coordinator: Cindy Gutierrez
E-mail: cgutierrez@co.walker.tx.us
Court Administrator: Sherry Fabre
E-mail: sfabre@co.walker.tx.us
Court Reporter: Sherry Stephens

**County Clerk: Kari French**
Suite 201
Phone: 936-436-4922
Fax: 936-436-4928
E-mail: kfrench@co.walker.tx.us

**County Judge: Danny Pierce**
Room 204
Phone: 936-436-4910
Fax: 936-436-4914
Administrative Assistant: Sherry Pegoda
E-mail: spegoda@co.walker.tx.us

**County Court at Law**
**Judge Tracy Sorensen**
Suite 101
Phone: 936-436-4919
Fax: 936-436-4920
E-mail: tsorensen@co.walker.tx.us
Court Coordinator: Casey Robertson
Phone: 936-436-4912
E-mail: crobertson@co.walker.tx.us
Court Administrator: Samantha Echtler
Phone: 936-436-4695
E-mail: sechtler@co.walker.tx.us
Court Reporter: Kathy Davis
E-mail: kdavis@co.walker.tx.us
Bailiff: Don Conover
E-mail: dconover@co.walker.tx.us

**STATE, DISTRICT AND COUNTY COURTS**

## WALLER COUNTY

Seat: Hempstead

836 Austin St.
Hempstead, TX 77445
www.co.waller.tx.us

**District Clerk: Liz Pirkle**
Room 318
Phone: 979-826-7735
Fax: 979-826-7738
E-mail: e.pirkle@wallercounty.us

**District and County Attorney: Elton R. Mathis**
645 12th Street
Hempstead, TX 77445
Phone: 979-826-7718
Fax: 979-826-7722

**506th District Court**
**Judge Albert M. McCaig, Jr.**
Room 307
Phone: 979-921-0921
Fax: 979-826-9149
E-mail: judge@court506.com
Court Coordinator: Susie Schubert
E-mail: admin@court506.com
Court Reporter: Robyn Wiley
E-mail: reporter@court506.com

**County Clerk: Debbie Hollan**
Room 217
Phone: 979-826-7711
Fax: 979-826-7771
E-mail: d.hollan@wallercounty.us

**County Judge: Carbett "Trey" J. Duhon, III**
Room 203
Phone: 979-826-7700
Fax: 979-826-2112
E-mail: t.duhon@wallercounty.us
Administrative Assistant: Cindy Jones
E-mail: c.jones@wallercounty.us

**County Court at Law**
**Judge June Jackson**
Room 216
Phone: 979-826-7762
Fax: 979-826-9119
E-mail: judge.jackson@wallercounty.us
Court Coordinator: Yesenia Pinon
E-mail: y.pinon@wallercounty.us
Court Reporter: Sheila May

## WARD COUNTY

Seat: Monahans

400 S. Allen St.
Monahans, TX 79756
www.co.ward.tx.us

**District Clerk: Patricia Oyerbides**
P.O. Box 440
Monahans, TX 79756-0440
Phone: 432-943-2751
Fax: 432-943-3810

**District Attorney: Randall W. Reynolds**
*Please see Reeves County.*

**143rd District Court**
**Judge Mike Swanson**
Suite 200
Monahans, TX 79756-0205
Phone: 432-943-2749
Fax: 432-943-5718
Court Coordinator: Cathy Adams
Court Reporter: Roger Epps
Bailiff: Breck Record

**County Clerk: Natrell Cain**
Suite 101
Phone: 432-943-3294
Fax: 432-943-6054

**County Attorney: Hal Upchurch**
201 E. 4th
Monahans, TX. 79756
Phone: 432-943-4211
Fax: 432-943-2423

**County Judge: Greg M. Holly**
Suite 100
Phone: 432-943-3200
Fax: 432-943-5010
Administrative Assistant: Linda Davis

## WASHINGTON COUNTY

Seat: Brenham

100 E. Main St.
Brenham, TX 77833
www.co.washington.tx.us

**STATE, DISTRICT AND COUNTY COURTS**

**District Clerk: Tammy Brauner**
Suite 304
Phone: 979-277-6200, ext. 153
Fax: 979-277-6239

**District Attorney: Julie Renken**
Box 303
Brenham, TX 77833
Phone: 979-277-6247
Fax: 979-277-6237
Email: jrenken@wacounty.com

**21st District Court**
**Judge Carson Campbell**
Suite 305
Phone: 979-277-6200, ext. 156
Fax: 979-277-6235
Court Coordinator: Lynn Mitchell

**335th District Court**
**Judge Reva L. Towslee-Corbett** sits as scheduled.
*Please see Burleson County.*

**County Clerk: Beth Rothermel**
Suite 102
Phone: 979-277-6200
Fax: 979-277-6278

**County Judge: John Brieden**
Suite 104
Phone: 979-277-6200
Fax: 979-277-6221
E-mail: countyjudge@wacounty.com
Administrative Assistant: Karen McGill

**County Court at Law**
**Judge Matthew A. Reue**
Suite 203
Phone: 979-277-6200, ext. 144
Court Coordinator: Peggy Wagers
E-mail: pwagers@wacounty.com

# WEBB COUNTY

Seat: Laredo

1110 Victoria St.
Laredo, TX 78042
www.webbcountytx.gov

**District Clerk: Esther Degollado**
P.O. Box 667

Laredo, TX 78042-0667
Phone: 956-523-4268
Fax: 956-523-5063

**District Attorney: Isidro R. Alaniz**
P.O. Box 1343
Laredo, TX 78040-1343
Phone: 956-523-4900
Fax: 956-523-5054

**49th District Court**
**Judge Jose A. Lopez**
Suite 304
Phone: 956-523-4237
Fax: 956-523-5051
Court Coordinator (Civil): Maria Rosario Ramirez
Phone: 956-523-4238
Court Coordinator (Criminal): Grace Solis
Court Administrator: Lisa Rogerio
Court Reporter: Cyndy Lenz
Bailiffs: Robert Reyes and Saul Rubio

**111th District Court**
**Judge Monica Zapata Notzon**
Suite 301
Phone: 956-523-4230
Fax: 956-523-5088
Court Coordinator (Civil): Abel Solis
Phone: 956-523-4226
Court Coordinator (Criminal): Gloria Hernandez
Court Administrator: Gracie Garcia
Phone: 956-523-4722
E-mail: gvgarcia@webbcountytx.gov
Court Interpreter: Merab Martinez
Court Reporter: Vincent Mendoza
Phone: 956-523-4229
Mental Health Court Coordinator: Javier Gonzalez
Administrative Assistant: Cynthia Olaez
Bailiff: Orlando Juarez and Fernando Ramos
Phone: 956-523-4227

**341st District Court**
**Judge Beckie Palomo**
Suite 302
Phone: 956-523-4325
Fax: 956-523-5055
Court Coordinator (Civil): Magdalena Martinez
Phone: 956-523-4328
Court Coordinator (Criminal): Raquel Carrillo
Phone: 956-523-4327
Court Administrator: Minnie Villarreal

**STATE, DISTRICT AND COUNTY COURTS**

E-mail: mvillarreal@webbcountytx.gov
Phone: 956-523-4329
Court Administrative Assistant: Martha Prew
E-mail: mprew@webbcountytx.gov
Court Interpreter: Blanca Canales
E-mail: bcanales@webbcountytx.gov
Court Reporter: Ana Laura Alcantar
E-mail: aloanales@webbcountytx.gov
P.O. Box 1598
Laredo, TX 78042-1598
Family Court Coordinator: Roberta Morales
E-mail: rmorales@webbcountytx.gov
Bailiff: Lorena De La Cruz and Doreen Hale
E-mail: ldelacruz@webbcountytx.gov
Phone: 956-523-4326

### 406th District Court
### Judge Oscar J. Hale, Jr.
Suite 402
Phone: 956-523-4954
Fax: 956-523-5074
Court Coordinator (Civil): Cruz Maldonado
Phone: 956-523-4957
Court Coordinator (Criminal): Marco Perez
Phone 956-523-4967
Court Administrator: Arminda Piña
Court Reporter: David Laurel
Phone: 956-523-4960
Bailiffs: Horacio Lopez and Juan Roycraft

### County Clerk: Margie Ramirez Ibarra
Suite 201
Phone: 956-523-4266
Fax: 956-523-5035

### County Attorney: Marco Montemayor
1110 Washington, Suite 301
Laredo, TX 78042
Phone: 956-523-4044
Fax: 956-523-5005

### County Judge: Tano E. Tijerina
1000 Houston St. 3rd Floor
Laredo, TX 78040
Phone: 956-523-4600
Fax: 956-523-5065
Executive Administrator: Adelaido Uribe
Phone: 956-523-4614
E-mail: auribe@webbcounty.tx.gov
Executive Assistant: Cordelia Valdez
Phone: 956-523-4677
E-mail: cvaldez@webbcounty.tx.gov
Court Administrator: Melinda Mata
Phone: 956-523-4622

E-mail: melmata@webbcounty.tx.gov
Communication Officer: Marah Mendez
Phone: 956-523-4620
E-mail: argarza@webbcounty.tx.gov
Bailiff: Blas Garza

### County Court at Law No. 1
### Judge Huge Martinez
Suite 303
Phone: 956-523-4340
Fax: 956-523-5058
Court Coordinator (Civil): Joann Ingunzo
Phone: 956-523-4346
Court Coordinator (Criminal): Jeremy Coss
Phone: 956-523-4341
Juvenile and Probate Coordinator: Juan J. Ramirez, Sr.
Court Reporter: Ginny Henderson
Phone: 956-523-4342
Bailiffs: Roger Benavidez, Gerardo Carmona and Pat Garza
Phone: 956-523-4343

### County Court at Law No. 2
### Judge Jesus Garza
Suite 404
Phone: 956-523-4332
Fax: 956-523-5075
Court Coordinator (Civil): Cindy Flores
Phone: 956-524-4376
Court Coordinator (Criminal): Nancy Rodriguez
Phone: 956-523-4333
Probate Coordinator: Christopher Casarez
Court Administrative Assistant: Ivan Flores
Court Reporter: Roxanne Soto
Phone: 956-523-4335
Bailiff: Albert Treviño

# WHARTON COUNTY

Seat: Wharton

103 S. Fulton St. Ste 100
Wharton, TX 77488
www.co.wharton.tx.us

### District Clerk: Kendra Charbula
P.O. Drawer 391
Wharton, TX 77488-0391
Phone: 979-532-5542
Fax: 979-532-1299
E-mail: Kendra.Charbula@co.wharton.tx.us

**District Attorney: Ross Kurtz**
210 S. Rusk St.
Wharton, TX 77488
Phone: 979-532-8051
Fax: 979-532-8467

**23rd District Court**
**Judge Ben Hardin** sits as scheduled.
*Please see Brazoria County.*

**329th District Court**
**Judge Randy Clapp**
100 S. Fulton St.
Wharton, TX 77488
Phone: 979-532-1514
Fax: 979-532-4752
E-mail: judge.clapp@co.wharton.tx.us
Court Coordinator: Cassie Ritler
Court Reporter: Sherri Johnson

## County Court
309 E. Milam St., Suite 602
Wharton, TX 77488

**County Clerk: Sandra K. Sanders**
P.O. Box 69
Wharton, TX 77488-0069
Phone: 979-532-2381
Fax: 979-532-8426
E-mail: sandra.sanders@co.wharton.tx.us

**County Attorney: G.A. Maffett, III**
100 S. Fulton St., Suite 105
Phone: 979-532-2591
Fax: 979-532-1251
E-mail: attorney@co.wharton.tx.us
Administrative Assistant: Donna Zahn

**County Judge: Phillip S. Spenrath**
100 S. Fulton St., Suite 100
Phone: 979-532-4612
Fax: 979-532-1970
E-mail: judge.spenrath@co.wharton.tx.us
Court Coordinator: Patty D. Shannon
E-mail: patty.shannon@co.wharton.tx.us
Administrative Assistant: Joyce Ferrell
E-mail: joyce.ferrell@co.wharton.tx.us

## WHEELER COUNTY

Seat: Wheeler

401 S. Main St.

Wheeler, TX 79096
www.co.wheeler.tx.us

**District Clerk: Sherri Jones**
P.O. Box 528
Wheeler, TX 79096-0528
Phone: 806-826-5931
Fax: 806-826-0346

**District Attorney: Franklin McDonough**
*Please see Gray County.*

**31st District Court**
**Judge Steven R. Emmert**
P.O. Box 766
Wheeler, TX 79096-0766
Phone: 806-826-5501
Fax: 806-826-5503
Court Coordinator: Dana Burch
Court Reporter: Toni McClendon

**County Clerk: Margaret Dorman**
P.O. Box 465
Wheeler, TX 79096-0465
Phone: 806-826-5544
Fax: 806-826-3282
**County Attorney: Leslie Standerfer**
P.O. Box 469
Wheeler, TX 79096-0469
Phone: 806-826-2042
Fax: 806-826-0717

**County Judge: Jerry D. Hefley**
P.O. Box 486
Wheeler, TX 79096-0486
Phone: 806-826-5961
Fax: 806-826-3282
Administrative Assistant: Carol Porton

## WICHITA COUNTY

Seat: Wichita Falls

900 Seventh St.
Wichita Falls, TX 76301
www.co.wichita.tx.us

**District Clerk: Patti Flores**
P.O. Box 718
Wichita Falls, TX 76307-0718
Phone: 940-766-8190
Fax: 940-766-8181
E-mail: patti.flores@co.wichita.tx.us

**STATE, DISTRICT AND COUNTY COURTS**

**District Attorney: Maureen Shelton**
Phone: 940-766-8113
Fax: 940-766-8102
E-mail: maureen.shelton@co.wichita.tx.us

**30th District Court**
**Judge Robert "Bob" Brotherton**
Phone: 940-766-8180
Fax: 940-766-8253
E-mail: robert.brotherton@co.wichita.tx.us
Court Coordinator: Helen Gass
Court Reporter: Leslie Ryan-Hash

**78th District Court**
**Judge W. Bernard Fudge**
Room 314
Phone: 940-766-8182
Fax: 940-766-8557
E-mail: barney.fudge@co.wichita.tx.us
Court Coordinator: Clara Little
Court Reporter: Sherri Harvey

**89th District Court**
**Charles Barnard**
Phone: 940-766-8184
Fax: 940-766-8114
E-mail: charles.barnard@co.wichita.tx.us
Court Coordinator: Denise Cope
Court Reporter: Joanna Beverage

**County Clerk: Lori Bohannon**
P.O. Box 1679
Wichita Falls, TX 76307-1679
Phone: 940-766-8195
Fax: 940-716-8554
E-mail: lori.bohannon@co.wichita.tx.us

**County Judge: Woodrow "Woody" W. Gossom, Jr.**
Room 202
Phone: 940-766-8101
Fax: 940-766-8289
E-mail: county.judge@co.wichita.tx.us
Administrative Assistant: Willie Wall
Executive Secretary: Joyce Gilleland

**County Court at Law No. 1**
**Judge Gary Butler**
Room 201
Phone: 940-766-8107
Fax: 940-766-8156
Court Coordinator: Karen Mortan
Court Reporter: Cayce Coskey

**County Court at Law No. 2**
**Judge Greg King**
Room 353
Phone: 940-766-8111

Fax: 940-766-8566
Court Coordinator: Gail Canady
Court Reporter: Carol Smith

# WILBARGER COUNTY

Seat: Vernon

1700 Wilbarger St.
Vernon, TX 76384
www.co.wilbarger.tx.us

**District Clerk: Brenda Peterson**
Room 33
Phone: 940-553-3411
Fax: 940-553-2316
E-mail: brendajean1953@yahoo.com

**District Attorney: John S. Heatly**
Room 32
Phone: 940-553-3346
Fax: 940-552-9630

**46th District Court**
**Judge Dan M. Bird**
Room 34
Phone: 940-552-7051
Fax: 940-552-0305
Court Coordinator: Sherrie Gibson
Court Reporter: Gloria Bourland
Phone: 940-552-0256

**County Clerk: Jana Kennon**
Room 15
Phone: 940-552-5486
Fax: 940-553-1202
E-mail: jkennon@co.wilbarger.tx.us

**County Attorney: Cornell Curtis**
Room 28
Phone: 940-553-3521

**County Judge: Greg Tyra**
Room 12
Phone: 940-553-2300
Administrative Assistant: Shanon Conley

# WILLACY COUNTY

Seat: Raymondville

576 W. Main St.
Raymondville, TX 78580

**District Clerk: Gilbert Lozano**
Phone: 956-689-2532
Fax: 956-689-5713
E-mail: gilbert.lozano@co.willacy.tx.us

**District and County Attorney: Bernard Ammerman**
2nd Floor
Phone: 956-689-2164
Fax: 956-689-5280
E-mail: bernard.ammerman@co.willacy.tx.us

**197th District Court**
**Judge Migdalia Lopez** sits twice a month, on a rotating basis.
*Please see Cameron County.*

**County Clerk: Terry Flores**
576 W. Main St.
Raymondville, TX 78580
Phone: 956-689-2710
Fax: 956-689-9849
E-mail: terry.flores@co.willacy.tx.us

**County Judge: Aurelio Guerra**
576 W. Main St.
Raymondville, TX 78580
Phone: 956-689-3393
Fax: 956-689-4817
E-mail: aurelio.guerra@co.willacy.tx.us

# WILLIAMSON COUNTY

Seat: Georgetown

405 MLK Blvd.
Georgetown, TX 78626-0405
www.wilco.org

**District Clerk: Lisa David**
P.O. Box 24
Georgetown, TX 78627-0024
Phone: 512-943-1212
Fax: 512-943-1222

**District Attorney: Jana Duty**
Suite 265
Phone: 512-943-1234
Fax: 512-943-1255

**26th District Court**
**Judge Donna King**
Box 2
Phone: 512-943-1226

Fax: 512-943-1188
Court Coordinator: Deb Lewis
Court Reporter: Cindy Kocher
Phone: 512-943-1228
Bailiff: Steve Miller

**277th District Court**
**Judge Stacey Matthews**
Box 6
Phone: 512-943-1277
Fax: 512-943-1276
Court Coordinator: Wanda Davidson
Court Reporter: Aimee Walker
Phone: 512-943-1288

**368th District Court**
**Judge Rick Kennon**
Box 8
Phone: 512-943-1368
Fax: 512-943-1285
Court Coordinator: Jennifer Tredemeyer
Court Reporter: Simone Wright
Phone: 512-943-1280
Bailiff: Jeff Lowey

**395th District Court**
**Judge Vacant**
Box 15
Phone: 512-943-1395
Fax: 512-943-1187
Court Coordinator: Vacant
Court Reporter: Vacant
Phone: 512-943-1178

**425th District Court**
**Judge Betsy Lambeth**
Box 22
Phone: 512-943-3380
Fax: 512-943-3383
Court Administrator: Marlys Tidrick
E-mail: mtidrick@wilco.org
Court Reporter: Lynette Thorpe
Phone: 512-943-3381
Bailiff: J.C. Weaver

**County Clerk: Nancy E. Rister**
P.O. Box 18
Georgetown, TX 78627
Phone: 512-943-1515
Fax: 512-943-1616
E-mail: nrister@wilco.org

**County Attorney: Dee Hobbs**
Phone: 512-943-1111
Fax: 512-943-1120

**STATE, DISTRICT AND COUNTY COURTS**

County Judge: Dan Gattis
1st Floor
Phone: 512-943-1550
Fax: 512-943-1662
E-mail: ctyjudge@williamson-county.org

County Court at Law No. 1
Judge Suzanne Brooks
Box 5
Phone: 512-943-1200
Fax: 512-943-1204
Court Coordinator: Fernanda Muñoz
Phone: 512-943-1201
Court Reporter: Sharon Huck
Phone: 512-943-1202
Bailiff: Arleen Reyes

County Court at Law No. 2
Judge Vacant
Box 4
Phone: 512-943-1410
Fax: 512-943-1414
Court Coordinator: Diane H. Lowder
Phone: 512-943-1411
Office Administrator: Kevin Kracht
Court Reporter: Carrie Townsend
Phone: 512-943-1412
Bailiff: Tammy Waton

County Court at Law No. 3
Judge Doug Arnold
Box 16
Phone: 512-943-1160
Fax: 512-943-1165
Court Coordinator: Brooke Daniel
Court Reporter: Karen Goh
Phone: 512-943-1163
Bailiff: Richard Tooley

County Court at Law No. 4
Judge John B. McMaster
Box 17
Phone: 512-943-1681
Fax: 512-943-1685
Court Coordinator: Sharrion Threadgill
Court Reporter: Tom McMinn
Phone: 512-943-1683
Bailiff: David Ruppard

# WILSON COUNTY

Seat: Floresville

1420 3rd St.
Floresville, TX 78114
www.co.wilson.tx.us

District Clerk: Deborah Bryan
110 S. Railroad St.
Floresville, TX 78114
Phone: 830-393-7322
Fax: 830-393-7319
E-mail: districtclerk@co.wilson.tx.us

District Attorney: Rene M. Peña
*Please see Atascosa County.*

81st District Court
Judge Donna S. Rayes sits as scheduled.
*Please see Atascosa County.*

218th District Court
Judge Russell Wilson sits as scheduled.
*Please see Atascosa County.*

County Clerk: Eva S. Martinez
P.O. Box 27
Floresville, TX 78114
Phone: 830-393-7308
Fax: 830-393-7334
E-mail: eva.martinez@co.wilson.tx.us

County Attorney: Daynah J. Fallwell
Suite 201
Phone: 830-393-7305
Fax: 830-393-7358

County Judge: Richard L. Jackson
Suite 101
Phone: 830-393-7303
Fax: 830-393-7327
Administrative Assistant: Dawn Barnett

# WINKLER COUNTY

Seat: Kermit

100 E. Winkler St.
Kermit, TX 79745
www.co.winkler.tx.us

**District Clerk: Sherry Terry**
P.O. Box 1065
Kermit, TX 79745
Phone: 432-586-3359
Fax: 432-586-2998

**District Attorney: Dorothy Holguin**
P.O. Box 1040
Kermit, TX 79745-1040
Phone: 432-586-3700
Fax: 432-586-3208
E-mail: dorothy.holguin@co.winkler.tx.us

**109th District Court**
**Judge Martin B. Muncy** sits twice a month.
*Please see Andrews County.*

**County Clerk: Shethelia Reed**
P. O. Box 1007
Kermit, TX 79745
Phone: 432-586-3401

**County Attorney: Thomas Duckwarth, Jr.**
P. O. Box 1015
Kermit, TX 79745
Phone: 432-586-2596
Fax: 432-586-3535
Assistant: Sheryl Wright
E-mail: sheryl.wright@co.winkler.tx.us

**County Judge: Charles Wolf**
P.O. Drawer Y
Kermit, TX 79745
Phone: 432-586-6658
Fax: 432-586-3223
E-mail: charles.wolf@co.winkler.tx.us
Administrative Assistant: Debbie Simmons
E-mail: debbie.simmons@co.winkler.tx.us

# WISE COUNTY

Seat: Decatur

101 N. Trinity St.
Decatur, TX 76234
www.co.wise.tx.us

**District Clerk: Brenda Rowe**
P.O. Box 308
Decatur, TX 76234
Phone: 940-627-5535
Fax: 940-627-0705
E-mail: districtclerk@co.wise.tx.us

**District Attorney: Greg Lowery**
101 N. Trinity, Suite 200
Decatur, TX 76234
Phone: 940-627-5257
Fax: 940-627-6404
E-mail: districtattorney@co.wise.tx.us

**271st District Court**
**Judge John H. Fostel**
P.O. Box 805
Decatur, TX 76234
Phone: 940-627-3200
Court Coordinator: Cathy Fostel
Court Reporter: Denise Hill
Bailiff: Dick Wood

**County Clerk: Sherry Lemon**
P.O. Box 359
Decatur, TX 76234
Phone: 940-627-3351
Fax: 940-627-2138

**County Attorney: James Stainton**
101 N. Trinity St., Suite 300
Decatur, TX 76234
Phone: 940-627-3321
Fax: 940-627-7194

**County Judge: Judson D. Clark**
P.O. Box 393
Decatur, TX 76234
Phone: 940-627-5743

**County Court at Law No. 1**
**Judge Melton D. Cude**
P.O. Box 901
Decatur, TX 76234
Phone: 940-627-5005
Court Coordinator: Debbye Barnett

**County Court at Law No. 2**
**Judge Stephen Wren**
1007 13th St., Suite 109
Bridgeport, TX 76426
Court Coordinator: Debbie Gardner
Phone: 940-683-0268

# WOOD COUNTY

Seat: Quitman

One Main St.
Quitman, TX 75783
www.co.wood.tx.us

**District Clerk: Jenica Turner**
P.O. Box 1707
Quitman, TX 75783-1707
Phone: 903-763-2361
Fax: 903-763-1511
E-mail: jdturner@mywoodcounty.com

**District Attorney: Jim Wheeler**
P.O. Box 689
Quitman, TX 75783-0689
Phone: 903-763-4515
Fax: 903-763-5105
E-mail: wcda@mywoodcounty.com

**402nd District Court**
**Judge G. Timothy Boswell**
P.O. Box 1707
Quitman, TX 75783
Phone: 903-763-2332
Fax: 903-763-1511
Court Coordinator: Joy Parker
E-mail: jparker@mywoodcounty.com
Court Reporter: Una Garland
E-mail: ugarland@mywoodcounty.com

**County Clerk: Kelley Price**
P.O. Box 1796
Quitman, TX 75783-1796
Phone: 903-763-2711
Fax: 903-763-5641
E-mail: kprice@mywoodcounty.com

**County Judge: Bryan Jeanes**
P.O. Box 938
Quitman, TX 75783-0938
Phone: 903-763-2716
Fax: 903-763-2902
E-mail: countyjudge@mywoodcounty.com
Court Coordinator: Kari Perkins

# YOAKUM COUNTY

Seat: Plains

Cowboy Way and Avenue G
Plains, TX 79355
www.co.yoakum.tx.us

**District Clerk: Sandra Roblez**
P.O. Box 899
Plains, TX 79355-0899
Phone: 806-456-7491, ext. 297
Fax: 806-456-8767

**District Attorney: Bill Helwig**
P.O. Box 359
Plains, TX 79355-0359
Phone: 806-456-7491, ext. 298
Fax: 806-456-2441

**121st District Court**
**Judge Kelly G. Moore** sits as scheduled.
*Please see Terry County.*

**County Clerk: Deborah L. Rushing**
P.O. Box 309
Plains, TX 79355-0309
Phone: 806-456-7491, ext. 294
Fax: 806-456-2258
E-mail: drushing@yoakumcounty.org

**County Judge: Jim Barron**
P.O. Box 456
Plains, TX 79355-0456
Phone: 806-456-7491, ext. 101
Fax: 806-456-6175
E-mail: jbarron@yoakumcounty.org
Administrative Assistant: Toni Jones

# YOUNG COUNTY

Seat: Graham

516 Fourth St.
Graham, TX 76450
www.co.young.tx.us

**District Clerk: Jamie Freeze Land**
Room 201
Phone: 940-549-0029
Fax: 940-549-4874
E-mail: j.land@youngcounty.org
Chief Deputy Clerk: Teresa Kilpatrick
Deputy Clerk: Karina Huerta

**District Attorney: Dee Hudson Peavy**
Room 206
Phone: 940-549-4132
Fax: 940-549-7151
E-mail: districtattorney@youngcounty.org
Legal Assistant: Terri Rhodes
Assistant DA: Phillip Gregory

**90th District Court**
**Judge Stephen E. Bristow**
Room 205

Phone: 940-549-0091
Fax: 940-549-4874
Court Coordinator: Beverly Ford
E-mail: b.ford@youngcounty.org
Court Reporter: Kim Reeves
Bailiff: Tommy Martin

**County Clerk: Kay Hardin**
516 Fourth St., Room 104
Graham, TX 76450
Phone: 940-549-8432
Fax: 940-521-0305
E-mail: khardin@yongcounty.org

**County Judge: John C. Bullock**
P.O. Box 298
Graham, TX 76450
Phone: 940-549-2030
Fax: 940-521-9482
E-mail: j.bullock@youngcounty.org
Administrative Assistant: Timi Hall
E-mail: ccadmin@youngcounty.org

# ZAPATA COUNTY

Seat: Zapata

200 E. 7th Ave.
Zapata, TX 78076
www.co.zapata.tx.us

**District Clerk: Dora Mtz. Castañon**
Suite 119
Zapata, TX 78076-0788
Phone: 956-765-9930
Fax: 956-765-9931

**District Attorney: Isidro R. Alaniz**
*Please see Webb County.*

**49th District Court**
**Judge Jose A. Lopez** sits as scheduled.
*Please see Webb County.*

**County Clerk: Mary Jayne Villarreal-Bonoan**
Suite 138
Zapata, TX 78076-0789
Phone: 956-765-9915
Fax: 956-765-9933

**County Attorney: S. Alfonso Figueroa**
Suite 305
Zapata, TX 78076

Phone: 956-765-9905
Fax: 956-765-9932
**County Judge: Joe Rathmell**
Suite 115
Zapata, TX 78076-0099
Phone: 956-765-9920
Fax: 956-765-9926
E-mail: zcjo@zapatacountytx.org
Administrative Assistant: Roxanne Elicondo

# ZAVALA COUNTY

Seat: Crystal City

200 E. Uvalde St.
Crystal City, TX 78839
www.co.zavala.tx.us

**District Clerk: Rachel P. Ramirez**
P.O. Box 704
Crystal City, TX 78839
Phone: 830-374-3456
Fax: 830-374-2632

**District Attorney: Robert Serna**
*Please see Maverick County.*

**293rd District Court**
**Judge Cynthia L. Muniz** sits as scheduled.
Also see Maverick County.

**365th District Court**
**Judge Amado Abascal, III** sits as scheduled.
Also see Maverick County.

**County Clerk: Oralia G. Treviño**
Suite 7
Phone: 830-374-2331
Fax: 830-374-5955
E-mail: countyclerk@zavalacounty.org

**County Attorney: Edward Serna**
Phone: 830-374-3734
Fax: 830-374-3007

**County Judge: Joe Luna**
Suite 9
Phone: 830-374-3810
Fax: 830-374-5634